Rocking My Life Away

Anthony DeCurtis **Rocking My Life Away**

Duke University Press

Durham and London

1998

Writing about

Music and Other Matters

For Rose Marie and Renato DeCurtis,

who would have glowed with pride to see it, and for Dom and Carmela,

who made me the person who could write it, with my deepest

love and gratitude

Contents

This is the hardest piece I've ever written. I've been avoiding it for several years. When I confided the difficulty I was having with it to my friend Frank Lentricchia, who teaches at Duke and whose advice on all matters concerned with writing is invaluable, he said, "Why don't you start by writing about the problems you're having with it?" That was more than a year ago. I remember thinking at the time that it was great advice. I also thought it would motivate me to begin writing. That didn't happen.

Maybe this project means too much to me. Ever since I started writing about music in 1978, when I was a graduate student in English at Indiana University—I wrote reviews and profiles for the town newspaper, then amusingly titled the Bloomington Herald-Telephone—I thought that one day I would love to publish a collection of my work. Years later when I discussed it with Ken Wissoker, my editor at Duke University Press, he expressed enthusiasm, and I became excited. I thought it would be revealing, and fun to put together. That was before I began the strangely complicated process of assembling my work, deciding what would be best to include and arranging it in some sensible order.

Essentially, the process broke down for me at that point. A notoriously generous reader of my own work, I liked—or at least felt a certain affection for—almost everything I read. Still, looking back disturbed me. I resented the implied suggestion that the glory days were behind me. The cliché about projects like this is that you feel as if you're writing your own epitaph. There's some truth to that.

Also, arbitrarily declaring a stopping point in my work seemed unnatural, counterintuitive. Through chance and the passage of time, a couple of natural breaking points occurred. First, in May 1995, I left my job as a writer and editor at *Rolling Stone* after nine years to take a job as on-air correspondent and editorial director at vh1. At that point Ken and I talked about using the move from print to television as a peg for this introduction. When I left vh1 a year later, Ken and I spoke again. I had gotten a deal to write a book about R.E.M. for another publisher, but, of course, I assured him, I would shortly be completing this introduction. Then I did nothing.

As all this was going on, I eventually dumped an enormous pile of stuff on Ken's desk. He read it, made some comments, and suggested an organizational plan. We then met in North Carolina and weeded through the pieces to give the book a more determined shape and bring it in at a manageable length. We refined that scheme a few times subsequently, incorporating suggestions from the press's readers, and finally came up with the work you see before you.

I introduce Ken's role here both to emphasize the deep sense of gratitude I feel and because, for whatever reasons, I doubt I would have been able to organize this collection myself. From an intellectual standpoint, I suppose my problem looking back on my work is that I don't come to music or any other subject from a specific ideological stance, and no such position emerges in this collection. That's partly because most of this work was written on journalism deadlines and partly because I prefer to *discover* a story—whether that story is a critical response to an album, an encounter with an artist, or an engagement with a social issue—rather than allow my preconceptions to "explain" it in advance.

What I like about these pieces is their sense of a drama unfolding, the palpable feel of a person rendering perspective on a series of experiences in a complex culture. I always liked writers and teachers who seemed to be thinking in front of me, and, to as great a degree as possible, my writing is done in that spirit. One of the titles I originally considered for this collection is "flashpoints," and that's how I see this work—as the sparks that flew when I rubbed up against the subject of the moment.

While social and political ideas inform my thinking at every second—I grew up in a working-class family, and that is the filter through which I view all my experiences—my writing tends to be governed more by aesthetic concerns. I'm far more interested in whether a subject excites me—and whether or not I can write well about it, whether I can make the reader feel or understand something—than whether it is "worthy" or "progressive," by whatever means such designations could be measured. As someone at play in the fields of popular culture, I care about everything that interests people. In a way that is antithetical to most rock criticism, I grow more curious about something the more popular it gets. Despite that, some of the subjects discussed here have faded from cultural view. Others have accrued greater significance. Prominence of subject was, of course, one factor Ken and I considered in assembling this book, but I think we both felt that if the writing in a piece really came across, then that piece would be included.

Given current academic fashions, my concerns and approach might be considered by some to be conservative. I don't see it that way—and the positions I take in the "Culture Watch, Culture Wars" section of this book bear me out, I think. But, if that's so, so be it. I've always enjoyed treating nontraditional subjects in traditional ways. As a graduate student, I wrote my dissertation about American fiction that, in almost every instance, had been written within the previous two decades. By the standard of the time—this was the late Seventies—writing about such "unproven" material was daring. Writing about it without hauling in an obvious theoretical frame was even riskier.

My approach was a kind of socially conscious new criticism—a concentrated focus on a text in the effort to coax out its cultural, political, psychological, and aesthetic meanings. That's still my favorite method. It implies that analysis is always a work in progress. If you keep thinking and paying attention, if you remain alert, meanings emerge and alter as times and cultural circumstances change. Sorting out the resonances of contemporaneous work is my greatest intellectual pleasure. It's a bit like walking on the wire. I love being free of the weight of previous readings, the precarious feeling that both my ideas and the subject in question must accept that there can be no firm footing on shifting sands.

The writing in this collection, too, is relatively traditional—perhaps even belletristic, as they say these days. I've never subscribed to the idea that writing about rock & roll somehow had to "capture the spirit" of the music. All writing should capture the spirit of its subject, obviously. In rock criticism, though, that goal typically provides the rationale for ridiculous adolescent excesses, creating a genre characterized by what Stephen Holden has described as "smart teen talk." Readers—and writers—who want to engage the spirit of the music really should go listen to it.

Nor am I, with relatively few exceptions, overtly present as a character in much of my writing. That's another absurdly self-indulgent tendency that has made rock criticism a laughingstock to virtually everyone who doesn't do it for a living. Writing about rock & roll, to the disappointment of most of its practitioners, is ultimately no different from writing about anything else. The same virtues apply—intelligence, clarity, grace, humor, and a concern for the reader.

As for the title, "Rocking My Life Away"—borrowed, of course, from the great Jerry Lee Lewis song (which was written by Mack Vickery and drops the "g")—that's another story. Six years ago, when I turned forty, that song—along with "Thirty-nine and Holding," another Jerry Lee Lewis signature—were my private, if somewhat ironic, anthems. They fiercely celebrate, with just the right undertones of arrogance and desperation, the contradictions of aging in a profession that worships youth. My favorite moment in "Rockin' My Life Away" comes midway in the first verse. Over a punishing piano rhythm, Lewis delivers the song's opening lines—first-rate examples of brilliant rock & roll nonsense—with who-gives-a-fuck off-handedness. "Fourteen, twenty-five, and forty, ninety-eight / I throwed a rock & roll party on my last birthday," he sings, "But it's good / I'm rockin' my life away."

From the fever of the performance, Lewis is clearly having a blast. So, why the "but"? What is the implied criticism to which he's responding? Should he have not thrown that "rock & roll party"? Why not? Is it morally wrong to be behaving at twenty-five or forty, let alone ninety-eight, the same as you did at fourteen? More likely, is rock & roll damning him to hell, as he once feared? For myself, I understood that "but" all too well. Among many other things, it meant, "even though I have a Ph.D.," or "even though I should have a grown-up job," or "even though I should be acting my age." I agree, though: It's good.

I never set out to be a "rock critic," a profession that did not exist when I was young. Sometimes it seems like a strange job to have as an adult. I've often told people that essentially I live the same way now as I did when I was seventeen (if not, fourteen)—I read, I write, and I listen to music.

That an entire intellectual culture would grow up around the music I love is something no one ever could have foreseen—certainly I didn't foresee it. Even when I was teaching literature and simultaneously writing rock criticism, I'd rarely introduce music into the classroom. I didn't want to be a "rock & roll professor," and, to tell the truth, that aspect of things still feels a bit funny to me. (Not that I'm snobbish about it, mind you. Not only have I written for virtually every mass market publication in existence, but, as I mentioned, I also worked in cable television.)

When I was younger, I believed that rock & roll, like sex, was something best learned on the street. I enjoyed the fact that my friends and I could have intense discussions about the music in ways that seemed far removed from any institutional structure. What's more, it always felt strange trying to contain the power of rock & roll in a classroom or lecture situation. I remember once playing Little Richard's "I Hear You

Knocking" during a talk I was giving to a group of arts journalists. It seemed surreal to be sitting still in a room in the middle of the afternoon earnestly listening to two of the most anarchic minutes in all of rock & roll.

These days, contradictions like that intrigue me more than put me off. Popular culture is a booming academic business—and it should be. I certainly do my share of lecturing and writing about it in serious contexts—like this one, for example. And I may eventually end up teaching it myself, quite happily.

Around the time of my fortieth birthday—the point of my realization that, for better or worse, I was rocking my life away—I made my peace with the notion that my professional life was largely devoted to a music that, to this day, many people associate exclusively with kids. While it embarrasses me to see some of my contemporaries—and even people in their thirties, for that matter—chasing every new trend, I still find myself moved and motivated by plenty of new music. And I ardently believe there are still plenty of interesting and important things to be said about the music that's been around for a while.

The nonmusic pieces in this collection demonstrate that my interests range far wider than rock & roll. But—that word again—sometimes your "career" chooses you, and I feel fortunate to have found a specialty that continues to provide gripping subjects and to renew itself for me. Some of the best results of that lucky fit are gathered here, for your pleasure.

Acknowledgments

Writing acknowledgments for a collection like this—essentially the work of a lifetime to this point—entails a certain degree of self-examination. What exactly is being acknowledged? While reading through these pieces, I felt both a bracing sense of continuity and a saddening awareness of how much breakage and loss shade even a relatively cohesive life.

A number of the people lurking around the edges of this collection—lovers, friends and colleagues, people who slept in our bed in the next room while I wrote, or helped form my ideas, or edited and inspired me, people who made me who I am—are no longer in my life for one reason or another: death or departure, bitter fallings out or the inevitable evolution of things. Do you write from the vantage of today or of yesterday, from a measured distance or from a place fraught with complex emotions? Do you simply leave out the hard parts, or risk darkening an occasion that might otherwise be a celebration or, at least, a straightforward recognition of help received and appreciated? My personal and professional lives wash over each other like rivers conjoining, and, for better or worse, are no more separable than that.

But not all of this is so complicated. When I told Jann Wenner that I wanted to use a number of the pieces I wrote for *Rolling Stone* in a collection of my work, his written reply was, "No problemo, as long as there is effusive and massive thanks to JSW." No problemo, indeed. Over the years Jann has made tremendous opportunities available to me, and this book would be a far more one-dimensional affair without his willingness to trust me on such a wide range of assignments. My "effusive and massive thanks" to him is merited and heartfelt.

When he was an editor at *Rolling Stone*, Jim Henke, who is now the chief curator of the Rock and Roll Hall of Fame, gave me my first national assignment. I was an unemployed English professor in Atlanta in 1980 who had written him a note asking if I could review a B-52's concert. One afternoon, to my amazement, the phone rang, and there was Jim. He said, "I have no idea who you are or what your writing is like, but go see the show and if your piece is good we'll run it." A little over five years later he hired me to work at *Rolling Stone*, taught me how to be a news reporter, and then turned me loose on some of my favorite pieces in this collection. I'm forever in his debt for taking a chance on me.

Another *Rolling Stone* editor, Bob Wallace, was primarily responsible for many of the nonmusic pieces I wrote for the magazine—no editor, before or since, has been as sensitive and receptive to my varied interests. There was simply no idea I couldn't suggest to him. Other editors at *Rolling Stone*—including Nathan Brackett, David Fricke, Lisa Henrickssen, Sid Holt, Mark Kemp, Bob Love, Susan Murcko, Barbara O'Dair, and David Wild—assigned and edited pieces included in this collection, and all have been a pleasure to work with. The same is true of editors at other publications, including Lois Fiore, Stacey D'Erasmo, Fletcher Roberts, and John Thornton, who worked with me on pieces included here.

The person who first put me on the map as a music writer was David McGee, who was editor of the late, lamented *Record*. Dave's confidence in me made me believe that I could earn a living as a writer, and he also gave me my first full-time job in journalism at *Record*. He continues to be a deeply valued friend and colleague.

Among my friends, Paul Evans has for many years now been the first among equals—"In my heart's core, ay, in my heart of heart." His intelligence and editorial sense have been eclipsed only by his love and loyalty. He is everywhere in this book. David Shumway launched my career as a journalist when we were both in graduate school by recommending me to the local newspaper as a pop music writer when he had to leave the job. Important as that casual decision has been in my life, it is the least of the reasons for my valuing his friendship of nearly twenty-five years.

When he directed my dissertation at Indiana University, Paul Strohm taught me more about editing than anyone I have worked with. Incredibly, he made writing my dissertation a pleasure, and I think of the lessons he taught me almost daily. Best of all, Paul has remained a dear friend and sage advisor. John McAlley has provided emotional support—and smart perspective—to me more times than I can ever repay. Abe Peck and Alan Light share a remarkable ability to penetrate to the heart of extremely complicated matters, and their good sense and sympathetic advice have often snapped me out of confusion and restored me to myself.

Holly George-Warren is my old war buddy and much prized confi- **xvii**
dante. Sarah Lazin, my agent, has helped me both as a writer and a
person. Elysa Gardner and Al Weisel deserve my thanks, as do John
Milward and Frank Cioffi, for many spirited conversations about music
and other matters. Andrew Slater also provided invaluable encouragement and advice during the time in Atlanta when I was wondering what
to do with my life.

As my preface makes clear, Ken Wissoker of Duke Press played a
crucial role, as a friend as well as an editor, in shaping this book and
bringing it into being. Two other friends helped as well: Stanley Fish,
director of the Press, chided my tardy soul, and Emily Young, head of
marketing, more gently urged me along.

My friendships with Dan Rubey and Frank Lentricchia have been
stormier than these others, but no less rich and important. Beyond my
abiding affection for them, they are my models for intellectual alertness,
emblems of how to see beyond clichés and convention to something
more profound. Frank, especially, has inspired me to strengthen the
bonds between what I've lived, what I think, and what I feel. In both
cases I know, as the song says, that "we'll meet again one day on the
avenue."

Tony Heilbut and David Gordon, in different ways, helped form my
thinking and suggested paths to follow when I was a student. Tony later
became a friend.

The final stages of work on this manuscript were completed with the
generous support of The National Arts Journalism Program at Columbia University.

Anne Buckley was a companion of inestimable worth for many years;
her contribution to creating the person who produced whatever is good
about this work cannot be overvalued. Martha Ropes and Kelly Scott
haunt many of the pieces in this book. Linda Kauffmann's energy and
readiness to laugh bring me pleasure both in memory and in our continuing, if intermittent, conversations. Kim Ronis and Jacki Lyden traveled journeys with me, and I often think of them. My fondness lingers
for Susan Richardson and her raucous posse of yore—Clio, Daz, Flav,
Supercat, and Snoop. Nancy Bilyeau has become a precious, close
friend—fun, eminently trustworthy, and a great support when I've been
in need.

Alphonse Calabrese first led me along the ever-winding road of self-discovery, but Robert Thorne was my most treasured guide, a man who more than any other human being shaped my sense of who I am and my way of seeing the world. I will miss him every day of my life, but he is with me at all times. Joan Robinson Thorne has proven a heartening, animating help to me.

My dedication of this book to them is a small honoring of what I owe my parents and my brother Dom and sister Carmela.

Finally, my love and thanks to Alexandra, for breaking on through.

Anthony DeCurtis September 1997

Sgt. Pepper's
Lonely Hearts Club Band
The Beatles

This piece, as well as the pieces that follow on the *Plastic Ono Band*, *Exile on Main Street*, and *Blood on the Tracks* were all written for a twentieth anniversary issue of *Rolling Stone* in which a poll of critics determined the hundred best albums of the previous twenty years.

"**I** *just listened to it* and said to myself, 'God, I really love this album.' Still, today, it just sounds so fresh. It sounds full of ideas. These guys knew what they were doing. They're good. And they're inventive. I haven't heard anything this year that's as inventive. I don't really expect to."

That's how Paul McCartney describes his response to hearing *Sgt. Pepper's Lonely Hearts Club Band* earlier this year, and it's hard to argue with him. The album he and those other "guys" in the Beatles released in 1967 revolutionized rock & roll. The "splendid time" McCartney, John Lennon, George Harrison, and Ringo Starr "guaranteed for all" has lasted more than two decades—and that immensely pleasurable trip has earned *Sgt. Pepper* its place as the best record of the past twenty years.

After the Beatles stopped touring in 1966, they had time to explore in greater depth the possibilities of the recording studio with producer George Martin. And removed, essentially for the first time, from the nonstop hoopla of Beatlemania, they also had time to question their identity as Beatles. A chasm had begun to open between their growing musical sophistication and the public's perception of them as lovable mop tops. The magnitude of the Beatles phenomenon was starting to encroach on the band—and their experience with psychedelic drugs made that phenomenon seem increasingly surreal. Already trapped, in their early twenties, the Beatles had to find a way out. *Sgt. Pepper's Lonely Hearts Club Band* was born.

"*Pepper* was probably the one Beatle album I can say was my idea," McCartney says. "It was my idea to say to the guys, 'Hey, how about disguising ourselves and getting an alter ego, because we're the Beatles and we're fed up. Every time you approach a song, John, you gotta sing it like John would. Every time I approach a ballad, it's gotta be like Paul would. Why don't we just make up some incredible alter egos and think, "Now how would he sing it? How would he approach this track?" ' And it freed us. It was a very liberating thing to do."

Clearly the *Sgt. Pepper* concept was more significant for the psychological escape route it provided the Beatles than for its specific use on the album. Apart from some relatively modest touches—the colorful uniforms, the opening theme song, the reprise near the end and Ringo's entertaining turn as "the one and only Billy Shears" in "With a Little Help from My Friends"—the alter egos make no discernible appearances on the album. But one look at the cover of *Sgt. Pepper*—festooned with the band's wildly eclectic gallery of heroes and with the wax figures of the youthful Fab Four standing next to their far more hirsute and serious-looking real-life counterparts—eloquently tells how greatly removed the group had grown from what they were. Under the guise of alter egos the Beatles had finally allowed their real selves to emerge.

Interestingly, however, the Beatles had freed themselves not merely to chronicle such weighty subjects as the joys of mind-expanding drugs, in "Lucy in the Sky with Diamonds," the paradoxical wisdom of Eastern religious philosophy, in "Within You Without You," or the sterile absurdity of mainstream values, in the astonishing "Day in the Life." On the contrary, *Sgt. Pepper* is filled with sly inside jokes, broad music-hall humor, and completely gratuitous novelties. It is not only the Beatles' most artistically ambitious album but their funniest.

Take, for example, the dog whistle—which humans can't hear—buried on the album's second side. "We're sitting around the studio, and one of the engineers starts talking about wavelengths, wave forms and stuff, kilohertz," McCartney recalls. "I still don't understand these things—I'm completely nontechnical. And as for John, he couldn't even change a plug—he really couldn't, you know. The engineers would be explaining to us what all this stuff was. An ultrasonic sound wave—'a low one, you can kill people with the low ones.' We were all saying, 'Wow, man. Hey, wow.' 'And the high ones,' he said, 'only dogs can hear it.' We said, 'We gotta have it on! There's going to be one dog and his owner, and I'd just love to be there when his ears prick up.' "

And the famous "Inner Groove"—the snippet of pointless conversation that sticks in the album's run-out groove and that was not included in the original American version of *Sgt. Pepper*—has an equally zany genesis. Around the time of *Sgt. Pepper*'s release, McCartney explains, "a lot of record players didn't have auto-change. You would play an album and it would go, '*Tick, tick, tick*,' in the run-out groove—it would just stay there endlessly. We were whacked out so much of the time in the Sixties—just quite harmlessly, as we thought, it was quite innocent—but you would be at friends' houses, twelve at night, and *nobody* would be going to get up to change that record player. So we'd be *getting into* the little '*tick, tick, tick*': 'It's quite good, you know? There's a rhythm there.' We were into Cage and Stockhausen, those kind of people. Obviously, once you allow yourself that kind of freedom . . . well, Cage is appreciating silence, isn't he? We were appreciating the run-out groove! We said, 'What if we put something, so that every time it did that, it said something?' So we put a little loop of conversation on."

These are minor points, perhaps, in the context of the enormous achievement of *Sgt. Pepper*. But such fun-loving experimentalism—born of the optimistic determination to blow away anything that "stops my mind from wandering where it will go"—is *Sgt. Pepper*'s best legacy for our time. In a decade of political conservatism and stifling musical formats, of sexual fear and obsession with the past, the hopeful message of *Sgt. Pepper*—that visionary breakthroughs are necessary to strive for and possible to achieve in every facet of life—is much more urgent now than it was twenty years ago today.

Rolling Stone August 27, 1987

Plastic Ono Band

John Lennon

Both Yoko Ono, who coproduced it, and Klaus Voormann, who played
bass on it, say they believe John Lennon's *Plastic Ono Band* is "timeless." Indeed, it sounds as if it could have been released yesterday. The
instrumentation—Lennon on guitar and piano, Voormann on bass,
Ringo Starr on drums—is stripped to the bone. In resonantly simple
language—language that deviates sharply from what Lennon dismissed
at the time as the "self-conscious poetry" of songs like "Lucy in the Sky
with Diamonds"—he takes on basic issues: death, isolation, anger, class,
fear. He attacks what he saw as the illusions of the Sixties, bidding
goodbye to that decade with the unsentimental announcement "The
dream is over." And when he declares, "Now I'm reborn," in "God," it
couldn't be any plainer: the Beatles are dead, and John Lennon and Yoko
Ono are standing alone.

Plastic Ono Band is dedicated to Yoko, who is also obliquely cited as the
album's inspiration in the credits: "Yoko Ono: Wind." Most of the songs
on the record were written while John and Yoko were undergoing
primal-scream therapy with Dr. Arthur Janov in California in 1970.
Primal-scream therapy, which Janov founded, asserts that people can
grow emotionally only when they break through the superficialities of
life and express their own personal pain, starting with repressed memories from infancy. Lennon had never resolved his feelings about his
mother, who died when he was a teenager, and his father, who abandoned him as a child. He had also recently divorced his first wife, had
split up with the Beatles, and had briefly been addicted to heroin. In
short, he had plenty of pain to confront—and all of it emerges un-
disguised on *Plastic Ono Band*.

After his time with Janov, Lennon was like a raw nerve; with characteristic honesty, he wanted to capture that rawness on record. He contacted Ringo and his longtime friend Klaus Voormann. He also brought
in producer Phil Spector, who had worked on *Let It Be* and "Instant
Karma." The album was recorded at EMI's Abbey Road studio, in London. "As soon as we came into the studio," Voormann says, "we noticed
that he was very much taken by that experience he went through [with

Janov], and he wanted, as quick as possible, to get this feeling down before it changed. That was his main thing."

For that reason—and also because Lennon wanted to shed the trappings of the Beatles' lush sound, which he associated with Paul McCartney and George Martin—the sessions proceeded rapidly and with little fuss. "He did not want to make a production with lots of instruments and great arrangements," Voormann says. "The main thing was that he wanted to do something as fresh and direct as possible. Just the fact that he asked Ringo and myself to play on the album meant to me that he wanted it to be a real close, intimate atmosphere. He did not say very much about what we played. He just played the song, and Ringo and I played the simple way we both enjoy playing. And it seemed to be exactly what he was looking for.

"The playing itself, to him, was not that important," Voormann says. "It was more important to capture the feeling. We did mostly one or two takes. There's a lot of mistakes on there and timing changes, but it was just like a pulse, exactly what John wanted. He loved it." According to Yoko, the sessions were infused with "an incredible feeling of energy, of starting something new." To keep things moving, Spector was doing mixes while the band was recording.

The simplicity of the arrangements on *Plastic Ono Band* only increases the power of Lennon's emotion. The anger Lennon had stored up for years—"so much pain / I could never show it," is how he puts it on *Plastic Ono Band*'s chilling coda, "My Mummy's Dead"—burst forth in his sessions with Janov. This passage from Lennon's interview with *Rolling Stone* shortly after the album's release demonstrates how extreme the passions were that he was tapping at the time: "One has to completely humiliate oneself to be what the Beatles were, and that's what I resent. I mean I did it, I didn't know, I didn't foresee; it just happened bit by bit, gradually, until this complete craziness is surrounding you and you're doing exactly what you don't want to do with people you can't stand, the people you hated when you were ten.

"And that's what I'm saying on this album—I remember what it's all about now, you fuckers—fuck you! That's what I'm saying, you don't get me twice."

Plastic Ono Band opens with "Mother," a stately ballad about the helplessness John felt at his mother's death and his father's departure. It ends with him screaming repeatedly, "Mama don't go / Daddy come home," as if he were wrenching the words from his guts. The riveting "Working Class Hero," which Lennon plays solo on acoustic guitar, grimly details how class oppression warps the people at the bottom of the social system: "They hurt you at home and they hit you at school / They hate you if you're clever and they despise a fool / Till you're so fucking crazy you can't follow their rules / A working class hero is something to be."

The merging of Yoko's and Lennon's lives is also an important aspect of *Plastic Ono Band.* According to Voormann, their intense bond was quite evident during the sessions, as it is on songs like "Hold On," "Isolation," "Love," and "Look at Me." "Ringo was a little confused," Voormann says, "because John's closeness to Yoko was sad to him. John was not one person; John and Yoko were one person, which was very difficult for him to accept."

"God," however, is the album's seminal track and definitive statement. Much as he peeled back the layers of his personality to reach emotional bedrock in his primal-scream therapy, Lennon rids himself in that song of every belief or idol he ever had. The song is Lennon's fervent, determined, almost willful effort to locate a sense of who he is independent of all externals. Over pianist Billy Preston's simple, emphatic chords, Lennon sings, "God is a concept / By which we measure our pain," and chants a litany of abandoned "gods" that concludes, "I don't believe in Elvis / I don't believe in Zimmerman / I don't believe in Beatles / I just believe in me / Yoko and me / And that's reality."

This was tough, uncut stuff, and it didn't send fans of Beatle John scurrying to the record store. "People underestimated it," says Voormann, "and they expected something else. But John couldn't care less." Yoko Ono agrees. *Plastic Ono Band* is, she says, "just as important as *Sgt. Pepper,* in terms of being a milestone and in terms of the direction that John took after that. The album characterized the direction we went in together, and because of that, a lot of people resented it. Like 'The dream is over / What can I say?'—and they were saying, 'Please, don't let the dream be over. Let us keep on dreaming.' They didn't want to know.

"I don't think that album sold more than *Band on the Run* or *Mc-Cartney.* We took a chance, in a way. But it was not a calculated chance. John could not be what he was not."

Rolling Stone August 27, 1987

"(I Can't Get No) Satisfaction"

The Rolling Stones

This piece was written for an issue of *Rolling Stone* in which a poll of critics determined the hundred best singles of the previous twenty-five years. "(I Can't Get No) Satisfaction" was voted number one.

I*t is the perfect riff:* tough, dramatic, and instantaneous in its impact— the rock & roll equivalent of the opening notes of Beethoven's Fifth. Perhaps the only person who wasn't knocked out the first time he heard the unforgettable fuzz-tone guitar line to "(I Can't Get No) Satisfaction" was Keith Richards, the man who wrote it.

"I actually didn't want it to be a single," Richards says about the song that became a Sixties anthem and the Rolling Stones' first Number One single in the United States. "I thought it was just filler."

The modest origins of "Satisfaction" may be one of the reasons Richards initially failed to respond. During their 1965 spring tour of America, the Stones were spending the night in a motel in Clearwater, Florida, when inspiration struck. "I was asleep," Keith recalls. "I woke up in the middle of the night. There was a cassette player next to the bed and an acoustic guitar. I pushed RECORD and hit that riff for about a minute and a half, two minutes. Then I fell back to sleep. The next morning when I woke up, the tape had gone all the way to the end. So I ran it back, and there's like thirty seconds of this riff—'*Da-da da-da-da,* I can't get no satisfaction'—and the rest of the tape is me snoring!"

Still, Richards liked what he heard that morning, and he turned the riff and key lyric over to Mick Jagger, who wrote the verses in ten minutes that same day by the pool. "It was my view of the world," says Jagger, "my frustration with everything. Simple teenage aggression. It was about America, its advertising syndrome, the constant barrage."

The Stones—Jagger, Richards, Brian Jones on guitar, Bill Wyman on bass, and Charlie Watts on drums—began working on "Satisfaction" a few days later, on May 10th and 11th, in Chicago's Chess Studios. Dissatisfied, they finished it at RCA Studios in Los Angeles on May 12th and 13th, with their manager, Andrew Loog Oldham, producing and Dave Hassinger engineering.

Productivity was dizzyingly high in those days. The Stones worked in the L.A. studio for sixteen straight hours, entering at 10:00 a.m. on the twelfth and leaving at about 2:15 the following morning. During that span and an eight-hour stretch on the thirteenth, they essentially completed seven songs, including "Satisfaction."

"When it was by the pool," says Jagger, "it was a rather lilting acoustic melody. It only got to the snarl when we got this fuzz box in the studio, which was the first time we'd used one." The song was released as a single two weeks later, on the twenty-seventh, and quickly became *the* song of that summer, staying at Number One for four weeks.

With its defiant lyrics about sexual frustration and the vapidity of consumer culture, "Satisfaction" sharpened the Stones' rebellious image and articulated the anger of the youth culture that was just beginning to take shape. Even two years later, *Time* magazine would fret that the Stones "write songs about 'trying to make some girl,' with supposedly coded allusions to menstruation, marijuana and birth control pills."

The Stones didn't take the criticism too seriously, Richards says. "We were just saying what anybody would say among their own generation," he says. "It was the reaction that was interesting: we were shocked to find out that *they* were shocked."

Two decades later, "Satisfaction" reigns. Jagger finds it "gratifying" that Aretha Franklin and Otis Redding both chose to cover it, considering that "it was a real white-middle-class song." And Richards now accords the song—and its killer riff—a seminal place in the Stones canon. "I hear 'Satisfaction' in 'Jumpin' Jack Flash'; I hear it in half the songs that the Stones have done," he says. "I'm almost to the point now, after writing songs for so many years, that there is only one song—it's just the variations you come up with." And the original is still the greatest.

Rolling Stone September 9, 1988

Exile on Main Street

The Rolling Stones

Raw, dense, uncontrolled, and feverish in its rhythmic momentum, *Exile on Main Street* is the only studio double album the Rolling Stones have ever made, and it's devastating to listen to from start to finish. It's the *sound* that hits the hardest—a sludgy, seductive, grinding groove that won't let up and somehow seems inseparable from the very idea of rock & roll itself. Mick Jagger's voice is not treated as a lead instrument; it's buried in the mix with Keith Richards's and Mick Taylor's interwoven guitars and with Bill Wyman's and Charlie Watts's rumbling bass and drums. Yet Jagger's singing has a feral conviction and works purely on a sensual level. To this day every album that abandons studio polish for sheer visceral attack—whether it's by the Replacements or Tom Petty and the Heartbreakers—draws comparisons to *Exile on Main Street.*

All this comes as something of an embarrassment to Jimmy Miller, who was the producer during the entire golden age of Stones records, from *Beggars Banquet*, in 1968, to *Exile*, in 1972. "*Exile on Main Street* was a difficult album from the technical side," Miller recalls, "because we were recording in a basement and in a very bad room for recording. I was never happy with the sound, and as a producer, I felt from the start we *should* be getting better sound. And yet through the years, people have come up to me and said, 'Wow, *Exile*, what a great record!' And they seem to love the *basementness* of it."

The Stones had become tax exiles from Great Britain by the time they started recording this follow-up to *Sticky Fingers* in 1971. So, along with a battery of fellow musicians and assorted friends and hangers-on, the band drifted to Nellcote, Keith Richards's house in the south of France. The Stones ended up making *Exile* in the basement of Nellcote, using their mobile recording unit, which had been set up outside the house.

In Barbara Charone's *Keith Richards: Life as a Rolling Stone*, engineer Andy Johns remembers that "Gram Parsons [was] sitting in the kitchen in France one day while we were overdubbing vocals or something. It was crazy. Someone is sitting in the kitchen overdubbing guitar and people are sitting at the table talking, knives, forks and plates clanking."

It's important to remember that rock & roll was still maturing in 1971—and fighting for some sort of respectability, albeit on the hippest possible terms. In the wake of *Sgt. Pepper*, records—even Stones records—were *supposed* to sound good. A raw sound wasn't a production choice, a sign of authenticity or ballsiness, as it is in the hypertech Eighties. It was just bad sound.

Thematically, *Exile* was notable because it carried the Stones' long-standing obsession with America to its furthest extreme. The Stones transformed themselves into a classic R&B band for the album's sessions by adding Nicky Hopkins on piano, Bobby Keys on sax, and Jim Price on trumpet and trombone. The Stones persisted in their love of the blues by covering Slim Harpo's "Shake Your Hips" and Robert Johnson's "Stop Breaking Down," and they worked blues, R&B, and gospel riffs into scorching originals like "Casino Boogie," "Ventilator Blues," "I Just Wanna See His Face," "Let It Loose," and "Shine a Light." The country strain in their music flowered with "Sweet Virginia," "Torn and Frayed," and "Loving Cup." They wrote "Sweet Black Angel" for black American radical Angela Davis, who was awaiting trial on charges connected with the murder of a California judge. The band even chose photographer Robert Frank—best known for his book *The Americans*—to do the album's artwork, which intersperses shots of freaks and characters from the margins of American life with photos of the band, blurring distinctions between the two.

If the Stones in 1971 were metaphoric "exiles"—British rockers obsessed with America and living in France—they were also, as one of the most popular rock & roll bands in the world, squarely on Main Street. They were burgeoning celebrities as well. Jagger divided his time between the raucous scene at Nellcote and visits with his pregnant wife, Bianca, in Paris, annoying the band with the unpredictability of his comings and goings.

Not that Keith, whose heroin addiction was raging, was much more reliable. "Keith would say, 'Just going to put Marlon [his son] to bed,' and then *disappear* for four or five hours," according to Andy Johns in *Keith Richards*. "At 1:00 a.m. he'd reappear. Everyone else would be bored to death or tired of waiting. Then Keith would want to work for the next eight hours."

Ultimately the Stones thrived on such chaos and confusion and forged their greatest and toughest album amid the mayhem. The soft-edged and high-minded Sixties were never really the Stones' time. As the Sixties ebbed and the Seventies—a time of cynicism, no-shit pragmatism, and narcissistic excess—rolled in, the Stones were perched swaggeringly on the cusp of the two decades. Beggars at the banquet on one end, exiles on Main Street on the other, the Stones faced down the cultural dislocation that shattered so many of their contemporaries, and it made their day.

Rolling Stone August 27, 1987

Blood on the Tracks

Bob Dylan

When **Blood on the Tracks** *was released* in 1975, it restored Bob Dylan to his standing as a preeminent artist. In a unique critics' symposium published by *Rolling Stone* to honor the album, writer Paul Nelson declared, "His marriage rumored troubled, his recent tour and albums treated somewhat indifferently by a less than worshipful press, Bob Dylan seems haunted and uncertain again, and that may be very good news." The album was roundly greeted as Dylan's return to the poetic force of his classic Sixties LPs *Blonde on Blonde* and *John Wesley Harding*.

Getting back was Dylan's clear goal on the record, his folkiest of the Seventies. Although the album's vision is expansive, the instrumentation is spare, often reminiscent of Dylan's pre-rock & roll narrative excursions: Dylan performs solo, accompanying himself on acoustic guitar and harmonica, on several tracks. "Tangled Up in Blue," "Idiot Wind," and "Lily, Rosemary and the Jack of Hearts" are rambling, intensely rendered, and completely spellbinding songs. To make the album, Dylan returned to Columbia Records' A&R Studios, where he had done his earliest recording.

"I want to lay down a whole bunch of tracks," Dylan told the late John Hammond, who had signed him to Columbia thirteen years earlier. "I don't want to overdub. I want it easy and natural." "That's what the whole album's about," Hammond said. "Bobby went right back the way he was in the early days, and it works."

"It was a theater experience as much as anything else," says Phil Ramone, who engineered the record. Dylan would start and stop songs at will and routinely run one song into another.

His idiosyncratic recording habits were regarded less kindly by Eric Weissberg, the banjo player whose band, Deliverance, backed Dylan on the sessions. "If it was anybody else, I would have walked out," Weissberg told *Rolling Stone* in 1974, before the album was finished. "He put us at a real disadvantage. . . . You couldn't really watch his fingers 'cause he was playing in a tuning arrangement I had never seen before." Dylan eventually recorded half of the songs in his home state of Minnesota, where he was living at the time.

Blood on the Tracks derives its power from Dylan's unmistakable commitment to his material—a quality that had often seemed to be lacking in his work after 1968's *John Wesley Harding*. The album's subject is love, and in the wake of his marital battles—the "blood on the tracks" of the title—Dylan seemed inspired by the complexity of the emotion in a more profound way than ever before. While "Idiot Wind" vents rage in an unrestrained manner that recalls "Like a Rolling Stone" or "Positively 4th Street," gentler songs like "If You See Her, Say Hello" or "You're Gonna Make Me Lonesome When You Go" suggest the possibility not merely of regret but of reconciliation and forgiveness based on the acceptance of loss. "Tangled Up in Blue" verges on the metaphysical in its stunning comprehension of how lost love haunts lives.

Ultimately, *Blood on the Tracks* is also a reflection on the passing of the Sixties, created by the man who was perhaps the decade's greatest pop-culture figure. Getting back meant—as it always does—learning once and for all that what's back there can never be fully recovered, only acknowledged and understood. When Dylan sang, with reeling energy, "There was music in the cafes at night / And revolution in the air," in "Tangled Up in Blue," or concluded that song with a verse that begins, "Now I'm going back again / I've got to get to her somehow / All the people we used to know / They're an illusion to me now / Some are mathematicians / Some are carpenters' wives / I don't know how it all got started / I don't know what they're doing with their lives," it stirred feelings and memories in an entire generation that had been frozen over in the real-life big chill.

Rolling Stone August 27, 1987

Bob Dylan's Blue Highways

The Bootleg Series, *Vols. 1–3*

Three CDs, fifty-eight tracks, nearly four hours of music—the first three volumes of *The Bootleg Series* stand solidly on their own terms as an essential statement of the breadth of Bob Dylan's artistic achievement. This collection is obviously not where a newcomer to Dylan—whoever such a person might be—should begin. These songs— outtakes from albums, alternative versions of well-known and lesser-known tunes, the occasional live track, demos Dylan recorded for his music publisher so his songs could be transcribed and made available to other artists—are not his greatest hits or his most influential work. They do not even demonstrate a definite creative progress, as do the songs on *Biograph*—despite the absurdly confused chronology of that earlier collection.

No, the tracks on *The Bootleg Series* document the blue highways of Dylan's imagination, the paths not taken, the back roads that sometimes run parallel to and sometimes veer away from the main road—songs from a planned live album that got scuttled, songs that seemed old-fashioned after fresher impulses gripped Dylan's restless soul, songs too similar to or too different from other songs on a particular album, sketches that never quite assumed full character. With the help of John Bauldie's excellent liner notes—detailed without being obsessive, interpretive without being bullying, appreciative without being fawning— listeners can get a distinct feel from this set for the kinds of decisions that make a song or shape a career.

But *The Bootleg Series* by no means requires such specialized interest in exchange for its pleasures. Hearing the songs without any reference to their standing in the Dylan canon is a spellbinding experience. In fact, it could even temporarily diminish one's enjoyment of a song like "Rambling, Gambling Willie"—even as it deepens one's understanding of Dylan—to know that the tune was pulled from *The Freewheelin' Bob Dylan* so that "Bob Dylan's Dream" could be included on the album. Without question, "Bob Dylan's Dream"—a dark, troubling reflection on innocence forever lost—is the superior song, but nearly thirty years later the comparison is important only to the most dedicated Dylan followers.

More casual fans can simply be swept up in the exuberant spirit Dylan brings to the outlaw ballad of "Rambling, Gambling Willie" and enjoy the charming innocence that Dylan, who was all of twenty-one at the time, felt he had outgrown.

Beyond that, some of the performances on *The Bootleg Series* are just extraordinary, up to the standard of Dylan's most profound moments on record. The contradictory emotions—longing, bitterness, affection, resignation—that inform Dylan's world-weary rendering of "Mama, You Been on My Mind," an outtake from *Bringing It All Back Home,* will be familiar to anyone who has been haunted by a former lover. "I'm just whispering to myself, so I can't pretend that I don't know," he sings, letting his pride slip and his honesty show, his voice lagging dreamily behind his own tempo on acoustic guitar. "Mama, you're on my mind." Another outtake from *Bringing It All Back Home*—the poetic "Farewell, Angelina," a surreal meditation on leaving love behind—is equally transporting. On the arresting "Blind Willie McTell," recorded with Dylan on piano and Mark Knopfler on guitar during the 1983 sessions for *Infidels,* Dylan transforms an oblique celebration of a dead blues master into a stark, existential indictment of the emptiness of life in the modern world.

Dylan's political aspect is also well represented on *The Bootleg Series.* Recorded in 1962, "Let Me Die in My Footsteps," with its stirring refrain, "Let me die in my footsteps / Before I go down under the ground," is a dignified response to the bomb-shelter craze generated by cold-war paranoia. On a similar but lighter note, "Talkin' John Birch Paranoid Blues," recorded live at Carnegie Hall, in New York, in 1963, skewers the lingering vestiges of McCarthyism in America. And Dylan's rendition of the slave spiritual "No More Auction Block," from a 1962 performance at the Gaslight Café, in New York's Greenwich Village, is riveting; he would later adapt the tune's melody for "Blowin' in the Wind." "Man on the Street" and "Only a Hobo," which, in a better world, might merely seem like sentimental holdovers from Dylan's fascination with Depression-era ballads, take on an unsettling contemporary resonance, given the problem of homelessness ravaging this country.

Meanwhile, Dylan the rocker steps forward on a torrid version of "Seven Days," recorded live in Tampa on the 1976 Rolling Thunder tour, as well as on the ardently sensual "Need a Woman," an outtake from *Shot of Love,* and "Foot of Pride," a blistering track left over from *Infidels.*

Guitarist Michael Bloomfield tears into a faster alternate version of "It Takes a Lot to Laugh, It Takes a Train to Cry," from the sessions for *Highway 61 Revisited*, while Dylan and the Band, then known as the Hawks, shake up the acerbic "She's Your Lover Now," recorded during the 1966 sessions for *Blonde on Blonde*.

Finally, however, *The Bootleg Series* is not about the rockers, splendid as those tracks are. With two exceptions—one being Dylan's nervous, moving recital of one of his poems, "Last Thoughts on Woody Guthrie," at a 1963 New York concert, the other being a song on which he is joined by a second, unidentified guitarist—the first twenty-eight tracks on the collection feature Dylan performing solo on acoustic guitar or piano, and on many of the other tracks the accompaniment is spare. Indeed, Dylan's vocals often take on the contemplative quality of someone thinking, rather than singing aloud.

These songs, then, are testament to an individual's struggle to bring meaning to experience, to an artist searching for a personal voice that can take the measure of an emotion and a time, to that voice rising to say what it needs to say. Traveling the hidden byways charted on *The Bootleg Series*, Dylan found his voice, and it's inspiring to hear it ring so true now, in all its starts and hesitations, its yearnings and disappointments—in all its triumphs.

Rolling Stone April 4, 1991

It's a Thursday Night in Athens, Georgia

This piece was commissioned by *Rolling Stone* in 1981, but it never ran. It appears here for the first time.

It's **a Thursday night in Athens, Georgia,** and Tyrone's, the town's major New Wave club, is packed. Well-scrubbed college kids and the town's bohemian contingent swelter alike in the June heat, but this crowd is poised. The four members of R.E.M., a local pop-oriented New Wave band, saunter out, and the audience clusters near the stage, prepared to hurl itself into Athens's major ideological act: *dancing.*

From the first note of "Radio Free Europe," the band's anthemic, independently released single, everyone is bopping. The dancing here is expressively free-form, blending Sixties' rave-up, disco sinuosity, and punk jerkiness. And through the entire rocking set it does not stop.

About five or six blocks away, the 40 Watt Club, a "refurbished" storefront that has become Party Central for the Athens New Wave crowd, is also jammed. Genial weirdness is the rule here. Vietnam, a funky jazz / punk band from Atlanta, conducts the dance. Techno-jungle rhythms, atmospheric keyboards, and bleating sax lines pull the strings of the thrift-store marionettes leaping about the dance floor. Shouts and squeals from floor and stage punctuate the music as saxophonist/lead singer Stan Saturi roams the stage like a spasmodic cadaver. The thumping encore of Sly's "Thank You (Falettinme Be Mice Elf Agin)" concludes the evening triumphantly.

Athens's Tyrone's and the 40 Watt Club, along with the Agora Ballroom and 688 in Atlanta, are key parts in a supportive network that has helped make the music scene here as exciting as anywhere else in the country. Even after the B-52's skyrocketed out of Athens in 1979 and Atlanta's Brains had begun taking their hard-hitting brand of New Wave on the road, there were still few places in this area where these bands, let alone their less established counterparts, could play. The B-52's had gotten their start playing at parties in Athens for their friends (a tradition still respected and practiced today), and the Brains would play the various progressive clubs in Atlanta that opened and closed with stupefying rapidity. Tyrone's did not exist while the B-52's were still in Athens, and the Agora, part of a national chain, was struggling to define its role on the local scene.

And more general problems existed. "The B-52's were always ecstatically received around here and never got a good review in the Atlanta papers," says Danny Beard, owner of DB Recs, the independent label that produced the band's first single. "There was no money to be made in clubs, here or in Athens. I didn't even bother with this area in trying to sell their single, and I was getting calls from all over the country. The audience was just not that large locally. The situation is improving now."

Indeed it is, for several reasons. The Brains' record contract and critical success authenticated what had happened with the B-52's. It could be no fluke: for two local bands to get so much national attention, something had to be going on. Then, a little over a year ago, 688 opened. A late-night New Wave club within four blocks of the Agora in downtown Atlanta, 688 provided the local scene with the center it had been lacking. "688 has been a godsend," states Atlanta musician Kevin Dunn. "I can't imagine what state things would be in if it weren't for that place. The Atlanta-Athens axis has its center at 688."

688 combines the techno virtues of a video screen and a great sound system with the hospitable squalor of an underground club. Crowds come here as much to dance and be seen as to see bands, and in its first year, the club has been a model of progressive national and local booking. Weeknight dates by local bands annihilate audience / performer distinctions. Conversations pass between the stage and floor, and an atmosphere of informal dress rehearsal pervades. The club has also had an important economic effect according to Dunn: "With 688, now everybody can find at least some work between here and the clubs in Athens. You don't have to be big enough to play the Agora."

Atlanta and Athens, about sixty-five miles apart, needed a fully developed club network to focus the scene that's been developing over the last two years. Following the success of the B-52's, bands began to form in Athens, seat of the University of Georgia, as quickly as pawn shops could put instruments in the hands of students who wanted more than a degree to show for their years at school. In their lack of technical training, the B-52's, and particularly guitarist Ricky Wilson, defined a spare, eccentrically rhythmic, and danceable sound that would be further developed by Pylon, the Method Actors, the Side Effects, Love Tractor, and

Current Rage. They also toppled Southern women off their pedestal and onto center stage. In the wake of 52-girls' Kate Pierson and Cindy Wilson, Pylon, the Basics, Kevin Dunn and the Regiment of Women, Vietnam, Limbo District, and Oh OK all feature women whose role has gone far beyond tambourine shaking. Avian of the Basics points out that "People are ready for a male/female balance on stage. Women are surfacing in everything now. They're getting more inspired, more ambitious. Women want to express their ideas as well as their feelings. They have to fend for themselves a lot more." In the New Wave South, even the girls can't help it.

But what the B-52's represented most to local musicians was that *it could happen*. That technique and years of dues-paying at the altar of rock & roll (a term these bands use only in tones of utmost contempt) could be circumvented by wit, conceptual adventurousness, and a willingness to ride the Athens-New York express the B-52's had established.

B-52's keyboardist Kate Pierson states that, "Our main influence on Athens has been in terms of attitude, a way of doing things. I sometimes wonder why so much seems to be coming out of Athens and not other, similar places. But all it takes is for one band to make it out. There's always been bands in Athens, but they used to just think of playing local places. People encouraged us to go up to New York and we went just for fun. We didn't we'd make it or anything. When it started to work, other bands got the idea that they could go up there. The trail had been blazed." "When I first saw the B-52's, I knew I had to form a band," states Vietnam's Stan Saturi. "I knew then that it could be done, that the art of doing it was the most important thing, not the music."

In Atlanta, things were and are more complicated. Whereas the B-52's established a tradition overnight in the hot-house, college-town atmosphere of Athens, Atlanta had its own history of rock acts like Billy Joe Royal, Tommy Roe, the Atlanta Rhythm Section, Kansas, the Dregs, Darryl Rhodes, and the Hampton Grease Band, against which aspiring New Wave bands had to define themselves. The rise of the B-52's profoundly affected Atlanta but was never regarded without ambivalence. Brains' lead singer Tom Gray tells how "The B-52's were an inspiration as far as their success, first in selling their own single and then with a major label deal. We followed in less than a year with our major label deal even though we haven't sold as many records as the B-52's. It used to bother me because everybody would say, 'Oh, the B-52's, Oh, the B-52's!' Everytime I did an interview it was 'You're from the same part of the country as the B-52's, do you know them personally?'"

Even Athens' bands have felt the need to separate themselves from the B-52's to establish their own identity. "It's real endearing to people in New York that all this new music could come out of the South," states Pylon bassist Michael Lachowski, "but really all the Athens bands have been interesting in and of themselves. We downplay the Athens connection now, primarily because it just makes people ask about the B-52's."

Yet after the signing of the B-52's by Warner Brothers and the Brains by Mercury (with whom they've since broken), major record companies have been reluctant to take on other aspiring local New Wave acts. The most recent Atlanta band to score a contract is the Producers whose debut album has just been released on Columbia's Portrait label. A bar band gone the skinny-tie route, the Producers play an infectious, innocuous brand of power pop, studiously incorporating influences from the Police, Cheap Trick, and the Knack. Regarded by industry people here as potentially the next big thing on the AM dial, the band is dismissed by cynical New Wavers as the Product. Vietnam's Stan Saturi describes Atlanta bands like the Producers as "bandwagon bands. They plan nothing from the heart."

As in other cities, however, the lack of major label interest has created an exciting independent recording scene here. The B-52's and the Brains first attracted national attention through independent releases, and other local bands have followed suit on the wings of hope and borrowed cash. Bands like R.E.M., RF and the Radar Angels, and the Basics have produced their own singles, while Danny Beard of DB Recs has established himself as a major independent producer, first with his release of the B-52's "Rock Lobster" and later with singles and albums by Pylon, Kevin Dunn and the Regiment of Women, the Swimming Pool Q's, and the Side Effects. A distribution arrangement with England's Armageddon Records provides Beard's bands with a transatlantic audience. *Gyrate*, Pylon's album, has sold about twenty thousand copies worldwide, a strong showing for an independent. A soft-spoken, shy man in his late twenties, Beard has few kind words for the major labels: "I'm amazed that companies aren't coming down here to sign these bands. It shows how irresponsible and lazy they are. Pylon was ready to do an album and no record company was close to making an offer. I'm not complaining though. I've decided to stop worrying about the big labels. Their hesitation leaves me free to do what I'm doing, what I have to do."

No doubt the economic depression in the recording industry has something to do with this record company conservatism. But, more positively, economics also plays its part in the New Wave Renaissance occurring in this part of the country. A strong economy makes rents cheaper and practice spaces more accessible here than in other regions. The constant influx of new people upsets balances and creates dynamism. "Not that many people know exactly what they're doing here," says Terry Coburn of the Regiment of Women. "There's a lack of precedent. It's fairly comfortable. You have to struggle a little bit, but you don't have to sacrifice everything decent in life to make an artistic statement."

Also, in the late Seventies and Eighties the Sunbelt boom cities began making their contributions to mass culture. These have involved a blending of the foreign influences bombarding these areas with aspects of the indigenous culture. Houston gave us the urban cowboy craze and Dallas gave us the cheerleaders and an obsessively popular TV series. However, Atlanta's proximity to the besieged industrial centers of the Midwest and Northeast called for something tougher, something that would reflect both the hopes and hidden fears of displaced Northerners who fled their native ground for the bright new southern frontier. Disruption breeds creation, and New Wave, in its combination of fun and meanness, of geniality and intimidating hipness, proved the right medium in which the area's optimistic boosterism and agonies of disorder could find their true expression. Here, indeed, you could dance the mess around.

Athens bands, particularly, capture the feel of the freewheeling Dada Sunbelt. Following the fun ethic handed down by the B-52's, Athens bands will try anything. Tom Gray describes the scene this way: "After the B-52's, bands like Pylon and the Method Actors began coming out of Athens making music like you'd never heard before. There was a band on every corner, all these great sounding weird bands of nonmusicians doing things that nobody'd ever thought of doing before." Before the Athens club scene formed, bands went public at the parties that go nonstop in the large ramshackle houses in and around the town. The B-52's started this way, as did newer bands like Love Tractor, Pylon, and Oh OK. Crowds ranging from fifty to several hundred would gather at these events and dance, dance, dance.

It's an odd distinction to make, but bands and their music were not the important thing: dancing was. This distinction underlines how conceptual a scene Athens is and explains such statements as this from Pylon's Michael Lachowski: "I have trouble with the term 'dance-oriented' music that people use to describe the sound of Athens bands. It doesn't describe our sound; it only describes the activity people engage in when they hear it."

This self-conscious distance is a hallmark of the Athens scene. Despite all the dancing, Athens is no *Dick Clark Show*. Those kids on the floor don't get on the good foot just because that new song has a hot beat you can really groove to. In Athens they do the Desublimated Dance, dancing that begins with a mental image of the self in motion and only later realizes itself in action. Talking about how much, with whom, how often, how wildly you danced at all tomorrow's parties is at least as important as dancing itself. In this hyperintellectualized college town, you dance *in order* to talk about it and fuel interest in the next party.

The word on the street that you are forming a band will produce a gig at one of these parties. This liberates bands in a number of ways. It puts off the hustle for club dates. Virtually everyone in the audience is a friend, so stage fright is held to a piquant minimum. The audience's tastes are arty and more zany academic than musical, so bands are free to experiment. Thus, the Method Actors form a band consisting entirely of a guitarist and a drummer. Limbo District dresses in Thirties' German regalia and stages No Wave cabaret. Oh OK constructs a sound solely out of drums, bass, and vocals.

The next step after playing parties is to arrange club dates in Athens and Atlanta, and then set sights on New York. There, three years of successful Athens bands has established a loyal, efficient network. From the B-52's on down, Athens bands nurture each other. Locally, they all go hear each other play all the time; pitch in with sound, equipment, lighting, and managerial help; critique each other's tapes; and talk each other up in interviews. Now living two hours outside New York City, the B-52's quietly put up bands when they're in town, move tapes around, help arrange bookings, and pass along the lessons of their experiences. "We still keep up with events in Athens because a lot of our friends in New York are friends who have moved up from there," explains Pierson. "We see them and share our information about what's going on there. And

when Athens bands come to New York, we go see them play and they
visit us. We're willing to help in any way we can."

As soon as they attain the leverage to do so, bands like Pylon and the
Method Actors request that Athens bands open for them at New York
dates. Transplanted Athenians in the Big Apple (not to mention those
who have gone along for the ride) mob the dance floor and once again
offer sanctuary, the occasional hot meal, and other amenities too frequently lacking for bands seeking exposure and experience in the city.

This focused support enables bands to view a New York gig as just
another party in a somewhat larger Athens. Protected against a too-
harsh awareness of the odds opposing them, they come on with an
engaging brashness that has invariably won them favor with crowds and
critics. So much so, that some Athens bands are girding themselves for a
backlash. "I hope people keep on liking Athens bands," says R.E.M.
guitarist Pete Buck, "but if I was in a New York band I'd be so pissed at
Athens. Here's a New York band that's been together for two years and
they can't get an audience. And here's an Athens band that's been together for a few months and they hit New York and everybody goes to
hear them and writes about them. I'd be pissed as hell."

But Pierson plays down the likelihood to such a backlash. "Ultimately,
I don't think people support these bands because they're from Athens,
although that does create initial interest. When we started out people
kept saying, 'how could *you* be from *there?*' It was like being from outer
space. But Athens bands are all very different. Bands like Pylon have
developed a following not because of where they're from, but because
they're good."

R.E.M.'s Brave New World

"**O** *kay, listen! we need everybody here* to act like professionals. We don't want to step on anybody's toes."

One of the few adults on the scene, Randy Terrell is trying to preserve order at the Basement, the Atlanta teen club that, to everyone's amazement, is about to be visited by R.E.M. Some sixty high-school photographers are standing in a roped-off area, cameras poised and hormones pumping, awaiting the band's arrival with barely suppressed hysteria. Crews from CNN, MTV, and local television stations are also at the ready.

Located behind the Lindbergh Plaza shopping center on Piedmont Road—the site, ironically enough, of the Great Southeast Music Hall, where the Sex Pistols had begun their volcanic American tour over a decade earlier—the Basement was opened last fall by Atlanta parents so their kids could have a place to go to hear music and hang out without the temptations of drink and drugs. Somewhat predictably, those high-minded origins have hardly made the Basement the hippest spot in town for older teens.

Terrell, the Basement's youth director, and the rest of the club's staff hope that today's event will change that. "We needed something that would attract the senior high-school kids, something that would make this place cool," says Miriam Lockshin, the Basement's promotion director. "Obviously, in Atlanta, R.E.M. is king, especially right now, because their album has just come out."

A call from one of the Basement's board members to Jefferson Holt, R.E.M.'s manager, elicited a quick agreement. Since R.E.M. was regularly coming to Atlanta to rehearse for its upcoming world tour, the group would stop by the Basement for fifteen minutes on the afternoon of January 19th to autograph a mural dedicated to the band. Pictures of R.E.M. at the Basement in school newspapers and other publications around the city would increase the club's cachet, and the members of the band, who live sixty-five miles away, in Athens, Georgia, would have done a bit of community service.

Suddenly, the R.E.M. boys—singer Michael Stipe, guitarist Peter Buck, bassist Mike Mills, and drummer Bill Berry—appear. They saunter in, their casualness and mild bewilderment a funny contrast to the jolt of energy that surges through the kids, who are crackling as if they'd been plugged into a live socket. After Terrell provides a brief tour of the club's facilities and explains the day's purpose—"We still haven't gotten to the kids who drink," he tells a politely nodding Buck—the band members seat themselves at a card table to sign autographs, pose for pictures, and chat with the students.

Then it's time for what Berry calls the Wall Scrawl. Berry and Buck hoist Stipe high into the air, and the singer begins writing with a black Magic Marker near the top of the mural, which is a light-green square inscribed with the orange letters R.E.M. When Stipe, who is still being held aloft by his band mates, turns around, raises his fist in the air, flashes a huge grin, and reveals his message—STIPE SAYS STRENGTH + PEACE—the room explodes with flashes. After a couple of short interviews—"I think it's a great idea, and I'm really glad we were able to do this," Mills says to a television reporter, while Buck laments that "there's too many tragedies that happen with drinking and driving"—the group heads for its van.

And what do the students think of their illustrious visitors? Fourteen-year-old Travis Peck of Pace Academy is only too eager to provide the answer: "R.E.M. is awesome!"

It's been a long, strange trip for R.E.M., since the release of "Radio Free Europe" on a minuscule independent label in 1981 first brought the group to national attention. Once the darlings of the underground, they are now solicited by parents' groups to improve the social habits of the young. College-radio perennials, they have now graduated—into high schools. Having signed a five-record deal with Warner Brothers last year for a reported ten million dollars, the members of R.E.M. are approaching the status of—can it be?—superstars.

Meanwhile, on the far less complicated trip across town to an industrial section of northwest Atlanta—where the band is renting the largest room at a studio complex called Rehearse Too Much—the mood is a bit charged. It's Thursday evening, and early Monday morning the band is flying to Japan to begin a yearlong world tour—R.E.M.'s first live shows in sixteen months—and nerves are somewhat frayed. The band members hadn't been told that the Wall Scrawl would include big-time media like CNN, and they are still bemused by the horde of younger fans they picked up after "The One I Love," from their 1987 album *Document*, became their first Top Ten hit.

During the ride, Stipe, whose political outspokenness tends to elicit the most painfully serious questions, laughingly recounts how one student asked him, "We just had a big argument in class about whether we should worship Karl Marx. What do you think, sir?" Munching on nuts, the singer, who is unshaven and characteristically decked out like a Beckett hobo, with the Eighties touch of a long, thin braid down his back, wonders, "Do I really merit the *sir*?"

At Rehearse Too Much, a stage is set up at the far end of a bleak, unadorned warehouse-style space with cinder-block walls. "About twenty-eight bands rehearse here, most of them thrash and metal," Stipe explains as he smokes one of his hand-rolled cigarettes and strolls through the corridors of the complex. That may account for the question one musician, whose band was rehearsing down the hall, asked R.E.M.'s crew while listening to the group run through its set one night. "Who is this fucking R.E.M. cover band?" he asked, his voice dripping contempt. "They play one R.E.M. song after another!"

"What! *Who* said that?" Stipe asks in mock horror when told of the comment. The singer was sufficiently concerned about rigidities in R.E.M.'s sound that, according to Mills, he told the other members of the band "not to write any more R.E.M.-type songs" when they began working on *Green,* the now-platinum album they released in early November. Consequently the remark has just enough of a point to sting Stipe a tad. He shakes his head as he walks away and says, "It's a perfect circle."

On the cramped stage, equipment is being readied for R.E.M.'s last rehearsal before the tour. Buck is huddling with Peter Holsapple, the former main man of the now-defunct dB's, who has been drafted to play guitar and keyboards for R.E.M. on this tour. They are sorting out an arrangement for "Academy Fight Song," a Mission of Burma tune that R.E.M. is covering in its shows. The other band members are cracking open cans of beer and soda and pulling slices from the eight pizzas that were ordered for dinner.

Bertis Downs IV, the band's lawyer and longtime friend, has torn himself away from last-minute tour preparations and driven over from Athens to catch the final rehearsal. R.E.M.'s set includes a healthy dose of songs from *Green,* and Downs, whose fresh-faced enthusiasm belies his profession, says, "I just had to come by to hear how the new songs sound." "After you hear 'Get Up,'" Holt assures him, "you're going to want us to make a live album."

Indeed, hearing R.E.M.'s power through some twenty-five songs in a space smaller than most clubs is undeniably, as Travis Peck might put it, awesome. Undistracted by an audience, gripped by the challenge of the impending tour, the band is totally concentrated in its musical force.

Dressed simply in black workout pants, a green shirt and a black cloth cap, Stipe stands virtually still, but his voice is strong and resonant. The band crunches the staccato rhythms of "Academy Fight Song" and then leans into muscular versions of "Pop Song 89" and "Stand," from *Green*. Buck's body rocks in emphatic time with his playing, and Berry and Mills build a solid bottom that gives the songs a tougher sound and a greater propulsion than they have on record.

After "Stand" closes, the band confers onstage, and Holt, ever protective of his charges, says to the four or five people sitting near him, "It must be pretty weird, playing these songs with everyone sitting around talking. We should all stand up and scream after they finish the next one." So when the group ends "Maps and Legends," an eerie tune from *Fables of the Reconstruction* that is much enriched by Holsapple's keyboards, it is greeted by a burst of shouts and raucous clapping from the dozen or so people hanging around the room.

The band members stare uncomprehendingly and then break into smiles. Buck waves, and Stipe says, "My first applause of the new year. Thank you!" Then he recalls that this night is the eve of George Bush's inauguration and adds, "My last applause of the Reagan era." Another volley of applause follows. "You've got to fuck with them every now and then," Holt says, satisfied.

The rehearsal resumes as R.E.M. fires up fierce versions of "Finest Worksong" and "These Days." The proceedings come to a brief halt when Buck pops a string during a particularly ferocious rendition of "Turn You Inside-Out"; and then "Sitting Still" and "Driver 8" follow, with Buck and Holsapple ringing out the signature guitar jangle of R.E.M.'s early sound.

The evening ends with "I Remember California," "You Are the Everything," another pass at "Academy Fight Song," the pleasing, untitled song that closes *Green* and "Time After Time," the evocative ballad from *Reckoning*. As the equipment is being loaded, Mills elects to stay in Atlanta, where his mother is about to undergo surgery. Stipe, Buck, and Berry climb into the van for the late-night drive back to Athens.

After they arrive, Buck drops in at the 40 Watt Club, which he describes as "purposely kind of a rock & roll dump," to catch the end of a set by an Athens band he produced called the Primates. "Their favorite bands are George Thorogood, Hank Williams, and the Minutemen," he says, "and they kind of sound like a combination of all three." Buck's wife, Barrie, a tall, dark-haired beauty who co-owns the 40 Watt, is behind the bar, and the guitarist orders a beer.

After the nightcap, Buck's mind drifts back to the rehearsal. "That's the way to see a band," he tells a visitor, "the way you saw us tonight."

Back in Athens for their last weekend before flying off, the band members and Holt are desperately trying to dispatch all the details that need to be dealt with before departure. Due to a bureaucratic snafu, a crew member's visa may not be ready in time, and Holt and Downs are pulling strings to make sure he is able to leave on schedule. At this point, R.E.M. is a sufficiently important Georgia industry—as he tries to check a friend into an Athens hotel, Buck unselfconsciously refers to the group as "our corporation" while negotiating with the desk clerk—that a U.S. senator intervenes in the band's behalf.

Stipe, who handles most of the band's visual imagery, needs to approve tour T-shirts. Mills is motoring back and forth to Atlanta to visit his mother and say goodbye to his family. Buck and Barrie are trying to find time to run off to the mall to buy luggage.

Finally, Holsapple and his girlfriend, Ilene, have agreed to headline a benefit at the 40 Watt for the Athens Pro-Choice Action League on Friday night. Buck rehearses with Holsapple earlier in the day and joins the duo onstage for ragged but right versions of such numbers as Marvin Gaye's "Sexual Healing," Dion's "Drip Drop," and the Flying Burrito Brothers' "Do Right Woman." A cheerful-looking Stipe drops in to catch the action, with a group of bohemian pals, known to more cynical locals as "diStipels," in tow.

With all the hubbub, it hardly seems only sixteen months ago that R.E.M. announced that the band would take a break from performing live and possibly even recording. R.E.M.'s steps forward have always been careful—the result of an intriguing blend of deliberation, intuition, and a staunch sense of integrity. The popularity that came in the wake of the platinum *Document* annihilated whatever vestiges remained of R.E.M.'s insulated cult status. The consequences of that change had to be analyzed and absorbed before the band could define a suitable direction.

"One thing that was affecting us was this blind acceptance and enthusiasm for anything that was said or done onstage," Mills says about the tour that followed the release of *Document*. "People are so frantic by the time you get into these larger halls that it's just a party no matter what you do. It makes you feel kind of weird about *meaning* what you do. You may put your heart and soul into something, but it doesn't matter because those people can't hear it anyway. Since it's something that we did love to do so much, we wanted to step back before we got burned out on it."

Another issue R.E.M. had to confront was the end of its contract with I.R.S. Records, the label that signed the band after the release of "Radio Free Europe." I.R.S. very much wanted to re-sign the group, and R.E.M. felt a great deal of loyalty to the label, which from the first endorsed and committed itself to the band's insistence on total creative control and progress at the band's own pace. When R.E.M. was first shopping for a contract, according to Buck, the folks at I.R.S. were "the only ones who didn't say, 'Boy, if you guys cut your hair and stop wearing dirty clothes, I can turn you into the Go-Go's.'" The band members all say that leaving I.R.S. was the hardest decision they ever made.

The key factor from the band's perspective was that I.R.S. and its overseas distributor, CBS International, had been unable to expand R.E.M.'s audience outside the United States. Says Berry, "We got really tired of going to Europe and pretty much being given an ultimatum by the record companies over there, the affiliates of I.R.S., who were saying, 'If you don't come over and tour, we're not going to promote your record. You won't even see it on the shelves.' Then we'd get over there, and there'd be absolutely no promotion at all." The band's core of followers never grew significantly.

Needless to say, news that R.E.M. was thinking of leaving I.R.S. excited interest from virtually every major record company. Ultimately, the band was impressed both by the assurances given by Warner Brothers that R.E.M. would be a top priority of the company's overseas division and by the label's artist-oriented reputation.

"They've had some of my favorite artists on the label for years and not really bothered them so much about selling records," Buck says of Warner Brothers. "Van Dyke Parks still puts out records. Randy Newman, sometimes he has hits, sometimes he doesn't—he makes great records. We figured that just looking at people's track records, you can understand what kind of business they're going to run." That Lenny Waronker, president of Warner Brothers Records, was himself a producer also weighed heavily with the band.

Still, it may be hard, at least in the public's estimation, for R.E.M. to maintain what Holt calls the "small, homey, hokey, *Mayberry R.F.D.* kind of feel to the way we live our lives" while earning millions of dollars, selling millions of records, pursuing international markets, and working with one of the largest entertainment conglomerates in the world.

From the questions they asked, according to Berry, the kids at the Basement seemed to "think of Warner Brothers as literally like a monster, just something that consumes and spits out. I think a lot of kids wonder how we fit." Sitting in his office, Holt halts a conversation about the move from I.R.S. to Warner Brothers, saying, "I feel completely uncomfortable discussing that situation, because I just don't think that anything said about it is going to translate, that there's any way for people to understand. It seems like you're either biased towards 'Well, they did what they had to do and went for the money' or 'God, they really did the underdog dirty.' "

In fact, nothing riles R.E.M. quite like the charge that the band has sold out. "My response is, like, Guns n' Roses," Berry says. "Great band, by the way. I love 'em. But it's like they've got this 'fuck you,' 'rock & roll kid' attitude, and they sell seven million records. Their *first* record. And here we are on our sixth record—*Document* was our fifth full LP, it sells a million records, and 'R.E.M. has sold out.' But Guns n' Roses gets all these accolades. I don't know what we're supposed to do. I really don't."

Never known for pulling punches, Buck hits the question dead on. "Pretty much all the extreme opinions about us I think are wrong," he says. "We're not the best band in the world—nobody is—so who cares about that? And all the people who think we've sold out, I don't really care much about them either.

"I know what I do, and I'll set my job up against anyone else's any day and say that I make less concessions to what people tell me to do than anyone else around—I mean, no matter *what* job they do. But, then, no one's going to believe that.

"There are a lot of people who like bands when they're smaller—and *I'm* one of them," he says. "I really love the Replacements, but I don't go see them now. I saw them in front of twenty people fifty times, and the same with Hüsker Dü. The last time I went to see Hüsker Dü, I was, like, eight hundred people back and getting elbowed in the gut by a fat guy with a leather jacket.

"So whenever people say, 'You're just too big, I don't enjoy going to your shows,' I say, 'That's fine.' I understand the people who say, 'You're too popular. I'm going to go follow the Butthole Surfers.' That's valid.

"Of course," Buck says, with a wry grin, "now the Butthole Surfers are getting a little too popular."

At a little after six o'clock on Saturday evening, Michael Stipe, driving a gray Volvo station wagon, pulls up in front of the two-story building R.E.M. has restored in downtown Athens for its offices and rehearsal studio. The street is deserted, the weather is uncommonly cold for Georgia, and the sky is darkening. Stipe, who is wearing his cloth cap and a long coat, suggests a cup of coffee, but when the coffee shop proves loud, brightly lit, and, most problematic, crowded, he wants to leave after about a minute.

Unlike Buck, Berry, and Mills, who are exactly the people they seem to be, Stipe, at twenty-nine the youngest member of the band, is much harder to fix—a fact that leads many people to dismiss him as pretentious or worship him as a mysterious god. With people he doesn't know very well, he is by turns remote and friendly. Anyone who grows used to one aspect of his personality is hurt or pleased, but always surprised, by the unexpected flash of the other. The emotional distance he seems to require, the imminence of departure that erases the threat of intimacy, is eloquently captured in lines from the song "Good Advices," on *Fables*: "I'd like it here if I could leave / And see you from a long way away."

It's the perfect attitude for a performer, and Stipe—perhaps inevitably and perhaps as a means of protecting himself—has made his personality part of his art. After climbing into a chair in Jefferson Holt's office and pulling his knees up to his chest, he says, "I can easily say, 'Which Michael do you want today?' "

The room is dim, and the window behind Stipe, lit with the day's last light, frames him, a dark silhouette surrounded by a waning brightness. As the interview continues and it grows darker outside, Stipe emerges more clearly among the room's shadows.

"It's so odd, I really don't have any idea how people look at me," he says, a cigarette in his hand and a cup of hot tea on the desk at his side. "I mean, I've always thought that the worst thing would be to be the court jester of a generation, and sometimes I feel like that, especially with the hats and tails onstage. But those are pretty simple devices, and they really stem from something that is a necessity for me. They also stem from an admiration and understanding of theatrics and the fact that you are in the public eye or the media and being able to utilize that."

During the week before November's presidential election, Stipe tried to utilize the fact that he was in the public eye by buying advertisements in college newspapers in Georgia and California that read, STIPE SAYS / DON'T GET BUSHWACKED / GET OUT AND VOTE / VOTE SMART / DUKAKIS. Green, with its suggestions of optimism, environmentalism, and innocence, was released on election day. The singer meant for the album to be a gesture of hope and encouragement.

"I decided that this had to be a record that was incredibly uplifting," Stipe says of Green. "Not necessarily happy, but a record that was uplifting to offset the store-bought cynicism and easy condemnation of the world we're living in now."

One dimension of Stipe's decision is that after years of being accused of obscurantism, he chose to print the lyrics to "World Leader Pretend"—a song that takes emotional honesty and directness of expression as its very subjects—on Green's sleeve. A number of the other songs on Green, like "Pop Song 89," "Stand," and "Get Up," are similarly straightforward and bracing.

But frustration over misreadings is another reason why Stipe went for greater sonic clarity and linear meaning on Green. "There was frustration," Stipe admits, "to the degree that I rewrote 'Green Grow the Rushes' two times—as 'The Flowers of Guatemala' and 'Welcome to the Occupation'—where I actually ghostwrote the bio that went out to the press, so that they would say that 'this is a song about American intervention in Central America.'"

Despite the general sense of uplift on Green, the album doesn't lack disturbing moments. "Orange Crush," about the herbicide Agent Orange that was used in Vietnam, was originally written around the time of Document. The haunted travelogue "I Remember California" chronicles the human wreckage, the "nearly was and almost rans," of the Los Angeles fast lane. The harsh, metallic "Turn You Inside-Out" also provides a menacing note.

"I understand that all high-school boys think it's about fucking," says Stipe with a chuckle. "That's the report I've gotten back from the grade schools. It's about manipulation and power. To me, it had a great deal to do, emotionally, with what a performer can do to an audience. A performer could be myself, it could be Martin Luther King, it could be Jackson, it could be Reagan, it could be Hitler—any preacher that is able to manipulate a large group of people."

Despite the urgency of his concerns, one of Stipe's more appealing qualities is his occasional willingness to poke fun at himself. He catches himself in the middle of an intense explanation of how "Oddfellows Local 151," on *Document,* was a "debunking" of the rural mythologizing of *Fables of the Reconstruction.* "Are you there?" he asks, laughing, and then admits, "I always get so serious in interviews, I think people think I'm a really serious person from that. My voice always drops way down to here, and I take on this Buckminster Fuller persona where the world hinges on my words."

On the other hand, Stipe *is* unquestionably a rather serious lad. Asked about R.E.M.'s impact, he says, "It's very hard for me to look at rock & roll and think of it as important in the world, because I just don't think that way. It's important in my life, because it's the arena I've chosen to move in.

"How serious can you be about a pop band?" he asks. "And then on the other hand, I see how music completely and totally affects people and affects their lives. It's nothing. On the other hand, God, look what it did for me, how much music has changed my life."

Buck comes at the issue of R.E.M.'s impact more frontally. "The influence that I'd like to think we have is that people saw that there's a way to go about doing this on your own terms," he says. "The thing is, you have to *not* worry about success. You can't do it and say, 'I want to make a million dollars tomorrow,' or 'I want to be as big as Madonna.' There's different ways to chase that. One of the things that's overlooked in music is that it's totally honorable to be a musician who does what he wants and doesn't make a lot of money.

"People tend to think, 'If you don't sell a million records, you're a failure.' Well, we didn't sell a million records until last year, and we were really successful. We didn't have a gold record until *Lifes Rich Pageant,* and that was five years down the line. We'd been touring, lots of people were coming to see us, and we were making a living. So I've never judged success in those kinds of terms, and hopefully we're an example that you don't have to be judged that way."

Buck lives about a mile outside of town in a large white Southern-style house, filled with books, magazines, guitars, and records, including a definitive collection of R.E.M. bootlegs. Against his better judgment, he recently purchased a "bottom of the line" CD player—his first—so that he'd be able to listen to the Mission of Burma CD compilation he just picked up. In his driveway sits a fancy Dodge jeep, a '57 Chevy, and a hearse.

Through the heyday of the Athens scene, when the B-52's, Pylon, R.E.M., and a seemingly endless stream of other bands managed to turn a sleepy Southern college town into a nonstop dance party, Buck lived in a single room that looked like a hip record store after an explosion. His house now, for all its beauty and tasteful appointments, is simply that room writ large. And while R.E.M. has achieved a prominence that none of the other Athens bands could attain, in their home town, Buck, Berry, and Mills are rarely bothered. Before he went onstage at the Pro-Choice benefit, the extent to which the patrons of the 40 Watt club permitted Buck to stand undisturbed at the bar seemed almost willful.

"The mayor says hello now" is how Berry describes how R.E.M.'s life in Athens has changed over the years. "It is real normal, except in the fall when the first batch of freshmen come in. They'll see us in the bars, and that gets a little weird, as far as people groping at us. That lasts for about two weeks, because then everybody realizes that we're out in the bars every single night!"

Stipe's life in Athens tends to be a bit more problematic, though even he can move around undisturbed much of the time. For all that the town's music scene has made Athens seem like a swinging place in the popular media, it's essentially still a small Southern backwater dominated by a conservative, football-crazed university. To the school's more Neanderthal frat boys, Stipe is not a mystical poet or a political progressive—or even a cool rock singer—but a geek to be abused. A recent column in a town paper that criticized Stipe prompted the following personal reply from him to the author: "Please cut the shit out. No matter what you think, I have to live in this town too. This is a reflection on me, not my 'image.' It's hard enough as it is."

On the opposite end of the spectrum, Stipe's enigmatic lyrics and

romantic persona often inspire slightly unhinged types to read their
own emotional difficulties into his songs. Such people are generally very
interested in discussing the connections between his work and their
lives when they run into him—to chilling effect. For the record, Stipe
refuses to discuss his life in Athens and is said to maintain a residence
out of state.

On the brighter side, tending a fire in his fireplace, sipping a beer late on
Saturday night, Peter Buck seems very much the contented lord of Buck
Manor, the affectionate name a fellow musician gave the guitarist's digs.
The impending tour recalls for Buck the days in the early Eighties when
R.E.M. first hit the road—the four members of the band in a small van
with Holt as their driver—for endless tours that have now become the
stuff of legend. The pilgrimage was gaining momentum, and for a considerable number of people across the country—in Nowheresville towns
and New Wave hotbeds—it was sometimes possible to believe that there
was nothing more important in the world than R.E.M.

Earlier in the evening, Stipe had described those days as "harrowing—
but a blast." "If there's an extension of *On the Road* and that whole
Kerouacian"—he began laughing—"Can I possibly use that term, Kero-
whack-ian? If there's an extension of that, probably forming a rock band
and touring clubs is the closest you could get. Peter and I certainly had
romantic ideas along those lines, and damned if we didn't do it. And
damned if it didn't pay off."

For his part, Buck says, "We really soon got the reputation of 'Well,
they'll do anything.' I mean, we're not going to do commercials, and we
wouldn't go on television and lip-sync, but as far as playing real places—
we had to. We were broke and we had to sell some fucking records, so
'Yeah, sure, we'll play the pizza parlor.' In the South there's a big thing
where every Tuesday gay bars would have New Wave Night, so we played
more gay bars than you could shake a stick at.

"If you ever saw *Spinal Tap*, we lived all of that, except for we're not
quite as ignorant," he says. "We played that same place where they were
second bill to the puppet show. It's Magic Mountain, I recognized it.
And we had the exact same crowd—people who would sit in front of us
only to give us the finger through our entire set."

The sort of experiences that would have broken up many bands—and
that did break up most of R.E.M.'s contemporaries—have managed to

bind R.E.M. together. The four band members and Holt and Downs still show a remarkable ability to close ranks, shut out the rest of the world and make decisions based solely on their personally determined criteria. And they take nothing about their relationship and their good fortune for granted.

"I most of the time feel like I'm not going to have a job next week," Holt says. "I always thought, 'They're going to get fed up, break up, and I won't have a job.' And I am amazed that it's however many years later and here we are. There's not a day that goes by that I don't think how incredibly lucky and thankful I am that things have worked out the way they are. And it wouldn't surprise me if they broke up tomorrow."

And yet there's a dizzying sense of a new beginning with R.E.M. "For me, *Green* had so many connections to *Murmur*," Stipe says. "It was very much in the back of my head the whole time we were working on it. From the album cover to the topics of the songs and the way the songs were carried out, to me, there's a great connection there. Signing to another label was a new start for us. It did offer us an opportunity to sit back, scratch our temples, and wonder, 'Where are we and where do we want to go?'"

With those questions answered for the moment, the pilgrimage is under way again. The members of R.E.M. are standing on the cusp of a brave new world they don't yet know. And they feel fine.

Rolling Stone April 20, 1989

Rock Criticism and the Rocker

A Conversation With Peter Buck

In *September 1994,* R.E.M. guitarist Peter Buck kindly took time off from promoting R.E.M.'s *Monster* album to do an interview for this book. Initially, I didn't want to include any interviews in question-and-answer format, but, because this is essentially a collection of writing about rock & roll, I wanted an artist's perspective on rock criticism. Peter was an ideal candidate for the job, both because R.E.M. is the very definition of a critic's darling and because he has a sharp critical sensibility himself. He keeps up with the music and with the writing about the music and loves to talk about both. In addition, I've known Peter since before the release of R.E.M.'s first independent single in 1981, and have always held his intelligence, humor, and passion for music in the highest regard. It's a pleasure to have any excuse to speak with him.

For this interview, Peter and I met in the bar of the Four Seasons Hotel in Manhattan, drank a glass of wine or two, and talked for about an hour. This conversation proceeds the way so many of our talks have. It begins with a focus, wanders through a variety of related topics, and eventually meanders back to our original subject. It was a fun trip, and I hope you didn't have to be there.

You read a lot of rock writing. It's obviously a different experience to read about yourself than it is to read about other bands or to read a review of somebody else's record. What's the difference between what you want to see when you're reading something about R.E.M. and what you want to see when you're reading about somebody else?

I do read a lot of music stuff, and I always have—it's not simply because I'm "in the business." And of course I always like to read about people who say controversial things and admit to drug problems and ornate sexual peccadillos. That's what you want to read—it just is. It's fun and exciting—and it's the *last* thing I want to have anything to do with my band.

The English press, especially, is focused completely on the personal. With the English magazines, it seems that if you sit in a room and you just want to talk about the music, they'll find a way to make it not about the music. Maybe it's because the magazines come out every week and you have to appeal on a flash level. I mean, a lot of the English press are closer to the *Enquirer* than to the *New York Times*. So every three years you get this generation of English bands who make absolutely great copy, and maybe not necessarily such great records.

Of course, when I read about R.E.M., I always want the writer to be a seasoned, knowledgeable person who respects and loves us and gives us the benefit of the doubt every step of the way—which isn't really what rock criticism is about.

What do you think it is about? What do you think it can do? Is it different from other kinds of criticism, like movie reviews or book reviews?

I think it's closer to movie reviews. With book reviews, most likely the writers aren't going to be much more literate than the readers. But the readers of rock criticism are definitely different. The person who reads *Rolling Stone* or *Melody Maker* isn't the person who reads the *New York Times Book Review*. I read them both, but I'm one person.

Rock & roll is first and foremost kids' music. Even though most of us are adults and we write about adult things, the records are bought and the reviews are read by teenagers who don't necessarily know who Kafka is—or even which college they're going to go to. So rock criticism tends to be about minutiae in a lot of ways. It's about small things. Especially the English reviews—you can read reviews of a record without ever finding out what kind of music it is. That always blows my mind. They'll review an album, talk about the lyrics, and personalize what they want to make of the record, and not say, "And by the way, it's an album of polkas." You just don't know. Sometimes I'll read a review and think, "Gee, that sounds pretty interesting—this record is about alienation and identity." Then I'll actually listen to it and go, "Whoa, it sounds like the Doobie Brothers."

What kind of impact do you think rock criticism has?

Again—I could be completely wrong—but with book reviews, there's kind of a received critical opinion about things that people tend to stick to. I'll read several reviews of the same book and they won't differ that much. People know good writing and bad writing. Whereas with rock & roll, sometimes bad playing is good playing. I mean, you would never find a guy who writes books the way the Ramones make records. And if you did, you certainly couldn't appreciate it. And yet the Ramones made pretty perfect records. So with rock criticism, there aren't rules and laws that can be followed. It's basically "Do I like it? Do you like it?" As for the audience, I think three quarters of them just look at the picture and the headline and see how many stars it got. You get to the point where you wonder how many people are influenced to go out and buy the record because of what they read.

I think it's cumulative. I think that most seventeen-year-olds won't go out and buy a record they never heard because they read one article. But if they see articles everywhere, the picture everywhere, they heard the single—you know, that's how Guns n' Roses happened. They were just everywhere all of a sudden. It's fascinating—I think about it all the time: What does this mean, the fact that we do these interviews, and they appear in the press, especially when it's in something like *People*, something that isn't necessarily for people who like music. You wonder, who does this reach? Does anyone say, "God, I have to buy that record because these guys talked about their personal lives."

Do you approach those kinds of interviews differently? What is your preparation? Do you think, "This is going to appear here, and these people might be interested in this and might not be interested in that?" You're obviously not going to talk about what kind of guitar strings you use to People.

No, not really. We have never actually talked to *People*—I don't know why. Generally we talk to the music media, although lately we've been doing things with *Vogue* and *GQ* and places like that. Still, the journalists for those stories seem to come from the same perspective—they're people who like music and get hired by those magazines to write about music. They tend to have to write more generally there. In *Vogue,* you have to explain when we got together and all that. So, for me, it's about understanding that it's going to be just the simple facts. Whereas *Rolling Stone* or *Melody Maker* has interviewed us every year since 1983, and I don't have to cover biographical data. I can feel a little freer free associating about what's going on with the new record or the new tour or whatever.

But we've never done a lot of press that was not music-oriented. I mean, Rod Stewart is a celebrity, and he gets celebrity things. We tend, at this point, to still get articles about music. Then there also are the specialist magazines, the guitar-player magazines, and that's something totally different. It's all right in those places to talk about effects and strings and picks, stuff that is boring to everyone in the world except the people who buy those magazines.

You were very influenced by rock criticism as a young person, but the cultural environment is different now from the way it was when you were growing up. Young people are much more likely to get most of their information from MTV and to a lesser extent maybe radio, and then magazines. Certainly when I was growing up, just to see a picture of a band was amazing. Now you've seen them a hundred times before you've heard three of their songs. Talk about the kind of impact that reading rock criticism had on you.

When I was growing up I lived in Georgia, and bands just didn't come down there. I mean, they really didn't. On TV—this is parenthetical—I remember when the New York Dolls were on Don Kirschner's rock concert in 1973. It was such a big event that a band I liked was going to be on TV that I had my three friends who also liked T-Rex and the Dolls over to my house. My parents had a basement, and we took old mattresses down there and brought the TV down and smuggled in a case of beer. I was about sixteen. We got drunk and watched the Dolls and it was an epochal event—real music on television. It wasn't just the usual suspects. Back then there were like two rock shows, and, you know, Helen Reddy would be hosting one. I remember that pretty specifically.

So I got a huge amount of information from the print media. I subscribed to the *Village Voice* for a couple of years, luckily enough for me, right when punk started happening in about '74, '75, '76. I always had access to the *Voice*. So I was reading Robert Christgau, and Lester Bangs writing about Blondie—I think he reviewed the first Blondie record. I found out about Television. I was buying those records the day they came out, which for Georgia was pretty different. I read *Creem* magazine. I hadn't discovered the English papers yet, because I don't think they came to Georgia in those days. *Creem* was a big one, because they liked Iggy and the Stooges. So I got turned onto a lot of stuff.

I lived in California for a year and a half when I was twelve and thirteen. There was a writer named John Mendelssohn, who was also in a band called Christopher Milk. He wrote for a magazine called *Coast*, which doesn't exist anymore, and he wrote articles about Iggy and the Stooges. I went out and bought the Christopher Milk records. This was like 1971. So I became a fan of Iggy, the Velvet Underground, the Nazz,

Crazy Horse. I'd be the only thirteen-year-old on the block going, "I think I need to buy this Iggy and the Stooges record." The guys at the counter would be like, "You better wear rubber gloves when you hold this album, kid." So I got turned onto a lot of stuff that was really foreign to me through print.

Mendelssohn actually was a big influence on me, as well. He was one of the first writers whose byline I learned to recognize. Much later, he said something nice about me in print, while disparaging a number of people I know, which only made it better, of course.

Of course.

In real life we tried to work together a few times, but it didn't really work out.

He wrote like what he thought he was: a rock star. I bought the Christopher Milk records when I was fourteen, and thought they were kind of cool. And they are kind of cool, but you can read their influences pretty easily. He reviewed for *Rolling Stone* in the old days—I've seen his stuff in the collections. I started reading *Rolling Stone* when I was thirteen, but still that was 1971 or whatever. But his stuff in the collections is really fascinating.

But criticism helped me elucidate a lot of things. Living in Roswell, Georgia, in 1971, everyone liked the Allman Brothers. I can't tell you why—that's all there was to it. It was a law. I didn't really have friends who could tell me why they liked something. I had two friends in Roswell who liked T-Rex, because they looked cool in make-up. I don't think it had anything to do with the way it sounded. It helps to have some kind of critical acumen about things when you're in a vacuum. I mean, *completely* in a vacuum. I had to define for myself why I thought T-Rex was cool and Sweet was less cool.

What do you think about the situation now? Does it make a difference if kids are not getting information from print, that they're getting their information visually, from television? At the same time, coverage of rock & roll is ubiquitous. Every newspaper has a rock critic, every TV show covers it, every news program covers it. Bands like Pavement play on The Tonight Show. How are people making sense of what's coming at them?

It seems that kids now are a lot more knowledgeable about the processes. MTV goes "backstage with so-and-so." I must admit to having been really naive about that kind of stuff. When I'd see a band open for another band at a place in Atlanta that held three hundred people, I just assumed that the opening band had a Lear jet.

Right. Exactly.

And that a limo would pick them up and they'd probably have an orgy with teenage girls in the back of the car on the way to the show. That's what I assumed. Now I realize that the *headliner* probably arrived in a station wagon. Kids today have a real understanding of the mechanics of the business. They know about sound-checks. I didn't know about sound-checks, I figured you just played. They know how people make videos, how people make records. They understand what demo tapes are. I had never met anyone who had been in a band who had even had a single out, ever, until the mid-Seventies, '76. I knew people who played in bands, but it was such a huge gap from playing Foghat covers to being one of the guys actually making records. You just assumed that gap was completely unbridgeable, that that would never be you or your friends. In a way it's really great that there's so much coverage now, because while the machine eats people up and spits them out, it still means that, well, Pavement is on Leno.

   That wouldn't have happened ten years ago. We were never on Johnny Carson. They would never take us. They would never take us right up until Jay was on. In '89, when everyone was fighting for us, they were like, "No, we're not really interested in having R.E.M. on." I can't say I blame them—we really weren't that big, and Johnny Carson had no knowledge of us. We weren't right for their audience. But Jay Leno probably listens to Pavement, or at least has heard of them. Still, I do think it's odd. When I was thirteen, forty-five-year-old guys didn't listen to what teenagers listened to. They just didn't. Forty-five-year-old guys, their experience was 1953 or something.

Along those lines, it was pretty amazing a while ago when MTV threw a party for R.E.M.'s work for Rock the Vote and President Clinton sent a videotaped message to the band.

Yeah. I know.

I mean, the president . . .

. . . knows who we are.

You've got to remember that up until George Bush, . . . you can guarantee that he never listened to anything. He didn't know who any of us were. He thought that Boy George was in U2.

Or even more incredibly, he denounced Elvis at the 1992 Republican convention. Who does this guy think his audience is? He's from Texas. Everybody in every state that is crucially important to him worships Elvis. And he referred to U2 as teeny-boppers, when they were calling the White House from the stage during the Zoo TV tour.

I guess U2 met with Clinton, and Bush said, "Well, George Clinton . . ."—great, *George* Clinton—"Well, Bill Clinton can talk to Boy George all he wants to." I'm sure someone thought that was a funny line, but it showed how out of touch he is. It's going to be a long time before I'm as old as the president. But it's really weird to think that those guys grew up and probably dated people who listened to the Grateful Dead and dropped acid.

Getting back to the earlier question, there's a sense now that everybody knows everything. Everybody knows what producers do. Everybody knows how a studio works. Everybody knows the kind of stuff that used to be specialist knowledge.

It's funny how that works. I was reading some article, this was years ago, it might have been in *Rolling Stone*. I think Ahmet Ertegun was cutting some record in Memphis, and he thought, "Let's get some kids off the street to hear what they think," and they brought some kids off the street. The first guy goes, "Man, I think this mix is EQ'd wrong. I think it's too high-endy." Ahmet says, "What the fuck are you talking about, mix, EQ? I pull some kid off the street and you tell me how to EQ a record?"

That is certainly the way it is now. In a way it's good. It demystifies it a lot. Kids understand more of what's going on. Think about Green Day for a minute—they're twenty-two and this is their third record. They were in bands when they were fourteen and put out their own record when the lead singer was seventeen. They're heirs to a tradition: you're sixteen, you're a punk, you write punk songs, you make your own record on a small label, you tour. I think they're all just legal-age for drinking now, after five years in the business. I just didn't have any awareness that you could do that when I was that age. I was kind of trying to write songs when I was seventeen, but I didn't know what I was doing.

The flip side of everyday people having specialist knowledge is that cult phenomena become totally mainstream. So someone like William Burroughs has become like a rock star.

That blows my mind, and this gets back to the media thing. William Burroughs is not the best writer in the world. People have a teenage fascination for his writing. I think he's interesting and has said some interesting stuff. He's gay or at least bisexual, a guy who was a junkie for forty years, way outside of society. And he's selling sports shoes right now! You turn the TV on and go, "What marketing whiz decided that an octogenarian ex-drug addict avowed homosexual beatnik is the guy to sell tennis shoes to seventeen-year-olds?" For me, it's totally great. But that was unthinkable twenty years ago. Twenty years ago, if they did sell tennis shoes on TV—

It would be a tennis player—

Or a basketball player. And he would have to be white, of course.

Well, we've drifted off from rock criticism to the media in general, though, obviously, they are connected. But it simultaneously seems that everything is closed down and everything is wide open. In a sense, there really does seem not to be any outside anymore. There's no real underground or counterculture that's thriving and really represents some kind of alternative stream. Maybe there never was. But on the other hand, it seems like consequently you do get William Burroughs in an advertisement. Everything is all up in the air, and no one knows exactly where things are.

Again, I hate to go back to when I was a kid, but all through the Seventies, Patti Smith was considered weird and scary, and she wouldn't have been in *People* no matter how many records she sold. Part of the reason for that is that the generation in control of things in the Seventies grew up in the Forties and Fifties, and they just didn't get it and didn't understand it and felt threatened by it. Anyone who's involved in the music industry now grew up in the Sixties or the Seventies even, and a lot of barriers did come down in those times. David Geffen is not going to be terrified of something new. He's seen it all. He probably dropped acid and ran around naked at Woodstock. David Geffen, what is he, maybe fifty-two? When I was a kid, a fifty-two-year-old man would send you off to Vietnam and get you killed. Now fifty-two-year-old guys, they're probably listening to whatever's happening and going, "God, that's really great. I wish I'd signed them."

So in a way it's good, because since everything is acceptable, the only thing that gradates things is cash. Everyone knows you can make money off this stuff, and anything can get in the back door. Anything. So G. G. Allin would have been on the cover of *People* if he'd sold a million records—it has nothing to do with how good or bad you are. And he would have made great copy. I'm actually surprised they didn't do an article about him.

Rock & roll is a demented, mindless business where there aren't principles you can follow. Rules that you think are hard and fast all of a sudden go right out the window. I think that's great. The fact that there is no outside anymore is cool because anything can really influence the culture then. Of course, most of the stuff that sells millions and millions tends to be lowest common denominator.

That's true of anything, though. That's true of books or movies, as well. Underground now has almost nothing to do with style; it only has to do with content. So if you're writing about some alienated twenty-five-year-old kid who's a junkie, even if you're the most clichéd writer who ever lived, you're underground. Whereas somebody who's stylistically adventurous but writing about a more conventional subject is regarded as mainstream. It's become almost a more conservative environment than in the past in a funny way, because then it was about stylistic innovation. So James Joyce writes Ulysses, *and it's just about a guy walking around Dublin, except in terms of its style and language. And that's a revolution. Whereas now, it's solely content-driven.*

Having gone through my teenage years, I know that the writing that appeals to teenagers tends not to be of the highest order. I can't tell you how many twenty-year-olds I know think Charles Bukowski is the best writer ever.

Perfect example.

He is the one. And I've read most of his stuff. I don't care for the poems. But I like it for what it is. But what it is is just kind of—

Yeah, it's the same book. I've read a couple of books, and I go, "Is this the same one I read before? Is he still working at the post office now?" I like the stuff near the end of his life when he was just this old drunken sot celebrity. *Hollywood* was pretty interesting. But all these kids will routinely name people who are not great writers, but who write about alienation or drugs or homosexuality or whatever. Whereas it's funny, any bookstore you go to now, there's a gay novelist section, which is totally fascinating and cool. Gay kids aren't reading it because it's not about being alienated. Most of it has to do with the past it seems to me, the things I've read. It's making sense of—

Finding your identity as a gay person.

And putting yourself in perspective. A lot of the ones I've read seem to deal with childhood. That doesn't seem revolutionary and wild. You get these teenagers as often as not gay or bisexual and they're going to read Bukowski, who's really kind of an old fart reactionary. And they'll go, "Man, this guy is totally wild." Why, because he drank and worked at the post office? I drink. I was a janitor.

Talk about the first times you were written about. Did it throw you to see yourself represented and discussed in that way? How is it different from seeing your picture or seeing yourself on TV?

I remember our first reviews. We'd just played around Georgia, so college juniors were writing about us and I was like, "This isn't the real deal." We were being written about in the *Red and Black,* the University of Georgia newspaper, and then the hippie alternative paper. We weren't on the cover of *Rolling Stone.* But I remember the first time I actually read an article about us, and I looked at it and I was like, "This is weird." I read it a couple of times and I was like, "God, I was there. I remember that." It was a review of the show that we did the day before. It's kind of off-putting.

Some of the English things were kind of odd. Those were around '83. We just came out of nowhere and we got really amazing reviews. Nobody should get reviews like that. One magazine reviewed our album twice, because the first guy didn't say it was the best album ever made. The editor went back and said, "I just want people to know how good this really is." And the first guy had given it the highest rating you could get—but that was not quite good enough. I appreciate that, because they were really on a mission to find new things to be excited about. But I had read these magazines, and I always tended to think that the people in them were to some degree—not special—but somehow validated. This must mean they're famous and big.

Someone sent me the Allan Jones review of *Murmur*, which was really good. But I was driving a van with no air conditioning to be sixth on the bill to the Police in Philadelphia. It was 110 degrees and we were also doing a gig that night somewhere else. I was like, "God, this doesn't validate us, because we're still poor and starving." I remember, we played Philadelphia, it was one hundred degrees, and there were ninety thousand people there. We went on, I think it was one o'clock in the afternoon, and it was so hot I threw up afterwards. And then someone gave me the Alan Jones review, and I'm reading it in the van on the way to the next gig, and I was like "Man, I wish I had an ice cold beer right now." In a way it's kind of distancing. Immediately, I thought, "Well, this isn't like the stuff I read when I was a kid." Because once you're in that position, unless you're a really shallow person, when you see yourself on the cover of a magazine, you don't feel validated. I mean, I don't. I try not to even read them anymore. I don't want to read about myself that much. It's just like anything else. You want something really bad, and then when you get it, you realize that it doesn't mean as much as you think it should.

The first time I published something in Rolling Stone, *I literally thought that people would recognize me on the street. And then you realize it's on the stand for two weeks, a few of your friends see it and then it's over.*

And you go on.

It was strange.

You know, what validates people to the outside world is television. When I was living in Athens, I used to walk downtown by the Coca-Cola plant everyday, and everyday there were the same fat guys with pot bellies. I had short hair and I'd wear sunglasses and a trench coat, and they'd be like, "Hey faggot, hey faggot, blow me, faggot." And I'd blow them kisses as I walked by—I wasn't going to let them drive me off the street. Then we appeared on David Letterman. I was home about a month later, walked down the street. The same guys who'd been going, "Hey, faggot," were like "Hey, I saw you on David Letterman. Way to go man, hey, cool." I liked it better when they were yelling "Hey fag."

At least it was sincere.

Yeah, it was real. Now it's like I'm a famous guy who was on David Letterman. And, again, being on TV, we did David Letterman that afternoon, then we played Maxwell's the next night. I was glad we were on TV, though. I thought it was kind of cool.

I remember seeing that performance.

I was the first person I knew who had ever been on TV—I guess maybe the B-52's were on *Saturday Night Live*. This is when there wasn't a world of difference between us and Pylon and Love Tractor. We all had record deals, we all had records out. R.E.M. worked harder.

And all the Athens bands got written about all the time.

Yeah, it wasn't that big of a difference. We'd go to parties, and if you liked Pylon better, then Pylon were the coolest people at the party. And then all of a sudden, being on Letterman made a big difference. We were perceived as big-time because we got on TV. To me, again, we were in the middle of a tour—taping that TV show was like having a night off. We played two songs and were done by six o'clock, and then we played Maxwell's the next night. But to the world, by which I mean, people on airplanes—because you always get "Who are you guys?" Obviously we're not a bowling team. In an airport, you always get people who walk up and ask, "Are you a band? Do we know you?" "Well no, not really." "Have you done anything I might have heard on the radio?" "No." "Have you been on TV?" "Well, yeah, we were on David Letterman once." And they'd go, "Wow!" They don't know who we are, never heard any of our songs, but I was on David Letterman.

I remember the first time I appeared on one of the morning shows. To the superintendent of my building I had just been another tenant—I might get my faucet fixed six months from now if I asked politely. But that night I was coming in at about one o'clock in the morning from being out, bleary-eyed. The super comes out of his apartment with his wife—they had waited up for me to get home, because they had seen me on Good Morning America. *I had no idea how significant television was. The degree to which it penetrates is amazing.*

TV does penetrate in a way that print never does. Nobody remembers the TV shows, though. I remember reviews of things that made me go out and buy the record. Steve Simels used to write about Patti Smith with a mission. He wrote for *Stereo Review,* which my father subscribed to. We didn't even have a stereo, basically, but we subscribed to *Stereo Review.* We had a mono, and I had a little Close 'n' Play. But I think the Patti Smith piece was in 1973, because he was just raving that this woman was going to be bigger than God. So I was fascinated. I had *Horses* on order before it was out, because I'd read reviews of the shows. I was seventeen. I was like, "Maybe I'll run away and go to New York." In a way, I wish I had. That kind of stuff can reach into your life—criticism can really change something and give you a perspective. Whereas with television, well, there it is. It is what it is. So with TV, it's almost like a celebration of celebrity-hood. You're not going to get any depth out of it. It's just a flat image. Whereas with print, I mean, I've read reviews that are better than the records.

Oh, well, that's very often true.

I'll buy the record, and go, "This guy loved this record so much that he produced a piece of art about it that is better than the record." I remember a review of Prefab Sprout that was just great. I bought the record and I kind of liked it. But if I hadn't read that review—let's just say I didn't get what the reviewer got out of it.

I assign and edit reviews all the time, and when they come in I often find myself thinking, "If only the record were as good as this." Rather than write what we think of as a review, they, as you say, create a piece of art about it. Since a magazine is about writing, I feel torn. Part of me is a person who, for so many years, was reading magazines and going out to buy those records with my spare money, and coming back and saying, "Man, this is disappointing." But then I'm also thinking, "Well, this is beautifully written, it's got some interesting ideas in it. It's 75 percent true." It's something I struggle with. I remember I had somebody review a Madonna record, and she attributed all these sophisticated cultural motives to Madonna. I said, "Look, I've spoken to Madonna, and I can tell you that none of what you're saying would ever have occurred to her in a hundred years. You can say that her record affects you in a certain way, or functions in the culture in a certain way, but it doesn't mean that she intended that. Your response is perfectly valid, but I'm not going to let you say she intended it because I know for a fact that that's not true."

I must say, we get away with that sometimes. When I feel the worst about the band, I think, "We're not as good as people think we are." Inevitably, then I'll read a review and someone will get something out of one of our songs that is totally unintentional. This is a good example: on *Monster*, "I Don't Sleep, I Dream." That's not an unintentional song, it's about sex and identity. I think it's supposed to be a little funnier than people think it is, but whatever. We couldn't think of a way of ending it, and for some reason we decided the bridge should be at the end of the song and we didn't want to fade it, so we just cut the tape. And Vic Garbarini was explaining why the song ends that suddenly, and he says, "The song is a dream state, and when the tape gets cut, that's when you wake up." And I went, "You know, Vic, that's totally great. I never would have thought of that." I guess unconsciously, we knew we wanted a fast ending to jerk you out of it, but I would never have associated that with sleeping and waking.

But I think that's a valid reading.

It's a valid point, and I said, "Vic, you can say that if you want to, but you'd be imputing more conscious motive than we put into it. We couldn't think of a way to end it, so we just cut the tape."

It seems to me that that's one of differences between art and criticism. An academic friend of mine once said that he was sure that Bob Dylan had read all of Ezra Pound. I said that I thought he had probably read the table of contents and flipped through a collection of Pound's poems while hanging out at Allen Ginsberg's apartment one day. Artists, people writing songs or poems, don't really have to be responsible to anything else when they're writing. What you want is something that gives you a vibe, something you can then take and do what you want with. So in a certain way critics both overvalue and undervalue what artists do. They overvalue it by attributing every conceivable intention to it. And they undervalue it because, essentially what they're saying is, that person thinks exactly the way I do. But they don't.

I would say probably 80 percent of the people who write rock criticism went to college and majored in English.

And they are more comfortable finding meanings than letting things be. In academic circles, you can't write a paper that says, "Well, it is what it is." So you tend to explicate things that should just stand as they are. Every lyricist, every single one, throws in lines that don't mean anything to flesh out a space, or just because they sound good. Like, in "Crush with Eyeliner" on *Monster,* there's that line "My kiss breath turpentine." That doesn't mean anything. I mean, it's evocative. It sounds great. It's stuck in there to fill the space. It doesn't take away from the song, but it doesn't have any literal meaning. If you were to find some literal meaning in it, that's your literal meaning. But English majors tend to think that everything means something.

One of my favorite discussions about that was in James Joyce's *Ulysses* apparently they found—do you remember reading this a few years ago?—they found some proofs? It turns out that people had been explaining what certain sections meant that turned out to be misprints. They had attributed full meaning to them—and that was not what was on the page. They had managed to explain typos as part of the process. You can just go too far with that.

Again, in academic circles, letting things be what they are is not a concern. You're either into the semiotics aspect of it, or you're deconstructing it. I've read real clever deconstructions of TV shows. I mean, like, the *Village Voice* has a TV critic. But I've met the people who do TV shows, and I know they're sitting there thinking, "We can sell a million dollars worth of Buick ads if we do this." That is what it's about. I'm not saying there isn't some good work on TV occasionally. But I've learned never to watch television, because what's on TV sucks. But I do read TV criticism, and every year I'll read something about a show that says, "This is a ground-breaking innovative show." And you turn it on and you go, "Wait a minute. It's a television show about cops." I just don't care if it's a really good television show about cops. There's a million of them.

Still, you can analyze television from a cultural perspective, even though attributing anything to the writers of those shows is ridiculous. There are reasons why a studio would spend tens of millions of dollars to make a particular kind of movie, for example. Take "Forrest Gump." It's brilliant, in a certain way. It's not brilliant as a work of art, but it manages to hit every hot button of American culture for the last twenty-five years without coming down anywhere or taking any positions at all, thereby not alienating one person who might be willing to spend eight dollars to see it. So you get the Vietnam war, race, child abuse, AIDS—all of these things that you would think, "No one could ever do that without alienating somebody." It's perfectly nuanced.

I had some real problems with that movie—it's a feel-good movie about the most horrific catastrophes that have befallen the country. And the guy who gets through it is really stupid, and it's all OK with him. He just walks through, leaving a pile of dead bodies every step of the way. Not that any of it's his fault, but the fact is here's this millionaire who's happy in his stupidity. How many people have to die for him to get to that place? How many people have to be victims of really awful circumstances?

The ultimate conservative message of the movie is that knowledge only fucks you up. The message is, "Your mother's aphorisms—that's all you need to get through life, Hallmark Card messages." Still, can you imagine the script meetings as that movie was being put together? Somebody must continually have been saying: "If we show the protesters this way, we also have to show the protesters that way. If we show this kind of political figure, we need to show that kind of political figure." Even down to the end where the question is raised, "Are we drifting through life without any kind of destiny? Or do we really have something that we're being propelled toward? Well, the answer is both." Well, of course it's both. Because, from a marketing perspective, you don't want any one person who believes one way or the other to leave the theater and not tell twenty of his friends to go see the movie—and that goes for every other issue in the movie, too.

It's certainly an odd movie. The messages in it were kind of scary. It's like, "Don't worry, be happy. Things will work out OK." And the fact is, they don't work out OK. There's a whole other movie in the Louisiana kid who gets killed in Vietnam and his family. What did they do? They were lucky enough that someone gave them a check for ten million dollars, but does that ever happen in real life? No. For me, the movie also didn't really work as entertainment, so philosophically, it doesn't really matter what it is. Forgetting all the theories about what the movie's about and why, I think it should have been thirty minutes shorter. That's my main critical carp about it. After Vietnam, it just started to get real slow.

Early on, before you began to sell a lot of records, R.E.M. was sustained by the response you were getting, both from critics and also just people who would go to your shows. How do you respond to writing about you now? You said before that you don't necessarily read all of it. What are your feelings about it?

It is different. When we started out, we didn't make any money, and we didn't really care. The critics who were in our peer group at the time— they were twenty-one, and we were twenty-one or twenty-two, or what- ever—could write these long passionate stories that would reach the thirty people in Pittsburgh who wanted to see us. And when you're not getting any financial rewards and have no comfort level, it makes it worthwhile to have your fans, whether they're critics or the people who come to the shows, as few as they are on occasion, to be really intense about it. I was always proud that we might get forty people, but they'd be like, "Wow, you're the best band in America—I can't believe you're only playing to forty people." That is sustaining. I have a lot of friends who've quit bands that were doing OK because they were nobody's favorite band. That was probably what happened to Guadalcanal Diary. They were slogging all over the world making OK money, but it wasn't like a celebration. The critics only gave the records three stars. Fans would come and maybe leave before the encore. It's hard to sustain it if you don't really feel that you're reaching people.

At our level, it's such a huge machine. It's odd, because I know it really affects some people, but if you sell ten million records, the odds are a huge portion of those people are gonna play it a couple of times, then file it under R. I mean, you can't change every person's life. It's different now. We get really good reviews, but the stakes are not as high. The record company's stakes are higher, because we're talking about mil- lions of dollars in marketing. But they're not as high for us, because we're being compensated financially—which is not the main reason we do this, by any stretch of the imagination. But we're making these rec- ords, we know their worth. The reviews now for us, all they can do is hurt the sales marginally. If every reviewer says, "This record really stinks," we'll still sell several million.

But, I mean, I want to get good reviews. I'd prefer to get good reviews and maybe sell a few less copies, because critics still tend to be my peer group. They're the people who listen to the same amount of music I do and get excited about new discoveries, but also have some kind of critical acuity to put things in perspective. That's why I get a kick out of the English mags, because they're always hiring a new generation of kids to write. They always have twenty-three-year-olds who've never heard of the Beatles.

There's actually an economic reason for that. Those publications pay so badly that only young people will write for them.

It changes the way the music business is over there. Here people still can remember Talking Heads when they were a brand new band. I mean, forget the Beatles—Talking Heads. Over there, they'll review things that are in every conceivable way not all that important or excit- ing, but they're brand new, and the writer is twenty-one years old and going nuts, so the Manic Street Preachers are the best band ever. Which is kind of good—you get people excited. But there is a lack of critical background. You read these things—"This performance by the Manic Street Preachers was the best performance ever." You read a real lot of those. Guys who are third on the bill get that. And then you buy the records and go, "This is second-rate Clash."

In a way, it's nice to have the press have an adversarial relationship to the bands because it keeps you on your toes. You can't get away with doing the same-old. The criticism you could make about American crit- icism is that established favorites get more latitude in making not-good records. I don't think that's happened to us yet, because we don't have any bad records. But certainly there are plenty of artists who make records that nobody really cares that much about, but because they're who they are, they'll get four stars and a big treatment and a big article about their personal lives. Whereas if it was a first record by a new band, it would be, "This is pretty OK. It's not that great." You don't tend to get that in England so much. Since they're a bit younger, they're totally willing to say how awful and old-fashioned we are.

I'll tell you why it works the way it does over here. Critics get excited about the opportunity to say something about a band they've loved for a long time and maybe rarely have had the chance to write about. So even if the new album by R.E.M. or U2 or whomever isn't their best work, it may well be that writer's best chance to say something about them. So between their desire to hang a bunch of major ideas on the album and their general enthusiasm about having the chance to do it, the review sometimes ends up sounding more positive than even the writer believes it should be.

It's understandable, and, certainly, history tends to color the present. I can't tell you how many records I've got where, if I were to divorce the band from its past work, I would go, "This isn't very good." But if you're fond of what the band does and willing to find the things you like—even if what you say is, "Well, there's two good songs, and the rest just sounds pleasant"—you're letting them get away with a lot.

It's also true that if you really like a band, almost nothing they do is uninteresting to you. You might like it or not, but after a while, if you're inside it, everything reveals something. And sometimes, because the bad records are less artful, they're more revealing. They open things up in a way, because the good stuff transcends category, and you don't necessarily know where it came from. But when you hear the three bad versions of a song, you go, "Oh, right, that was an attempt to do this, and that's how they failed, and that's how it works when it works." So if you like the best stuff, even the bad records can be intriguing.

Again, in England, they tend to go the other way. They don't have a lot of perspective on the past. You read reviews of solo records from guys in bands that never were all that good, and they treat it like this is the most amazing thing in the world. And you listen to it and realize, "It sounds kind of like Tom Waits." And yet Tom Waits was totally unhip over there until recently. Again, I'm one of those guys who buys records because of reviews, and I can't tell you how often there is a disparity between the rave review and the actual record that you listen to and go, "Well, that's just not there. This is a second-rate selection of imitative songs that sound kind of like Nick Cave."

Right. Or Van Morrison. Or the Velvet Underground. I wanted to ask you one last question about R.E.M. Ever since you began to sell records, there's been a sub-theme of negative writing about the band, a small backlash. But, apart from that, you've always been treated very generously by critics. Even in the English press, you've been immune to the kinds of attacks virtually every other band that's attained your level of success has undergone. Obviously, you believe the albums are good, but, as you know, that sometimes has nothing to do with it. So, setting aside the quality of the albums, why do you think R.E.M. has been treated so well?

In 1989, there was a period there when some magazines stuck by us, but a couple, one of which is not in business anymore, looked for someone who didn't like the record to assign it to. I talked to people who told me about this, and I'm not saying it's bad. It's fine, because the editor didn't feel it was a strong record. But I was talking to someone who told him, "I like that record." And there were plenty of people who would have written good reviews of it. They consciously wanted someone who wouldn't. They sent the nonbelievers to the shows. And that's fine. If we can only show people who like us that we're good, then maybe we're not that good. But they picked people who didn't like us. I accept that. I understood it, and I don't mind.

Funnily enough, then we stayed off the road and consciously turned our backs on what people expected us to be—a multiplatinum, billion-dollar touring machine. We could have turned into Pink Floyd if we'd done a tour after the *Green* tour. I think it was surprising to people that we just said, "OK, we're going to make a couple of weird acoustic records, and we're not going to tour." We then sold a boatload of records. But the idea is that we thought we were kissing our career good-bye to take some time to do what we wanted to do. Every record has been something we wanted to do. But we wanted to distance ourselves from the machinery a bit. And I think that was such a surprising move that we got a fair amount of respect for it.

I mean, *Automatic for the People,* for instance. It's a really good record. It's maybe the best that we've done. But it sold for almost two years in England. For like a year and a half it was on the charts, in the top ten. Everyone used it as a hallmark. I think we won Band of the Year in some magazine, and we didn't even do anything. We didn't tour, we did videos, we didn't do press, hardly. I think part of it is just that we took the unexpected choice at a point when most people would have gone for the throat and done a huge triumphant stadium tour, and the big rock record. I think it was great for us not to do that, but critically, I think that's why the press has stuck with us. Because at the point when almost any other band would have said, "OK, now, this is gonna be the big moment," we walked away from it.

It turns out record-wise it was the best thing we could have ever done. Band-wise it was the best thing we could have ever done. But that's not what everyone told us at the time. Our manager had meetings with us about how we were going to have to lay people off. We have a pension

plan; were we going to have to cut our pension plan? The record company people were like, "Well, you're not going to sell a million records
ever again if you don't tour." And, you know, they loved the records. But
it was not the way to go about it. And we all made the decision, "We'll
take a salary cut if we need to. We'll cut the pension this year, if it comes
to that, that's cool." Then we sold ten million records. In part, that's why
we've been seen as pretty hip, because we didn't embrace success. I like
it, I like being successful. But I did it exactly on my own terms.

*One last question: You have plenty of friends who are writers and critics,
which contradicts the idea that that relationship is adversarial. What do you
have in common?*

I do have a lot of friends who are critics, because our interests are the
same. If you name a band that's at our level, I doubt there are that many
of them who buy as many records and listen to as much different music
and read as many fanzines as I do. It's just something I'm fascinated by.
I still read those mimeographed fanzines—there's a bunch of them that
are really cool. I look for seven-inches on obscure labels and go to little
punk clubs to see bands. And at the shows I go to, I see music critics. In
Seattle, I see two of the four critics really often. I don't see the guys from
Mudhoney or Nirvana there. Those are my friends and my peer group,
but musicians tend to not go out and do this kind of stuff so much.
Thurston does, I see Thurston Moore at shows, and we have a lot of
things in common. But I see critics all the time. It's part of the world I'm
involved in. It has to do with getting advance cassettes and being excited
about new bands and seeing what's happening. So it's natural that you'd
be friends with these people. Not all of them—there's a lot of people I
disagree with. But, especially in Seattle, I keep seeing the same two
critics at every show I go to. I think it's interesting that they're there.
They'll write a review, and I'm there because I'm digging it. But we're
there for the same reason.

Lives and Deaths

Blues

Legends

This piece was originally written to accompany a series of portraits of blues artists by Albert Watson.

It *would be nearly impossible* to overestimate the importance of the blues in the formation of rock & roll, but the legendary figures of that seminal music still rarely get the opportunity to step out of the shadows of the artists they have influenced and stand alone on their own formidable terms.

Guitarists B.B. King and Albert King—the first a player of breathtaking sweetness and delicacy, the second a blazing virtuoso—and their musical heir Buddy Guy shaped the music of an entire generation of players, including Eric Clapton, Stevie Ray Vaughan, and the late Mike Bloomfield. One of the most significant songwriters in the history of the blues, Willie Dixon penned a cache of classic tunes—among them, "You Shook Me," "Back Door Man," "I Can't Quit You Baby," "(I'm Your) Hoochie Coochie Man," and "I Just Want to Make Love to You"—that provided crucial early material for Jeff Beck, Led Zeppelin, the Rolling Stones, and the Doors.

John Lee Hooker's insidious, sexually charged boogie—epitomized in songs like "Boogie Chillun," "Boom Boom," "Dimples," and "I'm in the Mood"—fired up everyone from the Animals and Van Morrison to Bruce Springsteen and Bonnie Raitt. Bo Diddley's propulsive, staccato beat drove songs like "I'm a Man," "Mona," and "Who Do You Love?" and provided a central link between the blues and rock & roll. Junior Wells, the wailing harmonica man best known for his insouciant version of "Messin' With the Kid," was a staple on the Chess Records studio scene in Chicago. For more than two decades, Wells, as part of a one-two punch with Buddy Guy, has led one of the most active touring blues bands in the country.

Along with the music they created, however, these bluesmen are the product of a world and of a time that has all but disappeared.

"I had two things to choose from," says the seventy-two-year-old John Lee Hooker, whose father was a sharecropper. "One was to stay there with the horses and cows and pigs and work on the farm and go to school and *not* be a musician. I felt from a kid up that wasn't my bag. I was gonna be a musician. I was different from any of the rest of the kids. I was *completely* different."

As a young black person deep in the segregated South in the early decades of this century, if you wanted to venture forth and re-create yourself as a blues musician, you had to have a vision of yourself as fated. You weren't choosing a "career," as pop musicians do today; you were choosing a way of life, accepting a destiny.

They weren't teaching the blues in college when John Lee Hooker was a boy in Clarksdale, Mississippi, and there were no museums to commemorate its history. You could hear it on the radio late at night, if your family had a radio and if you were allowed to listen to "the devil's music"—meaning music that wasn't church music. If you were old enough, you could hear it at fish fries and house parties. Perhaps a neighbor had a phonograph and some 78s by Robert Johnson, Blind Lemon Jefferson, or Lonnie Johnson.

Instruments weren't so easy to come by, either. Many players attempted to build their own guitars from whatever materials they could find—pieces of wood stuck in metal cans or nailed to cigar boxes, with chicken wire or wire from window screens serving as strings, or pieces of tubing nailed to barn doors. But if you were a "born talent," to use John Lee Hooker's phrase, the need for a store-bought guitar eventually became paramount. B.B. King tells a story that is by no means untypical of his time.

"While I was working for a family up in the hills of Mississippi, I was what you'd call a houseboy," recalls King, who was born in Indianola, Mississippi, in 1925. "I had found a guy that had a guitar, and I asked my boss if he would get the guitar for me. I was making fifteen dollars a month at that time, and the guitar cost fifteen dollars. I asked him to take out half of it the first month and then half of it the second month. That's how I got my first guitar."

A teenager with a guitar and a booming voice, King took the next step on the blues pilgrimage and hit the road. "On the weekends, after we'd get off work at Saturday noon, I would take that Saturday evening and go as far as I could go to be back home by the next morning," King says. Once he had arrived in a nearby small town, King would set up on a street corner that was likely to attract both blacks and whites and take requests.

King was versed in a variety of musical styles. "The blues we called 'the black man's music,' and country we called 'the white man's blues,' but everybody sang gospel," he says. King, in fact, considered himself a gospel singer at the time, but, he says, "if somebody asked me to sing a gospel song, usually when I finished, they would praise me, you know, pat me on the shoulder or the head and say, 'Son, if you continue, you're going to really be great one day.' But they didn't tip!

"But people that asked me to sing blues songs would always tip and maybe ask somebody around, 'Hey, *give* the boy something.' During this time, I worked on the plantation driving tractors, and prior to that, I had plowed mules. You name it, on the plantation I did it. I was making twenty-two dollars and a half a week, driving the tractor. Many Saturday afternoons I would make much more than twenty-two dollars and a half. So now you can see what motivated me to get into singing the blues!"

Entering the world of the blues typically required a kind of initiation, a process that often could be eased by the intervention of an acknowledged master. After John Lee Hooker left Clarksdale and ran away to Memphis, his family came and brought him home. He took off again, and after spending time in Memphis and Cincinnati, he finally moved to Detroit, where, he says, "I became the talk of the town around at the house parties. Finally, I met this very, very great musician, who I loved so much, I've treasured him like I would a jewel or a piece of gold, the great T-Bone Walker. He was the first person to get me my electric guitar." Fittingly, Walker had served his own apprenticeship to Blind Lemon Jefferson, one of Hooker's principal musical influences, when, between the ages of ten and thirteen, Walker guided the legendary bluesman through the streets of Dallas.

Buddy Guy, who was born in Louisiana in 1936, moved to Chicago in his early twenties to experience the burgeoning blues scene. After three days of no food in the Windy City, Guy was approached by a stranger who pointed to his guitar and, with characteristic big-city graciousness, inquired, "Can you play the damn thing?" When Guy leaned into some Jimmy Reed tunes and Guitar Slim's "Things I Used to Do," the man took him to the 708 Club, where the imposing Otis Rush commanded the stage.

"He had me by the hand and he's pointing at Otis," Guy recalls. "I'll tell you exactly what he said: 'I got a nigger here will run you *outta* here, man.' Otis Rush said, 'Bring 'im on up.'" Guy held his own and got offered a three-night-a-week gig for twenty-five dollars a night. "I was making twenty-nine dollars a week working at LSU when I left," Guy says about his previous job in Baton Rouge, Louisiana. "I thought, 'Seventy-five dollars for three nights! I can send my mama and them some money back home.'"

Muddy Waters heard about the new young guitarist in town who had no friends, no place to stay, and nothing to eat, and he showed up at Guy's first gig with a loaf of bread and some salami. "He slapped me and made me get into a red Chevrolet station wagon, made me eat the sandwich," Guy says. "I started crying, telling him I'm going back home, because I didn't know anybody and I was about to starve. He said, 'No, you're not gonna starve and you're not going back. You're gonna play this guitar, because everybody tells me how good you is. I'm here to hear you, and when *I* hear you play, you ain't goin' no-damn-where.'" Guy eventually recorded with Muddy Waters and virtually became the house guitarist for the Chess label.

Junior Wells, who was born in Memphis in 1934, recalls the friendly competition of the Chicago scene. "We'd have a Blue Monday party or a Sunday matinee, and a lot of the musicians that wasn't playing anyplace, if you had a gig, they'd come by your gig," says Wells, who replaced Little Walter as Muddy Waters's harmonica player. "Everybody'd just come by and jam. One would start it, saying, 'Well, Walter's coming in the house. Junior says that you could've left your harmonicas back home.' The guitar players would start talking about who could beat the other one playing the guitar. Oh, *man,* you talkin' about a *good* time! Everybody'd be jammin', and everybody'd be tryin' to see who's gonna win this fifth of whiskey or that twenty-five dollars."

As the main songwriter, bass player, and musical director at Chess, Willie Dixon, who was born in Vicksburg, Mississippi, in 1915, had to try to keep everybody happy. It wasn't always easy. "Muddy and Howlin' Wolf kind of had a thing against each other because they knew each other down South or somethin'," Dixon told *Rolling Stone* last spring. "And then, both of them wanted what they called 'the top spot in the blues.'

"When I first started giving them songs, nobody ever wanted the song you gave them," Dixon continued. "So I found out I had to use a little psychology on 'em. Since Wolf and Muddy both seemed to think that I was giving them the wrong songs, all I'd have to do is go to Wolf and say, 'Hey, man, now here's a song I made for Muddy. Muddy's gonna do this.' 'Oh, *man,* how come you give Muddy the best songs?' And Muddy would say the same thing about Wolf!"

When the Sixties rolled around, it became apparent that young English musicians had paid far more attention to American blues, R&B, and soul music than had their white American counterparts. All the new attention amazed, and sometimes confused, the original writers and performers. "It bothered me," says the sixty-year-old Bo Diddley, who came to Chicago from McComb, Mississippi. "It bothered me that people was covering my material. I didn't like it, see? I thought maybe they should write their own. But I learned different, that it was very good to have somebody think enough of your stuff to do it. When I understood that, it was a good feeling. It let me know that I had something special."

That "something special," unfortunately, was often something the original artists no longer owned. Many black songwriters were signed to exploitative publishing deals and cheated of royalties by the white-dominated music industry. The behavior of white artists who have benefited so much from the blues has sometimes been shameful. Willie Dixon was forced to sue Led Zeppelin after the band blatantly lifted from his song "You Need Love" for "Whole Lotta Love," the biggest hit of its career, and failed to credit him or pay any royalties. Settled out of court, the case was part of the reason Dixon established the Blues Heaven Foundation to help blues artists and their heirs recover copyrights and royalties.

As for the future of the blues, resilient as that form has proven, it's somewhat in doubt. While many of the greatest practitioners are still remarkably active, none of them, of course, is getting any younger. "I done did my part, and I'm getting ready to retire," says the sixty-six-year-old Albert King, who, like B.B. King, is a native of Indianola. Albert King now owns houses in Illinois and Memphis. "That's where I'm going to do my fishing from, Memphis," says King, whose signature tunes include "I'll Play the Blues for You" and his version of "Born Under a Bad Sign." "I've got my bus all fixed up. I got good electricity. I'm gonna put me a microwave oven in there and an icebox. Got my air conditioner and my heater all ready. I got an old bus, but it's in good shape. If I go down

---

on the riverbank and it come a rain and I can't get out, I just stay down there and go to bed!"

Both Buddy Guy and Junior Wells lament the absence of the blues from mainstream media, the difficulty blues artists have getting recording contracts, and the failure of young blacks—with Robert Cray the most prominent exception—to continue in the blues tradition. "Before Muddy died, he told me, 'Don't let the blues die,'" Guy says. "We as blues players don't have the recognition that I hope we could get. But who am I? I can't do nothing about it. All we can do is just play. . . . We write according to the facts of life, everyday life. If you live and die here, you got a part of the blues in you. Something you have to get up to do, it don't work, that's what blues is all about. I think a person will have the blues as long as he lives, but some people just don't want to bring it out like we do.

"It's something that belonged to the black man, because they invented it," Guy continues. "We carry it on. I just hope it don't die, but I don't see anything now saying it won't. Because me, Junior, and a few of us, we're not babies anymore, and I don't see a lot of young black people playing it. Quite a few white kids are playing it and carrying it on that way."

Whatever its future, the history of the blues will never die. "I left a trail," says John Lee Hooker. "When I'm gone, I won't be gone. Like Muddy Waters, you don't see him, but he lives on. That's the way it will be with me. I'm leaving something here for years to come. As generation and generation go by, they can say, 'I heard of John Lee Hooker, oh, yes. I never seen the man, but I would have liked to have seen him.'"

Rolling Stone September 21, 1989

Eric Clapton

A Life at the Crossroads

This piece served as the liner notes to the Eric Clapton retrospective *Crossroads*, which was released in 1988. The essay was awarded a Grammy in the "Best Album Notes" Category.

Over the past twenty-five years Eric Clapton's extraordinary career has traced a dramatic progression marked by musical pioneering, restless shifts of direction, spiritual awakenings, backsliding, and, at one point, a total retreat into isolation. Clapton's mysterious, internally determined moves from budding pop star to purist blues man to rock guitar hero to laid-back troubadour have challenged the faithful and won new converts at every turn.

Through all the personal and artistic upheavals, part of Eric Clapton has consistently remained detached and calm, as if he accepted in his heart that he was destined for such shocks—and that acceptance brought a certain peace. At the same time he has maintained a fierce, private idealism about his playing. "My driving philosophy about making music," he told *Rolling Stone* in 1974, "is that you can reduce it all down to one note if that note is played with the right kind of feeling and with the right kind of sincerity."

It makes sense, then, that Robert Johnson's tough, transcendent masterpiece, "Crossroads," has become Clapton's signature song. On the path of life, crossroads are where the breakdowns and breakthroughs come, where danger and adventure lie. As he has forged and disbanded musical alliances, altered his sound and his look, pursued and dodged fame, Eric Clapton has brought himself to the crossroads and proven himself time and time again.

Clapton's bold search for his own identity is the source both of his enormous artistic achievement and his inner strife. That search acquired its momentum in the earliest years of his life. Clapton was born on March 30th, 1945 in Ripley, a small village about thirty miles outside—and a universe away from—London. His mother raised him until he was two years old, at which point she moved abroad, leaving him in the loving hands of her mother and stepfather.

The elderly couple was indulgent of Eric—they bought him his first guitar on an installment plan when he was in his teens—but the stigma of being born out of wedlock in a small town made a forceful impression on him. The "secret" of Clapton's illegitimacy was a secret only from him. "I was raised by my grandparents, thinking that they were my parents, up until I was nine years old," Clapton explained to J. D. Considine in *Musician* in 1986. "That's when the shock came up, when I found out—from outside sources—that they weren't my parents, they were my grandparents. I went into a kind of . . . shock, which lasted through my teens, really, and started to turn me into the kind of person I am now."

Clapton was more pointed in Ray Coleman's authorized biography, *Clapton!*, published in 1985, about how hard it was to learn the truth about his background. "My feeling of a lack of identity started to rear its head then," he told Coleman. "And it explains a lot of my behavior throughout my life; it changed my outlook and my physical appearance so much. Because I still don't know who I am."

Like so many rockers, Clapton did a brief stint in art school—the Kingston College of Art, in his case. His formal education got derailed, however, when he was about sixteen and began to make the bohemian scene in London, where he discovered folk-blues. Eventually he would go on to play acoustic gigs in coffeehouses and pubs, accompanied by a vocalist and doing tunes by Big Bill Broonzy, Ramblin' Jack Elliott, and Blind Boy Fuller.

Another revelation struck around that time, as well. "Every Friday night, there would be a meeting at someone's house, and people would turn up with the latest imported records from the States," Clapton recalled in a 1985 *Rolling Stone* interview with Robert Palmer. "And shortly, someone showed up with that Chess album, *The Best of Muddy Waters*, and something by Howlin' Wolf. And that was it for me. Then I sort of took a step back, discovered Robert Johnson, and made the connection to Muddy." In later days, Clapton would come to refer to Muddy Waters as his "father." And Johnson's haunted country blues affected Clapton so deeply that he would tell Dan Forte in *Guitar Player* more than two decades later, "Both of the Robert Johnson albums (*King of the Delta Blues Singers*, volumes 1 and 2) actually cover all of my desires musically. Every angle of expression and every emotion is expressed on both of those albums."

The first band Clapton joined was the fledgling R&B outfit, the Roosters. The Roosters would last only a few months, from March to October of 1963, according to rock historian Pete Frame. But during that period the band's bassist, Tom McGinness, who later played with Manfred Mann and McGuinness Flint, turned Clapton on to blues guitarist Freddie King's instrumental "Hideaway," and another influential figure entered Clapton's pantheon. Playing John Lee Hooker and Muddy Waters's tunes with the Roosters sharpened Clapton's playing, according to the band's pianist Ben Palmer, one of the guitarist's oldest friends. "It was immediately obvious that he was something that none of the rest of us were," Palmer says in *Clapton!* "And he had a fluency and command that seemed endless. The telling point was that he didn't mind taking solos, which people of our standard often did because we weren't up to it."

Following an extremely short stay with the pop band Casey Jones and the Engineers—headed by Liverpool singer Brian Cassar, who was trying to cash in on the record-company signing spree in the wake of the Beatles' success—Clapton joined the seminal Sixties band, the Yardbirds, in October of 1963. In their early days the Yardbirds—who, in addition to Clapton, consisted of vocalist Keith Relf, guitarist Chris Dreja, bassist Paul Samwell-Smith, and drummer Jim McCarty—were an exuberant London R&B band that covered tunes like John Lee Hooker's "Boom Boom" and Billy Boy Arnold's "I Wish You Would."

On "I Ain't Got You"—and in his brief solo on the catchy New Orleans novelty, "A Certain Girl"—Clapton flashes the biting, fiercely articulate phrasing characteristic of his best playing. But in general Clapton was inhibited by the Yardbirds' harmonica-driven rave-up style. Despite his youth, Clapton was sufficiently confident of his musical tastes to become disgruntled when the Yardbirds, at the urging of manager Giorgio Gomelsky, edged away from the blues in order to pursue pop success. Clapton left the group by mutual agreement shortly after they recorded Graham Gouldman's "For Your Love" in quest of a hit.

Splitting from the Yardbirds on the brink of their commercial breakthrough was the first time Clapton displayed his willingness to pursue his own musical vision at whatever the cost—and it was far from the last. However high-minded and necessary such decisions were, Clapton is not beyond questioning them to a degree, in retrospect. "I took it all far too seriously," he states in *Clapton!* "Perhaps if I'd been able to temper it,

I might not have been so frustrated. . . . I still take it too seriously, in terms of relationships and being able to get on with other musicians. I'm far too judgmental, and in those days I was a complete purist. If it wasn't black music, it was rubbish."

Of course, seriousness about black music was hardly a problem during Clapton's tenure with John Mayall's Bluesbreakers in 1965 and 1966. A keyboardist with a vocal style derived from Mose Allison and Freddie King, Mayall was twelve years Clapton's senior and the father of the British blues scene. Mayall's Bluesbreakers were the proving ground for a host of ambitious young musicians in the mid to late Sixties, including Jack Bruce, Mick Taylor, Peter Green, Aynsley Dunbar, John McVie, and Mick Fleetwood.

Clapton raided Mayall's vast collection of singles, and the two men thrived on each other's enthusiasm, as is evidenced by the raw Chicago blues power of their duet on "Lonely Years" and the spry assurance of their instrumental jam, "Bernard Jenkins." Though barely into his twenties, Clapton shaped an aggressive, tonally rich playing style with the Bluesbreakers. Drawing on Freddie King, Otis Rush, and Buddy Guy in a way that blended respect with his own precocious mastery, Clapton unleashed some of the finest blues guitar playing of his generation on the 1966 *Bluesbreakers—John Mayall with Eric Clapton* LP. In addition, Clapton sang his first lead vocal on that record, a spare, eloquent reading of Robert Johnson's "Ramblin' On My Mind" that captures the song's edgy amalgam of anguish and submerged threat.

Clapton's scorching club performances in London during his time with Mayall—represented in this collection by his ignition of Billy Myles's "Have You Ever Loved a Woman," with Jack Bruce on bass— quickly established a cult following for the young guitarist. "Clapton Is God" graffiti began appearing around the city, defining a central tenet of the Clapton mythology to this day. And though the comparisons with God would prove to be a hellhound on Clapton's trail, he understandably received the adulation more positively at first.

"My vanity was incredibly boosted by that 'God' thing," Clapton says in Coleman's biography. "I didn't think there was anyone around at that time doing what I was doing, playing the blues as straight as me. I was trying to do it absolutely according to its rules. Oh yeah, I was very confident. I didn't think there was anybody as good."

However appealing, the adulation did not prevent Clapton from taking a three-month break from the Bluesbreakers in 1965, and it was during that period that Jack Bruce joined the band. Playing with Bruce upon his return spun Clapton's head around. Bruce's jazz background gave his playing an improvisational flair, and Clapton, who, despite his own purist impulses, had been feeling somewhat constrained in Mayall's strict blues format, felt a new sense of freedom. "Most of what we were doing with Mayall was imitating the records we got, but Jack had something else," Clapton told *Rolling Stone,* "he had no reverence for what we were doing, and so he was composing new parts as he went along playing. I literally had never heard that before, and it took me someplace else. I thought, well, if he could do that, and I could, and we could get a drummer . . . I could be Buddy Guy with a composing bass player. And that's how Cream came about."

Formed in 1966, Cream's impact on the world of pop music was immense. Rock bands to that point had played almost exclusively before crowds of screaming teeny-boppers—a major reason why live performance was beginning to seem pointless to bands whose music and ideas were becoming more sophisticated. Discussing rock & roll in musical terms was a joke to the mainstream media, and alternative media had not yet sprung up. Cream was a primary catalyst in transforming rock & roll into music that could be performed in concert before adults and analyzed with the same rigor that blues or jazz could be. The declaration implicit in the band's name was itself a demand to be taken seriously. In Coleman's terse summary, "They made musicianship hip." Clapton forever defined the role of guitar hero at this point, and with Bruce on bass and the redoubtable Ginger Baker on drums, Cream defined the power trio.

In their range and power, Cream forced a dichotomy between the studio and the stage. In the studio, the band was something like a later evolution of the Yardbirds. They could contain hip innovations within pop-song structures, as on "I Feel Free"; rework the blues, as on Willie Dixon's "Spoonful" and the Albert King-derived "Strange Brew"; journey into psychedelic wonderland, as on "Tales of Brave Ulysses" and "White Room"; or simply cut a radio-perfect, guitar-charged hit like "Sunshine of Your Love."

Live, however, Cream was essentially a rock & roll jazz band. Songs became thematic statements that provided the occasion for lengthy improvisational jams, with Baker and Bruce muscling each other into unexplored territory as Clapton wailed and roared above them. The propulsive live version of "Crossroads" included here is a Cream classic, and a masterpiece of concision—edited, as it was, by engineer Tom Dowd for the *Wheels of Fire* album—compared to the much longer renditions the band typically fired up.

The hero-worship Clapton had inspired when he was with the Bluesbreakers reached a fever pitch with Cream. The pressures of the inordinate praise heaped upon him, the wild improvisational competitiveness of Cream's gigs, and the fighting that resulted from Bruce and Baker's inability to get along gradually took their toll on Clapton.

"All during Cream I was riding high on the 'Clapton is God' myth that had been started up," Clapton told Robert Palmer. "Then we got our first kind of bad review, which, funnily enough, was in *Rolling Stone*. The magazine ran an interview with us in which we were really praising ourselves, and it was followed by a review that said how boring and repetitious our performance had been. And it was true! . . . I immediately decided that that was the end of the band."

Cream split up in November of 1968, about six months after that review appeared, and Clapton began jamming with Steve Winwood, the keyboardist and sterling R&B vocalist who had made his own youthful mark with the Spencer Davis Group and Traffic. The two men had played and recorded together two years earlier, and Clapton admired Winwood's tunefulness as a singer and songwriter—qualities that stood in sharp relief after the jazz-rock experimentalism of Cream.

But, given their musical pedigrees, Clapton and Winwood were hot commercial commodities. Because all three of its members had been eminent figures on the British scene, Cream had begun a trend toward supergroups, and the prospect of Winwood and Clapton teaming up was too hot a proposition for the business people to resist. What began idyllically with Clapton and Winwood jamming together at their homes in the country and searching for new musical directions quickly became a cash cow. Ginger Baker and Rick Grech, bassist of the English folk-rock band Family, were recruited as the rhythm section, and Blind Faith was born.

Formed in early 1969, Blind Faith debuted at a huge outdoor concert in London's Hyde Park in June of that year, recorded one album and then launched an arena tour in America. The band broke up in late 1969, and Clapton offered this bluntly honest obituary in *Rolling Stone* shortly afterward: "We didn't rehearse enough, we didn't get to know each other enough, we didn't go through enough trials and tribulations before the big time came."

Still, the *Blind Faith* album, recorded in February, May, and June of 1969, had a number of splendid moments. Steve Winwood's searching "Can't Find My Way Home," with Clapton on acoustic guitar, is a fine example of the kind of melodic, song-centered work Clapton was becoming more interested in after Cream. Among the earliest tunes Blind Faith laid down in the studio, Clapton's "Presence of the Lord" was the first non-instrumental song he ever recorded that he wrote fully on his own. It was also the first of the hymn-like spiritual songs of faith that would become a staple of his work in years to come.

The opening act on the Blind Faith tour of America in 1969 was a rocking R&B band led by Delaney and Bonnie Bramlett. Delaney and Bonnie played a loose, engaging blend of the full range of American soul music, and their unassuming, good-hearted shows seemed to Clapton a sharp contrast to Blind Faith's headline gigs. Clapton began spending more and more time with Delaney and his band, traveling from gig to gig on their tour bus and popping up on stage during their sets. In a 1970 interview in *Rolling Stone,* Clapton recalled that "on certain nights I'd get up there and play tambourine with Delaney's group and enjoy it more than playing with Blind Faith. . . . And by then I kind of got this crusade going for Delaney's group. I wanted to bring them over to England."

Blind Faith splintered once their blitz of America ended. At that point, Clapton not only sponsored a tour of England for Delaney and Bonnie, he played guitar with the band and recorded the infectiously upbeat single, "Comin' Home," with them. A live album from the tour was released later. More important, however, Delaney was the agent of a significant emotional breakthrough for Clapton.

Since about 1968, Clapton had been growing bored with virtuoso musicianship and more interested in songs that had clearly delineated structures and put across a pleasing groove. The Band's *Music from Big Pink,* which came out that year, made a striking impression on him and fueled his dissatisfaction with Cream. Discussing Cream's break-up in *Rolling Stone* in 1974, Clapton said "another interesting factor was that I got the tapes of *Music from Big Pink* and I thought, well, this is what I want to play—not extended solos and maestro bullshit but just good funky songs." The concise, melodic "Badge," which Clapton cowrote for Cream's *Goodbye* album with George Harrison, who also plays guitar on the song, was one product of this interest. Forming a band with Steve Winwood and serving as a guitar-slinger side-man to Delaney and Bonnie were other manifestations of it.

Yet despite his strong performances on "Ramblin' on My Mind," "Crossroads," and other tracks, Clapton was still extremely shy about his singing. Clapton told Robert Palmer that on the night he and Delaney met, "Delaney looked straight into my eyes and told me I had a gift to sing and that if I didn't sing, God would take it away. I said, 'No, man, I can't sing.' But he said, 'Yes, you can.' . . . That night we started talking about me making a solo album, with his band."

When Delaney and Bonnie's tour of England ended, the two men went into the studio in Los Angeles and began work on Clapton's first solo album, *Eric Clapton*. Delaney's influence on the record was considerable. He produced the album—which includes the joyful "Blues Power" and the fiery "Let It Rain"—and supplied most of the players from his own band. His hand is especially evident on the alternative version of J. J. Cale's "After Midnight"—which Delaney mixed and which features a horn section that does not appear on the LP track. With Delaney's encouragement, Clapton emerged as a front man for the first time since he had been propelled into superstardom with Cream. Clapton wrote or cowrote eight of the eleven tunes on the record, sang all the lead vocals, and played crisply and spiritedly. He was now ready to put together a band of his own.

When Clapton learned that three members of Delaney's band— keyboardist Bobby Whitlock, bassist Carl Radle, and drummer Jim Gordon—had had a falling out with their boss and were available, he scooped them up. The band came together and did their first recording while they were all working on the sessions for George Harrison's *All Things Must Pass* album, which Phil Spector was producing. They recorded a blistering version of "Tell the Truth"—backed with the salacious "Roll It Over," featuring Harrison and Dave Mason on guitars—as a single, with Spector at the board. But, at the band's insistence, the track was recalled within days of its release.

Still ambivalent about his rock-star status, Clapton avoided using his own name and debuted his new band at a benefit concert in London as

Derek and the Dominos. And rather than play large halls, he booked a club tour of England for their first trip out. As undisputed leader of the Dominos, Clapton was able both to play songs he felt comfortable with and to stretch out in solos when he desired. "It wasn't until I formed Derek and the Dominos and we played live that I was aware of being able to do exactly what I wanted and was happy with it," Clapton told Dan Forte in 1985. But Clapton's musical satisfaction contrasted with the emotional pain he was experiencing. He had fallen in love with Pattie Boyd Harrison, who at the time was married to his best friend, George Harrison. With the turmoil of a classic blues triangle worthy of Robert Johnson exploding inside him, Clapton left for Miami with the Dominos to make *Layla*.

Layla was recorded with legendary producer Tom Dowd under the most extreme conditions. Critic Robert Palmer visited the sessions and later recalled, "There was a lot of dope around, especially heroin, and when I showed up, everyone was just spread out on the carpet, nodded out." Shortly after the band arrived in Miami, Dowd took them to see the Allman Brothers, and Duane Allman was invited to play slide guitar on the album. Allman also teamed up with Clapton for a duet on Little Walter's "Mean Old World," which was not included on the LP.

Driven creatively by his new band, the formidable playing of Allman, and his own romantic agony, Clapton poured all he had into *Layla*'s title track, which was inspired by a Persian love story he had read, *The Story of Layla and Majnun* by Nizami. The song's extended lyrical coda was composed independently by drummer Jim Gordon on piano, and Gordon had to be convinced to allow the piece to be tacked onto "Layla."

After completing *Layla*, Derek and the Dominos launched a tour of America, from which the previously unreleased live versions of "Key to the Highway" and "Crossroads"—in a more churning, exploratory rendition than the one recorded with Cream—included in this collection are taken. The band then returned to England, and in April and May of 1971 attempted to record a second studio album—five tracks of which are presented in this collection for the first time: "One More Chance," Arthur Crudup's "Mean Old Frisco," the instrumental "Snake Lake Blues," a cover of Willie Dixon's "Evil," and an uncompleted studio version of "Got to Get Better in a Little While," which the band performed live on the album, *Derek and the Dominos in Concert*. In his 1985 interview in *Rolling Stone* Clapton told Robert Palmer that the sessions for a follow-up LP to *Layla* "broke down halfway through because of the paranoia and the tension. And the band just . . . dissolved."

Once the Dominos broke up, Clapton's drug dependence worsened and kept him virtually a prisoner in his home for the rest of 1971—though he did emerge to play at George Harrison's Concert for Bangladesh that summer—and much of the following year. During this period he felt both personally and emotionally adrift, and the long-standing identity issues arose once again. "The end of the Dominos came too soon, and that left me very high and dry as to what I was supposed to be," he told *Guitar Player* in 1985. "I'd been this anonymous person up until that time. It was difficult for me to come to terms with the fact that it was *me*, that I was on my own again."

Part of that difficulty may have resulted from the origins of Derek and the Dominos in Clapton's own psychic need. Despite the enormous satisfactions the band brought him, Clapton told *Musician* that Derek and the Dominos were "a make-believe band. We were all hiding inside it. Derek & the Dominos—the whole thing was . . . assumed. So it couldn't last. I had to come out and admit that I was being me. I mean, being Derek was a cover for the fact that I was trying to steal someone else's wife. That was one of the reasons for doing it, so that I could write the song, and even use another name for Pattie. So Derek and Layla—it wasn't real at all."

Clapton's good friend Pete Townshend of the Who organized a concert at London's Rainbow Theatre in January of 1973 to create some momentum for the guitarist's return to action. Clapton played at the highly emotional show with Townshend, Ron Wood, and Steve Winwood, and later that year took an acupuncture cure to end his drug addiction. Once that problem was behind him, Clapton contacted Tom Dowd and returned to Miami to record *461 Ocean Boulevard*.

Featuring a band of American musicians, including Carl Radle, brought together by Dowd, *461 Ocean Boulevard* is Clapton's great comeback LP. Appropriately, it opens with "Motherless Children," a traditional tune whose rollicking energy in Clapton's slide-guitar version counterpoints its relevance to the circumstances of his early life. The deeply felt "Let It Grow" finds Clapton once again "standing at the crossroads," and this time making a choice to affirm life, love, and, by extension, his ability to reach within himself and create art. And *461*

Ocean Boulevard contained Clapton's cover of Bob Marley's "I Shot the Sheriff"—represented here in a tougher, more expansive live rendition from the band's December 5th, 1974 concert at the Hammersmith Odeon in London—which exposed millions of Americans to reggae music for the first time when it became a Number One hit. During the *461 Ocean Boulevard* sessions at Criteria Studios in Miami, Clapton also recorded Jimmy Reed's insinuatingly seductive "Ain't That Lovin' You" with Dave Mason on guitar—a previously unreleased track included in this collection.

461 Ocean Boulevard re-established Clapton in both critical and commercial terms, but it also ushered in the phase of his career that engendered concern in many of his longest-standing followers. In their concentration on songwriting, vocals, and melody, *461 Ocean Boulevard* and the nine studio LPs that have followed it de-emphasize the pyrotechnic guitar work that characterized Clapton's tracks with the Bluesbreakers, Cream, and Derek and the Dominos—though there's certainly no shortage of excellent playing. Working with a variety of producers—including Dowd, Glyn Johns, and Phil Collins—Clapton alternated between American and British bands, experimenting with a wide variety of sounds and styles. Conventional pop songs and laid-back ballads of broad appeal appeared on those records and jarred the sensibilities of some fans.

A number of issues are important for understanding Clapton's music since 1974. One is that, while Clapton is still gripped by the blues and inclined to explore his favorite standards at length in live performance (note his probing reading of Otis Rush's "Double Trouble" in this collection), that impulse is no longer single and all-consuming. Since the latter days of Cream, the thrust of Clapton's music has been toward melody, and the artists that have interested him—the Band, Bob Dylan, Bob Marley, J. J. Cale, country singer Don Williams—are often more subtle than they are explosive. Taken together those artists and Clapton's blues idols are the influences behind his most notable work of the late Seventies and Eighties.

In 1985 Clapton spoke of a desire he felt during the Seventies "to be more of a composer of melodic tunes rather than just a player, which was very unpopular with a lot of people." The remark echoes something he said eleven years earlier, in expressing admiration for Stevie Wonder: "I think when it comes down to it, I always go for singers. I don't buy an album because I like the lead guitar. I always like the human voice most of all." The greatest blues guitar playing, after all, is modeled on the sound of the human voice.

Blues, country, folk, rock, and pop have come to share a place in Clapton's music. He offered a sensitive reading of Elmore James's "The Sky Is Crying" on *There's One in Every Crowd* (in addition to recording James's "(When Things Go Wrong) It Hurts Me Too" during the sessions for that album), and, in a live cut from 1977 included here, did an upbeat take on "Further On Up the Road," which over the years has become one of his signature tunes. Members of the Band were a prominent presence on the gently rolling *No Reason to Cry* album, which featured Clapton's optimistic "Hello Old Friend." Bob Dylan appeared on that record as well, sharing the vocal on his enigmatic song, "Sign Language."

Clapton also turned in fine versions of Dylan's "Knockin' on Heaven's Door"—another expression of the guitarist's spiritual side—and his swinging "If I Don't Be There By Morning." J. J. Cale's ominously enticing "Cocaine," included on Clapton's 1978 multiplatinum LP, *Slowhand*, has proven to be one of Clapton's most popular tunes, and Clapton's own catchy hit, "Lay Down Sally," from that same album, owes a clear debt to Cale. The affectionate "Wonderful Tonight," also from *Slowhand*, was simply born of Clapton's wish to write a love song.

Clapton's popularity as a live performer has consistently grown over the past ten years, and his videos and the pop-oriented LPs he has made with producer Phil Collins—*Behind the Sun* and *August* (which was co-produced by Tom Dowd)—have brought his music to a younger audience eager to learn about his past. He composed soundtracks for the BBC television series *Edge of Darkness*, which won prestigious BAFTA and Ivor Novello awards in Great Britain, and for the film *Lethal Weapon*. He contributed songs to films, including "Heaven Is One Step Away" for *Back to the Future* and two tracks for *The Color of Money*, directed by Martin Scorsese.

As a blues prodigy, Clapton built a commanding reputation very early in his twenties. By the time he was thirty he had, like many masters, become intrigued by simplicity—the one-note philosophy. The calm that he felt at his core—through the times of revolutionary innovation, through the drugs and the cure, through heartbreak and happiness, at the crossroads and further on up the road—finally entered his music.

In *Musician* in 1986 Clapton said, "I think that the ultimate guitar

hero should be a dispenser of wisdom, as well as anything else. . . .
That's the one thing I will say that I'm still striving after, outside of perfection as a musician: the attainment of wisdom, in any amount."

If wisdom can be reflected in the creation of a superbly accomplished body of work and in the defeat of personal adversity, Eric Clapton has already achieved the major portion of his goal. And the remainder has not escaped him. It awaits him—and us, his audience—at the spectacular series of crossroads to come.

Kurt Cobain

1967–1994

Kurt Cobain never wanted to be the spokesman for a generation, though that doesn't mean much: Anybody who did would never have become one. It's not a role you campaign for. It is thrust upon you, and you live with it. Or don't.

People looked to Kurt Cobain because his songs captured what they felt before they knew they felt it. Even his struggles—with fame, with drugs, with his identity—caught the generational drama of our time. Seeing himself since his boyhood as an outcast, he was stunned—and confused, and frightened, and repulsed, and, truth be told, not entirely disappointed (no one forms a band to remain anonymous)—to find himself a star. If Cobain staggered across the stage of rock stardom, seemed more willing to play the fool than the hero, and took drugs more for relief than pleasure, that was fine with his contemporaries. For people who came of age amid the greed, the designer-drug indulgence, and the image-driven celebrity of the Eighties, anyone who could make an easy peace with success was fatally suspect.

Whatever importance Cobain assumed as a symbol, however, one thing is certain: He and his band Nirvana announced the end of one rock & roll era and the start of another. In essence, Nirvana transformed the Eighties into the Nineties.

They didn't do it alone, of course—cultural change is never that simple. But in 1991, "Smells Like Teen Spirit" proved a defining moment in rock history. A political song that never mentions politics, an anthem whose lyrics can't be understood, a hugely popular hit that denounces commercialism, a collective shout of alienation, it was "(I Can't Get No) Satisfaction" for a new time and a new tribe of disaffected youth. It was a giant fuck-you, an immensely satisfying statement about the inability to be satisfied.

From that point on, Cobain battled to make sense of his new circumstances, to find a way to create rock & roll for a mass audience and still uphold his own version of integrity. The pressure of that effort deepened the wounds he had borne since boyhood: the broken home, the bitter resentment of the local toughs who bullied him, the excruciating stomach pains. He sought purpose in fatherhood. He wanted to soothe in his daughter, Frances Bean, his own primal fears of abandonment. He managed, finally, only to perpetuate them.

Cobain's life and music—his passion, his charm, his vision—can be understood and appreciated. His death leaves a far more savage legacy, one that will take many years to untangle. His suicide note and Courtney Love's reading of it say it all. In his last written statement Cobain reels from cracked-actor posturing ("I haven't felt the excitement . . . for too many years now") to detached self-criticism ("I must be one of those narcissists who only appreciate things when they're alone") to self-pity ("I'm too sensitive") to a bizarre brand of hostile, self-loathing gratitude ("Thank you all from the pit of my burning, nauseous stomach") to, of all things, rock-star clichés ("It's better to burn out than to fade away").

Left with that, Love careens from reverence ("I feel so honored to be near him") to pained confusion ("I don't know what happened") to exasperation ("He's such an asshole") to anger ("Well, Kurt, so fucking what? Then don't be a rock star") to sobbing, heartbreaking guilt ("I'm really sorry, you guys. I don't know what I could have done").

No answers are forthcoming, because there are none. Suicide is an unanswerable act. It is said to be the one unforgivable sin, though our age has sought to forgive it by explaining it away in psychological or chemical terms. Earlier eras were not so kind. Suicides were buried at the crossroads. The message was severe: You were at an impasse in your life and lacked the faith to make your way through it. Our lives are no easier to bear than yours. We may fall, but you chose to fall. We will make our way over you down the road of our destiny.

But suicide sends its own remorseless message. True, it is the ultimate cry of desperation, more harrowing than any scream Cobain unleashed in any of Nirvana's songs. True, he was in agony and saw no other way to end it. But suicide is also an act of anger, a fierce indictment of the living. If the inability to live is "sensitive," the ability to live comes to seem crass. "You're so good at getting over," the final message runs. "Get over this."

At twenty-seven years old, Kurt Cobain wanted to disappear, to erase himself, to become nothing. That his suicide so utterly lacked ambivalence is its most terrifying aspect. It all comes down to a stillness at the end of a long chaos: a young man sitting alone in a room, looking out a window onto Lake Washington, getting high, writing his goodbyes, pulling a trigger. You can imagine the silence shattering and then collecting itself, in the way that water breaks for and then envelops a diver, absorbing forever the life of Kurt Cobain.

Rolling Stone June 2, 1994

No Mercy

Leonard Cohen's Tales from the Dark Side

"**I always experience myself as falling apart,** and I'm taking emergency measures," says Leonard Cohen, entirely deadpan. "It's coming apart at every moment. I try Prozac. I try love. I try drugs. I try Zen meditation. I try the monastery. I try forgetting about all those strategies and going straight. And the place where the evaluation happens is where I write the songs, when I get to that place where I can't be dishonest about what I've been doing."

That penchant for unadulterated honesty is precisely what liberates Cohen's music from the tastes of the moment and renders it timelessly alive. Through a body of work that ranges from the somber folk meditations of his debut, *Songs of Leonard Cohen* (1967), to the jagged art songs of his current album, *The Future,* Cohen's resonant croak of a voice delivers lines like "Give me crack and anal sex / Take the only tree that's left / And stuff it up the hole in your culture" with the deranged authority of an Old Testament prophet battling an addiction problem. Self-described as "the little Jew who wrote the Bible," he informs his songs with the force of moral significance—though, as he would be the absolute first to insist, neither his work nor his life should be taken as a moral example.

The figure Cohen cuts in person counters his self-portrait of psychic dissolution. Seated at a corner table in the lounge of a garish midtown Manhattan hotel, nursing a club soda, leaning forward to make an urgent point, then settling back in the oversized chair to listen carefully and think, he could easily be mistaken for an editor at a small publishing house, visiting New York to meet with writers and agents to discuss deals. He appears more serious, more intent than the attractive, evening-hour fun lovers clustered around the bar and crowding the tables, but not at all out of place.

At fifty-eight, his black hair combed straight back and turned partly to gray, Cohen is handsome and fit. His gray pin-stripe suit, gray shirt, and dark, patterned tie are subdued but well up to the imposing local standard. He is gracious, even courtly, a gentleman, but his dark eyes fix you, looking directly into yours. He seems anything but out of control.

What finally distinguishes Cohen from everyone else in the room, of course, are his words. They come not in torrents—he does not speak especially quickly—but in a steady, relentless assault. He has a poet's instinctive sense of cadence. When a phrase or a rhythm catches his ear, he will seize it, turn it, reverse it, repeat it until its expressive potential is exhausted. His relationship with spoken language is at least as sensuous as it is intellectual—listening to his deep, grainy voice, you remember that speech is a physical act. The effect is hip and hypnotic.

Thankfully, the branches of a potted palm arching over his head add a suitably ironic note: Foretelling the apocalypse in the bar of a three-hundred-dollar-a-night hotel, Leonard Cohen is a desperado under the leaves.

Characteristically, *The Future*, Cohen's first album since the stunning *I'm Your Man*, in 1988, is simultaneously grim, hopeful, and stirring. "There is a crack in everything," he sings on "Anthem," a track produced by Cohen with his lover, the actress Rebecca De Mornay. "That's how the light gets in."

The record continues to chronicle the struggle between despair and human possibility that Cohen has made his subject, first in poetry and fiction (the best known of his literary works is the 1966 novel *Beautiful Losers*) and then in a series of gripping albums, including such classics as *Songs of Leonard Cohen, Songs From a Room* (1969), *Songs of Love and Hate* (1971), *New Skin for the Old Ceremony* (1973), and *Various Positions* (1984).

Not counting the in-concert *Live Songs* (1972) and *Best of Leonard Cohen* (1975), Cohen has made just nine albums in twenty-five years. It's not because he's lazy, and it's not because he does other writing, though a new anthology of his poems, tentatively titled *Stranger Music: Selected Poems and Songs*, is set for publication in the fall of 1993. He bemoans his painstaking methods as a songwriter and in the studio, dismissing them as "stupid," but then adds: "It's a serious enterprise. Some people write great songs in taxicabs, and some people write great songs in offices in the Brill Building. I wish I could work that way. For me, I've got to surrender to it, struggle with it, and get creamed by it in the process."

And it's also not as if Cohen is unaware of the disjuncture between the culture of violence he documents in "The Future" ("Give me back the Berlin Wall / Give me Stalin and St. Paul / Give me Christ / Or give me Hiroshima / Destroy another fetus now / We don't like children anyhow / I've seen the future, baby: / It is murder") and the comfortable, far safer world in which he typically moves.

"The sense I have as I sit here is very different from the sense of the man who was struggling with the material," Cohen says about the rigors of writing the songs for the album. "This is after the struggle. The man who sits here in the lounge of this hotel is somewhat more casual and less committed than the man who wrote the record. The record involved a four-year struggle; the songs, some of them, are eight, ten years in the works. The record is there for keeps. There's flesh and blood attached to it. I did what was necessary, and I sit here kind of wrecked."

Cohen makes statements like that as if he were simply enumerating facts. A certain amount of self-dramatization is at play, obviously. But equally involved is Cohen's dead earnestness about his work, his conviction that writing songs is a lethal matter, a process of artistic self-searching that must not in any way be compromised. It's an old-fashioned view of the artist as a kind of humanist hero, an intrepid explorer of the soul and the times. It's not a conception often encountered in the pop world or, for the most part, anywhere else these days.

"The song will yield if you stick with it long enough," Cohen says. "But long enough is way beyond any reasonable idea you might have of what long enough is. It takes that long to peel the bullshit off. Every one of those songs began as a song that was easier to write. A lot of them were recorded with easier arrangements and easier lyrics. A song like 'Anthem,' for instance, I recorded that song for each of the last three albums—with strings, voices, and overdubs. It didn't make those records, because the version was too easy. 'The Future' began as a song called 'If You Could See What's Coming Next.' That point of view was a *deflected* point of view. I didn't have the guts to say, 'I've seen the future, baby: / It is murder.' The song was more observational, on the edge of the action."

Driven by a surprisingly funky guitar-and-keyboard groove, "The Future" evokes a disturbing nostalgia for the iron hand, a collective state of profound emotional panic that yearns for ruthless order as a balm against the horrors of anarchy. It's a mind-set that Cohen feels has already taken shape, one that he understands and, to a degree, shares. It's a reality that has already arrived.

"It's true now," Cohen says plainly. "I think the future is here. It's like when I was standing on my balcony in Los Angeles, where I live, and I could see six good fires. My music store was on fire. Through some incredible, invulnerable optimism I didn't feel the fire was going to come to my house, although the air was full of soot. It was settling on my grass.

"Where I had to go for the song," Cohen continues, "there is not that optimism. You have to go to the truth of feeling. When I inhabit that place, I discard all the alibis. I'm talking about a collapse of perspective. The catastrophe has already happened on the interior plane. The world has already been destroyed. The mental hospitals are full, and people are copping to each other that they can't take it. Well, what *is* it that they can't take? The traffic lights are still running. The subways are still running. People still have jobs. What is it that people can't take? They can't take the reality they're living in.

"People seem to know what 'The Future' is about. It's humorous, there's irony, there's all kinds of distances from the event that make the song possible. It's *art*. It's a good dance track, it's a hot number. It's captivating—it's even got *hope*. But the place where the song comes from is a life-threatening situation. You've got to go to some risky terrain. That's why the record takes so long to make, and that's why you're shattered at the end of it."

One of *The Future*'s zanier aspects is a bonkers eight-minute R&B arrangement of the Irving Berlin standard "Always," complete with horns and background vocals. In one sense, the song is fatally (and intentionally) subverted both by its context—it's a heartfelt declaration of unconditional, everlasting love amid the modern ruins—and Cohen and the band's unhinged performance.

In another, possibly deeper sense, it's strangely affecting, no more anomalous (or less, to be honest) than the quotation from the Book of Genesis that dedicates *The Future* to De Mornay: "And before I had done speaking in mine heart, behold, Rebecca came forth with her pitcher on her shoulder; and she went down unto the well, and drew water; and I said unto her, Let me drink, I pray thee. And she made haste, and let down her pitcher from her shoulder, and said, Drink, and I will give thy camels drink also: so I drank, and she made the camels drink also."

"It's a song that was sung a lot in my house," Cohen says of "Always." "My mother loved the song. I guess it's one of the first songs I learned. I always thought the words were great: 'Not for just an hour, not for just a day, not for just a year'—that was my idea of poetry." The recording of "Always" on *The Future* was partly inspired, Cohen says, by "my drink, the Red Needle, which I invented in Needles, California: tequila and cranberry juice, a little Sprite and fresh fruit." "Juicing everybody up," he says, loosened the atmosphere in the studio considerably: "The reason we kept that particular version is that it's the shortest one we had! We have four that go the whole tape—twenty-five minutes or something. We couldn't stop playing."

If "Always" provides a kind of moving comic relief to the album's darker elements, "Democracy"—a skewed, knowing, good-hearted paean to the United States that features the march-time chorus "Democracy is coming to the U.S.A."—balances the dread of "The Future" with the potential of better days to come. "In Canada we're taught to observe America very closely," says Cohen, who grew up in Montreal and splits his time between that city and Los Angeles. "That's why I could write 'Democracy.' I've lived a lot of my life in Europe, and I always found myself defending America. I found that people didn't understand that this was the great experiment, as catastrophic as it's become. If there is any possibility, whatever dim possibilities are left—as I say in 'Democracy'—'it's here they got the range / And the machinery for change / And it's here they got the spiritual thirst.' In the hearts of the world some kind of prayer is being said for American democracy *everywhere*. This is where the eyes of the world are turned. Is it going to work? It's here that the experiment unfolds."

The question haunting the song and left provocatively unanswered is, if democracy is at long last coming to the U.S.A., exactly what sort of system has the country been living under to this point?

In the course of a quarter century as one of the most highly regarded, if not commercially successful, singer-songwriters in popular music— he is the composer of "Suzanne," "Bird on the Wire," "Hey, That's No Way to Say Goodbye," and "Sisters of Mercy"—Cohen has, of course, had any number of encounters with the pop elite.

One of them, a brief affair with Janis Joplin that is preserved in "Chelsea Hotel," is a source of embarrassment to him. A memoir of uncommon frankness ("Giving me head on the unmade bed / While the limousines wait in the street") and unsentimentality ("I remember you well in the Chelsea Hotel / That's all / I don't think of you that often"), the song now strikes Cohen as "an indiscretion." "I don't know how it got out, but it did," Cohen says of the song's subject. "I said it somewhere. I may have been juiced at a concert and spoken about it in a way that seemed appropriate at the moment—and I have regretted it. There's nothing I can do about it. If I could do it again, I would have kept my mouth shut."

Death of a Ladies' Man, the 1977 album produced and cowritten by Phil Spector, represents the oddest collaboration in Cohen's career. "It has its admirers," Cohen says, while calling it "a grotesque, eccentric little moment." Spector, Cohen says, "was in his Wagnerian phase, when I had hoped to find him in his Debussy phase." "I was holding on for dear life," he continues. "My family was breaking up at the time—just to show up was rough. Then I'd have to go through this ninth-rate military film noir atmosphere. I've never forgotten Phil coming towards me with a bottle of Manischewitz in one hand, a .45 in the other and putting his arm around my shoulder, shoving the gun into my neck, cocking it and saying, 'Leonard, I love you.' It wasn't that much fun."

Cohen's willingness to go to the edge—and even, on occasion, to tumble headlong over it—is part of what has made him one of the rare Sixties icons whose appeal extends well into the twentysomething crowd. In 1986, Jennifer Warnes released *Famous Blue Raincoat,* a splendid album of Cohen songs, and in 1991 a tribute album, waggishly titled *I'm Your Fan,* came out, featuring covers of Cohen's work by the likes of R.E.M., Lloyd Cole, John Cale, the House of Love, and Fatima Mansions. He couldn't have been more delighted.

"I was very pleased to hear my eighteen-year-old daughter say, several years ago, 'You know, Dad, a lot of young bands are playing your material,'" Cohen recalls. "Then *I'm Your Fan* came out. My critical faculties were suspended immediately. People say, 'Do you like so-and-so's version?' Yeah, I do—whatever it was. I got a kick out of it."

Meanwhile, Cohen is under no illusions about his status as a pop star or as a folk god. "People are always inviting me to return to a former purity I was never able to claim," he says. Instead he questions himself about his future, about his proper role in the ever-changing, ever-new world order. "What do you do when you get older?" he asks. "What is your work as you get older? Is it appropriate to be out carrying a guitar from coffee shop to coffee shop at sixty? What is a dignified position?

"I have a real appetite to *hear* work from people my age," Cohen continues. "I mean, it's wonderful to hear from a guy talking about his first love—especially if it's Rimbaud. If it isn't Rimbaud, it's not so interesting as you get older.

"Those questions are hammered out in the workshop," Cohen concludes. "They have urgency, because you really do see the years, you really see the end. I think as long as you can crawl into the workshop, you should do the work. I always saw those old guys coming down to work, whatever job I happened to be in. Something about that always got to me. I'd like to be one of those old guys going to work."

Rolling Stone January 23, 1993

Jerry Garcia

Don't Look Back

I *first saw the Grateful Dead* in June of 1967 at a free concert in New York City's Central Park, and I was disappointed. I was fifteen years old and was there to see the Jefferson Airplane, who, for reasons I couldn't fathom at the time, had opened for the Dead. I was confused. Why would the Jefferson Airplane—who had hits, who had a certifiable star in Grace Slick—open for a band I had barely heard of and whose six members seemed no closer to star charisma than I or any of my friends? I wish I could say that my eyes were opened that day, that the wonders of the Dead were forever manifested to me. But that's not what happened. After twenty minutes or so, I left.

The wonders of the Dead would finally manifest themselves to me a couple of years later—appropriately, through the efforts of a group of friends. I had started college, the counterculture was in full swing, I was still star-addled, and my new college friends couldn't believe I wasn't into the Dead. A group decision was made: The next time the Dead came to New York, my friends would buy me a ticket.

This time I got it—and the next time and the next time and the next time. The shows I saw over the next few years were mostly at the Fillmore East, where the late sets began at 11:30. With the Dead that often meant that I would reenter the grimy streets of the East Village near dawn, humming with good vibrations. Those shows, as I at long last came to understand, were not about star tripping or even, in many ways, about music—though musically they were transporting. They seemed primarily about ecstasy and community, about my relationship with my friends, about our relationship to the larger audience around us, about the deep bond between that entire audience and the Dead.

In my memory, those shows were also about redefining time and the meaning of performance. The band's sets evolved in ways that dissolved even the loosest, most progressive expectations. Extended jams that melted the boundaries between songs and improvisation, between structure and chaos, were followed by interminable breaks, during which the band seemed simultaneously to be relaxing, re-collecting itself, freeing the audience to its own devices, and determining the next stage of the night's musical journey.

In a way that was remarkable even in those remarkable times, the Dead resisted being elevated above their audience. During one of those interminable breaks between songs, Bob Weir—sensing a discomfort in the crowd, an impatience, a hint that the audience was passively expecting the Dead merely to provide the evening's entertainment—stepped to the mike and suggested that we find ways to amuse ourselves. In the future, he said, the utopian future we all fully believed would soon arrive, there would be no distinctions between musicians and audiences. We would all create for each other. To force the band into a prescribed role would be to deny our own responsibility for bringing that future about.

But if the Dead refused the easy appeal of stardom, one man still stood at the center of the Dead experience, first among equals: Jerry Garcia. Not that he sought the spotlight. Instead, the light emanated from him. That light helped guide the Dead through their most extravagant musical excursions, when they would wander far into places from which it would seem impossible to return. Suddenly, Garcia, with his Cheshire Cat grin, would reach into his bag of tricks for the move that would light the road home.

Maybe it's a cliché at this point to compare music to a drug experience, but the Dead's music always seemed an extraordinary rendering of what it's like to take LSD—and Garcia was a big reason why. That wasn't because of any self-conscious "psychedelic" effects, though Garcia could occasionally indulge in those. Mainly, it was because Garcia's consciousness was genuinely expanded: He saw vistas where others could see only barriers, windows where others saw walls.

He was endlessly curious. For him, every musical possibility, every variation, was worth exploring. The moment was everything. There could be no such thing as a mistake; every direction pulsed with potential revelation. No song structure was ultimately firm, everything solid would melt into air, disintegrate, yielding a freedom that was both spiritually transformative and a little frightening. Who would I be if I were to lose myself this completely? At those instants, everyone—the band, the audience—looked to Garcia for deliverance.

We looked to him and he looked into himself. Then, magically, form would return from formlessness, and you would be wildly exhilarated, yourself again but changed. Garcia's playing—that thrilling sorcerer's brew of casualness and wit, intelligence and complete openness, daring and ease, playfulness and desire for beauty—contained all that. And the sweet yearning of his voice, the way he loved to sing at the very top of his register, as if he were always reaching for something just beyond his range.

The only time I met Garcia was when I interviewed him for *Rolling Stone*. I was struck by how totally his personality and talk recalled the manner of his playing. Ideas suggested ideas, which led to more ideas and eventually wound back to the first idea—it was no surprise when he told me that he learned about "musical things . . . rhythm . . . motion, timing" from Neal Cassady. He talked about hating to make choices as a songwriter, hating to eliminate possibilities in favor of one decision, preferring to "make it up as I go along." That made it hard to write songs. Closure did not come naturally to him. Improvisation and discovery, optimism and vision, those were Garcia's instinctive virtues.

Now, the deal's gone down. It's hard to stand Garcia's loss and it's hard to mourn him. For one thing, like all people who feel truly and deeply, he despised sentimentality. So what is the best way to keep him present in our hearts? Garcia, of course, loved Dylan and these Dylan lines have been running through my head: "You must leave now / Take what you need, you think will last." Garcia gave us a lot. "Take what you have gathered from coincidence," take what you need, share it with friends, leave the rest for others, kiss the sky, don't look back.

Originally published in *Garcia* (Rolling Stone Press/Little, Brown, 1995)

Robyn Hitchcock

A Wry Poet to the Devoted

O_ften when musicians are said to_ have cult followings, it simply means they don't sell many records. The British singer-songwriter Robyn Hitchcock, however, is a cult artist in the truest sense. For nearly two decades his fans have displayed a loyalty rare in the fickle world of popular music.

In turn, he writes songs with immediately appealing melodies but with lyrics that read like letters from a faraway dreamscape, exquisitely wrought bulletins from the farthest shores of his imagination. Entering the world of his music is like stepping into the looking glass. It's exciting, but a little frightening too. And it requires the sort of commitment that creates devotees rather than casual listeners.

It would be lovely to think that Mr. Hitchcock's new album, "Moss Elixir," his first release since signing with Warner Brothers earlier this year, might significantly expand his audience. (His albums have tended to sell in the low six figures.) Even though the album ranks among the most satisfying work he has done, that prospect is farfetched. The title itself reveals a couple of reasons why, betraying, as it does, Mr. Hitchcock's obsessions with Surrealist punning and natural science. Not that the forty-four-year-old Mr. Hitchcock, who lives in London, has ever envisioned himself in the spotlight.

He seems almost to have been bred for his cult status. He and his two younger sisters—reared, he says, in a "relatively wealthy" London environment by a father who wrote and painted and a "pretty cosmic" mother—"were brought up to be beautiful, precious creatures strolling around on the lawn."

Even when the Beatles, Bob Dylan, and Syd Barrett, a founding member of Pink Floyd, led Mr. Hitchcock out of his hothouse background, inspiring him to form his first band, the Soft Boys, in the mid-Seventies, he had modest expectations. "I didn't necessarily want to be the face of a generation or change the world," he says "I was much too timid and inward-looking for that."

Lanky and shaggy, a look of perpetual puzzlement on his face, Mr. Hitchcock greets each moment of his life as if it were entirely new and entirely befuddling. His manner is that of an absent-minded professor, hipster genus. Offhand intimations of mortality litter Mr. Hitchcock's conversation, as well as his songwriting. And he has affected the music scene—through his work with the Soft Boys and his former backing band, the Egyptians, as well as his solo albums. Peter Buck, R.E.M.'s guitarist, cites the Soft Boys—whose albums rejected the punk esthetic to move in a more eccentric direction—as an influence on R.E.M. Mr. Buck sees Mr. Hitchcock's songs as having a literary ancestry.

"It's like Edward Lear, the continuation of an English tradition," says Mr. Buck, who has frequently played guitar behind Mr. Hitchcock. "I also like it that one or two themes keep cropping up. Death is in there, fear of the body, sexual terror. It's as if sex, like death and nature, is just another part of this gaping maw of existence."

The director Jonathan Demme, a Hitchcock fan since the early Eighties, intends to make a film of a performance by Mr. Hitchcock. "There's a wonderful performance-art aspect to Robyn, with all the stories he tells between songs," Mr. Demme says. "It's like something between Spalding Gray's 'Swimming to Cambodia' and Talking Heads' 'Stop Making Sense.'"

The musical interplay Mr. Hitchcock sets in motion between his whimsical lyrics, chiming melodies derived from Sixties folk rock, and a sense of dread inherited from Anglo-Celtic folklore persists on "Moss Elixir." But this time, he has streamlined his sound, jettisoning his longstanding backup band, the Egyptians, while opting for the occasional violin, saxophone, and horn or rhythm section to support his own deft guitar playing and singing.

"The basic idea was to make something that only had what was necessary on it," he says. "I decided to go for the old-fashioned approach that Dylan used to have, where you build it all up around the voice and guitar."

That approach has brought with it a greater degree of accessibility. "Like a chandelier festooned with leeches" is still the sort of disturbing simile that springs naturally to Mr. Hitchcock's mind. But "The Speed of Things" is a powerfully compressed—and moving—meditation on the passing of time, while "This Is How It Feels" artlessly captures the accidental nature of love as "a sideways glance in a full-on world."

But it is seldom easy to pin down the meaning of Mr. Hitchcock's songs. Those meanings are as elusive as the beautiful birds, skittering insects, or slippery sea creatures that are among his most recurrent images. "I think very often my words get in the way," he admits. "Maybe it's because I'm not really using words to say anything. They're just the words that come to me when I have a certain feeling."

"If you'd just had an orgasm," he continues. " 'There goes the fence' might come into your mind. You wouldn't necessarily know why. My words are just a reaction, rather than a way for me to hack my way through the jungle to tell the folks how I feel."

Mr. Hitchcock may be a cult figure, But he has something of a media assault under way. In addition to "Moss Elixir," Warner Brothers will simultaneously release a vinyl-only companion piece for collectors. Titled "Mossy Liquor (Outtakes and Prototypes)," it consists of alternative versions of six of the songs on "Moss Elixir," along with six additional tracks. In September, Hitchcock's former label, A&M, will release a compilation of his earlier work, and Rhino Records, which has reissued the bulk of his extensive catalogue, will release a compilation of its own next spring. In October, Mr. Hitchcock will begin his North American tour, and Mr. Demme will make his film that month as well for theatrical release next year.

So even if his audience is small by pop music's inflated standard, Mr. Hitchcock takes the long view. "I think if you look back on it all in fifty or one hundred years, my stuff will actually blend in very well with the late twentieth century," he says. "It's pretty emotionally accurate about these times. Because I don't appear to be an overt commentator, I'm not seen that way. That means I'm not trendy. But it does give me longevity."

The *New York Times* August 18, 1996
© 1996, Reprinted by permission

John Lennon

The Man

October 9th marked the fiftieth anniversary of John Lennon's birth. December 8th will mark the tenth anniversary of his death. It is somehow fitting that the two dates will proceed forever down the ages, each inspiring commemoration as they simultaneously reach round numbers, the sad reminder of a death following hard upon the celebration of a life.

Lennon's death still reverberates with stunning force; it has lost none of its impact over the past decade. For anyone who cared about the Beatles and Lennon's individual vision and political activism, his impulse to experiment, and his willingness to speak the unwelcome truth, the world is simply a less enjoyable, less engaging place without him. For those inclined to speculate, it is easy to imagine that his presence could have blunted the hard edges of the Eighties, that his humor, intelligence, and sense of integrity could have proven a strong tonic for the spirit in those cynical times.

With *Double Fantasy,* the album he and Yoko Ono released in 1980, Lennon was clearly ready to return to public action after a five-year immersion in family life. How would his music have evolved in the Eighties? Interested in film all his life, how would he have responded to the rise of video? Lennon's uncompromising voice has been sorely missed during the censorship controversy of the past five years. Wouldn't it have been amazing to see John Lennon walk onstage during Live Aid? And in the decade of comebacks and reconciliations, could the Beatles really have resisted a reunion if Lennon had been alive? Would he have wanted such a thing? The loss of one life can change the course of a whole world.

On October 9th, Lennon's life was celebrated in a brief ceremony, called Imagine All the People, at the United Nations. After being welcomed to the UN—"this House of Peace"—by Marcella Pérez de Cuéllar, the wife of UN secretary general Javier Pérez de Cuéllar, Yoko Ono read a prepared statement, played a tape recording of Lennon, in which he urged the world to recognize "the choice we have in front of us: war or peace," and then broadcast the song "Imagine" over more than one

thousand radio stations in one hundred thirty countries to an audience
of approximately a billion listeners.

Several hundred UN diplomats and delegates, journalists, friends of
John and Yoko's, and other guests gathered in an auditorium at the UN
for the ceremony. "The dream we dream alone is only a dream," Yoko
said during her introduction, invoking the more mystical aspect of her
and Lennon's shared sensibility. "But the dream we dream together is
reality." Indeed, like Martin Luther King, John and Yoko had a dream.

In both its scale and its simplicity, the event was an eminently appropriate tribute to Lennon, a man who never hesitated to exploit the plat-
form he enjoyed in the media to try to change the world. His blunt
messages—"All You Need Is Love," "Give Peace a Chance," "Power to
the People," "War Is Over If You Want It"—were essentially advertising
slogans in the service of social betterment. Even the tape of Lennon that
Yoko played was moving in the directness, the plain-spokenness, even
the naiveté, of its appeal.

"You have the power, you know, you have the vote," Lennon said,
speaking in his characteristically natural, unforced cadences. "Just *show*
your neighbors that you're trying to be peaceful, however hard it is. It's
hard for us all. Just pass the word around. . . . Just have one word, PEACE,
in the window. And even if you don't exactly know why you're putting it
in the window, it can't harm you. And then you'd come across other
people that have put PEACE in the window. They're all hoping for peace.
We're all together on this thing. We all want peace, whatever sort of job
we have."

We may all want peace, but ten years after Lennon's death, peace has
proven as elusive as ever. Looking ahead, it is difficult to be optimistic,
and it is difficult to assess the true quality of Lennon's impact on the
world he fought so incessantly to improve. Sitting in the living room of
the apartment she shared with Lennon for many years in the Dakota, in
New York, Yoko Ono discussed the legacy of John Lennon on the day
after the ceremony at the United Nations. Even Yoko had to admit that,
at least in the years immediately following her husband's death, it
seemed as if much of their work had come to naught—though, in her
view, that work bore fruit eventually and will continue to.

"John was saying in 1980, 'The Eighties are going to be a great, great
decade, a fantastic decade,'" Yoko said. "Mainly to project positiveness—
and I was saying that, too. But fans would write to me, saying 'Well, John

said the Eighties were going to be great, but what's *this?*' For one thing, to start the decade, John died. Then what happened was—I think it started with Band Aid and Live Aid. We had "We Are the World," Hands Across America, Amnesty International—all of these big things started to happen.

"Those things were the results of the grassroots movements of the Sixties," she continued. "The memory of that must have been there and started to blossom. Then there was a peace conference in Moscow. Then Gorbachev and Reagan shook hands. Then at the end of the Eighties—as if somebody was making a point to do it *within* the Eighties—suddenly the Berlin Wall disappeared, Eastern Europe was freed. I mean, it's *incredible!*"

The UN event grew out of Yoko's desire to commemorate Lennon's fiftieth birthday in a public, yet dignified, way. "Even before the year started, I thought that somehow I wanted to direct the celebration into a positive direction," Yoko said. "Already last year, people started to say, 'What about this, what about that?' The suggestions were made mainly from a business point of view. I didn't want the year to become a pandemonium of trying to sell Lennon out on the market. I wanted something that was more positive and in the spirit of 'Imagine.'"

One idea was holding tribute concerts in various cities, including Liverpool, Tokyo, and Moscow. Plans for the Moscow show eventually fell through because of the deteriorating political situation in the Soviet Union, but the Tokyo concert, featuring a bill consisting of both Japanese and Western artists, will take place this December. The Liverpool show, which was staged this past May, received a mixed response—an assessment Yoko regards as unfair. "It was nothing like the press reported," she said. "It was really a very positive, beautiful concert." A two-hour television special, originally planned for airing in October, will be broadcast in the United States this December, and a four-CD collection of Lennon's songs from his solo career was recently released by Capitol.

Still, the notion of one symbolic gesture that everyone everywhere could participate in held an allure for Yoko. "A lot of business ventures were suggested to me, but what I was looking for was one special event that would really unite Lennon fans throughout the world," she said. She explained her ideas to Los Angeles media consultant Jeff Pollack, who came up with the idea of a worldwide broadcast of "Imagine" after hearing the song on the radio while riding in a car in New York. Pollack also

suggested the United Nations as the site for the broadcast and arranged
for the event to be broadcast entirely without commercial sponsorship.

"He said, 'Do you think you could get the United Nations?' I thought
that was a bit much," Yoko said. "And also a bit much in terms of 'Well,
could I?' There's a long-standing grassroots feeling in me that made me
think, 'Why not Strawberry Fields? That stands for peace.' But then I
thought, 'It would be a very good thing if I did it in the United Nations. It
would be a symbol.' And Mrs. Pérez de Cuéllar just told me yes."

Though the decision to stage the ceremony at the un was made well
before Iraq's invasion of Kuwait, the event gained political resonance
because of the un's peacekeeping role at a time when war sometimes
seems just a shot away. "Even the way that both sides in the Middle East
crisis are dealing with the situation now is very sensible," Yoko said
cautiously, aware of the day-to-day shifts the problem takes. "So, hopefully, it will not go toward a violent situation but through discussion can
come to some kind of good result. In that sense, it shows the wisdom of
people now, even in a crisis."

Yoko's introductory statement at the United Nations was characterized
by a strong, if politely expressed, environmental stance, a position she
clearly perceives to be an essential component of shaping a legacy for
Lennon. "In celebration of John's life," she said, "let's use the power of
dreaming. Let's dream of trees growing in abundance, birds flying in
clear air, fish swimming in clear water, and our children living in joy."

Yoko has taken pragmatic steps to attempt to transform that dream
into reality. Last fall in Japan, she announced her desire to establish, in
cooperation with the Japanese government, Greening of the World
scholarships in Lennon's honor. The concert in Tokyo and the television
special in the United States are both designed to raise money for the
scholarship fund.

"The scholarships are for the children of the world, not just the Japanese," Yoko explained. "It would be given to Third World exchange
students. It doesn't specify what subject they should study, because the
greening of the world, I feel, is not just the *physical* greening of the
world, but it has to start with the mind, and education is very important.
And if there's enough money, I would like to give it to institutions that
do scientific research to make our lives easier in terms of pollution and
cleaning up the world. But it's mainly for children. Of course, I believe
in exchange programs, because it's one world, one people."

In her large, airy apartment, with its spare, white decor and floor-to-ceiling windows overlooking Central Park, overlooking Strawberry Fields, Yoko seemed delicate and slight. Now fifty-seven years old, smoking incessantly, she wore faded jeans and a dark blue shirt; she was slender, barefoot and, without her almost omnipresent sunglasses, she looked vulnerable, even girlish, far less imposing than she can sometimes appear in the media. She spoke softly and steadily.

She is an intensely private person and takes comfort in the organizational aspects of ensuring the ongoing significance of her and John's work. It is a way of giving public expression to deeply personal emotions. When Yoko, in the course of enumerating some of the most pressing issues facing the world today, suddenly said, "And violence in the streets is a very serious issue, as well—not just in New York, but in all cities, really," it was difficult not to feel a chill to the bone while remembering what took place just outside this very building one night ten years ago. That memory seemed just beneath the surface of her consciousness at every point, a presence hauntingly defined by its overt absence in her conversation.

"Well, I wasn't going to stand in front of the mike at the United Nations and start primal-screaming," Yoko said when asked about how she was personally feeling in the midst of the two anniversaries being commemorated this year. "I think that my feelings are probably obvious to a lot of people, especially the widows of the world, and I think they should remain private. Once I start to explain how I feel, it would probably be wrong, because my feelings are very complex, at this time especially. It's not like the initial shock at the initial loss. I pushed a lot of my emotions deeper inside, so it's more complex, and whatever I say about them does not sound right. It can't quite describe how I feel."

Nor did she feel comfortable discussing any of the myriad versions of "what might have been," the scenarios that the rest of us can't seem to refrain from spinning out. "I don't want to guess how he would have felt about it," Yoko said when asked how John Lennon might have perceived the culture of greed and materialism that coalesced in the early Eighties. "My guess is just as good as yours. We all know what he said and what he stood for and what sort of person he was. I think that it's very interesting that even in the Eighties his influence was felt, and also his songs were encouraging to a lot of people. So it's not like he stopped *working*."

She stopped and laughed. "It seemed like he was still working on the situation," she said. "So instead of thinking of 'What John would have felt,' or 'What John would have done,' I like to think of how *we* have felt his influence and how *we* have done."

She had struck a similar note during her press conference following the UN ceremony. "I think John's spirit is alive today," Yoko answered when she was asked what sort of things Lennon might be doing on this day if he were still alive. "And I think this celebration is a proof of that. I think that his music is still affecting people, affecting the world, and encouraging people to make a better world." She emphasized in particular Lennon's continuing importance to people who were only children when he was killed. "It seems like [young people] have their own way of being in touch with John's spirit," she said. "I have a teenage son, so I know that that generation seems to be very interested in, not John's only, but Sixties music."

Of course, Yoko, like everyone else, has her own favorite aspect of the legacy left by her husband. "The exchange of roles," she said that day in the Dakota, with evident fondness. "John's awareness about the roles of women and men and how to cope with each other and with a relationship. I think that affected a lot of couples and a lot of couples with children, too."

She still holds to the brand of personal politics that she and Lennon made a hallmark of all their activism in the Sixties and Seventies. Speaking about what ordinary people can do to help realize the ideals extolled by John and Yoko in their own lives, Yoko articulated a vision that inextricably linked the late Sixties with the early Nineties.

"I always get letters from people saying, 'I'm not famous, I'm not rich, and I'm just an ordinary housewife. What could I do?'" Yoko began. "I think this is an age when the issues are so big that, of course, one hero cannot take care of it. All of us have to be heroes in some ways. But we don't really have to be that *much* of a hero. What I learned from what we did in the Sixties—maybe we were young, too, but we were always in so much of a hurry. When I wrote the song, 'Now or Never,' I thought, 'Oh, well, with this song, everything is going to be all right by next year'—I was *that* naive, you know? And when I saw that nothing happened after writing a song or something, it was like 'Oh, it didn't work.' I think a lot of us were like that. We were very idealistic, and we wanted a result *now*. If we demonstrated, the war was supposed to end tomorrow. That's how it was.

"What I learned was, it's true that bettering the world to the point that the world is extremely healthy, clean and all of us can live fairly comfortably—I mean, that's a very ambitious thing to do. And for that, it takes a long time. And so each of us should not feel that we have to do it *now*, that we have to do a hundred percent *now*, because then we'll be out of breath. The way to do it is just relax about it a little and keep a good balance going, not put our energies too much on just the *cause*, but always remember about the people around you: your family, your friends. Keep having love for them and caring about them as well.

"And by the way," she continued, "maybe do one good thing a day, one especially good thing. And it could be a very small thing—it depends on the person. That's good enough. If all of us were to do that, the world would be pretty good, pretty soon."

Like Lennon himself in even his bitterest moments, Yoko maintains an essential optimism. "In the midst of the Reagan age," Yoko said, "When the Star Wars idea and all that was very prominent, I thought, 'Well, what can I do?' And so, when Strawberry Fields opened, I tried to plant a little seed about the fact that we're entering the age of wisdom. Friends said, 'Entering the age of wisdom? Are you *crazy*? We're not wise at all.'

"And I thought, 'But we *have* to be,' " she continued. "And I think that we could be. The age of wisdom is an age where we can change things by discussion, rather than fists, and by understanding each other, rather than trying to buy and control things. It's that kind of world. And I think that the Nineties will be that. I think that the Establishment and the people are going to use the maximum human wisdom to make a beautiful world. This is our mission of this decade: to greet the twenty-first century in peace and with a feeling of satisfaction."

It's a lovely vision, and one that John Lennon surely would have shared. Whether it becomes a reality or not, all of us can affirm the feelings Yoko expressed at the end of her speech at the United Nations, though none of us can feel it as profoundly as she does. "Happy birthday, John," she said, speaking slowly to prevent her voice from breaking. "The world is better today for having shared a time with you."

Rolling Stone December 13–27, 1990

John Mellencamp's
Void in the Heartland

"**W**as *Bruce Springsteen* really successful with *Born in the U.S.A.?*" asks John Cougar Mellencamp one crisp spring afternoon in Bloomington, Indiana. "Think so? I think the record was great—that has nothing to do with it. I wonder if he's the same guy he used to be. That's what success is about: happiness. I wonder if he's as happy as he was."

Mellencamp takes a pull on one of his ever-present Marlboros and continues. "I'm not bad-mouthing him. I like the guy. Every time I've been around him, he's been a blue chip fella to me, right? But I wonder about his happiness. I wonder about Madonna's happiness. I wonder about Michael Jackson's happiness. We put him down so bad that he feels he has to make a statement about it. Let's quit feeding off these people."

Mellencamp is looking at the big picture these days ("Is Madonna happy?"—now there's a puzzle worthy of a Zen master), and he doesn't like what he sees. He is full of questions—about his own identity, about the pop-culture world that envelops him, about the life he has led to this point—and that makes him extremely uncomfortable. It's not a place he's used to being. Growing up as a hell-raiser in a small town, playing in rock bands through your teens, and landing a record deal in your early twenties are not great incentives to the contemplative life.

Nor is the fiery singer suited by temperament to indecision and ambivalence. Confronted with a problem, Mellencamp is far more prone to ride roughshod over it than to analyze it coolly. Brash, even arrogant at times, he likes to shoot from the hip and from the lip. He can be stubborn and demanding, and his temper is legend. By the close of the seemingly endless world tour that followed the release of Mellencamp's album *The Lonesome Jubilee,* in 1987, Mellencamp's band had dubbed his dressing room Valhalla, in honor of one of the singer's favorite jokes: "You know what makes a good Viking, don't you? Severe mood swings."

As his raw, poignant new album, *Big Daddy,* indicates, Mellencamp's mood has swung into darkness. The bitterness that courses through the album's first single, "Pop Singer," in which Mellencamp excoriates the music industry and declares, "Never wanted to be no pop singer," is palpable—and some say hypocritical. There's no doubting that Mellencamp—the product of a pre-punk world in which bigger was better and it was assumed that rock & roll stars were *supposed* to be popular—ardently pursued mass success and occasionally made a fool of himself in the process.

Unfortunately, going after something doesn't necessarily guarantee that it will be what you thought it would be once you get it. Also, in Mellencamp's younger years *pop music* was a term that stood in direct opposition to *rock & roll*. Rock & roll was tough, Dionysian, and serious; pop music was light and frivolous. In Mellencamp's view, pop has won out.

"At thirty-seven years old, I am at total odds with the pop business," Mellencamp says. "That's what 'Pop Singer' is about. As I sit here every day, I just become at total odds with my generation, too. I hate to say this, but I feel like what John Lennon must have felt: I don't want to be in this race anymore, because it leads to *nowhere*.

"I'm living the dream of a nineteen-year-old boy from Indiana," he continues, "and I'm thirty-seven years old. Some people would say, 'Well, then, hell, you've got it made, man. You're young forever.' But what happens when you don't *want* to be young anymore? When the fascination of being a young man has left you?"

In the course of what Mellencamp will later describe as "probably the best Marlon Brando interview I've ever done, where you just hate everything," it becomes clear that the singer has arrived at the critical point reached by many rockers before him—Elvis Presley, the Beatles, and Bruce Springsteen among them. It's the point where, amid the delights, temptations, rewards, and horrifying fun-house reflections of media-driven celebrity, you either find yourself or lose yourself. It's growing up in public: the rock & roll midlife crisis.

As he nears forty, the self-mocking "Little Bastard"—a sobriquet Mellencamp borrowed from that other Indiana icon, James Dean—finds himself facing some hard realities with nothing but wildly contradictory emotions to support him. Despite a string of first-rate albums—*Uh-Huh, Scarecrow, The Lonesome Jubilee,* and now *Big Daddy*—Mellencamp is rarely regarded with the seriousness accorded the likes of Springsteen and U2, and it bothers him.

"There was a writer who likes my music—I know this guy—and I'm reading one of his articles about another artist, right?" Mellencamp says.

"He says, 'Well, it was a good record, but it was like a John Mellencamp record.' It wasn't what they *should* have been doing. I'm thinking, 'Man, there's a thousand guys that sold out—use *their* name, don't use mine, like I'm a second-rate artist.' And he *did*, and it was like 'Well, thanks, bub. Appreciate it.' That hurt me."

Mellencamp's uncompromising stance against corporate sponsorship has made him feel anomalous in an age when even esteemed figures like Lou Reed, Steve Winwood, Robert Plant, and Eric Clapton have hawked products. The trivializing of rock & roll is a problem he sees in the media as well. "Nothing against *USA Today*," he says, "but that's what people want—'Let's cut to the chase, give me the dirt.' This is *our generation* doing this. It's sad. And, like, *Rolling Stone*, there's the Critics Poll, and then there's all those advertisements around it. How are we supposed to take you guys seriously when you've got a corporate sponsor underneath your names?"

Other difficulties plague Mellencamp. Early on in his career, he signed a disadvantageous publishing deal, and to this day he does not own his own songs. "I had to give up something to get something when I was twenty-two years old," he says wearily. "And at thirty-seven, it's pretty disheartening to me to write hundreds of songs and not own them."

Finally, Mellencamp, in the wake of tabloid reports about his womanizing, is currently separated from his second wife, Vicky, the mother of the two youngest of his three daughters. Mellencamp's eldest daughter, now nineteen, from his first marriage, is about to be married.

"Oh, I'm the world's worst at relationships, are you kidding me?" Mellencamp says ruefully. "I'm retarded. I've been married two times— and both times married to wonderful women—and I've managed to fuck those up somehow. Relationships—yeah, they'd mean a lot if I knew how to have one. To really relate to a woman—*ah*, I don't know how to do it."

On the new album's "Big Daddy of Them All," a grim parody of all the self-congratulatory "my way" songs, Mellencamp, the rock & roll star and former paterfamilias, sings, "You did it your way and, man, you did it all." His voice is filled with a sad but unsentimental irony. "How does it feel to be the big daddy of them all?"

And if all this sounds to you like nothing more than the self-pitying posturing of a pampered celebrity, a kind of rock-millionaire version of *thirtysomething*, Mellencamp's got a characteristic reply. The singer ponders how his situation might look from the outside and concludes, "Anybody who thinks, 'Well, Mellencamp's rich, he ought to be happy, fuck him'—well, fuck *you*."

Amid his problems, consolation has come to Mellencamp in the form of art—or, as he puts it, "this painting shit." These days, of course, every socially aspirant philistine twit in the music business who earns a six-figure salary is an art collector. The fashionable taste tends to run toward contemporary painting that is abstract but pretty and unthreatening—and, needless to say, a sound investment. Speculating on the careers of younger painters—an extension, really, of the market-think that determines the signing of new bands—has eclipsed stock speculation as a hip money sport for record-industry executives and artists alike.

Typically unpretentious and almost willfully self-confident, Mellencamp has avoided such nonsense. Instead, beginning last August, he started to paint himself—a fact amiably noted by Lou Reed, who refers to Mellencamp as "my painter friend Donald" in "Last Great American Whale," on the album *New York*. Mellencamp is drawn less to contemporary art than to late-nineteenth-century European masters, and his own work strives for a style that, like his songs, "is impressionistic but at the same time has a certain realism to it and creates a mood."

"If an art critic came in and looked at my paintings," Mellencamp says, "he'd go, 'Man, you are so old-fashioned and you are so behind the times that this has nothing to do with contemporary art.' Sorry—I'm not dying to be hip." On the other hand, he understands how incredulous people will be about his new interest. "I'm sure people reading this are going to have a good laugh," he says at one point.

Wearing a gray turtleneck and black jeans, his brown hair cut back to medium length after it grew past his shoulders on the last tour, Mellencamp sits at a table in the art studio he recently had built next door to his house in Bloomington. "It's been here since Christmas," he says of the studio. "I was tired of painting in the garage. It was winter, and there's no heat in the garage. I'd get the oil on the palette, and the fucking oil would freeze. I dig the struggling-artist stuff, but this was a little ridiculous. I said, 'If I'm gonna paint, let's try to get some place where it's a little more comfortable.' "

Set close by the woods on Mellencamp's property, the studio building is pristinely white, with high ceilings and light streaming in from the windows that line the studio's southern wall. The space is large, open and airy, and canvases of Mellencamp's paintings, along with art books and supplies, are everywhere. Significantly, even in this environment, which is a kind of hymn to the ideal of fine art, one rock & roll note intrudes and dominates. Virtually surrounded by canvases beside the door stands Mellencamp's enormous, gleaming black motorcycle.

"My mom painted when I was a kid," Mellencamp says, over a lunch of ham-and-cheese sandwiches, barbecue potato chips, melon, and Perrier. "I thought oil paintings took forever to paint. She had a little studio set up downstairs in our basement. She'd do florals and still lifes—pretty boring stuff, I thought. But she had to take care of us kids, so she'd paint for fifteen minutes, and then the painting would sit for three weeks. I thought, 'Man, this is fucked. This oil painting takes too long.' But that was a kid's perception. The reality is, I never spend more than a day on a painting. That's my problem with this art: I don't have the patience to do what I need to do."

Nor does Mellencamp have any interest in taking formal lessons. "I think lessons screw people up," he says. "I know a girl here in town, she's my age, and she just started painting. She was a pretty good painter till she took a couple of classes. Now she's all balled up in what's right and what's wrong. And what they teach in school now, I'm not interested in learning. I'm not interested in drawing a guy's dick, you know? That's one of the things she had to do."

For Mellencamp, painting has become a retreat from the pressures of his life on the pop roller coaster. Increasingly, his world has narrowed to his home, the art studio, and his recording studio, Belmont Mall, located about seven miles away, where he records with his band and produces other artists. The pleasure he takes both in his own work and in encountering the work of the masters lends his conversation the conviction of a convert.

"I think you can say much more in a painting than you can in a stupid song," he says. "I just went to Chicago to see a painting by Renoir. I've gone to Chicago four times to see it. I wouldn't go to Chicago to see any rock band, but I'll go up there just to look at that painting. It's thrilling. It's what rock & roll used to be to me when I was younger. I mean, my heart beats fast, I get excited, I break out in a cold sweat. It's called *Two Sisters on the Terrace*—the most beautiful painting ever painted. The first time I saw it, I cried. It's so fucking beautiful."

About his own painting, Mellencamp says, "It's honest. There's no commerce involved—there's nothing for fucking money. I don't know, it's just a much better medium. I'm thirty-seven now; hopefully by the time I'm fifty-seven, I'll be . . ." He doesn't allow himself to complete the thought.

"All these paintings are just John practicing—I mean, you're looking at *Chestnut Street*, right?" he continues, alluding to his critically devastated 1976 debut album, *Chestnut Street Incident*, which he recorded as John Cougar. "And I think that I'm ahead of *Chestnut Street*, as far as painting goes. So we'll see what happens in ten years, if I can keep with it.

"Some days I start at seven o'clock in the morning, and I paint until five, eat dinner, and come back and paint till midnight. I don't have to see anybody. I don't have to talk to anybody. It's better than sex, for me.

"The songs, it's like 'Oh, I don't know, this guy already did this.' 'What are they gonna think about this?' All these fucking things that come into your head that limit you as a songwriter. Then you've got your stupid image that people are thinking about. All that garbage. It kills every artist's songwriting eventually."

Mellencamp's acrid perception of the vagaries of the pop world has formed at a time when he arguably could be poised to goose his record sales into the tens of millions. Instead, he has refused to tour in support of *Big Daddy*—"It's not that type of record," he says, with a knowing chuckle, "there's no 'R.O.C.K. in the U.S.A.' on it"—and he is doing relatively few interviews.

"What's the point?" Mellencamp asks. "This other step that people keep wanting me to take to become another level of recording artist—to be *Madonna*? To sell out? To bend over? To kiss somebody's ass? I ain't gonna do it. I don't want nothin' to do with it."

Even so, Mellencamp has always been fiercely competitive—he is managed, for example, by one of the most high-powered management firms in the music industry. While the commercial aspects of the music business may disgust him, he acknowledges that he is not fully indifferent to the standards set for him. "I'll say, 'I don't give a fuck if the record sells or not. If people like it, they buy it. If they don't, they don't.' But the minute it comes out of my mouth, I know I'm lying—to myself. 'Who you kidding, Mellencamp? If this record doesn't sell a certain volume, you're gonna be bummed out.' I'll sit there and contradict

myself about what I believe over and over and over again. And I haven't
really found a place where I'm comfortable with it."

And, as you might think, Renoir and the high-art tradition are not the only cultural beacons by which Mellencamp measures his dissatisfaction. Another one is much closer to home, and much more intimately related to the cultural heritage of which Mellencamp is a part: the imprisonment of his idol, James Brown, on misdemeanor weapons and traffic charges, in South Carolina. If James Brown, "the greatest fucking soul songwriter in the world," can be allowed to languish in jail, Mellencamp seems to think, what possible value can American society be said to place on the popular arts?

"Don't we respect *anything?*" he asks, his voice rising from a whisper to a shout. "Don't we respect what James Brown gave us? I just can't believe that there hasn't been 90 million letters written to the governor of South Carolina saying, 'You should pardon this guy.' I mean, they're gonna pardon Ollie North!

"You should pardon James Brown, give the guy some help, because he has given *his life* to us. He gave us 'Papa's Got a Brand New Bag.' You know what that song meant to me? *Everything.* 'I Feel Good' means *everything.* The minute James fucks up, 'Take this, motherfucker.' It ain't right. It just ain't right."

A few moments later, Mellencamp collects himself, pauses for a second and, his blue eyes flashing, cracks his infectious smile. "You didn't know this was going to be so much fun, did you?" he says.

You can only fall as far as you rise, and the depth of John Mellencamp's disillusionment is partly a reflection of how completely he embraced the rock & roll dream. The working-class Midwestern culture in which Mellencamp grew up was as far removed from insider status as it could be, and the singer's early notions about how the music business worked were touchingly naive.

"I figured if a guy made a record, it was on the radio," he says. "I thought all disc jockeys were handsome. I thought the record business was run by kids. I was shocked when I got my very first record deal: I went out to California, MCA, to meet the president of the company—he was an *old man* my dad's age. I couldn't believe it. It really threw me for a loop."

But as with many outsiders trying to penetrate a more sophisticated world, Mellencamp's naiveté was laced with a suspicion that what separates insiders from outsiders is not talent but a knowledge of how to play the game. To get his break, Mellencamp sought out Tony DeFries, the Svengali manager who had helped transform a hippie-ish London R&B fan named David Jones into the androgynous glitter rocker David Bowie. DeFries thought he had found his next mark in Mellencamp, whom he rapidly dubbed John Cougar and signed to a record deal.

"Let's face it, I got out of Vincennes University," Mellencamp says, referring to the two-year college in southern Indiana that he graduated from, "and I had a record deal like that [*snaps his fingers*]. I'd written, like, three songs. I got a record deal for all the wrong reasons. This guy sees me, he's from England, he thinks my accent's funny, and he didn't give a fuck what the songs were like. 'A real *American*'—and I'm thinkin', 'Man, they're all *over* the fucking place!' So it never was the music in the beginning to me. It was a hustle. . . . I mean, Larry [Crane, Mellencamp's guitarist] was still in *high school,* and we're making records."

Mellencamp began to attract attention when Pat Benatar covered "I Need a Lover," from the album *John Cougar;* his own version of the song cracked the Top Forty in 1979. Three years later his album *American Fool* yielded the Top Ten hits "Hurts So Good" and "Jack & Diane," but it wasn't until 1983 and the bracing populist rock of "Pink Houses," from the album *Uh-Huh,* that Mellencamp began to achieve critical respectability—a process he encouraged by actively courting the press. That stature was enhanced when his next album, *Scarecrow,* articulated a bleak vision of Midwestern farm culture in crisis; Mellencamp then turned art into action by helping Willie Nelson and Neil Young organize the first Farm Aid show.

On both *The Lonesome Jubilee* and *Big Daddy,* Mellencamp seems, in the aftermath of his political awakening, brought up short by the elusive nature of human happiness. "I went through a period in '84 and '85 when I was in a real positive frame of mind," Mellencamp says. "My personal life was great, my career was going well. But in 1989, I'm not that positive about anything. It seems real complicated to me now. Back then, when I wrote 'Pink Houses,' it was pretty simple. When *Scarecrow* came out, it was pretty simple. I fell back into that idealism of the Sixties for a while. I liked being there—but it was false. I do think that music can change things. But not now. Not with the way it's going now."

Mellencamp and his stalwart band—guitarists Larry Crane and Mike Wanchic, bassist Toby Myers, violinist Lisa Germano, accordionist John Cascella, drummer Kenny Aronoff, and background singers Pat Petersen and Crystal Taliefero—recorded *Big Daddy* in their "spare time," often laying down basic tracks in one evening. Mellencamp produced the album himself, bypassing his coproducer Don Gehman for the first time since 1982. As on *The Lonesome Jubilee,* the group's lean, gritty sound is embellished by a variety of folk instruments; this gives the music a haunting flavor that suits the album's emotional terrain well.

"I got off *The Lonesome Jubilee* tour, and I just started to look at myself and evaluate my life, trying to see what it meant," Mellencamp says about the genesis of *Big Daddy,* for which he wrote about thirty songs. "I say it in 'Void in My Heart': 'Hundred dollars in my pocket / And it didn't buy a thing.' I'm just real discouraged about it. That's where this record comes from."

Out of a kind of inverse respect for the edginess of the feelings he's expressing on *Big Daddy*—and with a nod to records by Bob Dylan and the Rolling Stones that he's admired in the past—Mellencamp did not include a lyric sheet with the album, and he buried his vocals in the mix. Most of the songs are sung in a grainy, world-weary drawl.

"As far as the singing goes, I can't wait to read some of the reviews," Mellencamp says. " 'Mellencamp's flat on the first song.' I just know some kid somewhere is going to write that. For me to go up there and sing 'Big Daddy' in my best voice is kind of silly, isn't it? A lot of those songs shouldn't even have been sung; they should have been spoken— *quietly.* That's the way it felt."

Still, Mellencamp has been gratified by the early responses to *Big Daddy.* "It verifies everything that I've always thought: When you don't try so hard, it just turns out better," he says. "See, I was so afraid when I made records when I was twenty-five years old, thirty years old. I'm not afraid any more. What can you do to me? So you don't like the record? The record don't sell? Those things will hurt, but I've got a thick motherfucking skin. Afraid of what—making a bad record? I made a hell of a *bunch* of them. And I made some good ones."

Our car pulls through the electronic gate that encloses the grounds of John Mellencamp's house, and a pile of disassembled wooden crates, packing materials, broken screwdrivers, and a hammer come into view, littering the ground outside the studio. "Uh-oh," says Rick Fettig, a large, friendly guy who went to high school with Mellencamp in Seymour, Indiana, and now works as his assistant. "John's paintings must have arrived, and he couldn't wait."

Inside the modest, attractive house, done in muted tones, Mellencamp is admiring five paintings he purchased from a gallery on his recent trip to Chicago. They are propped up in the living room, which is dominated by a large piano, and in the adjacent den, which contains a pool table. Gold and platinum records line one wall of the den, and Mellencamp suggests that they be taken down to make room for art.

Three of the newly acquired paintings are by an artist whom Mellencamp describes as "a forty-year-old hippie girl from Ireland or Wales," and two are by an eighty-year-old male artist. The woman's paintings are quiet, romantic, and personal—impressionistic scenes of children eating cake at a table with their mother in a country house or of a woman walking through a gorgeously colored field with a young girl.

Mellencamp is enthusiastic in his praise of all the paintings, and in his bluff way he wants that enthusiasm shared. Rick and a young woman who also works for Mellencamp seem slightly uncomfortable. They want to participate, and they want to say the right things, but they seem a bit out of their element amid all the art talk.

One of the paintings is meant as a gift for Vicky, who is coming by to see it. As she pulls into the driveway and walks through the door, Mellencamp watches her intently through a window, as if there were something to be learned from the mere sight of her.

A slender blonde whose features are, no doubt, as lovely now as when she was a teenager, Vicky looks sad, determined, and mildly careworn. Mellencamp's natural energy and charm are blunted by his desire not to assume too much from the fact of her presence. The playful domestic joke of the sweatshirt Vicky is wearing—THOROUGHBRED SPENDING TEAM, it reads—is almost heartbreaking in this context.

The lines between intimacy and distance have been blurred, and no one quite knows how to act. Mellencamp presents the painting hopefully, and Vicky accepts it graciously. As Mellencamp walks her to her car, they talk, and he puts his arm around her shoulder. The intent of the gesture and its stiffness seem separated by an abyss of unstated emotion.

Asked when he's alone about the possibility of a reconciliation, Mellencamp says, "Well, I don't know. I mean, that would be nice, but I have to look at the situation and wonder, if we got back together, what would be different? I don't want to hurt this woman any more. She doesn't deserve it."

The scene at the house and the feelings that churn beneath its surface recall a moment from the day before when Mellencamp pulled out a book of Degas paintings. "When is it *ever* going to work?" he asked, speaking about the struggles of men and women in relationships as he leafed through the text. "Degas was an artist that had a great understanding of that conflict between man and woman that basically governs our entire living, breathing moment."

As Mellencamp turned the pages, one scene after the next depicted men and women occupying the same physical space and different emotional worlds. "It's like the battle of the sexes," Mellencamp said, looking at one work. "Men taunting women and women taunting men. He painted that as a young man." He continued to flip through the book, stopping when something caught his eye. "The conflict between man and woman is in every single painting," he said, stopping again. "I mean, this is a sexually charged situation. This is like . . ."

He stopped himself, and we both silently stared at the image of a man and woman in a room, neither looking at the other. Then Mellencamp looked up and whispered, "I mean, *me* and *you* are going to solve *this* problem?" Then he broke into laughter.

Rolling Stone June 29, 1989

Father of Bluegrass Is Dead at 84

Bill Monroe

"**H**igh Lonesome**"** is the term that has often been used to describe his sound, and he was a dignified loner who rose from hardscrabble obscurity to the highest places. He is one of the handful of Americans justly credited with forging an entirely new musical genre. And now he is gone. Bill Monroe, the undisputed father of bluegrass, a peer of such giants as Louis Armstrong, Duke Ellington, and Miles Davis, died of complications from a stroke Sept. 9, 1996, four days shy of his eighty-fifth birthday. We will not see his like again.

Monroe's early life hardened and strengthened him. He was born in 1911 to a farming family, the youngest of eight children, near the small town of Rosine, Kentucky. "I started to work when I was eleven," Monroe once said, "and there wasn't a lot of playtime for me. . . . The evenin' would be lonesome, you know. Well, that's in my music."

John W. Rumble, who assembled the superb four-disc set *The Music of Bill Monroe: From 1936 to 1994,* assigns Monroe's "complex, moody" personality, as well as his determination to excel, to the conditions of his upbringing, "Rural life, when he grew up, was relatively isolated," Rumble says. "All of his brothers and sisters were considerably older. He was cross-eyed, and people often made fun of him. He lost both parents by the time he was sixteen. So there was a lot of anger, loneliness, forced self-reliance, and pride in him. He could never have done what he did without those aspects of his personality."

Monroe channeled all of his troubling emotions into his music, a subject in which he received an early, thorough education. His mother was an accomplished fiddler, as was her brother, Pendleton Vandiver, whom Monroe later commemorated in his bluegrass classic "Uncle Pen." Monroe learned to play fiddle, too, and accompanied Vandiver on guitar when the older man entertained at local square dances. When the family played together at home, however, Monroe's older brothers monopolized the fiddle and guitar, leaving Monroe the far less desirable mandolin.

Characteristically, Monroe seized the small, seemingly limited instrument with a vengeance but gave up nothing stylistically. In later years,

Monroe made his name with the mandolin, exploiting all of its possibilities for melodic precision while firing off lightning runs more characteristic of the fiddle, and unleashed a percussive, rhythmic propulsion more characteristic of the guitar. His playing was charged with a ferocious momentum far more aggressive than anything heard in country music to that point. Eventually every player who came after Monroe would have to contend with the mandolin style he defined.

Monroe learned gospel songs in his local church and listened to contemporary country artists, particularly Jimmie Rodgers, the "Singing Brakeman" whose yodeling style was deeply informed by the blues. Monroe was also powerfully influenced by an unrecorded black blues guitarist named Arnold Schultz, whom Monroe accompanied on mandolin. Gospel, country, and blues—along with Anglo-Celtic folk songs, stringband music, sophisticated Tin Pan Alley pop, and jazzy improvisation—would find their way into Monroe's conception of bluegrass.

"He brought a drive to his sound," says Emmylou Harris, who worked with Monroe over the years. "There was an arrogance to his music—and I don't mean that in a bad way at all. There was an energy that I don't think had existed before. It predated rock & roll. His music always had a hard-driving edge, and he probably could have made more money if he softened it. But he stuck by it."

Monroe worked at an oil refinery outside of Chicago through the early years of the Depression. In 1934, he and his brother Charlie, who played guitar, formed the Monroe Brothers and made their mark as one of the finest harmony duos popular at the time. When the two men split acrimoniously in 1938, Bill formed a group called the Kentuckians, which also broke up. He then organized the first version of the Blue Grass Boys, choosing the name to honor his origins in Kentucky, the Bluegrass State.

In the defining moment of Monroe's professional life, an uproarious version of Rodgers's "Muleskinner Blues," with Monroe's spectacular yodeling tenor soaring to the heavens and his rhythm guitar driving the tune, won the Blue Grass Boys a permanent spot on Nashville's Grand Ole Opry radio broadcasts in 1939. "They said I could go work any other place I wanted, but if I ever left there, I'd have to fire myself," Monroe recalled. The weekly slot made Monroe a national star, and he would remain with the Opry until his death.

The lineup of the Blue Grass Boys shifted continually, largely because

Monroe was a rigorous taskmaster. He worked the band at a relentless pace—Monroe lived for live performance—and held his players to the same exacting standard he demanded of himself. It was Monroe's way *and* the highway—no one was ever permitted to slack off.

Monroe turned the Blue Grass Boys into a kind of college for aspiring musicians. During the last three decades of his life, he became a figure regarded with an almost religious reverence by bluegrass fans and musicians alike. He was tireless in his willingness to teach, and visitors to his annual bluegrass festival, in Bean Blossom, Indiana, would bring their instruments for him to bless.

Guitarist Peter Rowan, who played with Monroe in the mid-Sixties, says that Monroe "was kind of like a mentor figure, a guru. If you really wanted to tune into him, you faced that fire that was in him—and it would burn. But it would also light *your* fire." Rowan laughs. "I think I got over my fear and awe of him only last year," he says.

Two notable players who felt the heat of Monroe's flame were guitarist Lester Flatt and banjoist Earl Scruggs, who both joined the Blue Grass Boys in 1945. Together with fiddler Chubby Wise and bassist Howard Watts, this quintet achieved the essence of what Monroe had been striving for musically. Its ensemble talents helped the Blue Grass Boys to achieve an unprecedented degree of subtlety, texture, and force. Though the term would not become current until the early Fifties, this was bluegrass music.

The twenty-one-year-old Scruggs, in particular, was a virtuoso who defined a more aggressive, modern style for the banjo, just as Monroe had done for the mandolin. Predictably, Monroe was upset when, in 1948, Flatt and Scruggs, tired of the sixty-dollar-per-week pay and the grueling travel, left the Blue Grass Boys and formed their own combo, the Foggy Mountain Boys. "I was just burned out, I guess," Scruggs recalls. "It wasn't ill feelings toward Bill." Monroe, however, always ruthlessly competitive, saw the departure as a betrayal and the new band as a rival.

"I guess it's well-documented that he didn't speak to us for over twenty years," says Scruggs resignedly. But after he and Flatt split up in 1969, Scruggs mended his friendship with Monroe. "I just walked over and said, 'Hi, Bill,' and stopped to shake his hand," Scruggs says, "and he hugged me like a brother. We were friendly from then on. I never did have any hard feelings toward him."

Despite the departure of Flatt and Scruggs, the late Forties and early Fifties were a period of enormous popularity for Monroe. Intriguingly, his visibility as an Opry star put him in a unique position to influence the generation of young white Southerners who would upend Nashville with the tumultuous new sounds of rockabilly and rock & roll. Monroe was a figure of tremendous significance to the Everly Brothers, Buddy Holly, Johnny Cash, Carl Perkins, and, especially, Elvis Presley. "Upon meeting Elvis—and here's the historical fact—Elvis said to me, 'You like Mr. Bill Monroe?'" Perkins recalled. "I said, 'I love Mr. Bill Monroe.' Elvis said, 'Man, I do, too.'"

The fierceness and intensity of Monroe's playing, and the gorgeous yearning of his high Appalachian tenor are, no doubt, the main reasons for that appeal. Another, perhaps, is the reputation he had already earned for refusing to bow to the powers that be—in Nashville or any-where else. He stood apart, always independent. He rarely gave inter-views and certainly never gave much mind to tailoring his ideas or his music to suit the tastes of the times.

"He reminded me so much of my redneck people back home," says Dolly Parton, who first met Monroe when she was a young girl and who says he looked after her like an "old uncle." "Bill just had a real back-woods, country way about him. He was a character. He said exactly what was on his mind and didn't think he had to flower up nothin' or be diplomatic. Whatever popped out of his mouth had just popped out of his mind. I always loved him for that."

"His songs were always sad and dark," says Emmylou Harris. "They never got syrupy. He never tried to whitewash life. He sang the blues, really, and he never wavered from it."

It can hardly be surprising, then, that on the second day of his legend-ary 1954 sessions at Sun Studio, in Memphis, Tennessee, Elvis Presley recorded a supercharged version of one of Monroe's signature tunes, "Blue Moon of Kentucky." Presley released the song as one side of his first single, which also included an equally blistering version of Arthur "Big Boy" Crudup's "That's All Right, Mama." Presley and his band wondered how their raucous treatment of what already was a country standard was going to be received. "After we cut it, we said, 'Good Lord, we're liable to get run out of town,'" says Scotty Moore, the guitarist on the session. "We'd heard that Bill was kind of disturbed by the way we did the song."

At his only appearance on the Grand Ole Opry, Presley, ever the polite Southern boy, apologized to Monroe. Monroe was gracious. "He had no need to apologize," Monroe said. "It was a big boost for the song and me." Perhaps Monroe also remembered that he had launched his own career with a similarly revved-up version of Rodgers's "Muleskinner Blues." And perhaps the royalties Monroe knew he would earn from Presley's rendition also factored in. "They was powerful checks," Monroe later marveled. "Powerful checks."

In any event, Monroe was enough of a showman to make Presley's version of "Blue Moon of Kentucky" a centerpiece of his own live sets. He would start out playing the original arrangement and then kick into overdrive. He was not a man to be outdone.

Still, in the Fifties and early Sixties, rock & roll forever altered the popular music scene, and Nashville in particular. Country artists were encouraged to incorporate electric instruments into their arrangements and "modernize" their sound. Bluegrass in the unadulterated acoustic form that Monroe played it was perceived as old-fashioned. For the most part, however, Monroe had no inclination to pander. "I have willpower," he later said. "There's nobody I know could change me. I was going to play it the way I thought it should be played, the way I knew my friends and fans would want me to play it."

The folk revival of the Sixties brought Monroe a new audience, mostly made up of college students, outside of the South. Drawing on the folk festivals that helped build a community of like-minded fans in the early Sixties, Monroe established his bluegrass festival in Bean Blossom in 1967. There are now more than five hundred such festivals in the United States alone every year.

Regardless of who was listening—and regardless of the failure of mainstream country-radio stations to play his music at all—Monroe soldiered on, incapable of slowing down even as he entered his sixties. Official recognition eventually came. Monroe was elected to the Country Music Hall of Fame in 1970. When country star Ricky Skaggs won a 1984 Grammy for his version of Monroe's "Wheel Hoss," on which Monroe played mandolin, Skaggs gave the prize to Monroe, partly because Skaggs's idol had never received a Grammy himself. "I love him more than any kind of an award," Skaggs said at the time. In 1989, Monroe received the first Grammy in the category of Best Bluegrass Recording, and in 1993, the National Academy of Recording Arts and

Sciences honored Monroe with a Lifetime Achievement award. And shortly after his death, it was announced that he would be inducted into the Rock & Roll Hall of Fame.

Despite his advanced years and illnesses that would have caused a lesser man to fall—he'd had bypass, colon, hip, and kidney surgery—Monroe continued to perform, sometimes taking the stage in a wheelchair. Finally, the stroke he suffered in April brought his career to a halt.

"He had a long life, he had a good life, and he leaves behind a legacy," says Emmylou Harris, who performed at the memorial service for Monroe, in Nashville. "The sad part for most of us, besides just losing him, was knowing that since he had the stroke, he had not been able to perform. I think all of us would have hoped that Bill Monroe could have gone down swinging. We all knew that if he ever got to the point where he couldn't perform, that he wasn't going to make it. That really was his connection to life. Music was his life."

"He was never what you'd call a family man," says Rumble of Monroe. "Both his marriages ended in divorce. He didn't see much of his kids. He paid an emotional price for that, as anybody would have to. But he was married to bluegrass."

"I wanted a music of my own," Monroe once said, and he created it. His family will gather whenever and wherever bluegrass is played, and it will be played forever. Bill Monroe will be present then. "It's a wonderful music," he said. "It's got a lot of meaning in it; it's a music that brings people together and makes friends."

As for his death, the stoic words of the great Earl Scruggs might just as well have come from Monroe himself. "I don't have much of a way to express my feelings," Scruggs says. "I wish I was a good philosopher. I'm sad that he's gone—it's the end of an era. But time keeps goin'."

Rolling Stone October 31, 1996

"**We still all right?**" asks O(+>, the Artist Formerly Known as Prince, with a maniacal grin on his face. "Let me know when I start boring you."

Not any time soon. O(+> leaps off the arm of the couch where he had perched and bolts across the room to his CD player. He presses a button to interrupt his lovely version of the Stylistics' 1972 hit "Betcha by Golly, Wow," and then selects a fiercer, guitar-charged track called "Damned if I Do, Damned if I Don't."

It's the sort of scene you've been in a hundred times: A music-crazed friend ricochets between his seat and the stereo, torn between the song he's playing and the greater one you've just *got* to hear, between explaining what you're listening to and just letting you listen to it. Two exceptions distinguish this situation: First, this isn't one of my friends, this is O(+>; second, the songs he's playing are amazing.

Of course, no such scenario would be complete without someone in the role of the indulgent girlfriend. Cast in that spot is O(+>'s gorgeous and very pregnant wife, Mayte, 22. Wearing a short black dress with white trim, the word *baby* stitched across her chest in white above an arrow pointing to her stomach, Mayte sits quietly and smiles, shaking her head fondly at O(+>'s uncontrolled enthusiasm.

"I'm bouncing off the walls playing this," O(+> says, acknowledging the obvious. His sheer white shirt, lined with pastel stripes, is open to the middle of his chest and extends to his knees. The shirt, open below his waist as well, contrasts starkly with O(+>'s tight flared trousers. Black-mesh high-heeled boots complete the ensemble.

O(+>, who is now 38, is previewing tracks from his upcoming triple CD, *Emancipation,* which is set for release on Nov. 19. We're in the comfortable apartment-style office quarters within O(+>'s Paisley Park studio complex, in Chanhassen, Minnesota, just outside Minneapolis, his hometown.

Eager to reassert his status as hitmaker, O(+> is verbally riffing in a style that recalls one of his heroes, the young Muhammad Ali. "I ain't scared of *nobody*," he claims at one point, laughing. "I wanna play you the *bomb*. You tell me how many singles you hear—I wanna *read* that. The only person who kept me down is R. Kelly, and when I see him, he's gonna pay a price for that!"

Producer and songwriter Jimmy Jam, whom ⚥ fired from the funk band the Time, in 1983, also comes in for some of ⚥'s good-natured rivalry. Jam, along with his partner, Terry Lewis, has produced gigantic hits for both Michael and Janet Jackson, as well as many other artists. Like ⚥, Jam has remained based in Minneapolis. But the town isn't big enough for both of them: ⚥ sees the days of Jam's chart reign as numbered.

As "Get Your Groove On" booms out of the speakers, ⚥ screams over the sound: "You can tell Jimmy Jam I'm going to roll up to his driveway with this playing real loud! *Honk! Honk!* What do you think he's gonna say about that?"

⚥'s energy is so high because he has finally negotiated his way out of his contract with Warner Brothers, for which he had recorded since his debut album, *For You,* was released, in 1978. In his view, he is now free at last—hence the title of his new album. When I comment on the relaxed, easygoing groove of the new song "Jam of the Year," ⚥ smiles and says simply, "A free man wrote that.

"When I'm reading a review of my work," he adds, referring to some of the negative comments garnered by his previous album, *Chaos and Disorder,* "this is what I'm listening to. They're always a year late."

⚥'s struggles with Warner Brothers have wreaked havoc on his career in recent years. He could see no reason why the company could not release his albums at the relentless pace at which he recorded them. Meanwhile, Warner Brothers, which had signed ⚥ to a hugely lucrative new deal in 1992, believed the singer should put out new material only every year or two, thus allowing the company to promote his albums more effectively and, it hoped, to recoup its enormous investment.

Matters deteriorated to the point where, in 1993, ⚥ disowned the work he had recorded for Warner Brothers as Prince and adopted his new, unpronounceable name. He later scrawled the word *slave* across his cheek in frustration over his inability to end his relationship with the company and to put out his music the way he wanted to. Such moves have caused many to question not only ⚥'s marketing instincts—his album sales have plummeted—but his sanity.

For *Emancipation,* which will be released on his own NPG Records, ⚥

has signed a worldwide manufacturing and distribution agreement with Capitol-EMI. While neither he nor Capitol-EMI would disclose financial terms, such an arrangement typically means that the artist delivers a completed album to the company and assumes the cost of recording it. For ⚥, those costs are relatively minimal, since he plays virtually all the instruments on his albums and owns Paisley Park, the studio where he records.

Capitol-EMI receives a fee for every copy of the album it manufactures, with the costs of the initial pressing possibly absorbed by the company in lieu of an advance to ⚥. In addition, the company will assist in promoting and publicizing the album, which should retail for between twenty and twenty-five dollars. If *Emancipation* sells well—mind you, a triple album is a risky commercial proposition—⚥ will make a great deal of money. There can be no question that he is determined to do all he can to make sure that the album finds its audience: ⚥ is abandoning his reclusive ways and planning a live global simulcast from Paisley Park and a Nov. 21 appearance on *The Oprah Winfrey Show*. He will also launch a two-year world tour early in 1997.

⚥ is clearly stung by the skeptics who believe that he will never again achieve the aesthetic and commercial heights he scaled with such albums as *Dirty Mind* (1980), *1999* (1982), *Purple Rain* (1984), and *Sign 'O' the Times* (1987). At one point, as we stroll through Paisley Park, he gestures toward a wall of gold and platinum records.

"Everything you see here is not why I created music," ⚥ says. "Every human being wants to achieve clarity so that people will understand you. But when the media tell somebody what success is—Number one records, awards—there's no room for intuition. You've put words in their heads. For me, the album is already a success when *I* have a copy. *Lovesexy* is supposed to be a failure, but I go on the Internet and someone says, '*Lovesexy* saved my life.'"

As for people making fun of his name change—"The Artist People Formerly Cared About," in Howard Stern's priceless slag—and his branding himself a slave, ⚥ says, "The people who really know the music don't joke about it. A lot of black people don't joke about it because they understand wanting to change a situation that you find yourself in."

⚥ has erased *slave* from his face, and he now sports a neat, carefully trimmed goatee. Blond streaks highlight his brown hair, which is slicked back. He is delicate, thin and slight, almost spritelike—you feel as if a strong gust of wind would carry him across the room. But, far from seeming shy or skittish, as he's often portrayed, he burns with a palpable intensity. He looks me in the eyes when he speaks, and his thoughts tumble out rapidly.

It is indicative of the idiosyncratic way ♀'s mind works that he does not permit journalists to record interviews with him because he is afraid of being misrepresented. His fear isn't so much that he will be mis-quoted as that he will be trapped within the prison house of his own language, frozen in his own characterization of himself. For an artist who has built a career—and, to some degree, unraveled a career—by doing whatever he felt like doing at any particular moment and not looking back, that fear is deep.

Still, ♀ is sufficiently concerned about saying nothing that will dam-age the truce he's struck with Warner Brothers that he initially requested that a court stenographer be present during our interview. Sure enough, when I arrived at Paisley Park, the stenographer was sitting in the recep-tion area, transcription machine at the ready. But after ♀ came out to greet me and took me on a tour of the studio, he felt comfortable enough to abandon the idea. The stenographer was sent away.

"It's hard for me to talk about the Warner Brothers stuff because I start getting angry and bitter," ♀ explains before beginning to play some of the songs from *Emancipation*. "It's like, to talk about it, I have to get back into the mind state I was in then. It's frightening."

Making a triple-album set, it turns out, was one of ♀'s long-standing ambitions—and one of his difficulties with Warner Brothers. "*Sign 'O' the Times* was originally called *Crystal Ball* and was supposed to be three albums," ♀ says of the double album he released in 1987. "'You'll overwhelm the market,' I was told. 'You can't do that.'

"Then people say I'm a crazy fool for writing *slave* on my face," he continues. "But if I can't do what I want to do, what am I? When you stop a man from dreaming, he becomes a slave. That's where I was. I don't own Prince's music. If you don't own your masters, your master owns you."

As part of the deal to end ♀'s relationship with the company, Warner Brothers retains the right to release two compilations of the music that the singer recorded while under contract to the label. In addition, ♀ has provided Warner Brothers with an additional album of music from the thousands of hours he has in his own vaults; this album would be released under the name *Prince*. "The compilations don't concern me," says ⚥ dismissively. "They're some songs from a long time ago—that's not who I am."

Despite all the bad blood that has flowed between them, ⚥ insists he bears no grudge toward his former label. He views his battles with the company as part of a spiritual journey to self-awareness. "What strengthens is what I know," he says. "It was one experience—and it was my experience. I wouldn't be as clear as I am today without it. I don't believe in darkness. Everything was there for me to get to this place. I've evolved to something—and I needed to go through everything I went through.

"And that's why I *love* the folks at Warner Brothers now," he says with a laugh. "You know that Budweiser ad—'I love you, man'? I just want to go there with them!"

Asked about the concept behind *Emancipation*, ⚥ says, "It's hard to explain in sentences." The album is based on his complicated—not to say incomprehensible—sense of the relationship among the pyramids of Egypt, the constellations, and the dawn of civilization. Each CD is exactly an hour long and contains twelve songs.

"Recently I thought about my whole career, my whole life leading up to this point—having a child helps you do that—and I thought about what would be the perfect album for me to do," ⚥ says. "People design their own plans. That's when the dawn takes place. The dawn is an awakening of the mind, when I can see best how to accomplish the tasks I'm supposed to do. I feel completely clear."

⚥'s marriage to Mayte and the impending birth of their child were two of the important inspirations for *Emancipation*. It's no coincidence that what ⚥ describes as his "divorce" from Warner Brothers has occurred right around the time of his marriage and Mayte's pregnancy. "I don't believe in coincidence," he says flatly.

Along with covers of such smoochy ballads as "Betcha by Golly, Wow" and the Delfonics' "La-La-Means I Love You," *Emancipation* is filled with what ⚥ sheepishly calls "sentimental stuff." Discussing how he has been affected by the prospect of fatherhood, he says, "You'll definitely hear it in my music." For the song "Sex in the Summer," which was originally titled "Conception," ⚥ sampled his unborn baby's heartbeat. "Of course, that's a tempo," he says. "The baby set the groove for this song. Mayte always smiles when she hears it."

⚥ may have used his baby's ultrasound as a rhythm sample, but he and Mayte did not ask to know which sex their child is. "It doesn't matter," ⚥ says. "We all have the male and female with us, anyway. We'll be happy with whatever God chooses to give us." And just as ⚥ has no intention of once again taking the name Prince—the people around him refer to him simply as "the Artist"—he says, "The baby will name itself."

As he prepares to preview a song called "Let's Have a Baby," ⚥ turns to Mayte and says, "You're gonna start crying—you better leave." Then he explains to me, "I got my house fixed up and put a crib in it. Then I played this song for her, and she started crying. She had never seen my house with a crib in it before." "Let's have a baby," the lyrics run. "What are we living for? / Let's make love." As for the song's spare arrangement, described by ⚥ as "bass, piano, and silence," he says, "Joni Mitchell taught me that. If you listen to her early stuff, she really understands that."

He points to a portrait of Mayte that is framed in gold. "I can't wait for my baby to look up and see Mayte's eyes," he says, his voice filled with wonder. "Look at those eyes. That's the first thing the baby is going to see in this world."

⚥ has transformed Paisley Park in anticipation of the birth of his child. What had been a modern industrial park has become more playful and vibrant, like the psychedelic wonderland implied by its name. And it would warm the heart of Tipper Gore, who was inspired to found the Parents Music Resource Center when she overheard one of her daughters listening to the masturbatory imagery in the Prince song "Darling Nikki," to hear the singer talk about how he now sees things through the eyes of a child.

"When I looked at some of the artwork around here from that perspective, *pfft*, it was out of here: 'Those pictures got to go,'" ⚥ says. "I also wanted to make this place more colorful, more alive. This place was antiseptic—there's life here now."

The memory of the violence that his father introduced into the household when ⚥ was young preys on his mind. "How do you discipline a child?" he asks. "You have to imagine yourself as one of them. Would you hit yourself? You remember the trauma you suffered when you suffered that."

For all of the drama he has created around himself, ⚥ is about music.

The only time he seems completely relaxed is when he is jamming with his band, the New Power Generation, in a rehearsal space at Paisley Park. The band—including Kathleen Dyson on guitar, Rhonda Smith on bass, Eric Leeds on saxophone, and Kirk Johnson on percussion—sets up in a circle, with ⚥ facing the indomitable Sheila E. who is sitting in on drums.

Playing his ⚥-shaped guitar, the singer smiles and leads his crew through a series of rock-funk improvisations. He roams the room calling for solos, pointing at whichever player is taking the music to a higher plane so everyone can follow on that journey. They goof around with a James Brown riff. Then, when Sheila E. introduces a syncopated Latin groove, ⚥ blasts off on guitar in the roaring style of Carlos Santana.

"We don't really know any songs yet; we're just recording everything," ⚥ explains to me at one point, nearly apologizing. But the music just seems to course through him, and he fairly shimmers with happiness as he drifts from guitar to bass to keyboards as his mood dictates.

During a short break, ⚥ asks Leeds to play the theme of John Coltrane's immortal "A Love Supreme." As Leeds articulates the line, ⚥, sitting at the keyboards, crumples with joy. "It's that one note," he says, laughing, isolating the highest-pitched tone in the sequence. "That's what tells you a madman wrote it."

⚥'s identification with Coltrane—a driven musical genius and spiritual quester who seemed intent on playing himself out of his skin—is plain. ⚥ had spoken about the saxophonist earlier in the day. "John Coltrane's wife said that he played twelve hours a day," he had said. "I could never do that, play one instrument for that long. Can you imagine a spirit that would drive a body that hard? The music business is not set up to nurture that sort of spirit.

"Let's see," he continued. "According to some people, I'm bankrupt and crazy. I woke up one day, and the radio said I was dead. People say, 'He changed his name; he doesn't even know who he is.' "

The very notion that ⚥ could be perceived that way seemed painful to him. But then his spirit ascended. "I may not be like Muhammad Ali—I ain't predictin' no rounds," he said, looking me directly in the eyes. "But I'm pretty well-focused. I know exactly who I am."

Rolling Stone November 24, 1996

As *they relax backstage* at the Pontiac Silverdome, outside Detroit, Mick Jagger and Keith Richards burst into giddy laughter at the very idea that the North American leg of the Rolling Stones' *Steel Wheels* tour—sixty shows in three and a half months—is within two weeks of closing. The prospect of life at home for the Christmas holidays seems welcome—and strange—after the rigorously structured life of the road.

"It's got that end-of-term feeling," Jagger says.

"We were just talking about that," Richards says. "Having to go to the kitchen from the bedroom without a police escort."

"Should I *really* go to the restaurant without my bodyguard?" Jagger asks, with feigned superciliousness. "It's so stupid. My old lady says, 'You're going to be impossible for the first week and for the holiday. I know you are. I'm going to be as patient as . . .'" He catches himself careening into the genre of domestic comedy and brings himself up short, with a smile. "No, I'm sorry," he says, ready to resume the interview. "Carry on."

Jagger is draped along a comfortable gray chair, his back against one arm of the chair, his legs, crossed at the ankles, dangling over the other. Wearing black trousers and a green sweater and shirt, his hair cut short, he looks like a mischievous English schoolboy surprised by middle age. Richards, in a black leather jacket over a white T-shirt, sits opposite him a few feet away in the small room, smoking, nursing a drink.

If they aren't the inseparable Glimmer Twins of old, Jagger and Richards are easy and familiar around each other. The differences that have developed between them over the years are obvious and, neither man being a fool, they are both aware of them. Their bond at this point seems to rest more on mutual respect than affection; they are partners, no longer soul mates.

But their partnership, which had looked to be on the point of a permanent severing, has instead proven to be the driving force behind one of the most successful years in the Stones' tumultuous history. *Steel Wheels* won positive reviews and achieved double-platinum sales; *The Rolling Stones Singles Collection: The London Years,* assembled by the band's former manager Allen Klein, was a mainstay on the charts, and the *Steel Wheels* tour, marred, though it was, by a shameless marketing campaign, was an unparalleled musical and commercial triumph. Both the critics and the readers of *Rolling Stone* voted the Stones Artist of the Year; both groups also cited the Stones for the year's Best Tour, and the readers named the Stones Best Band. All the honors are well deserved.

Jagger and Richards say that writing and recording the album *Steel Wheels* was the crucial first step in making 1989 such a stellar year. "We had to prove to ourselves—as well as proving to other people—that we wanted to do new songs," Jagger says. "People will like them or not, depending on their own personal tastes. . . . People said, 'Oh, they only did three numbers from the new album.' Bullshit. In reality, you don't want to do a hell of a lot more than that at the beginning. You know they like 'Start Me Up' and 'Angie,' but how are they going to like 'Mixed Emotions'? That's the thing that you want to know. In the beginning, they don't."

"That little bit of fright on a new number, breaking it in the first night, you're really going out there on the tightrope," Richards says. "It saves the show from becoming stale to the band. If you've got one or two things that keep everybody on their toes, playing new stuff, then they'll play the old stuff with a fresher aspect as well. It winds them up just that little bit extra, that little bit of chance."

Along with the challenge of making an album and presenting some new songs onstage, the Stones were determined to perform material from every phase of their career. That meant going so far as to include a touchstone from the band's largely discredited psychedelic period: "2000 Light Years From Home," from the 1967 album *Their Satanic Majesties Request.*

"I knew that one was going to come up," Richards says, when asked about the song.

"We made that album, for better or worse," Jagger says about *Satanic Majesties.* "I didn't know if '2000 Light Years' would work, but I wanted to give it a shot, just so that period was in there, and we didn't, as we'd done before, gloss over it"—he begins laughing—"because it was an embarrassing moment we rather wanted to forget. Maybe it was, but, fuck it. People actually do like it."

"Trying to *remember* making it was the hard part," Richards says, laughing.

Partly because they tend always to perceive the Stones as embattled—a holdover from the long period in which that was the case—Jagger and Richards are almost humorously disinclined to give outsiders the benefit of the doubt. Media coverage of the tour was "overly reverential," Jagger says, while Richards quickly adds, "And the criticism we did get wasn't really valid. It was obviously some guy, like, the only way he could get the review in was by panning us." Asked if, given the enormous scale of the venues the band chose to play, he and Jagger attended many stadium shows themselves, Richards says, "I've done, once or twice. I'll go and see some band, if somebody says, 'Oh, they'd like to see you,' or if I'd like to see them. I just hope they don't do a four-hour show."

Jagger agrees. "I don't have that long an attention span," he says. "I've seen Bruce Springsteen's show in two parts."

Richards breaks up, saying, "Come back tomorrow for the other half."

Jagger did go to a number of stadium shows to see what other bands were doing and to generate ideas for the Stones. "To be honest, I would never go to the Pink Floyd show," Jagger says. "The show, just musically, leaves me cold. That's just a personal take. But when they add the whole spectacle, its great. The Who has done great shows."

Richards found the high-tech logistics of contemporary stadium performance somewhat inhibiting. "With the technology," he explains, "it's no longer five people in this band—it's like three hundred. The coordination has to go down. You can't get up there and jam, because then the computer's out and the lights."

"That was a criticism: 'Spontaneity was lacking,'" Jagger adds. "You don't come to the Rolling Stones in a stadium for spontaneity. You go to a jazz club. 'Spontaneity' usually means 'mistakes,' I find."

As for the countless sponsorships, presentation arrangements, and marketing deals that made the *Steel Wheels* tour, estimated to gross as much as 140 million dollars, perhaps the most lucrative venture in rock history, the Stones—with a characteristic blend of defiance, charm, pragmatism, and sheer nerve—want to have it all ways.

"I don't know about the appropriateness of it . . ." says Richards.

"I don't think you should be defensive about it," Jagger says.

"After all, if there's anybody to blame for sponsorship, you can blame us, because I think we were probably the first—with the perfume," continues Richards, alluding to the Stones' groundbreaking sponsorship deal with Jovan in 1981. "You see, ideas get perverted. The idea was to get somebody to front the bread, so that you could keep the ticket prices down. Then other people take the idea over. They take the sponsorship money and still jack the ticket prices up. But if you want to put on a show like this in places of this size, you need some financial help."

"I have another point on sponsorship—which I don't really like," Jagger says. "I think Keith and I both agree. I would personally prefer to do the show without sponsorship, and I told Anheuser-Busch the same thing when they asked me. But for the people with our Canadian promoter, it's useful for them, because it gives them a lot of TV presence and awareness.

"You can sell two million tickets quite easily," Jagger continues. "But when they want to get out there and do three million-plus tickets, that's the bit that's hard to sell. The *last* bit, you know what I'm saying? So their attitude, which they sell to us, is that you get that TV sponsorship, which is money that they could never use for advertising, because it's so expensive, and with that you get the awareness. You never know how much you would sell without it. Yes, you would have sold two million tickets— but would you have sold three?

"That's America in the Eighties. Now it's another question, whether you like it or not. If you're under thirty, I don't see that you'd have any problem with it. The people that are over thirty, like probably all of us are, have a different attitude. . . ."

"We have a lot of problems with it, you know?" says Richards.

"The Sixties people, we don't like it," Jagger continues. "In the way that we were growing up, we have all kinds of objections to it."

"It's the sellout clause we're talking about," Richards says.

"And we don't want to do ads," says Jagger. "We say, 'Sponsoring the tour only. When the tour's gone, you're gone.' You never see us with a can saying, 'Drink this.' You might say, 'Well, that's a bit splitting hairs,' but to us, it isn't."

"Hey, I don't mind taking the companies for a ride," Richards says, laughing.

"But we're not taking them for a ride, because they're getting something out of it," says Jagger.

"And they think they're taking *us* for a ride, and so . . ." says Richards.

"I don't think they're taking us," Jagger says. "I don't *think* they think that, anyway. *I* don't think that."

"I don't know," Richards says, wearily. "You never know. Who knows the inside of the corporate mind?"

"They're *pleased* with it," Jagger says.

"All we say is we want to build a stage like this, and it's going to cost us so much to do it, and we've got to build two of them—how can it be done?" Richards says. "After all, you know, this is America. And I find it funny—it's always the Americans that get up in arms about sponsorship—and it's their system."

After Jagger wanders off to attend to some Stones organizational matters, Richards continues the conversation. "He's a smart little motherfucker, I'll give him that," Richards says about Jagger, with an appreciative laugh, after the singer leaves the room. Despite his 1988 solo album and tour with his band the X-Pensive Winos, Richards is still a Rolling Stone to his bones. For all their differences, he admires Jagger deeply and speaks of the group in almost mystical terms.

"To me, a great band is a miracle," Richards says, "because you really need to stick together. You never think about it when you start off. You think a year or two's a long time. I remember distinctly when we got our first record contract. In a way, there was a sense of dismay among the members of the band, because you felt in those days, even if you really hit it big with the first couple of records: two years. It was like 'We've only just started, and we're already watching the downside.' "

Similarly, the Stones' success has lost none of its rush—and none of its mystery—for him. "The amazing thing about this band," says Richards, "I look around, say, like when I go up onstage. 'Mick. There's Charlie. There's Bill. There's Ronnie. I know I'm here.' It's like 'Is that *all*?' " He shakes his head and laughs. " 'Is this what all this is about?' You're still looking for someone that really knows what's going on, because nobody does."

For years, the Stones earned a reputation as the bad boys of rock & roll, and Richards was the baddest of the lot. He's taking it a good deal easier these days. "I recognize that I'm not twenty or thirty anymore," Richards says, almost wistfully. "I make sure I get . . . a *little* sleep." He chuckles. "Not a lot, but at least a bit. It's the longest show we've ever done, and you want to do it right. There's this incredible feeling amongst the band: We've got to deliver. Instead of hanging out for that extra five minutes—

which usually means five *hours* by the time that five minutes is over, because that's the killer five. You say, 'Oh, one more drink,' and then suddenly, 'All right, who fancies a game of poker?' 'Well, why *not?*' And then five hours later, you've blown it. They don't do that. It's amazing to me to watch this lot's self-discipline come down."

In the early days, when the Stones came to a city, the band incited a heady combination of arousal and fear, as if a street gang had blown into town. Asked whether he missed that aspect of the Stones' appeal, Richards laughs and says, "The Wild Ones? Not really. You get older, you know? You've got families and kids. It will happen to the best of you, baby, don't worry. The one thing I can guarantee is you're gonna get older—if you're *lucky.* If you're really bad, you get older; only the good die young. But I've known a few exceptions to that rule, as well.

"There's no point at this point of life still trying to play bad boys just for the sake of it," Richards continues. "I was as bad as you could get. I look back, and I say, 'I was trying to commit suicide for ten years.' But I couldn't kill it. So I came to terms with myself: 'Okay, well, then, we'll get on with living.' Now I want to see how far I can take this thing. If I can grow up, then surely my music can."

Richards knows that the context in which that music will grow up is somewhat in doubt. Jagger, while fully committed to the Stones for the present, isn't saying much about the future of the band. Such reticence used to make Richards's skin crawl; now he accepts it. "From the very minute that I waltzed into this joint in Barbados with my little bag, thinking, 'Mick and I are gonna write some songs,' I'm taking it a day at a time," Richards says, adding significantly, "at the moment."

Taking it a day at a time has, so far, produced an album and a North American tour. The Stones have played Japan and will likely go to Europe in the summer. Jagger is fronting the band and doing an extraordinary job of it. For Richards, that's enough—at the moment.

Still, Richards values the time he spent away from the Stones. "The Stones, it's a weird thing, it's almost like a soap opera," he says. "We needed a break to find out what you can and what you can't do on your own. I had to find myself a whole new band. Hell, I've got another band round the corner that's damn hot. And they're still there; my guys are still there. I kind of provoked the Stones with the Winos. Before I did that, the idea of doing something like that meant to me 'You failed to keep your band together.' I thought I always could. But then I realized maybe that's the way to keep the band together: leaving for a bit."

Clearly, however, the absurd amounts of money and the hoopla of the past year mean far less to Richards than the fact that, in 1989, his real band, the *Rolling Stones,* won the battle of the bands hands down. Of skeptics who had written the Stones off before the tour, Richards says, "*Loads* of people have tried that. That was the idea: Saying, ' '*Ey,* I've got a good band here. All you've got to do is come and see them. We'll take you down in the basement and show you what's what.' And try and make a basement out of a football stadium, get back in the garage. Get that *feel* going. I never doubted the band, personally—but I'm an incredible optimist where this band is concerned. It never occurred to me that they might not be able to cut it. Absolutely not."

"Back out on the killing floor," Richards says cheerily as he sets off to prepare for the first of the two Silverdome shows. But first he goes looking for Jagger with the words "I'll send Her Majesty back over."

Referred to earlier by one member of the Stones entourage as "The house of God," Jagger's dressing room is not especially posh, just a rigged-up space off the sterile corridors within the bowels of a stadium, outfitted with a couch, a table, some chairs, and a humidifier. Jagger's assistant, Miranda Guinness, kneels on the floor preparing a pot of tea to his specifications; someone else's previous effort had proven unsatisfactory. She will later bring him a plate of fish that he will pick at as he speaks.

Sitting on the couch, Jagger is wound up much tighter than he was just an hour ago. It's nearing show time, and he's pulling into himself. When the Stones hit the stage a little over an hour later, fifty-five thousand people will roar at the mere sight of Mick Jagger and will follow his every move, blown larger than life on the video screens, for two and a half hours. It's not the sort of prospect that makes you want to kick back, get vulnerable, and bare your soul—or makes you feel that you need to.

Despite his obvious intelligence, Jagger is impatient with introspection and speculation. He doesn't question his desires—he wants them *satisfied*—and, as a result, he exudes an extraordinary air of self-possession. The world and what can happen in it—that is, the present and, as concerns his specific plans, the future—are his exclusive focuses. What might have happened, could have happened, should happen, or, even more improbably, whatever you might feel about any of those issues, are quite beside the point.

"I hate talking about future plans, because if they don't work out, you look like a cunt," Jagger says, while discussing his interest in television production. "Then you'll say, 'What happened to that idea?' It didn't *work*, you know?"

When talk turns to the Stones, he again emphasizes the band's currency, "As I said to you when we were talking with Keith," says Jagger, "I was so insistent that we put out a new album, because I thought the Stones were becoming just a nostalgia thing. And they are nostalgia. They're out there selling their catalog and we're playing these old songs because a lot of them people want to hear. But you've got to put out new things. You've got to think for the future. The past is the past. It's gone, thank you very much.

"I hope younger people just see the band as a band, without the baggage of history," Jagger continues. "You can't deny the history's there; I'm not denying it's there. But I'm not really interested in the history of the band. I'm not really interested in what happened then. I'm still interested in the songs—if they hold up. I'm not interested in doing them just as history. I'm more interested in doing new things. I'm just not that orientated toward the past. I think it's a waste of time. It's dumb. It's done, nothing's gonna change it."

As for the Stones' future, Jagger addresses that in pragmatic terms as well. "You can't particularly plan the future that hard and fast," he says. "I mean, they want us to go and tour Japan, which is easy, lots of money, so you say, 'Yeah, okay.' And then Europe. You say, 'Well, yeah, but not *hundreds* of shows,' because Europe is, like, a terrible nightmare compared to this. It's not so much money, it's much harder work, it's endless border problems, it's huge tax problems. No one gets that much money, you never know how much you're going to get, the stage can't be as good. It's a logistical nightmare. I was just doing that before you came in: How many thousands of hours can the stage be put up and how can we do it and on and on.

"I hate doing these other things," continues Jagger, "because America's like A and everything else is B—and living with B is never as good. It's like you rent a Ferrari and you have to be in a Honda the next day, and it just isn't very good. And you have to live with it.

"I don't know. After that, I don't know what happens, really. I've got enough planning to get to the end of this monstrous week: pay-per-views, special guests, song lists for Axl." Jagger suddenly brightens, his hard, blue-gray eyes lighting up. "It's quite amusing, really. It always comes out right at the end, right?"

But isn't it hard shifting gears between the business and the artistry of the Stones? "Not really," he says, stirring his tea. "I'm used to doing it. I mean, people say, 'You shouldn't do it. Mick does too much.' But if I don't do it, it'll get fucked up. I read these things always: 'Mick's the one calculating; Keith's *passionate.*' But, I mean, I'm really passionate about getting things *right.* And if I'm not passionate about the details, some slovenly person that's employed in this organization will just let everything go, and you'll end up with a lot of crap. It degenerates very, very quickly. To be honest, no one can do that for you. Maybe that's one of the reasons the Rolling Stones thing comes off."

Without a doubt. And Jagger is as proud of his version of the Rolling Stones as Richards is of his. "This was the huge challenge, to do a good record and a good tour," Jagger says. "And I think we've done really well. I mean, the record could have been *better;* there could have been more *hits* on it; it could have *sold* more. But, apart from that, the tour did really well. There's not been one night—and I'm a terrible critic of the Rolling Stones, I've said when they've been fucking useless—where I've felt that the band has not been worth the money paid. I'm quite pleased. I think the Rolling Stones have been very, very professional and kept a very high standard."

Rolling Stone March 8, 1990

Phil Spector

Back to Mono (1958–1969)

This essay was commissioned to accompany *Phil Spector: Back to Mono (1958–1969)*, a box set released in 1991. Spector rejected the notes—who knows why? They appear here for the first time.

"**W**hen I go into a recording studio I make Art,** and I changed rock & roll into a form of Art, and I made the rock & roll music and the role of the producer credible," Phil Spector told British journalist Roy Carr in 1976. "I gave it credence." The statement is quintessential Spector: brash, overreaching, provocative, and, in the main, true. A genuine modern master, Spector approached the raw materials of the pop culture mass market—compose-to-order songwriting teams, studio musicians and singers, teen-age emotions, ruthless commercial constraints—with the visionary boldness of a hip Michelangelo standing before a virgin block of marble. Where others saw only disposable novelties and easy profits, Spector saw the possibility of crafting perfection, of shaping a three-minute song in such a way that it could last forever, of creating an eternal moment. And he never sought anything less. "They never seemed to believe what I always thought," he said to Carr in the mid-Sixties about the established powers of the record industry, "that every every record can be a hit if you concentrate on it enough."

Spector proved that point in 1958 when, at the age of seventeen, he recruited Marshall Lieb and Annette Bard, two friends from Fairfax High School in Los Angeles (where Spector was known as "Mr. Music"), and recorded the spare, elegant "To Know Him Is to Love Him" as the Teddy Bears at the cost of forty dollars. Written and produced by Spector—the title is derived from the epitaph on the grave of Spector's father: "to know him was to love him"—the song soared to Number One and sold well over two million copies worldwide. Though its airy arrangement bears little resemblance to the dense, tumultuous "Wall of Sound" with which Spector would eventually become identified, "To Know Him Is to Love Him" looks forward to his later, more definitive work in essential ways: lyrics that state a recognizable emotion honestly and directly; a simple, unforgettable melody; the use of hypnotic repetition ("to know, know, know him is to love, love, love him") to burn a hook indelibly into the listener's soul; a female vocal that oozes unquestioning devotion; allusion to marriage ("and I do, and I do") as a potentially Edenic state.

The Teddy Bears disbanded in 1959, and Spector pursued other interests—he enrolled at UCLA, worked for a time as a court reporter, and nurtured hopes of a career as a French interpreter at the UN—before deciding to re-enter the record industry. While working for and absorbing valuable lessons from producers Lester Sill and Lee Hazelwood, he returned in 1960 to New York, the city he had left with his mother at the age of twelve after his father died, and took up with songwriters and producers Jerry Leiber and Mike Stoller. The endless hustle of the New York music scene offered myriad opportunities, and Spector took advantage of them. In 1960 he produced Ray Peterson's pretty version of "Corinna, Corinna," which made the Top Ten. That same year, in his first great artistic triumph, he cowrote (with Mike Leiber) and produced "Spanish Harlem," the first solo release by Ben E. King, who had left the Drifters.

Distinguished by the spectacular understatement and effortlessly original phrasing of King's vocal, "Spanish Harlem" is also notable for its delicate Latin touches and for its proud celebration of urban minority life. Like the Crystals' "Uptown," it is a song that subtly makes an important point while providing the pure sensual pleasure of an undeniable radio hit.

Spector's hit-making efforts continued through the following year, when he produced Curtis Lee's breathlessly energetic "Pretty Little Angel Eyes," Gene Pitney's passionately overheated "Every Breath I Take" (written by Gerry Goffin and Carole King), and, most significantly, the Paris Sisters' dreamily erotic "I Love How You Love Me." The top-five success of "I Love How You Love Me" put Spector, who had not yet turned twenty-one, in the position of being able to form his own label and attain the absolute degree of creative control he had been striving for. In late 1961 Spector and Lester Sill formed Philles Records (the name being a combination of Phil and Les), and one of the most dramatic periods in the history of popular music got underway.

The first Philles single to send shock waves through the music industry was the Crystals' "Uptown," which was released in March of 1962. Written by Barry Mann and Cynthia Weil, "Uptown" was a powerful love story set squarely in a social context, and, sung by five black schoolgirls from Brooklyn, its racial and ethnic implications were unmistakable. Basically, the song told the tale of the humiliations suffered by young minority men in the " downtown" world of white corporate power, while it simultaneously exalted the freedom and individuality they could express in their "uptown" neighborhoods. "Uptown" was unsentimental, fresh, and daring in its perspective.

But if the song's themes were potent, Spector fashioned a musical setting that dramatized them ideally, as Alan Betrock has pointed out. Describing Spector's "tremendously innovative arrangement" for the song in his book *Girl Groups: The Story of a Sound,* Betrock writes, "There's a downbeat *pizzicato* musical setting and tone to the 'downtown' verses, and a completely different uplifting quality to the 'uptown' sections. With the complex string arrangements, background vocals, castanets, and mandolins blended together into a three-dimensional mural, few listeners noticed the complete absence of drums on the record. . . . In this song, a bass and rhythmic sand blocks took their place, letting the strings and mandolins drive along and soar without obstruction."

By this point Spector was fully, even obsessively, committed to exploring and establishing the artistry of production, the effort to impart deep emotional meaning to the sound of popular, commercial music. He insisted that rock & roll songs could meet the measures typically reversed for more traditional art forms. His motto was "Tomorrow's Sound Today," and he would tell writer Bob Rolontz, "You see, I don't want to follow anyone, I want to create things that other people want to copy." All the while, however, Spector was looking to the classical composers of the past for inspiration; he was determined to validate "a Wagnerian approach to rock & roll: little symphonies for the kids."

The Crystals' next release, the disturbing "He Hit Me (And It Felt Like a Kiss)," written by Gerry Goffin and Carole King, was withdrawn after radio programmers objected to the song's matter-of-fact presentation of violence against women as an expression of male affection ("He hit me, and I knew he loved me," one verse concludes). But after that came another seminal single: "He's a Rebel," which rose to Number One. Written by Gene Pitney, "He's a Rebel" came to be seen as something of a theme song for Spector, whose independent ways, outspoken opinions, and, worst of all, extravagant successes, had hardly endeared him to his more entrenched and conservative elders in the record industry.

In the wake of "He's a Rebel," Spector bought out Sill and a later investor, Harry Finfer, and assumed sole ownership of Philles. And he *still* had not turned twenty-one.

Put out as a Crystals single, "He's a Rebel" in fact featured Darlene Love, then of the Blossoms, on the captivating and dignified lead vocal. (The Spector version blew a rendition by Vicki Carr that came out at the same time on a competing label completely off the charts.) Love also sang lead on the group's splendid 1963 single "He's Sure the Boy I Love," on Bob B. Soxx and the Blue Jeans' "Zip-A-Dee-Doo-Dah," and on a number of songs released under her own name, including such savories as "(Today I Met) The Boy I'm Gonna Marry," "A Fine, Fine Boy," "Christmas (Baby Please Come Home)," and "Wait 'Til My Bobby Gets Home." (*Back to Mono* also contains a version of "Chapel of Love," best known as performed by the Dixie Cups, that Spector recorded with Darlene Love.) The artistic freedom that Spector fought to win as a producer would not be attained by artists until later in the decade, thanks largely to the Beatles, Bob Dylan, and the Rolling Stones.

By establishing his own independently distributed label, Spector had liberated himself as a producer economically as well as artistically. Generally, producers worked for a fee, not royalties, and Spector was among the first to list his producer's credit on a record. His recording genius, his immense vision of what a song could be, his skills as a musician (he played many sessions as a rhythm guitarist) and arranger, and his characteristic impulse to control made Spector a formidable figure in the studio. The comparison most frequently cited by Spector himself, as well as others, is to the "auteur" theory of cinema, in which certain distinctive film directors are seen as the "author" of their movies, even though actors, screenwriters, studio heads, technical people, and any number of other participants help bring the director's vision to the screen.

"I always liked talent, but then I always knew how to use talent and whatever ability an artist possessed," Spector told Roy Carr. "When you see a Kubrick movie, you tell me how many names you immediately remember in the cast—say of *2001* and *A Clockwork Orange*. One, two? It's the same thing with Fellini, and that's what I wanted to do when I directed a recording session. . . . I used voices as just another instrument. . . . Singers are instruments. They're tools to be worked with."

This is not to underestimate the contributions of the individual artists and songwriters: It requires great scripts and actors to meet the standards and accomplish the goals of a great director. The tracks Spector recorded between 1962 and 1966 with the Crystals, Bob B. Soxx and the Blue Jeans, Darlene Love, and, of course, the Ronettes (whose lead singer, Veronica Bennett, Spector eventually married and, later, divorced) are among pop music's greatest achievements, indisputable masterpieces of the girl-group genre. The Crystals' "Then He Kissed Me" and "Da Doo Ron Ron (When He Walked Me Home)," both written with Spector by Ellie Greenwich and Jeff Barry and released in 1963, simply could not be improved upon. Their exquisite evocation of the chance instant of meeting the true love of your life ("Well, he walked up to me and he asked me if I wanted to dance") or of the heart-racing erotic thrill that can transport you beyond mere language, beyond making sense ("And when he walked me home / Da doo ron ron ron / Da doo ron ron") has yet to be matched in the world of art. The only adequate comparison these songs can brook is the experience in life itself of the emotions they describe.

In the ardent yearning of the Ronettes' "Be My Baby" and "Baby I Love You" or the Crystals' "Little Boy"—again, all released in 1963 and written by Greenwich and Barry, with Spector—Spector found an emotional field large enough to contain his most compelling notions about how songs could communicate, could mean something in people's lives. While lesser talents believed that the youth market represented some sort of lowest common denominator, Spector shunned that idea and believed that, because everyone experiences youth, the emotions of that time of life are basic and universal.

It can sometimes be difficult, here in the last decade of the twentieth century, a time perilously infected by irony and attitude, to credit the degree of hope and conviction with which the songs included in this collection imbue such matters as romantic love and marriage. That's our loss. Marriage in these songs is treated in an uplifting manner reminiscent of the endings of so many classical comedies; in a song like Darlene Love's "(Today I Met) The Boy I'm Gonna Marry," written with Spector by Ellie Greenwich and Tony Powers, it takes on the shimmering quality of a wedding day itself ("He smiled at me and then the music started playing / 'Here Comes the Bride' when he walked through the door"). In Spector's hands even the pragmatism of the Crystals' 1962 single "He's Sure the Boy I Love"—a song that, written by Barry Mann and Cynthia

Weil, recalls the antiromantic playfulness of Shakespeare's sonnet, "My mistress' eyes are nothing like the sun"—can be raised to delirious romantic heights. "He'll never be a big businessman / He always buys on the installment plan / He sure ain't the boy I've been dreaming of," the song's heroine admits, "But he's sure the boy I love."

Finally, for all the analysis, Spector was ultimately drawn to clear, carefully crafted, economical songs. "Now I'm getting tired of hearing about, you know, everybody's emotional problems," Spector told Jann Wenner of *Rolling Stone* in 1969 in a discussion of songwriting. "I mean it's too wavy. Like watching a three- or four-hour movie. I'm getting so fed up with it. No concept of melody—just goes on and on with the lyric, and on and on with the lyric. . . . They are going to really *kill* the music if they keep it up, because they're not writing songs anymore. They are only writing ideas."

The Righteous Brothers and Ike and Tina Turner stand as the concluding twin peaks of the opening phase of Spector's career. In the voices of Righteous Brothers' Bill Medley and Bobby Hatfield, Spector found the consummate vocal correlatives to the instrumental extremes he loved to explore. Medley's sonorous bass could penetrate the fullest depths of Spector's thunderous arrangements, losing none of its richness, while Hatfield could soar as high as the most lyrical strings. Spector searched out the full emotional range of the duo's impressive gifts in such unrestrainedly ardorous tracks as "Just Once in My Life," "Hung on You," "Ebb Tide," and "Unchained Melody."

Of course, the apex of the Righteous Brothers' career was the first single they recorded with Spector: "You've Lost That Lovin' Feelin'." Written by Barry Mann and Cynthia Weil with Spector and released in 1964, "You've Lost That Lovin' Feelin' " is a stunning journey through the desperate abysses (Medley: "Baby, baby, I'd get down on my knees for you") and manic emotional highs (Hatfield: "If you would only love me like you used to do") that accompany a growing awareness of the loss of one's love. The dramatic shifts in the song's wonderfully complex arrangement—from nearly isolated voices articulating a kind of sung speech to stormy crescendos and towering choruses—helped rocket "You've Lost That Lovin' Feelin' " to Number One.

But not without some problems, as Spector explained to Robert Hilburn, music critic of the *Los Angeles Times*, in 1977. "You've Lost That Lovin' Feelin' " clocks in at 3:50, quite long by 1964 standards, so Spector initially listed the time as just over three minutes in the hopes that once disc jockeys played the song, its length wouldn't matter. Then, when Spector first played the completed track for cowriter Barry Mann, Mann was thrown by the eerie mood Medley's singing creates at the start of the song. "Barry thought I had it on the wrong speed," Spector told Hilburn. "I showed him it was on 45, not 33. Then he said to check the needle. It got me worried."

If one track can stand as a pinnacle, a summary of everything Phil Spector has sought to achieve in pop music, it's "River Deep Mountain High." Written by Spector with Ellie Greenwich and Jeff Barry and released in the spring of 1966, the song is a prodigious declaration of undying love in which Tina Turner's incandescent vocal, burning with a gemlike flame, and Spector's epic arrangement combine to ecstatic effect.

Spector had seen Ike and Tina Turner perform and determined that he wanted to record Tina. She was perhaps the only person in the music industry at the time who was unaware of who Phil Spector was—the boy genius who had not yet turned twenty-five, the "First Tycoon of Teen," in Tom Wolfe's immortal phrase—and what he had done. "I hadn't even known who Phil Spector was when I first met him," Tina told writer Kurt Loder in her autobiography, *I, Tina*. "He said he wanted to produce me . . . I didn't even know what a 'producer' did in those days anyway. Then I was told there would be two weeks of rehearsals, from twelve to two every afternoon. Ike was not to be there. I liked that. For the first time, I really felt like a professional."

Bob Krasnow, who is now the president of Krasnow Entertainment and who at the time of "River Deep—Mountain High" ran the small California label for which Ike and Tina Turner recorded, recalls the sessions for that song. "At the early sessions, Phil had every big studio musician in Hollywood there—Glen Campbell, Sonny Bono, Hal Blaine. I think Barney Kessel was one of the guitar players—there were like five of them. And Leon Russell on piano—there were all kinds of piano players, too. There were like fifty guys in the studio—the whole room was just jammed full of musicians. And this went on for weeks. I mean, who knows what this record cost—maybe twenty grand. In those days, you could make five albums for twenty thousand dollars. And this was just a single—*one side* of a single."

At first, Tina was intimidated by the massiveness of the production and the mammoth number of musicians around the studio and couldn't deliver the vocal Spector wanted. He then sent her home, worked on other aspects of the song and brought her back a week later. When she returned to record her final vocal, only Spector and his engineer, Larry Levine, were present. "I was very comfortable with Phil, and he was very patient with me," Tina recalls. "But did he work my butt off! That intro— 'When I was a little girl . . .'—I must have sung that five hundred thousand times. . . . I would sing it, and he would say, 'That's very close, very close. We'll try it again.' . . . Pretty soon, I was drenched with sweat. I had to take off my shirt and stand there in my bra to sing, that's how I was working on that song."

That "River Deep—Mountain High"—an altogether magnificent performance, surely one of the most majestic pop singles ever recorded— never made it past the highest reaches of the Top One Hundred was a crushing disappointment for Spector. It's one thing to say that the track was ahead of its time. That would have been no surprise to him; he was, after all, the man who had promised "Tomorrow's Music Today." He had made few friends among the moguls in the music industry; consequently, few people in radio were willing to smooth the way for a song that annihilated virtually all the accepted notions of what a pop song was supposed to be.

The failure of "River Deep—Mountain High" to reach an audience— and for all his artistic aspirations, Spector was no hermit in a garret: reaching an audience was the very point of his work—contributed to Spector's decision to withdraw from the music business for a time.

Spector would return, certainly, in the late Sixties to work with the Beatles and to record solo albums with John Lennon and George Harrison, among other artists. The musical environment then would be different. The revolution Spector launched was over and it didn't matter whether or not "River Deep—Mountain High" was a hit. He had won. Artists and far-seeing people in the new music industry that was taking shape knew the scope of Spector's triumph—to them "River Deep – Mountain High" was, in the words of George Harrison, "perfect"—and he would be part of the music they would go on to create.

It is impossible to overestimate the influence of the songs included on *Phil Spector: Back to Mono (1958–1969)*. But their influence is only a small part of their worth. How can you measure the rush of hearing the opening of "Da Doo Ron Ron," "Uptown," "Be My Baby," "Spanish

Harlem," "He's a Rebel," "Baby I Love You," or "Then He Kissed Me"? Those songs are woven into the fabric of our lives in the most profound ways. That is the meaning of Phil Spector's work. They may have charted this or that week or affected the work of this or that artist, but they are important because we can hear them in our minds at the most intimate times. They resonate in our very souls, as he intended them to.

"**T**his is my dog Willie** and his brother Hector," Sting explains as his two dogs careen down the road ahead of him, barking wildly, delighted to be liberated from the house. "They actually love each other, but they're tearing each other apart right now. They're a bit crazy— apparently it's the breed. They're springer spaniels. I'm told Willie is very like me; he's my familiar. They want to get him doctored, but I refuse to have that happen."

Sting seems no less pleased than Hector and Willie to be outdoors; when the time came to start this interview, he suggested that we talk while taking a stroll. Wearing a brown suede jacket, brown suede boots, and black jeans, the stubbled outline of a beard along his cheeks, he walked at a brisk pace, relishing the cold afternoon air and the physical movement.

The London home where Sting lives with Trudy Styler, their three children, and one of his two children from an earlier marriage is no secluded pop star's paradise. It sits only slightly set back from a very busy street, with houses right next to it on either side (perhaps appropriately, one of those houses was once the home of Samuel Taylor Coleridge, the poet and critic who blazed the trail for British romanticism two centuries ago). Outside the door is the familiar urban world of traffic, honking horns, construction sites, pedestrians, and pets. Around the corner and a few blocks down a hilly street, however, lies Hampstead Heath, a rolling, verdant landscape ribboned with walking paths. This balance of the country and the city suits Sting fine. "If you look out the back window, all you can see are trees," Sting says of his home. "And yet we're right smack in the middle of the city."

Sting seems to enjoy the common perception of himself as a man who has everything. A framed *New Yorker* cartoon in the downstairs bathroom of his home depicts two businessmen calmly chatting at a bar. One says to the other, "Oh, I'm pretty happy—I just wish my life were more like Sting's." The cartoon neatly encapsulates the degree to which Sting's varied accomplishments—not to mention his looks—can incite envy even among the relatively satisfied.

Sting is the pop idol adults can admire. His infallible instinct for hooks made the Police one of the world's biggest bands, but his ventures into jazz-inflected rock on *The Dream of the Blue Turtles, Bring on the Night,* and . . . *Nothing Like the Sun* made him an acceptable figure even to the most recalcitrant members of a thirtysomething generation that has turned its back on the adolescent excesses of much rock & roll. He is an active and highly visible supporter of Amnesty International and the preservation of the Brazilian rain forest. Now thirty-nine, he is handsome, but no pretty boy, and his movie roles and appearance on Broadway last year as Macheath in a production of Bertolt Brecht's *Threepenny Opera* attest to a range of talents that is increasingly rare in what often seems the increasingly one-dimensional world of pop culture. Indeed, Sting's life seems charmed.

But the hanging of the cartoon on the wall of a bathroom, like glorified graffiti, demonstrates Sting's ability to acknowledge the perception of his life as ideal and, simultaneously, to mock it. It also shows the singer's willingness to make fun of his own self-absorption. Sting finds few subjects as intriguing as himself, but that doesn't mean he is uncritical of his own foibles.

Nor do the command and personal control that Sting projects at all times come without a price. While walking along the side street that leads to the heath, Sting begins speaking about the difficulties he experienced writing the songs for *The Soul Cages,* his first new album since . . . *Nothing Like the Sun* in 1987.

"It's afflicted me every time I've tried to write something, but never to the extent where I haven't written *anything* for three years," Sting says about the writer's block that crippled him after his tour in support of . . . *Nothing Like the Sun.* "Not even a couplet, not an idea. Obviously, if you make your living writing, as you know, and you can't write anything, it's *over.* It's very frightening. Hence you have to really start working out *why,* and I think once you discover why you're not writing, that's the key to finding out how you *can* write."

The search for the cause of his literary paralysis—interestingly, he continued to be able to write music—forced Sting to address some painful emotional issues. "I think it really goes back to what I did at the end of the last record, which was done over three years ago," he says. "I immediately went to work and did a mammoth tour. At the same time, I was just getting over the death of my mother, and my father died about six months later. I figured the modern way to cope with death is to ignore it, just work through it. It's the modern thing to do—you go to work. Really, I think, it's fear. You're scared to actually deal with the enormity of what's happened and you try and pretend it *hasn't* happened.

"So I did that," he continues. "I worked my butt off, and I got to the end of the tour, and I went off on some rain-forest project, and I just didn't stop. I didn't want to think about it. Then, having done all that, I said: 'Well, I have to make a living here, I have to make a new record. What will I write about?' Nothing. There was nothing. I was punished, in a way, because I didn't actually go through the mourning process."

The friendship Sting established with chief Raoni and other members of the Kaiapó Indian tribe in Brazil in the course of his rain-forest work bore personal, as well as environmental, results for him and helped him break his creative logjam. "Having lived and spent a lot of time with these so-called primitive people," Sting says, "I realized that death is something that is obviously important to them, because they mourn. I figured that I'd have to go through some sort of process where I would get this stuff out. Once I'd worked that out, I realized that I was going to have to write a record about death. I didn't really want to."

Sting dedicated *The Soul Cages* to his father—along with two colleagues from *The Threepenny Opera*, director John Dexter and actor Ethyl Eichelberger, both of whom died last year—and the album is suffused with imagery drawn from the singer's childhood in Newcastle, a shipping town in the north of England. As it often does, struggling with the notion of death for Sting meant coming to grips with the notion of his own mortality and led to a questioning of his life and its purpose. While many may wish their lives were more like Sting's, Sting's own life, in this sense at least, proved no different from anyone else's.

"I'd reached the age of thirty-eight," Sting says, "and I wanted to assess my life—figure out what had gone wrong, what had gone right. I started at the beginning; I started with my first memory. As soon as I remembered the first memory of my life, everything started to flow. The first memory was of a ship, because I lived next to a shipyard when I was young. It was a very powerful image of this huge ship towering above the house.

"Tapping into that was a godsend. Once I began with that, the album just flowed. It was written in about three or four weeks. Having written all these words in a big burst, I then fitted them in with the musical fragments I had and put it together. I'm fairly pleased with the record. I think it achieved what I wanted it to achieve in that I feel somehow, I don't know, like I've done the right thing."

The ship image sits at the center of "Island of Souls"—the haunting opening song on *The Soul Cages*, which depicts a son grappling with his father's death and desperately seeking to avoid following his father's footsteps to a grim life in the shipyards—and it recurs in the album's title track and elsewhere. The memory of the towering ship recalls the earliest years of Sting's life, a working-class life of limited promise that he feared was going to overwhelm him and that he felt compelled to rebel against. His occasionally haughty manner and aristocratic airs are perhaps the last remnants of that rebellion. The ship also encompasses the notion of travel—and escape. The memory that freed Sting to write returned him to the deepest source of his identity and at the same time suggested access to a broader world in which that identity could be shed, in which a provincial schoolteacher named Gordon Sumner could become the international rock star Sting.

As a younger man, Sting could be merciless in his observations about his background. "I suppose that part of my egocentric drive is an attempt to transcend my family," Sting told *Rolling Stone* writer Kristine McKenna in 1980. "I come from a family of losers—I'm the eldest of four—and I've rejected my family as something I don't want to be like. My father delivered milk for a living and my mother was a hairdresser. Those are respectable occupations, but my family failed as a family. I grew up with a pretty piss-poor family life. I lived in Newcastle, which would be like living in Pittsburgh, and the whole thing for me was escape."

Two and a half years later—in a *Rolling Stone* article in which he described Sting, the character that he had invented, as "this monster"—the singer was penitent. "Candidly, that article you wrote quoted some things I said about my childhood that hurt my family deeply," Sting told McKenna at that time. "I learned a big lesson there and had to work very hard to repair the damage done by the article. It wasn't your fault; it was purely my own arrogance and lack of thought. I've become more aware of the possible consequences of what I say to the press."

These days Sting is philosophic about the contradictory nature of his feelings about his past. "Well, again, it's the old ping-pong of wanting to escape and then having to go back and face it," he says. "Wanting to escape the idea of death, yet having to go back and face it. Wanting to escape where I come from, yet having to come back and face it. I don't think we ever leave; I think everything's a big circle. My relationship with my father was complex, and it wasn't resolved. It needed to be resolved. I think now, through some psychic working, it seems to be resolved. I feel as if something has balanced out now, by having done this record. It's the only way I can do it."

"All This Time," the album's second song and the bouncy first single, takes another long-standing symbol of permanence and departure—the river—as its central image. Like "Island of Souls," it is about a young man whose father has died, and it also takes on the religious training that troubled Sting's childhood –he has credited the Jesuits for "my venomous nature"—as its subject. In fact, *The Soul Cages* is rife with biblical and specifically Catholic imagery, from "The Jeremiah Blues (Part 1)," with its tongue-in-cheek nod to the Old Testament prophet of doom and its allusions to crucifixion, to the title of the instrumental "Saint Agnes and the Burning Train."

"I was brought up in a very strong Catholic community," Sting says. "My parents were Catholic, and in the Fifties and Sixties, Catholicism was very strong. You know, they say, 'Once a Catholic, always a Catholic.' In a way I'm grateful for that background. There's a very rich imagery in Catholicism: blood, guilt, death, all that stuff." He laughs. "I'm not sure it goes far enough to explain our situation. At my age, I feel some of it is inadequate to explain a lot of things. So the album, although it has this religious element, is about a deeper religion.

" 'All This Time' sounds kind of poppy," he continues, "but it's a serious attempt to look at ritual and the inadequacy of ritual in our lives. The young guy is trying to deal with the death of his father, and instead of going through the Catholic last rites, he wants to bury his old man at sea. He looks at the river as a symbol of continuity. The song basically says, 'Well, the Romans were here two thousand years ago and their religion was very important, but it went. Then Christianity happened and that seems to be inadequate now. Let's look for bigger systems of continuity, like the river, this old religion.' The song is a kind of black comedy. I'm not really antireligious. I'm just poking some lighthearted fun at religion and also asking pragmatic questions about it."

Sting's sense of the "pretty profound" inadequacies of Catholicism and Christianity is intimately linked with the passion for the environment that has consumed him in recent years. "I've come to believe that we made a mistake in trying to imagine God outside of nature, that God doesn't exist in nature," he says, emphasizing his remarks with gestures that call attention to the natural beauty of Hampstead Heath. "Therefore to find God, we have to destroy nature. I think that's a Judeo-Christian idea, and it's not in any of the other religions of the world. I think that is the key to our disastrous treatment of the world. We don't see God in this *tree*—God is somewhere else. Therefore why should we respect the tree? Why should we respect the Earth, the river, the sea? 'Man is the most important thing,' they say. 'The animals are at our beck and call, they're at our service.'

"*Wrong!* Absolutely wrong. 'We can have as many people on the Earth as we can possibly make.' *Wrong.* I'm sorry, I just don't agree with it anymore. I think it's bullshit, and I think if we carry on thinking like that, we're doomed. We have too many people—we *have* to use birth control. We are not the most important thing on the planet, we're *part* of the planet, and until we realize that, we're in big trouble."

Sting's work in support of the preservation of the Brazilian rain forest has not, however, been universally lauded. Critics have questioned how appropriately the funds raised by the Rainforest Foundation, which Sting established, have been used. In addition, some observers claim that Sting's international jaunts and high-level diplomatic meetings in the company of Raoni are the best public-relations gambits the Brazilian government could hope for. A great deal of worldwide publicity attended Sting and Raoni's meetings with José Sarney, who at the time was president of Brazil, creating the impression that the Brazilian government was seriously attempting to address the rain-forest issue. President Sarney failed to keep his promise to demarcate the 19,000-square-mile area that Sting and Raoni wanted set aside as a preserve for the Indians who live in the rain forest. Now Brazil's new president, Fernando Collor de Mello, is having similar meetings and making similar promises.

When asked about the charge that he is being exploited by the Brazilian government, Sting first laughs with a kind of glee—a master of control, he seems almost titillated by the prospect of being outmaneuvered—then bristles. "I think I'm a focus for international attention," he says. "The Brazilian government, if they don't want to change anything, does not welcome any kind of focus on that problem. I don't think I'm being used at all; if anything, I'm an embarrassment.

"I was in the jungle last week, and I took Raoni to a meeting place in the jungle to meet with Collor," he continues. "I didn't want to meet the president particularly, but I wanted Raoni to meet him, because Collor was making a big publicity move by going to the jungle. The military told me I couldn't stay in that village because I was a danger to national security! I laughed at them—I said, 'Are you kidding? I'm so proud of this.' Nonetheless, I had to go spend the night in another village nearby. I left Raoni, who spoke to the president, who promised that he would demarcate the land. I actually think he wants to. There are forces in Brazil that *don't* want him to—obviously, the military being one of them, because they see the jungle as their last vestige of power. They see it as their personal property."

While Sting is a longtime supporter of Amnesty International, having played benefits for the organization in England well before it was fashionable, the ardency of his activism in recent years is notable because it represents such a departure for him. This is a man, after all, who, in his conviction about the importance of the spiritual world, declared in one song that "there is no political solution" and titled another one "History Will Teach Us Nothing."

"I'm still, in a sense, a believer in transcendent cures for various problems," Sting says. "Contemplating your navel will *perhaps* move the mountain one day. I think people can change one by one. If you work on yourself, you change the world in a microcosmic way—but it's getting a bit late, unfortunately. I feel that with certain issues, like the environment, for example, you *have* to be active. You can't just sit there with your legs crossed and hope that the air is going to be fit to breathe tomorrow. I think we don't have very long left, frankly."

Back at his home, Sting starts a fire and sits on a sofa in front of the fireplace in his den. Though it's only midafternoon, it is also December in England, and the gray sky outside is already beginning to darken, deepening the shadows that take shape along the room's dark, wood-paneled walls. It's warm in the room, and Sting, drinking tea with honey, wears a black T-shirt.

The talk turns to "Mad About You," a brooding ballad on *The Soul Cages*. "That's another one in the lust-power-jealousy genre," Sting says, smiling. "I think it's a fascinating genre." It's suggested that "Every Breath You Take" is perhaps the classic of the idiom. "It's funny, I got a

British Music Industry award last night for two million plays of that record, which, added up, is about seventeen years of continuous radio play!" Sting says incredulously. "It would be a pretty boring radio station, but the staggering idea is that this song, which is so ambiguous—it's seductive, but it's also quite pernicious . . . it *works*. This may sound highfalutin, but it's probably *the* song of the Reagan years—this idea that you'll be looked after by this patronizing, beneficent figure. Like Star Wars: You'll be under surveillance but also . . . *protected*. That mixture of sex and power is very compelling."

Sting might have added ambition to the list. In the same 1980 interview in which he insulted his family and hometown, Sting declared: "Success always necessitates a degree of ruthlessness. Given the choice of friendship or success, I'd probably choose success." Sting laughs, collapses into the couch, and buries his head in the pillows when asked what he thinks about that statement now.

"Well, I was the Sinéad O'Connor of the time," he says wearily as he begins to sit up again. "I might have believed it." He hesitates. "I *might* have believed it. One of the reasons you're successful in many ways is you're *burning* with this stuff. You're tied to the stake of your own career and you have a match and you set fire to it: 'Awright, I'm gonna *make* it!' And that's what the Police did. We thought about nothing else but making it—making records and being the biggest group in the world. Even if it only lasted for six months, 'We *did* it!'

"You come out with polemic statements like that because people remember them and it's a good headline or whatever—and I might have meant it at the time. I wouldn't say that now—friendship's much more important to me than what I thought success was. Luckily, I've succeeded and managed to keep some of my friends. I believe the opposite now—but then again, it's easy for me to say because I've been successful and I have a nice life. When you're struggling, *no*, success is vitally important."

Sting remembers the early days of conquering America with his mates in the Police—guitarist Andy Summers and drummer Stewart Copeland—with evident pleasure. The three musicians came to this country for a club tour in 1978, very much against the advice of their record company and well before the single "Roxanne," from their debut album, *Outlandos d'Amour,* began to attract attention.

"It was right in the middle of corporate rock & roll, where to tour in America, you had to support Foreigner," Sting recalls. "You'd go on as the doors opened, people would be eating popcorn or whatever and would hate you. Instead, we *headlined* every night—but sometimes to three people. We played to three people in Poughkeepsie, New York, and two of them happened to be DJs, and they added our record because of that show. It was a *great* show. I remember coming off the stage and introducing these three people to each other, who had sat alone in the Last Chance Saloon—it was actually called that, I think it might still be there. That gig has entered legend now—hundreds of people come up to me and say, 'I was at the gig in Poughkeepsie,' and I *know* they weren't!

"That sort of energy that we had as a band—we did four or five encores for those three people—was what did it," Sting continues. "We were a tough little unit. We carried the gear, we drove hundreds and hundreds of miles, we slept in the same bed. It was like being at war. We were out there fighting a war—and we won! I'd never been to America—America was a dream for me. The first night I arrived from London, they drove us to the Bowery. The streets were steaming and full of bums—you know where CBGB is, it isn't one of the *best* streets. I thought, 'Man, this is incredible, it's like *Hades!*' And the club is even *worse*. And we go onstage and we tear the place up. We really thought, 'Fuck it, we've got to survive here.' Stewart and I had a fight in the dressing room after the show—I thought he was speeding up, he said I was slowing down. We were strangling each other, and then we heard the calls for an encore. We stopped strangling each other, did an encore and then came back, had another fight and then back for another encore. *That* was our first night in America."

Fond and furious memories aside, don't hold your breath waiting for a Police reunion. "In our final year, it was very clear to me that for the sake of sanity, for the sake of *dignity*, we should end it," Sting says, laughing. "We had the big song of the year, the big album of the year, the big tour of the year. We were *it*. We'd made it—everything we attempted, we'd achieved to the power of ten. That was the time to say, 'Now we'll go off'—and we did. We haven't made a comeback tour or anything like that. I'm very proud of the legend of the Police—I think it's intact. And I want to keep it intact. I'm very proud of the work we did, and I'm proud of my association with Andy and Stewart. I've no regrets about it—but it's in the past. I don't want to return to the Police for nostalgic reasons or for money. That would spoil it."

Despite his expressed "grave philosophical doubts about video," Sting is swaddled in elaborate Moroccan-style robes and standing in front of a dark blue desert backdrop to film a clip to accompany "Mad About You," one of the four singles—along with "All This Time," "Why Should I Cry for You," and the title track—planned for release from *The Soul Cages*. In this get-up, Sting looks like a dissipated cleric. He is still unshaven and—bearing out his reputation for scruffiness—beneath the robes he is wearing exactly the same clothes as the day before. When an assistant on the set gently asks, "Are you going into makeup or anything like that?" Sting replies, with slightly offended disbelief, "I just *came* from there." Meanwhile, a beautiful, enormous white horse has just been led into the sound stage and is being groomed and patted. Like all of England in winter, the set is freezing. "That's why the English set out to conquer the world," Sting jokes while hugging himself against the cold. "Every place else is preferable to here."

Sting will have the opportunity to put that theory to the test when he embarks on a yearlong world tour in February. This time out, he will head up a tough, streamlined, four-piece band in which he will play bass, Kenny Kirkland will play keyboards, Dominic Miller will play guitar, and Vinnie Colaiuta will play drums. The band will whip itself into shape during short stands in small theaters in San Francisco, Los Angeles, Chicago, and New York before moving into arenas.

"The strategy is that the music can grow in the small venues," Sting says. "If we immediately start in arenas, then it's arena music, so I want to start off small. I think it's your job as an artist to make every basketball arena as intimate an occasion for the ticket buyer as you can. They deserve more than being treated like cattle. A lot of the arena shows I've been to lately had industrial levels of noise without any letup. They were basically just MTV stage shows. It's like a video: wonderful dancing, incredibly loud sound—but no one playing and no one singing! I'm not making a value judgment here, it's just not what I want.

"What I find entertaining is, instead of trying to reproduce the record, you're saying to the audience, 'Look, there's four guys here onstage, we *can't* reproduce the record. We could mime to it, but here's how we'll tackle the problem of reproducing the album, given the limitation that we're only four guys.' I think it's entertaining to see people cope with those limitations, and often transcending the album. The album is just a starting point that you can grow from. You have to trust the ability of bands to interpret music. The album isn't the be-all and end-all of the music. We've got a pretty good little combo. We played in Chile at the Amnesty show this fall and we tore the place apart, so I have no fears."

Nor does Sting, unlike many other rock stars his age, harbor any fears about his ability to carry his music with some measure of decorum into the future. "A rock & roll band is essentially a gang, an adolescent gang," he says. "You get together when you're teenagers or in your early twenties—it's a kind of male thing, even if you have females. It's macho, a tribal thing—which is great. It works, and the music reflects that tribalism, a sense of having to have a rite of passage to adulthood.

"Once you've *reached* adulthood and you're still in the gang, you tend to be a bit dysfunctional because you're pretending that you're going through a stage which you've already gone through. You know, you watch MTV and you see these reconstituted bands who were successful in the Seventies or the Sixties, and they're getting a bit jowly and they have less hair than they used to, there's a bit of a belly—but there's these beautiful models wandering around, blowing kisses at them. It's not *true!* In truth, those girls wouldn't look twice at those guys—it's perfectly obvious. I feel a bit sad when I see that. There is a way of getting older and being a performer without embarrassing yourself. It's the gang thing—you don't have to be in a gang when you're an adult. You can be on your own. And that's why I'm not in a band."

On the set, Sting and the horse are building a relationship based on artistic necessity, physical proximity, and what clearly seems to be a burgeoning mutual respect. Through at least two dozen takes the duo attempts to walk together on a treadmill to create the impression that the two are trekking through the desert to the stately strains of "Mad About You." Sting's training as an actor and innate sense of discipline stand him in good stead. Time after time—as Sting tries simultaneously to maintain his grip on the horse's bridle, lip-sync the song's lyrics, strike suitable facial expressions, walk on the treadmill in time, and keep his place in the shot—the horse nuzzles his snout against the singer's face, steps off the treadmill with his hind legs, or sends Sting staggering out of the camera's frame with a friendly nudge. The bond between the two appears sealed when, after the horse grinds the proceedings to a halt by abruptly urinating on the treadmill, Sting struts over to where the horse had been standing, hitches up his pants, and starts to unzip his fly, as everyone on the set bursts into laughter.

During a break on the set, Sting sits in his dressing room and assesses his attitude about his career to this point, casting a cold eye on the future. "I've tried very consciously to break the mold, to do things that rock stars don't normally do or aspire to," he says. "Of course, you end up being called pretentious. I'm not pretentious. I'm just willing to take a lot of risks, to the extent where I don't mind being ridiculed and I don't mind failing, because I think the process of trying to burst out of the stereotype is worth doing.

"The standard you measure yourself by is, Have you learned something? Often you learn more from failures than you do from success; they're often more interesting experiences in retrospect. You learn to obey your instincts. The *logical* process will often be the *safe* one. I tend, when I'm given that choice, to go the way that's *not* safe.

"I don't really think that people know what to expect from me now," Sting continues. "I don't think this album is going to conform to any of their expectations—I think they're expecting a record about ecology or something. If they're surprised, then I'm pleased. And the next record will hopefully surprise them again."

Rolling Stone February 7, 1991

10,000 Maniacs Break Loose

"**I**'m glad you guys** made it where you've gone so far. That's really terrific. Probably the name is what did it, right? I mean, it's very catchy."

Late on a rainy Monday night at Joyce's Keg Room, in Jamestown, New York, Joyce's boyfriend, Paul, is trying to explain the success of 10,000 Maniacs, western New York's most celebrated export since the late Lucille Ball barreled out of nearby Celoron half a century ago. The Keg Room is a solidly working-class gin mill where, between rolls of dice for free drinks at the bar, men in painters' caps and women with teased hair are far more likely to spin a record by Patsy Cline or the Georgia Satellites on the jukebox than anything like the Maniacs' highminded folk rock. Mention "Like the Weather" in here and someone is apt to respond, "It hasn't been too bad."

But Maniacs keyboardist Dennis Drew and bassist Steve Gustafson are conducting an alcohol-soaked tour of landmarks in the band's history, and the Keg Room figures prominently. The bar's small back room, with its patterned, opaque windowpanes and carpeted door frame, was the site of some of the band's earliest gigs. Despite his absolute unfamiliarity with the Maniacs' progress since they last played the Keg Room years ago, Paul, a white-haired wag with a penchant for ribald jokes (at one point, nodding toward a house regular, he says, "Someone came up and asked Rose, 'Do you have two nipples for a dime?'"), continues to speculate on the role of the Maniacs' name in their eventual good fortune.

"All you have to hear that name is once," he says. "And you think, 'Who's that crazy bunch?'"

"Weren't you afraid when we came down that first night and said, 'We're 10,000 Maniacs'?" asks Gustafson, whose blond, curly hair and boyish good looks suit his mock earnestness well.

"I didn't know whether to open the door or what," Paul says. "Yeah, my God!" He pauses a beat for effect. "I said, 'Do they all have money?' Then you wonder: How do you get all 10,000 people on the stage?"

Such jokes—and, believe it or not, many worse ones—have followed the Maniacs since they took their name in 1981, after earlier incarnations as Still Life and the Burn Victims. The moniker is a mistaken borrowing from the cult horror film *2,000 Maniacs*; Drew says it was chosen so that locals would know "that we weren't going to do Led Zeppelin covers." It hasn't always been an advantage. Radio programmers often ignored the Maniacs' records in the belief that they were a hardcore or novelty band. Even a sax player who was once in the group used to take the stage wearing pink slippers and a spaghetti colander on his head. According to Gustafson, he would say to the others, "We're maniacs, aren't we? I thought we were supposed to be funny."

The Maniacs—whose lineup, in addition to Drew and Gustafson, includes singer-lyricist Natalie Merchant, guitarist Robert Buck, and drummer Jerry Augustyniak—finally proved they were more than a joke last year when their third album, *In My Tribe*, propelled by the video for the near-hit single "Like the Weather," took off, nearly six months after its July 1987 release. Before that, the band had put out a string of intriguing records—the EP *Human Conflict Number Five* (1982) and the album *Secrets of the I Ching* (1983), both released on the band's own label, Christian Burial Music, and, after the Maniacs were signed to Elektra, *The Wishing Chair* (1985)—all to resounding commercial indifference.

Now, with *In My Tribe* nearing platinum status, the Maniacs have released *Blind Man's Zoo*, a provocative album that includes songs addressing the legacy of the Vietnam War ("The Big Parade"), toxic spills ("Poison in the Well"), intervention in Nicaragua ("Please Forgive Us"), teenage pregnancy ("Eat for Two"), religious zealotry ("Jubilee"), Western imperialism in Africa ("Hateful Hate"), and the hard times that have hit once-proud manufacturing towns like Jamestown ("Dust Bowl"). The lyric sheet, which Merchant designed, makes each song appear to be the chapter of a book, a specific drama in a chronicle of chaos. At 10,000 Maniacs' point of greatest professional optimism, *Blind Man's Zoo* is a starkly pessimistic statement.

"I think that was a conscious effort on our part—well, maybe more so on my part," says Merchant, twenty-five, one afternoon in her kitchen. "A lot of songs were written, and I had in my mind this feeling that there should be a consistency between all the songs, that there should be some kind of thematic unity. And the songs that I liked the most were the ones that were heavier, more powerful lyrically and musically and, I'd say, darker than the others. The most uplifting song is 'Trouble Me,' which seems like the antidote for all the rest of the album." The album's first single, "Trouble Me" is a striking ballad that was written while Merchant's father was in the hospital. In it, she pleads with him to share the weight of his illness: "Why let your shoulders bend underneath this burden," she sings, "when my back is sturdy and strong?"

Unlike many songwriters, Merchant does not hesitate to discuss or even interpret her work, and she offers a penetrating reading of *Blind Man's Zoo*. "The theme that I keep returning to with every song is betrayal," she says. " 'Eat for Two' is self-betrayal. 'The Big Parade' is a nation betraying its citizens. 'Please Forgive Us' is a nation betraying another nation. 'Hateful Hate' is a race betraying another race. 'Jubilee' is, first, a man who's betrayed by nature or God, because he's deformed, and then he's misled and betrayed by the envoy of God, a mad preacher who's obsessed with retribution and vengeance. 'Poison in the Well' is the question of corporate culpability when there's a toxic-waste dump that suddenly is seeping into the main water supply of a neighborhood. That corporation has betrayed those people."

Natalie Merchant lives in an apartment on the top floor of the house in which she grew up—her mother still owns it—on a residential street in Jamestown. In general, the apartment is plain, almost austere, but there's a sense of playfulness in childlike touches like the Peter Rabbit china in which she serves tea and the honey bear that accompanies the service. The title *Blind Man's Zoo* itself is drawn from a game in a children's book—a genre well represented in Merchant's library. Merchant herself plans to write an illustrated book for children later this year, after the Maniacs' tour is over. A note of single-girl self-deprecation sounds in the label on one of her file drawers, which reads, SHE WAS UNLUCKY IN LOVE. (In fact, Merchant is at the moment happily involved with an executive at Elektra.)

Although Merchant is not conventionally religious, her apartment is filled with remnants of her Catholic girlhood. Above the doorway of the room in which she designs the Maniacs' artwork and records demos on a portable four-track machine is a sign that reads, THE BLOOD OF JESUS CHRIST CLEANSETH FROM ALL SIN. A crown of thorns is draped almost jauntily atop a framed portrait of a saint contemplating a crucifix. In the kitchen stands a statue of St. Anthony holding the infant Jesus.

Trying to recover from the cold she caught during the filming of the video for "Trouble Me" and a series of outdoor photo shoots, Merchant attempts to explain what the Christian iconography means to her. "I started collecting it mostly because my grandmother had a lot of it," she says, "and when she passed away, no one else in the family wanted it. It reminded me of her.

"I went to see *The Last Temptation of Christ,* and I cried hysterically when he was being tortured," she continues. "I couldn't stop crying. To me, Jesus Christ is the symbol of what is unjust in the world—from what I understand from the myth, he was a kind man who saw injustice in the world, and he was also a political subversive. There was the Jewish hierarchy, and there was the Roman police rule, and he was against both. So he was a political and religious martyr.

"When I saw the torture scene in *The Last Temptation of Christ,* I was thinking, 'I'm sitting in this theater, and what's happening to him is happening right now in the Middle East; it's happening in Central America and South America; it's happening in Russia and the Eastern bloc. It's happening right here in America for all we know.' That's what struck me."

Merchant's fascination and identification with victims of violence, pain, and disaster is reflected in her songwriting—from early songs like "My Mother the War" and "Grey Victory" to later ones like "What's the Matter Here?" and "Please Forgive Us." The obsession goes back as far as her childhood reading. "I loved beautiful old picture books—we inherited some from my grandmother," she says. "But aside from that, I jumped right into reading *Helter Skelter,* the biography of Mussolini, and *The Hiding Place.* I became very interested in atrocity at a young age, and I don't know why I was drawn to it. I read *The Bell Jar* when I was twelve.... And a lot about the Holocaust."

She recalls watching war movies on television and confusing them with the images from the Vietnam War that she would see on the news. When a cereal company held a Stick Up for Breakfast poster competition, the young Merchant's entry was a collage of malnourished children under the slogan STICK UP FOR BREAKFAST BECAUSE SOME PEOPLE CAN'T. "I got a Tony the Tiger kite and 'Thank you very much, but you're not even a runner-up,'" she says, laughing.

Merchant's relentlessly acute sensitivity to political and moral issues—along with her general abstemiousness—sets her apart from the other members of the band. In a meat-and-potatoes region like western New York State, Merchant's vegetarianism and animal-rights activism are anomalies, to say the least. Drew and Gustafson joke in a friendly way about how their views are far more conservative than Merchant's. In addition, the boys in the band will drink you under the table and blithely leave you for dead; Merchant steps into a bar with only the greatest reluctance.

"I feel close to them because of all the things that we've done together," says Merchant, who is also the youngest member of the band by at least five years. "But I don't feel like we have anything more than that experience in common. That's partially because I'm a female, the age difference, the environment."

Merchant has known the boys since summer 1980, when, as a precocious sixteen-year-old student at Jamestown Community College, she met Gustafson, who ran the campus radio station with Drew. In January 1981, Gustafson and Drew joined Still Life, which included Buck on guitar. They invited her to sing with them at a party solely because of her great looks, her wild dancing in local clubs, and her taste in music (she was a big fan of Bryan Ferry, Brian Eno, and reggae). Asked about the venturesome choice, Gustafson says, "She *had* to be able to sing better than I could play the bass."

"I went with some other people, and we were all taking turns at the microphone," Merchant says, laughing at the memory. "I had just been to a thrift store, and I bought a social-studies book from the Fifties. There was a whole chapter on Lapland, so my first song was 'Reindeer Are the Cattle of Lapland.' I started improvising—'*Reindeer are the cattle of Lapland*'—and then I sang the whole paragraph. They said, 'Great. We're going to play a gig pretty soon, and we want you to be there.'"

The band soon added rhythm guitarist John Lombardo, who would write music for many of the Maniacs' early songs and who, ironically, would quit the band just as they were beginning to work on *In My Tribe*. The band's sets were something like Jamestown happenings, with movies and slide shows running while the group played. Merchant would whirl and dance like a dervish. Her tenuous connection to what was happening around her seemed nearly autistic, though her very willingness to enact a fiercely private vision onstage made her an astonishing performer.

Drew and Gustafson, who have known each other since high school and have built up an inimitable, rapid-fire conversational style over the years, say that Merchant's impact on the band was explosive.

"She wouldn't officially say that she was in the band," Drew says, "but she never missed a gig."

"She used to sneak out of the house," says Gustafson. "Her mother hated us. She thought we were having all these orgies and selling drugs from our warehouse. . . ."

"We were just *buying* them," Drew says, laughing.

"And we only had *one* orgy."

"*Not* with her, believe me."

"So she used to have to sneak out of her house," Gustafson says, "to come down to the bar at the Hotel Franklin to play. And her mother used to come down and drag her out. Her mother would come down and yell at her and make her go home."

"Natalie would leave in the middle of gigs quite often," Drew says fondly. "*Oh*, the time she slapped Rob? Did she slap him or pull his hair out?"

"No," Gustafson says helpfully, "she was pulling *her* hair out."

"She was pulling her hair out," Drew says. "We were playing at the Rusty Nail. She was an emotional young woman, of course. . . . She doesn't like people who are drinking. She didn't like the bar scene at all. She went over to Rob while we're playing this song and *boxed* him right on the ears. And ran out. This was in the days when we've got to do three sets. She's gone, man. We're doing 'Motor Booty Affair,' with John Lombardo singing. I had to sing 'Guns on the Roof.' "

Still, the band offered freedom and excitement—and the possibility of a life beyond Jamestown. *Human Conflict Number Five* and *Secrets of the I Ching*—both recorded as projects for the sound-engineering program at the State University of New York at Fredonia—garnered the Maniacs attention from alternative radio in the United States and England. In an effort to capitalize on that attention, the band—which now included Augustyniak, who joined up just in time to record *I Ching*—briefly relocated to Atlanta, where a plan to record with the independent label that released R.E.M.'s single "Radio Free Europe" soon went awry; the Maniacs then traveled around the country on the New Wave club circuit.

"We used to live out of an old school bus," Merchant says. "We had to paint it, because it's illegal to drive a school bus, so we painted it Rasta colors. Then we wrote, SING OUT WITH JOY! on the side, because we said, 'Oh, no, we're going to the South. We'll masquerade as a Christian rock band.' "

"In the wintertime it was great," says Buck, his voice laced with sarcasm. "Steve and I would do most of the driving. In the front of the van, you'd have to turn the heat all the way up. It would be like ninety-five degrees, and the driver would have a T-shirt on rolled up to his chin, sweating. And in the back seat people would, honest to God, be in parkas with sleeping bags wrapped around them. No matter how hot you had the heat turned up, in the back it was still below freezing."

While the band toured, Drew assiduously worked the college-radio and rock-critic rounds in every town the Maniacs visited, making sure the band's records were being played and written about and that its gigs were being publicized. Peter Leak, an Englishman based in New York, started working as the Maniacs' manager in 1983 and quickly arranged for their first British tour. He eventually guided them to their contract with Elektra in early 1985.

To produce their first Elektra album, the Maniacs selected Joe Boyd, who had worked with the British folkrock group Fairport Convention, whom the band idolized. "Elektra gave us a bunch of names, and we had a bunch of people on a list, and Joe Boyd was one of the main ones," says Buck, sitting at the dining-room table of his parents' house in Jamestown with Augustyniak, as a tape of Caruso, Buck's favorite opera singer, wails in the background. "All of a sudden we found out he was available. 'Joe Boyd, yeah, *yeah.*' Of course, the record company is going, 'No, *no,* please, no.' But finally they let go of it. They probably said, 'We'll let them go ahead for their first record. They'll learn.' "

The Maniacs spent nearly four months in North London recording *The Wishing Chair* with Boyd. Though the band still enjoys the album— and Buck, in fact, prefers it to *In My Tribe*—Boyd's easygoing work habits did not win admirers. "What I learned from Joe Boyd," says Merchant, "is that producers don't do very much but sit around, read the paper, and say, 'It's your album, do what you want.' "

"Joe, I don't know if I'd describe him as a record *producer,*" Buck says, searching for the proper term. "He was, like, a good help at decision making. He didn't know anything about music, really, or songs or songwriting or arranging. But if there was a controversy, he was a good guy to say, 'Okay, how many votes do we got on this side?' I'd be doing my guitar overdubs, and he'd be in there on the couch, with the paper over his face, snoring. Or else, 'Hey, where's Joe?' 'Oh, he's out getting a curry.' "

Boyd views the Maniacs' dissatisfaction as the result of a misunder-standing of his "laissez-faire" approach to making records. He describes their attitude as "This is the great Joe Boyd producing our record: Well, isn't he going to do more than what he's doing?"

"In no record that I've ever done have I changed arrangements or done what a lot of producers do in terms of restructuring songs," Boyd says. "The way I worked with them on that record is no different from the way that I've worked with any artist on a record, including all the records they *liked* that I did, which is the reason they wanted me to do the record in the first place."

The Wishing Chair, a splendid folk-flavored album that captures the Maniacs at their most charming, was a commercial disaster. (Elektra, perhaps stinging from the band's insistence on using Boyd, did not exactly pull out all the stops to promote it.) The group was disappointed, strapped for cash and exhausted from touring—all pressures that con-tributed to John Lombardo's decision to quit the band. Because he had been one of the group's main songwriters, his departure generated a fair amount of anxiety.

Elektra also started getting tough. The company rejected the demos the Maniacs submitted for their next album, saying the group was lazy and uninspired. Elektra also wanted a big-time producer to give the band a more contemporary—read salable—sound. The label suggested, of all people, Peter Asher—a mainstay in the L.A. mellow-rock mafia who was best known for his work with Linda Ronstadt (whom he also manages) and James Taylor, as well as for his recordings in the Sixties as half of Peter and Gordon. The Maniacs were philosophical, if skeptical.

"I didn't care much for Linda Ronstadt," Merchant says, "and it took me a little bit of concentration to get beyond her and the material she recorded and her voice to actually listen to the production. The only thing I really could notice about it was that it was very clean. You could hear every instrument very clearly, and the instruments had dimension. And the voice was recorded well."

"We were afraid of that L.A.—that slick sort of thing," Gustafson says. "We were really worried about that, but we thought that he's worked with singers—"

"He's worked with some mediocre artists and made them million-aires," interrupts Drew, laughing, "so we figured, 'What the hell?' "

Asher wanted to work in L.A., so the Maniacs relocated to the West Coast for four months—an experience that deepened their dislike of L.A., which shows up in the mournful "City of Angels," on *In My Tribe*. No one was sleeping under the newspaper or slipping out for curry this time around. Asher and his engineer, George Massenburg, were far more comfortable recording solo artists and studio musicians than bands, and they made it clear that if the Maniacs were not prepared to play exactly what was asked for, in tune and in time, other musicians would be called in to play for them. Some of the drum parts on *In My Tribe*, in fact, are computerized. Asher's discipline was bracing and educational, but the band can still summon up some bitterness about his intimidating ways.

"A lot of times he'd treat *us* like we were studio musicians, which got kind of weird," Buck says. "You'd be in there doing a guitar part, and Peter Asher would go, 'Hey, you're fucking up. What's wrong? Are you a jerk? Are you an asshole? A *fuck-up*? What the fuck's wrong? Are we going to have to call someone else in to do this?' He'd be yelling at Natalie, going, 'You keep fucking up. Are you an idiot? We're wasting *time*.' Then all of a sudden he'd realize what he was doing." While acknowledging the many arguments the band had with Asher, Merchant herself describes the producer as "diplomatic."

Seeking a hit single, Elektra pressured the Maniacs into recording Cat Stevens's "Peace Train," which the band now refuses to play live. Earlier, Elektra had tried to have the band undergo an image make-over.

"The record company wanted to make us look like the Human League," Buck says, laughing. "They called in a stylist in England. This guy comes in with a leather dress on and a samurai haircut—he has a bald head with a thing coming out on the top. He walks into the room, and he starts laughing, and we start laughing at him. He was really nice about it. He's going, 'I'm sorry. There's obviously nothing I can do for you. You people are just hicks. The best thing you can do is *accentuate* the fact that you're hicks—and I can't do that for you.' "

In My Tribe was slow getting out of the gate, but opening dates on R.E.M.'s 1987 fall tour and appearances on *The Tonight Show* and *Late Night with David Letterman* built momentum. When Elektra chairman Bob Krasnow attended a tumultuous Maniacs show at the Ritz, in New York, his enthusiasm for the band blossomed, and the company began to push the album hard. "Like the Weather" hit, the band toured end-lessly to larger and more enthusiastic crowds, and, at long last, the Maniacs arrived.

Success has a way of setting things right and smoothing the rough edges of past experiences. *Blind Man's Zoo* shows every sign of being yet an-other breakthrough for the band, and at the very least, the Maniacs are all confident now that they can make a living making music. Merchant, who nearly quit the band herself after *The Wishing Chair*, says she never believed that the band would be her life before *In My Tribe*.

"When John quit," she says, "I told everyone, 'I think I'm almost done too. I think it's time for me to go to school and start my pension plan because I'm getting old now. I need an IRA account.'" She laughs. "I was getting encouragement from my family, too: 'Quit. Quit now. You had fun, you learned a lot, but you can live a long time, and you need security.' And I was beginning to believe it."

In their various ways, the Maniacs have settled into new relationships and new homes. Augustyniak has moved back to Buffalo, and Buck has relocated to Albany. Gustafson got married and bought a house last year. "I guess it was the ultimate being-an-adult thing to do," he says. "I called my dad and said, 'Dad, I bought a house.' He said, 'I never thought you'd buy a new suit!'"

Last year, when it came time to pick a producer for their follow-up to *In My Tribe*, the Maniacs chose, of all people, Peter Asher. With a gold record behind them, the band and Asher were able to meet as equals this time around. The Maniacs recognized how Asher had sharpened their studio skills, and on his end, Asher consented to leave L.A. and record at Dreamland, an unpretentious studio in Woodstock, New York, much closer to the band's turf.

The Maniacs will tour the United States this summer and then go on to Europe, Japan, and Australia. After that, they'll take some time off. Merchant, who has written songs for a couple of benefit albums, will write her children's book and possibly another book of prose.

She also may record a solo album. "It's crossed my mind," she says, "because some of the favorite things I've done have been the scaled-down songs. I did a show in London, the only solo show I've done, and there's something really gratifying about a quiet evening of music, rather than a rock concert. There will always be another 10,000 Maniacs record, but I think it would be interesting."

The others seem to be content with the simpler rewards of success. "It's nice to be able to earn enough money so that we can actually live like thirty-year-old adults," Augustyniak says, "instead of saying, 'I've got to get home before my mom locks the door.' "

"We can actually look our friends in the eye," Buck says happily, "and say, 'That's okay, this time I can buy lunch.' They've been buying me food for the last ten years. 'It's okay, pal, *I'll* buy the six-pack.' "

Rolling Stone June 15, 1989

U2

Zoo World Order

"Uncertainty . . . can be a guiding light."
—From "Zooropa,"
the title track of U2's latest album

S **itting in the Ferryman,** a dockside Dublin pub, U2's guitarist, the Edge, speaks about the political crisis in Europe: "The single most powerful feeling we have is of the uncertainty of the situation here.

"Nothing really can be taken for granted anymore," he goes on, a Guinness close at hand, as strains of traditional Irish music float in from the bar's main room. "The old ideologies have fallen away. Capitalism won out. You can't even say it was democracy, because ultimately the ground upon which the battle was fought was economics—it was about money. And the West's economy won, and communism is pretty much over."

"Money, money, money
Always sunny In the rich man's world."
—From "Money, Money, Money," one of the many ABBA songs played
over the PA on the Zoo Plane, U2's private tour jet

"But rather than the sense that 'Well, that's over—now we can move forward with certainty,' the opposite has happened," the Edge continues. "People are perplexed. Maybe the stability that the Cold War created was the foundation of the West's movement forward, and now that that's gone and we have the resurgence of radical nationalism, people in Europe don't know who they are trying to be. Not only do they not know who they are, they don't know who they want to be. They don't know whether they want to be Europeans, part of the European community or whether they should be fighting to protect their national and ethnic identities.

"Even national boundaries don't mean much anymore. You've got the movement in Italy to partition the country into two or three autonomous states. There's the Basque-separatist movement that's alive and kicking. Northern Ireland is still no closer to a real solution. And Yugoslavia is the most obvious example of where things are starting to dissolve. Sarajevo has been a symbol of this."

> "We would like to hear the music, too, but we hear only the screams
> of wounded and tortured people and raped women."
> —A Bosnian woman speaking live by satellite from Sarajevo to 35,000 people
> at the U2 concert in Glasgow, Scotland, Aug. 8

To the inattentive eye of the Irish regulars and German tourists sucking up beer and whiskey at the Ferryman a few feet to his left, the Edge might have seemed like just another bar-stool philosopher gassing about the issues of the day before heading home to pass out in front of the telly. True, he and his three comrades in U2—Bono, Adam Clayton, and Larry Mullen Jr.—have spent plenty of time in front of televisions lately.

For the band, however—and in particular the Edge, whose increased musical and conceptual input earned him a coproduction credit on the new *Zooropa* album (he also sang lead on the first single, "Numb")—the pangs of European politics have been anything but remote. In retooling the Zoo TV stadium extravaganza that blitzed the United States in the summer of '92 for European audiences, U2 charged straight into the belly of the beast. The show's opening visual assault on gigantic vidiwalls and banks of televisions now included dramatic footage from *Triumph of the Will*, Leni Riefenstahl's Nazi propaganda film from the 1930s. Huge flaming swastikas and burning crosses appeared on the vidiwalls during "Bullet the Blue Sky." Meanwhile, *Zooropa*, the *Achtung Baby* follow-up the group released in July, chillingly evoked the exhilaration and fear of Europe in the throes of the new world disorder.

During the Zooropa '93 tour, U2's frequent live-satellite transmissions from Sarajevo—in which residents of the besieged city spoke uncensored to stunned stadium crowds—triggered a heated media debate abroad about the ethics of mixing up rock & roll special effects with heart-ravaging disasters.

At one of the Wembley shows in London, Salman Rushdie—who has been in hiding since the late Ayatollah Khomeini sentenced him to death three years ago for blasphemies against Islam in his novel *The Satanic Verses*—joined U2 onstage in front of seventy-two thousand people. And as if to assume the role in which many commentators were casting the band, Bono replaced his glitzy Mirror-Ball Man persona, the preening narcissist who closed the Zoo TV shows in the United States, with Mister MacPhisto, an aging, world-weary theatrical devil, complete with horns.

> "Ranking with the major megagigs of the 1970s and '80s, Zoo TV is the best live-music act in yonks. But again, it's like watching and rewatching atrocity footage such as, say, the Zapruder film, and trying to force the reality of it into your head. To paraphrase Bowie: In this context, whether it's Nazi Germany or Sarajevo onscreen, 'this ain't genocide, this is rock & roll!!!' "
> —Mic Moroney, "Irish Times," Aug. 24

> "What's the difference between Sarajevo and Auschwitz?"
> "What?" "In Auschwitz they always had gas."
> —Popular joke in Sarajevo, where gas supplies have been cut off

Bono is stretched out on the Zoo Plane, his legs resting on the seat opposite his own, as the band flies from London to Dublin. It is the evening after the fourth Wembley show—a truly spectacular performance in which Bono and the lads seemed only to gain inspiration from the steady rainfall—and he is tired and hoarse.

He is also hungover. After the show the previous night, the band threw a bash at the Regent Hotel, and given that it was closing night in London and one of the band's management crew was celebrating a birthday, the partying was especially intent. At about 3:30 a.m., Bono switched from beer to whiskey. I left at about 5:30; Bono was still going strong. He's suffering now. The couple of glasses of wine earlier in the day evidently didn't help. "Does anyone feel sick besides me?" he asks no one in particular.

Adding insult to injury, seated next to him is drummer Mullen, official U2 hunk, who always looks fit, groomed, and at the peak of health, regardless of the hour, location, or extent of alcohol intake.

MULLEN: The essence of good rock & roll—it's about confusion on every level. That's what makes Zoo TV so odd. On one hand, you can have Sarajevo, which is real, and then you have to continue on with the show. I mean, even for us, after the Sarajevo linkups we did, carrying on the show was incredibly difficult. People took it in different ways. People took it as "How can you have irony and then be serious?" But that is the point.

BONO: That's TV!

MULLEN: That *is* TV. You can switch the fuckin' channel any time you want. So I think a lot of people missed the point. I understand and accept the criticism, but it's not meant to be easy. It's not like going to a theater show, where you've got a beginning, middle, and end. It's a different journey. This is coming to a rock & roll show and watching TV and changing channels.

BONO: It's about contradictions. It's about all those instincts—we have all of them.

> "Serious shit—fan letters and murder in the same sentence. I don't like It."
> —Bono, *switching Zoo* TV *channels at Wembley, Aug. 21, after a news report about a woman who shot an abortion doctor in Kansas. She had sent fan mail to a Florida man who is charged with murder in the death of a doctor outside an abortion clinic.*

Bassist Adam Clayton is standing in a gazebo on the estate of Chris Blackwell, the founder and CEO of U2's label, Island Records. It's not a gazebo in the sense that you may have come to understand gazebos. It's shaped like a gazebo, but it's really more like a study, enclosed by glass on all sides, comfortably furnished, and perched, surrounded by trees, on the edge of a large pond. In a silent way, the scene is breathtaking.

The U2 gang has driven some forty miles south from London to spend this gray, cool Sunday afternoon enjoying Blackwell's tasteful hospitality and the secluded beauty of his home and grounds. Strangely, in this serene atmosphere, everyone seems a bit shellshocked.

Clayton, smoking, sporting his dyed semi-mohawk haircut and decked out in purple pants, black hiking boots, and black vest, takes in the enormous drooping willows, the people pushing small boats out onto the pond, the calm inside this room. He shakes his head.

"I haven't been programmed for an experience like this of late," he says with a laugh. "I feel quite vulnerable. I mean, there's not a TV in sight."

How did you hook up Salman Rushdie with your man MacPhisto?

BONO: In his isolation, I guess he gets to listen to a lot of music [*laughs*], so he's pretty tuned in. He turned up at our Earls Court show in London last year. We've kept in contact with him here and there. The issue of freedom of speech should be very close to rock & roll. At one stage we talked about sending him a satellite dish, and we would speak to him. We knew he was coming down to the show—which is very rare for him— and so we thought, "Well, look, if you're up for it . . . you *did* write *The Satanic Verses.*"

> "I also owe U2 a debt of gratitude for the gesture of solidarity and friendship they made by inviting me to join them onstage at Wembley. Not many novelists ever experience what it's like to face an audience of over seventy thousand people—and, fortunately for everyone, I didn't even have to sing.
>
> "Afterward I suggested that perhaps we could rename the band U2 + 1? ME2?—but I don't think they were for it. Still, one can always hope."
> —*Salman Rushdie, "Irish Times," Aug. 24*

> "Rock & Roll—it's the new religion, rock & roll. I have a great interest in religion. Some of my best friends are religious leaders. The ayatollah, the pope, even the Archbishop of Canterbury—I think he's fabulous. They're doing my work for me. . . . Nobody's going to church anymore. Shall I give the archbishop a call?
> —Bono as MacPhisto, *while dialing the Zoo telephone onstage, Wembley Stadium, Aug. 20*

> "We're not scared of dying, but you can't get used to seeing wounded people everywhere. . . . Something has to be done to help us."
> —*A Bosnian woman speaking live by satellite from Sarajevo at the U2 concert in Glasgow, Aug. 9*

THE EDGE: One of our Sarajevo connections had three women. One was a Serb, one was a Croat, one was a Muslim—all Bosnians. All in Sarajevo, all with their own story to tell. One of the girls said the thing that we'd always hoped no one would say—but she did. She said: "I wonder, what are you going to do for us in Sarajevo? I think the truth is you're not going to do anything."

It was so hard to carry on after that. It killed the gig stone dead. It was so heavy. I don't know how Bono managed to carry on singing. It was such a crushing statement.

—Bono, while channel surfing onstage at Wembley, Aug. 20

Bill Carter, a startlingly fresh-faced twenty-seven-year-old filmmaker and relief worker in Sarajevo, sits in the bar at the Conrad Hotel in Dublin and describes how, after he'd traveled from Sarajevo to Verona, Italy, to interview Bono for thirteen minutes, the plan for the live-satellite hookup was hatched.

"I had a real serious conversation with Bono and Edge about what was going on," Carter says. "They said, 'Well, what can we do?' That hit me with a huge trip—the largest rock band in the world is asking me what can they do. They wanted to play—Bono and Edge, all of them, really—wanted to come play in the disco in Sarajevo. But it was a difficult time then: a lot of shelling. I went back to Sarajevo and thought about it.

"A few days later, someone in their office called me and said, 'They really want to come—bad.' I wrote a long fax explaining why that shouldn't happen, but what about linking up to the show? They said, 'Let's do it.'

"We'd talk to seventy thousand people and hit them with reality on their rock & roll fantasy. That's a huge medium. . . . In Sweden we got the fiancee of a guy in Sarajevo—she lives in Sweden, his family, too—to come to the stadium. He talked very powerfully about what was happening, and then he spoke to her. She hadn't seen him in seventeen months. There she is, a refugee in Sweden, being feted backstage, and then looking up at him on the video. That was a heavy thing.

"We were offering a true human reality. This is one fact that is really important: No one in seventeen months had allowed Bosnians—besides the politicians—to speak live to the world. When I first went back to Sarajevo with this idea, ABC News and all the rest, they were like 'Are you nuts? You're going to let someone from here speak live?'

"The trust from U2 to me was tremendous, to say, 'OK, go ahead—you're in a war zone, speak live to us.' They didn't know me. They knew me for one evening."

THE EDGE: The Sarajevo connection was so different from what you were seeing on the news. It underscored for me the difference between the reality of people telling their stories and the editorialized sound-bite style of most TV news programs, where everything is packaged and contextualized through some sort of journalistic narration. This was raw, unedited, live, and at times almost unbearable. It suddenly dawned on me—actually it's something that I've probably known for a long time—that the TV news is now entertainment."

> Art is manipulation
> Rebellion is packaged
> Rock and roll is entertainment
> —*Mottoes flashed on the video screens during U2's Zoo TV shows*

CLAYTON: It's taken a long time for television to be thought of as rock & roll.

U2's last show at Wembley was attended by, among seventy-two thousand others, Eric Clapton, Robbie Robertson, and French singer and film star Charles Aznavour. Aznavour, sixty-eight, was asked if he wanted to leave the stadium early in the show when rain began to pour, but he refused, insisting on staying till the end. Among his other current projects, Aznavour is recording a duet with Frank Sinatra for his upcoming album of duets. So is Bono.

Bono wanted to do a version of Nancy Sinatra's "These Boots Are Made for Walkin'." "That could have been good," he says, preposterously. Sinatra, displaying his characteristically impeccable taste, refused, suggesting Cole Porter's "I've Got You Under My Skin" instead. Understandably, Bono is concerned.

"I don't know what I can do with that," he says. "I'm not going to croon it next to him. I might talk. I want to spook it up, because those Cole Porter songs are spooky. I don't know if you heard that 'Night and Day' thing we did [on the album *Red Hot + Blue*]—that's where we connect with Cole Porter. They're spooky, fucked-up songs of obsession. Some people perform them so fruity—[*belts in lounge-lizard fashion*] 'Night and day / You are the one'—it's like *whoa!* These are really dark pieces of work."

"I listen to Sinatra a lot," Bono continues. "Miles Davis was a great appreciator of Sinatra's phrasing. That turned me on to him, listening to him in a different way. I've seen him about five times. We met him in Vegas—we went backstage, and we were hanging out with him. It was like Rent-a-Celebrity, and we were like gyppos, just knackers. Larry was talking to him about Buddy Rich, who'd just died, and he didn't want to talk about anything else. He came alive. You got the feeling that maybe not a lot of people talk to him about music, and maybe that's what he's most interested in. There were people knocking at the door, big names, and he wouldn't go out. He wouldn't leave the dressing room.

"Then there was a very amusing incident in Dublin. We all went to see him in this big stadium. He was with Sammy Davis Jr. and Liza Minnelli—that tour. We didn't go backstage; we didn't think he'd remember us. But the lord mayor went back to see him, to have his photograph taken with him. When the lord mayor came back to his seat—and this is very Dublin—he kind of leaned over a few rows and said, 'Oh, Bono, Frank was asking for you all.' *That* might have been the moment!"

Did your role in the band shift during the making of "Zooropa"?

THE EDGE: Quite why on this record I've taken a production credit and not on other records is hard to explain. I don't think my role has changed that much. But we're in an age where it's very hard to be clear about people's roles in the making of records.

I suppose I took on a level of responsibility that I haven't on previous records. That meant sitting in with Bono on lyric-writing sessions—just being the foil, the devil's advocate, bouncing couplets around—down to completely demoing some pieces, establishing their original incarnations, which then served as the blueprint when we began to formally record them. And then, generally, just worrying more than everyone else.

We're at a point where production has gotten so slick that people don't trust it anymore. This is something that we were really feeling over the last two records. We were starting to lose trust in the conventional sound of rock & roll—the conventional sound of guitar, in particular—and, you know, those big reverb-laden drum sounds of the Eighties or those big, beautiful, pristine vocal sounds with all this lush ambience and reverb. So we found ourselves searching for other sounds that had more life and more freshness.

That's something we were talking to Wim Wenders about. He's finding that—because of the way certain images have been stolen by advertising or bad movie makers—that it's increasingly difficult to use imagery to tell his stories. He's now resorting much more to music and dialogue. He said that on his first movie he spent all his time editing and ten percent of the time working with music and dialogue. Now it's the reverse. He spends very little time editing—he gets it so that he's happy with the overall series of images, but then he spends all his time working on music and getting the dialogue the way he wants it.

It's really bizarre how things are melting into one another. We're now using imagery to underscore our songs.

Tell me, what was the Edge's role in the making of "Zooropa"?

BONO: When we start records, Edge is a slow starter. He's not quick to be enthused about a project. But at the end, when everybody else is fading, he's the guy who's up all night for weeks. I mean, I'm allergic to the studio after a few weeks. We wanted to acknowledge the baby-sitting that Edge does.

Brian Eno was coming and going. Flood went to the end when there were mixes to do. I mean, we're all a part of it—we always have been. But Edge is the guy with the screwdriver.

MULLEN: And the patience of a saint.

BONO: One of the things that worked about this record is that it was so quick. Edge is so good with the screwdriver, but we didn't give him much time to use it—which was great. He had more of an overall picture because he wasn't so taken up with the details.

There was a lot of publicity around the time "Achtung Baby" was released about your separating from your wife, Aislinn. How are things going for you personally?

THE EDGE [*long silence*]: It's a learning experience, Anthony [*laughs*]. I'm really no closer to bringing my private life to a conclusion than I was a year ago. I'm getting on really well with my wife, actually. I don't know, I'm feeling very positive about life in general, and that includes my private life. Whatever way it pans out, it's going to be OK. That's another thing that being off for nine months will help to clarify.

When you get off the road, you've got to reintroduce yourself to all your friends and family. We're lucky—we have a lot of very good friends and very patient families. But there is a limit [*laughs*]. And I think we passed that limit a long time ago.

So when are you and Naomi Campbell getting married?

CLAYTON: I really don't know. I would say it would be some time next year. We'll take January to have a clear break away from everything. I

think in that time we'll decide what's best and how we want to do it. It's **181**
kind of a scheduling thing [*laughs*].

You're taking a rehearsal break, then playing Japan and Australia for five weeks. That will take you till the end of the year. What then?

BONO: One of us has to die in a car accident. One of us has to book into the Betty Ford clinic. One of us should get married. And one of us has to become a monk. We'll have nine months off.

MULLEN: It'll be time to do things that we haven't had the opportunity to do—and I'm not necessarily talking about solo projects—so that we'll come back with new ideas and start up again. That's the idea. It's not nine months' holiday.

BONO [*incredulous*]: Jesus!

MULLEN: Bono thought he was going to have his holidays [*laughs*]. I really noticed while we were making *Zooropa*—because we were all in the studio at the same time—that there were things I wanted to say on a musical basis that I couldn't articulate. I could only say what I felt, and it took so much time to explain. What I'd really like to do is . . .

BONO: Learn how to speak.

MULLEN: What's your problem [*laughs*]? I'd like to learn how to talk in basic musical terms. The great thing about U2 is that there are no rules: Everyone has the chance to contribute as much or as little as they wish. After ten years of being on the road, it's time now to advance a bit musically. I really want to learn how to explain myself in musical terms, the basics of music theory.

> "The catatonic note-repetitions of the voice part in 'Numb' add up to a clear effect. The use of different texts simultaneously in 'Lemon' works well. It is a technique that seems to have been out of favour since the medieval motet. A lively song this, with its repeated-note accompaniment."
> —*Dr. Seorise Bodley, composer and associate professor of music, "Irish Times," Aug. 24*

The U2 management crew, friends, and hangers-on pile on a bus that will travel from Wembley to the Regent Hotel in London, about a half-hour trip. It's about 1:30 a.m., the third Wembley show ended a few hours ago, only three shows remain until the end of the European leg of *Zooropa '93*. It feels like the last week of school.

Bottles of wine are being passed around and someone shouts for music. Someone else pops a cassette in the deck. Over the speakers comes the fanfare that begins "Daddy's Gonna Pay for Your Crashed Car," on *Zooropa*. An instant collective drunken groan: "Oh, nooooo!"

The Zoo TV show, which starts out so explosively, fades out on a far more ambiguous, introspective note. A desperately searching "Ultraviolet (Light My Way)" is followed by an equally desperate, equally searching "Love Is Blindness." Then comes Bono's eerie, falsetto rendering of Elvis Presley's "Can't Help Falling in Love." "Elvis is still in the building," Bono says softly, as U2 exits the building and Elvis' own version of the song comes up on the PA. Through all this Bono is dressed as the devil.

What's the meaning of all that Elvis business at the end of the show?

THE EDGE: Well, we wanted to move away from the well-established and long-standing tradition of ending on "40" [*laughs*]. It seemed like the only way to make sure we didn't have to.

Really, who else but Elvis could have made that possible? You have to call in the big guns, it always comes down to that.

I think at this stage, yeah. People still start singing "40" at the end of the set. I guess it'll be a while before we can lay that one to rest. People come to the shows who have seen U2 before, and you're constantly having to deal with their expectations as opposed to what you're trying to do. I know there are a lot of people who come away disappointed from the *Zooropa* show because we didn't play "Sunday Bloody Sunday" or whatever other old song they wanted to hear.

But you close the set proper with "Pride." How does a song as emotionally direct as that fit in with all the irony and media chicanery in the rest of the show?

At the beginning we weren't sure if that was going to work. I think it does work. It may be a bit of a jump to go from something as ironic as Bono as MacPhisto or the Fly and yet pull off "Pride," complete with Martin Luther King on the video screen. But it comes at a part of the concert where to make a connection like that is important. Amid the uncertainty there are certain ideas that are so powerful and so right that you can hold onto them no matter how screwed up everything else is.

> "Everybody wants a long life. Longevity has its place.
> But I don't care about that now. I may not get there with you, but I
> want you to know tonight that we as a people will get to the promised land!"
> —*Passage spoken by Martin Luther King on the vidiwall*
> *during U2's version of "Pride"*

There's a really theatrical element to that MacPhisto character.

BONO: The cabaret aspect . . . I was called by a tabloid photographer, who said, "You know, the fellow you do in the fin-ah-lay" [*laughs*]. I thought, "Oh, wow."

It's great, your singing an Elvis song in the fin-ah-lay, too.

For me, MacPhisto is sort of sad, bad, not so funny but might be. It's like taking the rock jerk that the Fly is and—if you're going to play him—take him to his logical conclusion, which is when he's fat and playing Las Vegas. It's a bookend to the funky and fucked-up swagger of the Fly.

It's rather poignant. Also, whoever he is now—Jesus or whoever—Elvis once was the devil.

The "devil's music"—that was the thing, wasn't it? The beat. The sadness of that last song, though, that child's voice, that falsetto as the song ends, is the most poignant moment of the show, because, in among all those fucked-up qualities, there's just that little childlike voice. That voice to me is the cover of *Boy*. If you study those films of Elvis—and I have— there were some very powerful moments as he was in decline. Maybe more powerful than when he was the svelte pop hero.

What's your feeling about the future of U2?

THE EDGE: I think with *Zooropa* we were reminded in a very nice way of how special the chemistry is between the musicians in the band. That was an unanticipated surprise, to rediscover how unique this collection of individuals is. I'm feeling very positive about our collaboration— there's a lot more there.

When things get really hairy, you start to think, "Well, maybe I should just excuse myself and wander off into something a little less hectic." Then I start to think, "Well, what would I like to do?" Well, I'd like to play guitar still. And I'm really not into working alone, so I'd like to get a group of people to work with. "And what sort of people would I like to work with?" Well, there are these other three guys that I've been getting on with really well for a while . . . [*laughs*]. You end up redesigning the band—again.

What would you like to see happen now as far as U2 and the situation in Bosnia is concerned?

BILL CARTER: The ultimate connection would be for whoever in the group wants to come to Sarajevo. But it's critically important that it not be a circus and that nobody know about it. The connection is not for the media, the connection is for the people in Sarajevo. The point is not to announce, "We're going to Sarajevo"—that's pure bullshit. That's useless. They should go in a way that's very personal, to solidify the connection. It would be very powerful.

What would it mean for the people there?

It means a great deal. They have no faith in politics anymore at all. But it's a very cultured city. The Olympics were there ten years ago. It's like Vienna—it's a beautiful city. U2 are huge cultural heroes, so the connection is important spiritually. They know that U2 speak to a lot of people, especially young people. And if they care, then that means people will remember Sarajevo for at least that little while. Because they're afraid that people are forgetting that they're there.

CLAYTON: Although it's a confusing time, I think it is genuinely exciting. I think the world is filled with possibilities at the moment.

Any final thoughts as we land?

BONO: How is my hair?

Rolling Stone October 14, 1993

After midnight at Absolute Audio studios, in midtown Manhattan, a few members of Wu-Tang Clan are lounging in the lounge. Marijuana smoke clouds the air, the result of the incessant burning of blunts. "What's that, Tical?" says Raekwon, addressing Method Man by another of his tags—a synonym for weed—and gesturing toward the television set hanging in a corner of the room. "Strange Universe" is on the box. "You ain't seeing what I'm seeing?" Meth's lanky frame is stretched out on a chair; the rapper is deeply immersed in a movie script that he's considering for an acting role. Aptly enough, the subject turns to the Heaven's Gate suicide cult. "They was dropping it on '60 Minutes,' God," Ghostface Killah says with characteristic fervor. "They had the other niggas that were saying shit like, 'I wish I was there.' Like they was down wit' the shit, but they just happened to miss it that day." "Bad," says Meth, shaking his head. "Damn," says U-God. Their disbelief is tinged with respect.

That respect, however, is short-lived. "You said they all had Nikes on," says Raekwon.

"They *all* had Nikes on, G," Ghost assures him.

"What? The aliens had Nikes on?" Meth asks, still distracted by his reading.

"No, the niggas that killed theyself," Raekwon explains to him.

"They all had black Nikes on, God," Ghost continues. "They had the wack pair of Nikes on, too." He's beginning to chuckle. "You know, the regular joints? The first pair, probably."

"The doofus shit," says Meth, dryly, his disbelief now veering into a weary contempt.

"The Smurf shit?" says U-God. They all collapse in hysterics, clapping and slapping hands.

"It looked like they was on their way out," says Ghost, mimicking the calm, take-me-away-from-all-of-this posture of the corpses. He stops laughing, finally, and takes a moment to collect himself. "Those niggas was buggin' the fuck out, G," he says, in conclusion. "They ain't went nowhere."

The last place Wu-Tang Clan, the most significant posse in hip-hop, is going is nowhere. Still, it fits that they would be fascinated by Heaven's

Gate, however lame the California cult's sense of style. Wu, too, sees itself and its extended crew as a secret society united by a deep bond, a "sword family" in the parlance of the martial-arts movies it loves. The nine members—RZA (pronounced *Rizza,* a rendering of razor), the Genius (GZA), Method Man, U-God, Raekwon, Ol' Dirty Bastard, Ghostface Killah, Masta Killa, and Inspectah Deck—are all relations or friends who grew up together. Each goes by a variety of identities, and they maintain a large home in rural New Jersey that serves as a kind of communal clubhouse.

"We are a group of men who came together for a common cause," says RZA, the group's main producer, its business leader, and the person who, in the group hierarchy, is the first among equals. "We can't split up—we don't really got too many friends besides us. We may have a thousand people around us, but there's nobody like *us.* That's the circle right there—that's how come it's so powerful. It ain't brought together for money or women or drugs. We're one in the heart and one in the mind. That's the power of Wu-Tang."

The common cause uniting the clan at the moment is completing *Wu-Tang Forever,* the double album that is among the music world's most anxiously awaited events. The album has been delayed innumerable times, partly because despite their being "one in the heart and one in the mind," it's virtually impossible to bring them together in one place for any extended period of time. But steadily moving forward within a whirl of barely controlled chaos has been Wu's highly successful MO ever since its audacious debut, *Enter the Wu-Tang (36 Chambers),* rocked the hip-hop world in 1993 with its grimy beats, cinematic conception, and raw, raucous MC'ing. It had the same impact that Run-D.M.C. had ten years earlier—it stripped away everything extraneous and refocused hip-hop on its DJ/rapper essence. The album, like all dramatic musical innovations, draws on the past to shape the future—it sounds both shockingly original and thrillingly reminiscent of the anything-goes energy of hip-hop's earliest days.

But *Enter the Wu-Tang* was just the start of something no one could have anticipated. In an arrangement that set a standard for boldness, Wu's contract with Loud/RCA allows the group's members to negotiate solo deals with any label of their choosing. "You got cats comin' to record labels now, talkin' 'bout, 'I want a Wu-Tang deal,' " says Method Man of the group's influence in business affairs. "They might as well put it on

the contract like that." The result has been a steady stream of hit side
projects from the Wu-Tang camp: *Tical,* by Method Man (Def Jam, 1994); *Return to the 36 Chambers: The Dirty Version,* by Ol' Dirty Bastard (Elektra, 1995); *Only Built 4 Cuban Linx . . . ,* by Raekwon (Loud/RCA, 1995); *Liquid Swords,* by the Genius (Geffen, 1995); and *Ironman,* by Ghostface Killah (Razor Sharp/Epic, 1996).

Each of those albums—none of which has sold less than 600,000 copies—has established its maker as a solo star. But all of them feature guest appearances by other Wu members, all were produced by RZA (who also owns half of Razor Sharp Records, in partnership with Sony), and all of them came out under the banner of Wu-Tang Productions. Each member contributes 20 percent of his earnings back to that company, and all of the members share equally in the profits, regardless of how well their individual albums sold, or whether or not they even made an album.

Such a share-and-share-alike arrangement might seem like a blueprint for jealousy and competition—and it may eventually prove to be. But, so far, it's helped to hold Wu together. In fact, they don't really view their individual efforts as solo albums. "It's like chapters of a book," says Method Man. "Or like when you look at *Pulp Fiction*—you got all the characters together, but you also got the background behind what each of them was doing. That's how we treat these solo albums—you've seen us all together, now it's what goes on with us as individuals."

The Wu-Tang tale is a compelling story that begins in the rugged housing projects of Staten Island, New York. It is a chronicle of street lives shaped by poverty, violence—RZA, for one, was acquitted of murder on the grounds of self-defense—drug dealing, and incarceration. But it is also a story of family values, Wu-Tang style. "I only had a mother," says U-God (born Lamont Hawkins), who grew up in the Park Hill projects—dubbed Killa Hill. "She was like Dr. J. in the house; she was my idol. I praise her for the goodness in me. When I went to junior high, I met people from the Stapleton projects—that's how I met Ghost, RZA, and Dirty. I knew Raekwon and Meth from Park Hill. To top it off, my mother knows Raekwon's mother and RZA's mother, from Brownsville, in Brooklyn. Our mothers is happy now, because we was some bad little boys. They didn't think it was gonna be a good sight with us. This life is crazy."

"I got a song called 'All That I Got Is You,'" says Ghostface (born Dennis Coles) when asked about his life growing up. "I wrote that from the heart. My father left me when I was six. My mother tried to take care of all of us on public assistance. We couldn't get fresh for Christmas. I took that with me—that's what gives me inspiration. All this could go tomorrow, and I would still know how to function, because I never had nothing before. I went through the struggle—it was a rough life. Outta my crew that I used to run with back in the day, all them niggas got locked up. I don't know, something kept me alive on the streets, and I'm just grateful for being here like this. It's a blessing."

The story continues to unfold, and now it often is set in the gleaming boardrooms of the overwhelmingly white music industry. That move has required certain emotional adjustments. "It's a bugged-out feeling sometimes, because you know you never was around people like that," says Raekwon (born Corey Woods) about his interaction with the corporate world. "But those people have a lot of importance to do with your career, so it's only right to deal with them." He thinks for a moment, then adds philosophically, "Shit, it beats being on parole."

True, the transition hardly has been seamless. When writer Cheo H. Coker's complimentary story about Wu in *Rap Pages* came out accompanied by illustrations the group didn't like, Masta Killa warned Coker that "Wu-Tang Clan ain't nothin' to fuck with" and blackened the writer's eye. One record-industry executive recalls Ol' Dirty Bastard calling her over to him one night in a club because he wanted her to witness another woman performing oral sex on him. Method Man missed the photo session for *Enter the Wu-Tang* because he was arrested for smoking a blunt; U-God was in jail when the album was released. Promoters who tried to renegotiate after one of the group's notoriously unreliable live shows early in its career risked a beat down. Wu can still get nasty with photographers, blatantly intimidating one woman at a recent shoot.

Most of that isn't much beyond the sort of thing that built the reputations of Jerry Lee Lewis, Guns n' Roses, and other white rockers with an appetite for destruction. But when rappers act up, it's seen less as a mark of their rock & roll authenticity than as proof of their sociopathology. Regardless, Wu claims it is trying to change. "When we started out, we was young," explains U-God. "We did so many bad things. Now that we're older, we want to show the world that Wu ain't bad. People can trust us. It took me two times going in and out of prison to realize I had to stop doin' what I was doin'. RZA showed me the way. He said, 'Would you rather risk your life on the streets, holdin' guns and doin' your wild thing, or would you rather go to London and lay up? Tour for the money we make?' It was like a transformation."

Talks with Wu are rife with such declarations. RZA (born Robert Diggs) is the keeper of Wu-Tang's mystic knowledge—a highly idiosyncratic blend of kung-fu discipline, the numerological speculations of the Five Percent Nation (a split-off sect from the Nation of Islam), chess lore, street smarts, the Bible, mafia mythology, black capitalism, millenarian anxiety, extraterrestrial visions, and superhero fantasies. "You got the Abbott [another of RZA's IDS] hittin' deep science," says CappaDonna, a member of Wu's extended clan, speaking of RZA's contribution to the Wu chemistry. "Telling you how much the earth weigh. Telling you how to break down a solid into a liquid. Telling how the baby was born, where it comes from."

In the course of a long night in the studio, each of the clan—except for Ol' Dirty Bastard (born Russell Jones), who, characteristically, never showed up—sits down for an individual interview on a catch-as-catch-can basis. Somehow, it's understood that RZA will speak last, partly because he's still busy overseeing the production of the album and partly because his entrance must be prepared by the others.

Indeed, RZA and GZA (born Gary Grice), who are cousins, both had record deals before Wu-Tang, and their negative experiences gave birth to Wu's approach to the music/business equation. "RZA and Genius were already in the industry, and they seen the bad parts of it," says Method Man (born Clifford Smith). "So we came prepared. We wasn't goin' for that bourgie shit. Don't try and make me up to be what I'm not. We gonna do it without compromising a goddamn thing."

When RZA does appear, it's close to 4 a.m., but he's bursting with energy, hyped about the range of moods that *Wu-Tang Forever* contains. "We tackle a lot of different subjects," RZA says about the album. "We got shit like 'Reunited.' That's the first rap on it: 'Reunited, double LP / World excited / Struck a match to the underground / Industry ignited.' Those are GZA's lyrics. We got a song called 'A Better Tomorrow,' where the hook tells you, 'You can't party your life away / Smoke your life away / Drink your life away / Fuck your life away.' We got a song called

'It's Yourz' that's for partying. But inside the party there's a little trouble—some chump niggas are tryin' to act too tough; we gonna have to smack them up.

"We come to peace," he continues, defining the Wu ethic, "but we always come prepared for war. You see, Shaolin warriors were different from Wu-Tang warriors. Shaolin warriors stay so humble that they might commit suicide before they would go against you—just so you could feel that ultimate pain. They're like Gandhi, a nonviolent approach. Wu-Tang come in that form, but you ain't gonna push us past the limit. We gonna serve you justice. If we gotta break your arm, we'll break your arm. But we ain't come to do that—we came to help shed light. Our album describes us like that, man—every angle of it."

CappaDonna (born Darryl Hill) puts the theory into active practice. "You know what my joy is?" he asks, laughing, as he strolls through the studio brandishing a baseball bat. "When I'm making somebody else happy, I love that. See this bat right here? This is for whoever's *stopping* me from making somebody happy."

"I feel the world needs this right now," says Masta Killa (born Elgin Turner) about *Wu-Tang Forever* and then draws on language derived from the Five Percent Nation to describe the album's purpose and intended impact. "I feel the world is in a state of confusion. We lost two great heroes: Biggie Smalls and Tupac Shakur. The world needs guidance. We the gods that gotta come through with mathematics to set everything straight, to give condolence to the world."

Wu is well aware, however, that for many people, the Notorious B.I.G. and Shakur are not heroes but outlaws who died by the sword they lived by. For those people, far from providing condolence, rap is seen as the source of the problem, the match that lights the fire of violence, then fans the flames. Method Man rejects the charge in no uncertain terms: "We the street news. What the cameras don't show, we tell. That's the reason they wanna stop it—it's straight at you, hardcore, and the truth hurts.

"I get upset," he continues, nearly shouting, "when I see people like Dionne Warwick and other people who came before us in the music business [put down rap]. Shit, they seen what state the black nation was in, and they didn't do a goddamn thing. Dionne Warwick ain't never come to my motherfuckin' avenue and threw a free concert. But I tell you who did: Doug E. Fresh. KRS-One. These rap niggas. Then we get criticized for our lyrics, for telling the truth, bottom line."

Raekwon leaps equally hard to the music's defense. "This is another frame of education," he says. "People may look at it like, 'Some of them talk about violence,' whatever—but first say the nigga's a poet. To flow— that shit is not easy. You can never get it no fresher, comin' up out the projects, twenty or twenty-one years old, and you start rhymin', and that's how you make your money—by speaking your lingo. Rap, to me, is slang poetry. It answers your questions: why young kids is doin' bad, why they turn to drugs to get away from their misery. This is the shit we talk about—and how to escape it.

"You'll never be able to stop this," he concludes, laughing, "because imagine if we didn't have no music—we'd be some miserable mother-fuckers."

And the reunified Wu-Tang Clan has no intentions of stopping. U-God, Inspectah Deck (born Jason Hunter), CappaDonna, and RZA all are slated for solo albums this year. "The Wu-Tang story still ain't told fully," RZA says. "My solo album will give more vision on my side. I already got the lyrics and the music. It's gonna be some shit." The next Wu-Tang album will not appear until the year 2000, at which time, predicts Cap-paDonna, "the world is coming to an end. What's bringin' it down? All the negativity. I don't want to get too deep into that. I don't fear that. I'm waitin' for that. I'm waitin' patiently."

Back on earth, however, the clan continues to evolve. "After this Wu-Tang album, I'm gonna pull back some from producing any album," RZA says. "I think I laid down a good pattern of hip-hop production for the whole world. Anybody can listen to our songs and generate some-thing of their own. Take 'Ice Water' [from Raekwon's *Only Built 4 Cuban Linx . . .*], with that voice going 'Ahhhh,' or 'Bring the Pain' [from Meth's *Tical*]. How many songs come out, man, with voices going like that? [Blackstreet's] 'No Diggity,' for example—a Number One hit based on the sound that I heard first. I brought strings into hip-hop. The heavy piano loops—I got everybody runnin' back to snoop for piano loops. So, with that foundation laid down, I think Ghostface, Raekwon, and Meth could produce their own albums. Then, on the next Wu-Tang album, we'll come back and put that into one big bowl of soup for you again."

For now, RZA is content for *Wu-Tang Forever* to sound the whistle of the underground railroad. "This album will spark the hip-hop nation," he says. "Radio stations these days don't even know what true hip-hop is. They playin' this regenerated R&B with somebody rapping over it, artists who sell with their looks, the same familiar looping of songs that people grew up with or that already was famous on the radio.

"There's only two things that can happen," RZA concludes about the future of hip-hop in the wake of *Wu-Tang Forever*. "One: Wu-Tang takes over and brings back hip-hop to its true form. Or, two: The media dogs hip-hop to the utmost extremity to where only the Hammer-type sound gets through, and hip-hop becomes an underground thing. And if it goes underground, it's only gonna grow more. Either way it goes, it's all right with me."

Rolling Stone June 10–24, 1997

Recordings

The Bristol Sessions

Various Artists

For the past few years a "new traditionalism" has been in vogue in country music—a welcome antidote to the stupefying commercial formulas that had infected Nashville music making. But before those formulas hardened and before traditionalism became new, there was simply a country music tradition, and *The Bristol Sessions* represents one of its earliest, most pristine expressions.

In 1927 a record-industry talent scout named Ralph Peer set up a makeshift studio in the town of Bristol, Tennessee, and in two weeks recorded seventy-six tracks by nineteen different performers. Among the artists discovered at those sessions were Jimmie Rodgers and the Carter Family, and every significant strain of what we now call country music was captured on tape. In his excellent notes for this double-LP selection of thirty-five songs from the Bristol sessions, Charles Wolfe asserts that once these recordings hit the stores, "country music . . . was about to go into high gear." In terms of artistic achievement and influence—as well as commercial impact—he couldn't be more correct.

All the artists who participated in the sessions are included here, and obviously the quality and force of the performances vary. "The Jealous Sweetheart" and "A Passing Policeman," by the vaudeville duo the Johnson Brothers, for example, will likely prove cloying even for the most generous modern listener. Just about every other track on this double album, however, has something to recommend it—and many are simply stunning.

The extraordinary richness of Jimmie Rodgers's singing, including a lovely yodeling stretch on "Sleep, Baby, Sleep," distinguishes his two songs. The Carter Family's contributions showcase the raw beauty and stark mountain conviction of Sara Carter's voice.

But the virtues of country music's greatest pioneers should come as no surprise, and *The Bristol Sessions* teems with other pleasures. B. F. Shelton's "O Molly Dear" is a riveting love-and-death ballad, part of a tradition that reaches back to the Middle Ages. Henry Whitter's breathless exclamations on "Henry Whitter's Fox Chase" turn his careening harmonica solo into a cheerily erotic set piece. "Walking in the Way with

Jesus," by Blind Alfred Reed, and "I Want to Go Where Jesus Is," by Ernest Phipps and His Holiness Quartet, are only two of the bracing—even jaunty—declarations of spiritual faith in this collection.

What is most uplifting about *The Bristol Sessions,* however, is its uncompromised human dimension. These songs are rooted in essential concerns: desire, love, jealousy, fear, death, and the hope for redemption. Similarities and consistencies within these performances did not result from the advice of record-industry consultants or hitmaking producers. They are the product of a cohesive Southern culture that saw the world clearly and simply and rendered that dangerous, wonder-filled world in song. Alfred G. Karnes's splendidly optimistic "I Am Bound for the Promised Land" concludes *The Bristol Sessions,* but by the time you get to that track, you'll feel as if you've made your visit already.

Rolling Stone May 24, 1988

Autobiography of Mistachuck
Chuck D

Chuck D's debut solo album opens with an excerpt from the discussion that begins Spike Lee's movie *Clockers*—a group of black kids arguing about whether Chuck D still matters as a rapper. After the excerpt fades, Chuck's voice comes into the foreground, noting what they have to say. Then he blasts in with "Mistachuck," a blistering claim to his accomplishments in the world of rap and a State of the Hip-hop Union address.

That segue sums up the perspective of *Autobiography*. On this album, the thirty-six-year-old Chuck D speaks as a rap elder statesman, not so much embroiled in the music's ongoing controversies as commenting on them from a distance. He lectures the young gangstas of "Generation Wrekkled," as one title puts it, from a similar remove, urging them like a benevolent uncle to set aside the blunts and the guns, to forget the East Coast/West Coast rivalries and study their history.

Though such messages don't make for much cultural heat, Chuck certainly has the shoulders to carry their moral weight. As the leader of Public Enemy, he was in the thick of the anti-Reagan charge in the Eighties, articulating a vision from the urban battle zone that was both incendiary and inspiring. Chuck has lost none of his anger, but he sets his sights lower now, preoccupied as he is with preserving his reputation and combating a fictional character he calls Big Willie, a black record-industry executive desperate to cater to the white power structure. And in a surprising move, Chuck reunites with ex-Public Enemy member Professor Griff, whose anti-Semitic comments plunged PE into controversy in 1989, on "Horizontal Heroin," a Last Poets-style antidrug riff.

Working here with producers Gary G Wiz and Eric "Vietnam" Sadler, Chuck successfully reinvents the sound he defined with Public Enemy, slowing the beats down and introducing stylish R&B elements like sampled horn parts and vocal choruses. Seventies soul singer Isaac Hayes even steps up to the mike on the fearsome "But Can You Kill the Nigger in You?" And Chuck can still cram more meaning into a telegraphic phrase—"Metaphors be passin' you like taxicabs," as he puts it in "Generation Wrekked"—than any other rapper on the scene.

Chuck insists that Public Enemy will be back next year with an album called *Afraid of the Dark?* If that title reminds you of *Fear of a Black Planet*, that's part of the problem with *Autobiography* as well. A song like "Talk Show Created the Fool" is funny and sharp ("Ricki Lake is eating mad steaks off your bad breaks"), but Chuck already covered this ground in 1988 on "She Watch Channel Zero." It's time for this "incredible rhyme animal" to go on a fresh hunt.

Rolling Stone   October 3, 1996

Woody Guthrie's
Dust Bowl Ballads and
Library of Congress Recordings

Perhaps the lone salvation of human tragedy is that occasionally it finds its poet, the one person who lends enduring meaning to suffering and rescues dignity from disaster. The Dust Bowl crisis of the Thirties found its poet in Woody Guthrie, as the recently re-released *Library of Congress Recordings* and *Dust Bowl Ballads* demonstrate with overwhelming clarity.

The *Library of Congress Recordings* are particularly remarkable. The three-record set, which was recorded for a radio show in 1940 at a studio owned by the Department of the Interior, runs nearly three hours. It consists of Guthrie performing twenty-eight songs during the course of a rambling interview with musicologist Alan Lomax and Lomax's wife, Elizabeth Littleton.

In response to Lomax's questions, Guthrie, who was born in 1912, chronicles his harrowing family life in Oklahoma, his days of "hoboin'," and his experiences with the Okies who traveled the hard road to the promised land of California. His songs weave in and out of the conversation.

Guthrie seems incapable of discussing a subject without striking a resonant moral chord. Early on he drifts into talking about "the colored situation" and tells how he came upon a wailing harmonica instrumental he calls "Railroad Blues." He first heard the piece, he tells Lomax, while walking past a barbershop in Oklahoma as a young black man played it. Guthrie describes the tune as "undoubtedly the lonesomest piece of music that I ever run into in my life." He asked the man where he learned it. "I just lay here and listen to the railroad whistle," the man explained, "and whatever it say, I say too." "He never did play the same piece no two days alike," Guthrie says of the man, "and he called them all 'Railroad Blues'!"

In the Dust Bowl migrations, Guthrie discovered his own version of the blues, one on which he'd play endless variations. As Southern and Great Plains states became unlivable because of drought and the Depression, California came to seem like the land of milk and honey to desperate farmers. In song after song—"Talking Dust Bowl Blues," "I Ain't Got No Home," "Will Rogers Highway"—Guthrie captures the hopelessness of the crop and bank failures, the rigors of the journey west, and the crushing disappointment that ensued when California offered a reality nearly as harsh as the land left behind.

Horrifying as the situation was, Guthrie was capable of perceiving the absurdities of it. In "Do-Re-Mi" he can barely suppress his chuckles as he advises westward-bound refugees that "California is a garden of Eden / A paradise to live in or to see / But believe it or not / You won't find it so hot / If you ain't got the do-re-mi." Such tough knowledge doesn't prevent him, however, from being obviously moved sometime later as he describes an old man hitching to California and refusing to believe that his hardships are not about to end.

Among its fourteen superb selections, *Dust Bowl Ballads* offers better-recorded versions of many of the songs on the *Library of Congress Recordings*, without the conversation. Because of the circumstances under which it was made, the three-record set, unlike *Dust Bowl Ballads,* is sonically subpar. Also, Guthrie occasionally makes false starts, hits bum notes, and goes out of tune in this one-take setting. Still, the substance and historical import of the *Library of Congress Recordings* by far outweigh its technical shortcomings. And, to emphasize a point that was made when Bruce Springsteen, U2, and Bob Dylan paid tribute to Guthrie on *Folkways: A Vision Shared* last year, the importance of Guthrie's music is not exclusively historical. The lessons his songs teach are essential in a time that has its own problems with homelessness, displaced workers, bank failures, and farm crises.

As usual, Woody said it best. "Wherever people ain't free / Wherever men are fightin' for their rights," he sings in "Tom Joad—Part 2," on *Dust Bowl Ballads,* "That's where I'm a-gonna be." That's as true now, more than twenty years after Woody Guthrie's death, as it ever was.

Rolling Stone May 4, 1989

Ice-T Fires:

Black Rage, Dope Beats

Home Invasion

Dead cops litter the nineteen tracks on *Home Invasion*—just in case you thought that in the wake of his split from Time Warner, Ice-T was backing down. Released on his own label and distributed by Priority Records, the album is a furious declaration of independence; as he says, "We always knew it was gonna come to this point sooner or later." The mood is frank, realistic, and uncompromising, born of the cold knowledge that as Run-D.M.C. put it years ago, "It's like that / And that's the way it is."

"I own my own label, put my own shit out," Ice raps on "It's On," *Home Invasion*'s first song, "so no one tells me what the fuck to talk about." "It's On" was a last-minute addition to *Home Invasion*. A commentary on Ice's grim, determined frame of mind after the "Cop Killer" debacle, it's one of the most arresting tracks he's ever recorded. Over an itchy guitar figure, an eerie keyboard sample, and relentless gunfire, Ice tears off staccato lines, insisting that "you're best to let me rap / Ice back on the streets? You don't want that / Cause I'll break ill / And you'll really have to body-count the cops I'll kill / It's *on*."

The voice of "It's On" is the voice of undeniable experience, and for all its topical immediacy and outrageous gang-banging, *Home Invasion* is a curiously mature work, the sort of album you could make only after fully establishing a successful, multifaceted career. Having penetrated deep into the white community, become a movie star, and ventured into thrash rock with his band Body Count, Ice-T is now making a back-to-basics roots move, issuing a call to "real motherfuckers" of whatever color. Its bass tracks cranked up far into the red zone, *Home Invasion* is made to boom out of Jeeps and blasters, to solidify Ice's street cred, to crush any doubters among the hard-core.

Prominent among Ice-T's targets are that noted defender of corporate morality Charlton Heston ("I might cut his head off") and rappers who cross over to pop. Reporters who criticize him are gleefully blown away—should journalists start harassing Priority's executives? And perhaps most significant of all, on "Watch the Ice Break," upstart rappers nipping at Ice-T's heels get a stern history lesson: "In case you forgot, I invented this gangsta shit / You wanna step to me, new jack? Walk / Come back in five LPS, then we can talk / You're just new, kid—you got a hit out / In interviews you talk a lot of shit out / You got paid, you really made out / You went broke when your one jam played out."

Beyond conventional rap boasting, Ice-T seems to understand that he has earned the right to look past the streets and take himself as his subject, which he does to chilling effect on "That's How I'm Livin'." A piano drones, a flute phrase drops, and a bone-dry percussion pattern beats hypnotically as Ice-T intones his life story in virtual spoken-word style. The tale is tense and affecting—"I speak on this with hesitation/Even though we're past the statute of limitations"—as introspective and personal a track as rap has ever seen.

Unfortunately, not everything on *Home Invasion* rises to this level—and at close to eighty minutes, it would have been astounding if the album had maintained that standard. On "Pimp Behind the Wheels," Ice-T takes over the turntables and passes the mike to his DJ, Evil E, for a track that's fun but inessential. Ice also gives over the nearly five minutes of "Funky Gribsta" to Grib, a fourteen-year-old female rapper; her caterwauling is unlistenable. And Brother Marquis from the 2 Live Crew shows up for the pointless, if guiltily pleasurable, bitch catalog "99 Problems."

Home Invasion goes out on a note of extreme strength, though. On "Message to the Soldier," an atmospheric midtempo track spiked by a jazzy saxophone sample, Ice-T kicks a first-rate definition of hard-core rap and its cultural meaning: "But rap hit the streets / Black rage amplified over dope beats / Now they wanna shut us down / And they don't fuck around / Check the history books, son / Black leaders die young / They tell us that our words are scary / They're revolutionary."

Ice-T knows that—to use his phrase—he's "trapped in a paradox." If he hadn't attracted a large audience among young whites, he would still be a Warner Brothers recording artist—even though his potential to pull that audience is what got him on the label in the first place. To his credit, he hasn't distanced himself from those fans—in fact, he's embraced them. *Home Invasion*'s title track describes this original gangsta's crime as stealing America's children, "so they know the noise you talk is lies."

As militant as *Home Invasion* is, as fully as it is the product of an artist under siege, it is still driven by an imagined ideal of racial harmony. Track after track—"Home Invasion," "Gotta Lotta Love," and, despite its title, "Racewar"—asserts that. It's a harmony in which people are judged not by their color but by their willingness to treat others with respect. That's the vision on which America claims to have been founded but that it never has come close to achieving. It's also what makes Time Warner's refusal to stand behind Ice-T so shameful and what makes his work so admirable and important.

Rolling Stone April 1, 1993

Flying Cowboys

Rickie Lee Jones

Flying Cowboys simultaneously bears the distinctive mark of Rickie Lee Jones's wild, unruly talent and continues the steady process by which her art is achieving a stunning, mature force. While it explores a wealth of themes and musical styles, the album unfolds with the ongoing grace of one long song. What provides unity to the album's varied elements is its seductive rhythmic flow, the down-home surrealism of Jones's lyrics, the clarity and intelligence of Walter Becker's production, and, of course, the sensual elasticity of Jones's extraordinary singing.

The album—Jones's first in five years—opens with the easygoing groove of "The Horses," a song addressed to a young girl, perhaps Jones's daughter, as well as to the young girl that Jones herself once was. Over simple, eloquent piano and percussion accompaniment, Jones begins the song as if it were a bedtime story—a story that evokes the twilight world between sleep and waking in which the willingness to believe and let go is all that separates a person from a realm filled with wonder. The song builds to a rolling chorus, and Jones assures the young girl: "We'll be riding on the horses, yeah / Way up in the sky, little darlin' / And if you fall I'll pick you up, pick you up."

In the song's concluding chorus, Jones wails with improvisatory fervor: "I was young myself not so long ago. . . . And when I was young, oh I was a wild, wild one." This acceptance of her past—and Jones has been a wild, wild one, indeed—at the same time that she assumes adult responsibilities toward the young girl makes for a human fullness that helps keep *Flying Cowboys* emotionally grounded even in its boldest flights.

"The Horses" also demonstrates the subtlety and appropriateness of Becker's production—and calms anyone who feared that the cofounder of Steely Dan might suffocate Jones's hipster looseness in icy musical perfectionism. No fewer than sixteen musicians play and sing on "The Horses," and the arrangement still seems open, comfortable, and endlessly inventive. Working in the same manner as the record's themes, Becker's settings provide Jones with enough structure to make her vocal pyrotechnics meaningful.

Jones again recollects the wild days of her youth in the title track, a

song that, like "The Horses," conjures up a vision of spiritual deliv- **205**
erance ("We come to the river / We'll walk away from all this now") from
a world that is "a desert." "Flying Cowboys" is also one of the four songs
on the album that Jones cowrote with her husband, Pascal Nabet-Meyer.
"Away From the Sky," a quiet meditation in which Jones's voice floats in
a melancholy atmosphere created by two guitars and two synthesizers,
and "Atlas' Marker," a jazzy number on which Randy Brecker plays
trumpet, end the album on a note of yearning for a place that's "somewhere better than the world where we live."

But not all of *Flying Cowboys*, whose very title is a fusion of the ethereal
and the earthy, is so deeply suffused with a desire for transcendence. The
lazy, soulful saunter of "Just My Baby"—underscored by the fetching
slur of Jones's vocal—suggests that physical attraction ("My heart's just
flying when he walks by") is itself a kind of ideal.

The encouragement offered in "The Horses" finds more straightforward expression in Jones's stirring cover of Gerry and the Pacemakers'
"Don't Let the Sun Catch You Crying," while "Satellites," with its Sixties-
pop choruses, imagines two lovers "born forever . . . twinned in a fugi-
tive mind." Two reggae-inflected tunes—"Ghetto of My Mind," a jaunty
street anthem in the manner of Jones's songs from a decade ago, and
"Love Is Gonna Bring Us Back Alive," which foregrounds Jones's belief
in the restorative powers of love—rock with a sunny exuberance. In fact,
the album's only false note is the self-consciously eerie "Ghost Train,"
which revives the myth of the down-bound mystery train in a film noir
setting to no particular effect.

Since her superb 1979 debut album, *Rickie Lee Jones*, and her powerful
1981 follow-up, *Pirates*, Jones has failed to meet her early promise,
though she has never failed so totally as to call that promise into question. Now, with *Flying Cowboys*, she is back at the very height of her
considerable powers, having crafted a record that makes an indelible
impression on first listen and retains its ability to startle long after that.
For fans who have hoped for just such an album from Jones, *Flying
Cowboys* is her much welcome, long-awaited wild gift.

Rolling Stone November 2, 1989

One from the Heartland

John Cougar Mellencamp's

Scarecrow

"*Life sweeps away the dreams* that we have planned," sings John Cougar Mellencamp on *Scarecrow,* but this powerful, ambitious LP is ultimately about people, ideals, and relationships that fight life's sweep and proudly endure. Like Bruce Springsteen, Tom Petty, and John Fogerty, Mellencamp has taken one weave of the American tapestry—in this case, the farming communities and small towns of the Midwest—as the theme for his album, and as a means of exploring the national jitters underlying the new jingoism abroad and self-serving self-reliance on the domestic front. As on 1983's *Uh-huh*—Mellencamp's breakthrough to seriousness—it's still the simple man, baby, who pays the bills, but *Scarecrow* takes greater care to acknowledge the dignity those men and women achieve through the suffering they undergo.

Scarecrow finds its focus quickly in the opening track, "Rain on the Scarecrow," which evokes Dylan's harrowing "Ballad of Hollis Brown" and details the plight of America's farmers—a problem Mellencamp addressed in more than song with the Farm Aid benefit he helped organize. An ominous, insistent guitar intro sets the stage for Mellencamp's intent vocal and grim, folkloric imagery, delineating a wasted land:

Scarecrow on a wooden cross, blackbird in the barn / Four hundred empty acres that used to be my farm
I grew up like my daddy did, my grandpa cleared this land / When I was five I walked the fence while grandpa held my hand
Rain on the scarecrow, blood on the plow / This land fed a nation, this land made me proud
And son I'm just sorry there's no legacy for you now / Rain on the scarecrow, blood on the plow.

The spirit-chilling visual force of this tune, which Mellencamp wrote with long-standing collaborator George Green, turns out to be quite consciously intended. " 'Scarecrow' is probably one of the more cinematic songs that we did on the record, as far as really trying to create a picture, a moving picture, especially," says Don Gehman, Mellencamp's co-producer since the 1982 multiplatinum *American Fool* LP. "The arrangement was brought in pretty much as it stands on the record, and the idea we were trying to get across was something very stark, very rural." Gehman describes his studio work with Mellencamp as the attempt to create "sonic pictures" of the songwriter's ideas, and Mellencamp's own conversation about his record is littered with references to films.

"You ever see that movie *Hud*?" Mellencamp asks, in trying to describe his growth from the cynical, if endearing, chip-on-the-shoulder buffoon who once titled an album, *Nothin' Matters, And What if It Did* to the committed, socially engaged grown-up of *Scarecrow* and *Uh-huh*. "The old man is talking to Hud about his principles—Hud has just taken his brother's son out and got him drunk. The old man's talking to Hud, and he says, 'You know, you have a way of being nice and cordial and'—I'm trying to paraphrase this so it makes sense—'it makes you seem glamorous to younger people. But slowly and surely, this nation changes by the men that we admire, and men like you, who are unprincipled, are not fit to live with.'"

To make himself "fit to live with" and more than a glamorous rube rock star fit to be idolized by people who don't know any better, Mellencamp has made "generations changing hands" a virtual obsession on *Scarecrow*. This concern informs "Rain on the Scarecrow"; the self-conscious nostalgia of "Grandma's Theme," sung by Mellencamp's own grandmother; the gentle, rootsy boosterism of "Small Town"; the stalking social dislocation of "The Face of the Nation"; and the guitar-powered, though heavy-handed political allegory of "Justice and Independence '85."

In strongest expression, however, is "Minutes to Memories," the other tune on *Scarecrow* cowritten by George Green. A lonely, lyrical guitar figure sets the song's mood, as Mellencamp unwinds the tale of a young man's meeting on a Greyhound bus with a seventy-seven-year-old former steel worker. The old man conveys his life's wisdom in the workaday poetry of the song's surging chorus: "Days turn to minutes, and minutes to memories / Life sweeps away the dreams that we have planned / You are young and you are the future / So suck it up and tough it out, and be the best you can." The story assumes an added, moving resonance when its last verse makes clear that the "young man" on the bus ride is now himself a parent, remembering the old man's unheeded advice ("I do things my way and I pay a high price," he wearily admits) and passing it along to his own son. The point of the song—and of the entire album, really—is that the process of looking out for the people who come after you is itself a kind of sentimental wisdom; the affection in the exchange is remembered from generation to generation even when the good advice, however heartbreakingly, is ignored. Each person matures into a simultaneous recognition of loss and connection.

Scarecrow was recorded in a new studio Mellencamp built in Belmont, Indiana, a short distance from his home in Bloomington. Although Gehman unironically states that "John's got a terrific eye for decor," he goes on to say that "the concept for the whole studio was definitely simplicity. . . . The shack that we put together for the *Uh-huh* record was such a shack. It was about as sloppy as you could do anything. I mean, it was clean, but it was definitely making a record in a construction site. We wanted to take all the elements that we had gotten sonically out of that environment and make them look good. Also, the control room that we had for the *Uh-huh* record was a kitchen, and it was less than ideal to listen in, as to whether you were getting the real thing out the door."

Before going in to record *Scarecrow,* Mellencamp gave his band a list of ninety-five classic rock songs to learn, according to Gehman, the idea being "to learn all these devices from the past, and then use them in a new way with John's arrangements." With that groundwork laid, the band then worked up the new songs Mellencamp had written, and he taped the instrumental arrangements refined in rehearsal and played them for Gehman, singing the vocals as his co-producer listened and absorbed. Gehman continues, "Then he'll say, 'I want this to be like an Animals record. And I've also got these ideas, I think we oughta have percussion in these sections that's really featured, and maybe in this breakdown over here, the drums have gotta sound absolutely monstrous. And I want the overall record to have this kind of a tone, like maybe it was a modern-day Dylan record.' "

In this sense, the cross-generational message of *Scarecrow*'s lyrics gets reinforced in its music, which is an upscale take on Sixties grunge rockers like the Stones, the Animals, and even the Troggs (who are hilariously quoted in the album's closing rouser, "R.O.C.K. in the U.S.A."), with some folkish earnestness thrown in for good measure.

The insistent Sixties ambience of *Scarecrow* reflects something more than a sound, however. "I was really, really, *really* gung-ho in the Sixties," Mellencamp recalls. "I really thought the war was gonna end, we were gonna change the world. You know, I was seventeen years old and I bought the whole thing hook, line and sinker. And then what a thing to turn twenty-one and realize, huh, this is a bunch of commercial *junk*, life is commercial junk, this whole *world* is run on commercial junk, you know, souped-up expense accounts and all that kind of stuff. And I was really disillusioned throughout my entire twenties. I said things in the press like, 'Ideals are for teenagers.' It sounds fucked, but at that point in time that's what I thought. I thought, man, there's no *place* for ideals in this world, you know, ideals'll turn around and bite off your face. Then I got a little bit older and, about a year or two ago, I started thinkin', yeah, John, you can go ahead and just hate everything forever if you want to, but you're not a very happy person because of it. You gotta start tryin', and reevaluate your outlook on everything. I know this is a strong statement, but I really did, like, *hate* everything."

As Mellencamp's hatred, which encompassed himself as well as "everything," softened into a generous social vision, he also opened up the personal dimension in his writing. As a tender balance to the larger, public issues it explores, *Scarecrow* takes a giving view of two estranged lovers holding onto what they can in the hit single "Lonely Ol' Night," the vagaries of personal contentment in "Between a Laugh and a Tear" (where Mellencamp is backed on vocals by Rickie Lee Jones), and the sturdy hopes of a likeable loser in the rocking "Rumbleseat." "I know there's a balance, I see it when I swing past," Mellencamp and Jones croon affectingly on "Between a Laugh and a Tear," and the distance he's traveled since the "hang on to sixteen for as long as you can" ethic of "Jack and Diane" is nowhere clearer.

"I realized that there were people out there who were really listening to what I was saying," Mellencamp states. "At first I didn't want that responsibility, and it was, like, 'Hey, you're making a mistake.' But there was not really any way I could run away from it. So, like the old man said to Hud . . .

"I had a song called 'Jack and Diane' once," he goes on, "and I had a real silly line, it said, 'Oh, yeah, life goes on, long after the thrill of livin' is gone.' And I was *amazed* at how many letters . . . and people just walked up to me, and said, you know, my dad just died, or my grandfather just died, or I'm sick, or I'm real depressed and that line really made a difference to me. And when I *wrote* that line, it was like, *phht,* that was kinda cute. That was like all of the commitment that I had put into the thing. But this record, it was a little different story. Look, what it boils down to is I can't *believe* a lot of the songs I used to write. But, it was like, well, if I'm gonna live with these things, I'm gonna have to at least try to write stuff on this record that I *can* live with, as opposed to hiding from two years later."

This willingness to stretch and test himself is finally most impressive in Mellencamp because of the effort it required to defeat the powerful forces within him—and within the culture at large—encouraging him to remain a dismissible American fool from the boondocks. Instead, with *Scarecrow,* he sounds a warning from the heartland—as serious, broadminded, compassionate, and enduring as the people whose lives he's given voice to, and taken so totally to heart.

Record November 1985

Life After Death

The Notorious B.I.G.

In *a frightening way,* the current hip-hop scene recalls the end of *Good-Fellas:* The major players are turning up dead, heading off to prison, or lying low, waiting for the smoke to clear. As for what brought things to this horrific pass, those who know don't speak, and those who speak don't know. Everybody who cares about the music is exhausted and confused. Is it greed? Jealousy? A turf war? An urge to self-destruct? One thing, of course, hasn't changed: It ain't white folks dying. Meanwhile, in a cultural situation that is essentially unprecedented, young African American artists are being killed, and seemingly nothing—not their fame, their money, their bodyguards, their own willingness to shoot—can protect them.

Into this epidemic of violence comes the double CD *Life After Death.* The album is riddled with chilling ironies in the wake of the recent murder of its creator, the Brooklyn, New York, rapper Notorious B.I.G. (a.k.a. Biggie Smalls) in Los Angeles. On the cover, Biggie stands solemnly next to a hearse; the hottest track is titled, with a nod to L.L. Cool J, "Going Back to Cali" and lifts its Zapp-derived vocoder sound from "California Love," the ferocious single by Biggie's slain left coast rival, Tupac Shakur; the last song, unbelievably, is called "You're Nobody (Til Somebody Kills You)," a wry acknowledgment that at least in the rap (and rock) world, larger-than-life figures become larger still in violent death.

But Biggie was somebody while he was still alive, and the ambitious *Life After Death*—a worthy and more mature, if less uniformly spectacular, successor to his 1994 debut, *Ready to Die*—demonstrates why. Like virtually all double albums—whether by Guns n' Roses, Bruce Springsteen, the Smashing Pumpkins, or 2 Pac—this one probably would have been more aesthetically satisfying as a carefully shaped single CD. But there's considerable pleasure and fun to be had when an artist feels free to stretch out and try anything, and those pleasures are available in abundance on *Life After Death.*

Like, for example, the coolly disorienting New Age keyboard sample that underlies the off-kilter time signature and rapid-fire rhymes of

"Notorious Thugs," on which Biggie is joined by Layzie, Krayzie, and Bizzy Bone of Bone Thugs-n-Harmony. Other guests also excel. The lubricious Lil' Kim more than holds her own, so to speak, in a funny he said/she said matchup with Biggie on "Another." And R. Kelly continues his dismantling of the ultraromantic loveman ballad on "#!*@ You Tonight," with its immortal opening lines: "You must be used to me spendin' / And all that sweet winin' and dinin' / But I'm fuckin' you tonight."

It can be no surprise, though, that the real stars of *Life After Death* are the Notorious B.I.G. himself—whose flow can seem both declamatory and sensually deft—and his producer, Sean "Puffy" Combs, the man who for all too many reasons is now sitting at ground zero of the hip-hop nation. Together they constructed a sprawling, cinematic saga of the thug life, a conscious continuation of *Ready to Die*. *Life After Death* captures crime's undeniable glamour ("I Love the Dough," "Sky's the Limit") but doesn't stint on the fear ("Last Day"), desperation ("Niggas Bleed"), and irretrievable loss ("Miss U") that the streets inevitably exact.

"I don't wanna die / God, tell me why," Combs whispers in the background of the chorus on the death-haunted "You're Nobody (Til Somebody Kills You)." It's a simple prayer, and its emotional directness undercuts—and reveals the terror underlying—much of the mack posturing that precedes it. Those lines resonate eerily after the album concludes, and the listener returns to the real world to wonder when all this will end. Or when the shots will ring out again.

Rolling Stone May 1, 1997

Graham Parker Squeezes New Sparks

The Mona Lisa's Sister

he Mona Lisa's Sister, Graham Parker's most compelling record in nearly a decade, is a raw meditation on desire and disappointment from a man who has felt—and *feels*—with a fierce intensity. In song after song, Parker examines how media images conspire with our own fantasies to create insatiable needs—and to drain satisfaction from any pleasure that is merely human scale. The wonderful paradox is that even as Parker has fashioned an album whose tough resignation is a razor's edge removed from despair, he finally manages to meet the torturous standard of his own ambitions.

By now, everyone who cares knows how Graham Parker and his backing band, the Rumour, became critics' darlings in 1976 by blending R&B soulfulness and punk insurgency on their first two albums, *Howlin' Wind* and *Heat Treatment.* As Parker got mired in battles with his record company—"I'm the best-kept secret in the West," he later complained on the aptly titled "Mercury Poisoning"—Elvis Costello outflanked him and quickly assumed the role Parker had vacated, that of the pun-loving angry young man.

When the powerful 1979 album *Squeezing Out Sparks* failed to win him the audience he deserved, Parker sank into creative confusion. The albums kept coming—*The Up Escalator* (1980) and, after the Rumour split up, *Another Grey Area* (1982), *The Real Macaw* (1983), and *Steady Nerves* (1985)—but no combination of producer and players seemed able to unlock Parker's heart.

Consequently, *The Mona Lisa's Sister* had all the fervency of a last-ditch effort. It is a record that, like John Lennon's *Plastic Ono Band,* Bob Dylan's *Blood on the Tracks,* and Bruce Springsteen's *Tunnel of Love,* is driven by a purpose that is as much personal as it is artistic. Clearly, Parker is out to prove something to himself as well as to say something to the world.

To ensure that he'd stand or fall on his own efforts, Parker seized control of all aspects of *The Mona Lisa's Sister.* He coproduced the album with Brinsley Schwarz, one of the Rumour's original guitarists; Andrew Bodnar, also from the Rumour, plays bass. When Atlantic, Parker's label, began to suggest changes, Parker bolted to RCA and made the company promise to release the album his way.

That was quite a demand. Unlike Parker's recent albums, this record is stripped to the bone, and the lack of fussiness underscores its serious intent. Parker's acoustic guitar provides the primary instrumentation, giving the record a folkie, intimate feel. Schwarz on electric guitar, Bodnar on bass, James Hallawell on keyboards, and Terry Williams on drums play virtually all the rest of the music, and they perform with a sensitivity to nuance and a respect for Parker's songs indicative of a band, not a gathering of studio professionals.

Parker's furious struggle with self-doubt provides the drama at the heart of *The Mona Lisa's Sister.* The opening track, "Don't Let It Break You Down," starts out sweetly as a message of encouragement in the face of the world's "everyday evil." But when Parker tears into his critics ("They have the nerve to / Rip up a man's life / In a paragraph or two"), bemoans the elusiveness of success ("You'll see a winning post / In the distance / That you'll never reach"), and brays the song's title with gathering urgency, he could be singing into a mirror. The anger he summons on that track finds expression again on the simmering single "Get Started Start a Fire," where he tells the tale of three victims, including Marilyn Monroe, and recommends the purifying power of revenge over passive suffering.

The ballad "I'm Just Your Man"—a lovely call for levelheaded romance—is haunted by a touching sense of regret. Even as Parker tells his lover, "I'm not a page in history. . . . I'm not a hero. . . . I'm not a burning comet that / Fell out of the sky," his very insistence on being seen in human terms is partly fueled by his own disappointed aspirations to greatness. For his lover to see him as more than what he is would stir ambitions that have been uncomfortably laid to rest—and that might prove too painful to arouse. In a strange way, the song is as much an apology as it is an eloquently direct declaration of love.

Given this rich emotional density—in which love, identity, and achievement are inextricably bound, and sometimes indistinguishable—it's fitting that the album's most gripping moment is a song titled simply "Success." The tune begins quietly, with Parker intoning the opening verse: "The dreams and hopes of men / Are powered by addiction / And who am I to say that / This is an affliction / When everybody gets /

Of success."

The bitterness heightens as Parker chants the song's title over and over, frequently pronouncing it "*suck*-cess," his voice seething with a lacerating contempt. But at times the repetition edges close to invocation, as Parker's dashed hopes lace his vocal with an unmistakable longing for the rush success inevitably brings to those who, like him, are addicted to it.

"Success" is followed by "I Don't Know," where a Buddy Holly lilt and catchy "dum-dum-da-dum-dum" background vocals counterpoint lyrics that abandon the possibility of self-knowledge. "I don't know why it's not enough / To feel moments of mighty love," Parker sings. "I can't know why my heart is chilled." The song's effect is a kind of stunned cheerfulness.

Yet after such staggering journeys through a jungle of contradictory emotions, Parker ends the album on a surprising note. Despite the insufficiency of those "moments of mighty love," Parker hauls out Sam Cooke's "Cupid" for the closer—as unambivalent a prayer for undying romantic love as American vernacular music has produced. Parker's rigorously faithful, deeply felt reading of the song is not ironic in the least- and it suggests the necessity of maintaining ideals, however troubling and difficult that might prove to be.

That sentiment echoes "Fool's Gold," *Heat Treatment*'s closing number, which Parker alludes to on this record when he sings, "There must be gold where fools are," in "Blue Highways." In the earlier song, Parker passionately vowed to "keep on searching for that fool's gold"—vehement conviction in quest of ambiguous goals being about as characteristic a Graham Parker stance as you could imagine. But on *The Mona Lisa's Sister*, Parker, like an alchemist, has transformed his fool's gold into the quintessential real thing—and fully justified his search.

Rolling Stone May 19, 1988

Songs for a Blue Guitar

Red House Painters

Covers of **Paul McCartney's** "Silly Love Songs" and Yes' "Long Distance Runaround"; a title that nods to the poet Wallace Stevens; a chord progression nicked from Led Zeppelin's "Bron-Yr-Aur"; lyrics that coolly recall, "I felt nervous when you shook and cried"—you know, some albums just don't lend themselves to casual summary.

But then Red House Painters have never been easy to categorize. On *Songs for a Blue Guitar,* the Painters' singer and guitarist, Mark Kozelek, embellishes his typical graveyard folk with a Buddy Holly-ish rocker ("I Feel the Rain Fall"), a female-harmony vocal ("Song for a Blue Guitar"), and storms of Neil Young-style guitar distortion ("Make Like Paper"). The effect is freshening, at once looser, more varied, and more textured than the band has often sounded in the past.

Have no fear, however. Kozelek continues to view the world through a dark glass, documenting the descent of love into loss with unsettling detachment, as if emotion were something that could only be imagined, not felt. The singsong melody and childlike strumming of the album's concluding track, "Another Song for a Blue Guitar," reinforce that chilling distance: "And the one thing that I found / As I gazed at the sea / Was that she lost all hope / All hope in me." Finally, only Kozelek could transform McCartney's breezy query "How can I tell you about my loved one?" into an anguished statement about the impossibility of one person conveying his feelings to another.

Still looking for a quick summary? Aptly, Wallace Stevens best evokes the impact of these songs in his 1937 poem "The Man With the Blue Guitar": "The blue guitar / After long strumming on certain nights / Gives the touch of the senses, not of the hand / But the very senses as they touch / The wind-gloss." Exactly.

Rolling Stone August 22, 1996

Their Way: Frank Sinatra and Johnny Cash

Sinatra and Sextet: Live in Paris, Frank Sinatra, and

American Recordings, Johnny Cash

Testosterone, alas, has seen better days. Male rock stars appear in magazines wearing dresses, advertise themselves as losers. Shoegazers trip over mope rockers in their effort to flee reality's bite. Inarticulate fury substitutes for focused masculine force. Grrrls get to riot; boys—apart, of course, from gangsta rappers, bless them—whine about their confusion, especially over (sigh) success.

Frank Sinatra and Johnny Cash stand to remind us that such was not always the case. In his best singing—which is to say, the best popular singing America has produced in this century—Sinatra epitomizes an urban ideal of manly sophistication. Poised and assured, he inhabits songs of immense complexity, remaining alert to their formal structure while gracefully intuiting the demands of the emotional moment.

Sinatra was not born to such a polished manner. He is the son of immigrants and sensed a route out of his narrow world in the style of his perceived social "betters." Cole Porter, he seemed to believe, would lead him out of Hoboken. That made for contradictions. Throughout his career, Sinatra has never been fully able to conceal the ingratiating working-class kid ("everybody's 'Pal Joey,' the King of Ring-a-ding-ding," as James Isaacs puts it in his superb liner notes to Live in Paris) who lurks within the supreme mastery of his art.

Cash is cut from a deeper and perhaps darker source in the American grain. The son of an Arkansas sharecropping family, he is an unapologetic loner, the fabled man in black, battling for his soul against demons both outside and within him. He has rambled through a lifetime of grimly indulgent Saturday nights, driven to further excesses by the ravaging moral glare of Sunday morning coming down.

Cash is Southern, so his strength lies in a polite reserve that masks an implacable will. A hardscrabble life taught him early on to do without and not complain, so he has made the absolute most of the very least—specifically, he has made a rumbling baritone voice with nonexistent range and a limited guitar technique expressive of a dignified worldview.

If aspiration excited Sinatra's genius, it has injured Cash's. When Cash has tried to modernize, to sweeten his sound—or, worse, to embrace an image of himself as a churchgoin', crowd-pleasin', aw-shucks family man—he has betrayed his art.

Two new albums capture each of these complicated men near their peaks. *Sinatra and Sextet: Live in Paris,* recorded in 1962 and now released for the first time, offers the finest available glimpse of the singer onstage: easy, affable, and in command. The instinctively tasteful six-piece combo supporting him—distinguished particularly by pianist Bill Miller and guitarist Al Viola—may well prove more congenial to contemporary ears than the orchestras that typically back him. And as for the Voice, well, what need be said? It's Sinatra, at forty-six, exploring the mature phase of his extraordinary power. Teen idol Frankie's angelic yearning had long been left behind, replaced by a more knowing, if equally rapturous, vision of adult romance. "Love is lovelier the second time around," he sings, and in this set consisting almost exclusively of love songs, he makes a moving case.

As does every live album, *Live in Paris* exchanges the aural perfection of the singer's classic studio performances for the immediate rush of the creative instant. It's fascinating, from that vantage, to hear Sinatra race through a jumpy 1:11 rendition of Johnny Mercer's "Goody, Goody" as a kind of warm-up before settling into more measured takes on "Imagination" and "At Long Last Love" and then a transporting "Moonlight in Vermont."

Given a microphone to speak into, however, Sinatra can always be counted on to embarrass himself. He follows a spellbinding "Ol' Man River" with an asinine comment that the song is about "Sammy Davis's people" and interrupts a gently swinging "They Can't Take That Away From Me" to complain that the onion soup he ate before the show is repeating on him.

The concert's spectacular defining turn comes in a duet with pianist Miller on Johnny Mercer and Harold Arlen's "One for My Baby." After a stupefying introduction (*"cherchez la femme,* which means in French 'Why doncha share da broad wit' me?' "), Sinatra delivers the song—long one of his signatures—as if he'd never sung it before in his life.

Miller's playing is astute and conversational, commenting on, responding to, highlighting phrases of, and even, at times, seeming to chuckle sympathetically at the singer's unfolding tale of loneliness and vanished love. "I could tell you a lot / But that's not in a gentleman's code," Sinatra sings, but by the time he warns that "this torch that I've found / It's gotta be drowned / Or it's gonna explode," the depth of the singer's pain—and his potential for violence, self-directed or otherwise—is palpable. Sinatra ends the tune with a haunted look down the "very, very long" road home, and this stunning remembrance of things past is complete.

If anything, Johnny Cash's *American Recordings* is an even more crowning achievement than *Live in Paris*, due in large part to the album's producer (and American Recordings owner) Rick Rubin. Rubin's résumé as producer of groundbreaking records by Run-D.M.C., the Beastie Boys, the Black Crowes, the Red Hot Chili Peppers, and Mick Jagger is stellar, and Cash can now be added to that list.

A noted (and somewhat self-conscious) firebrand, Rubin not only had the intelligence to sign Cash, who is now sixty-two, to his label of hormone addled upstarts, but he knew exactly the sort of album Cash needed to make. *American Recordings* is that album in spades: Cash, alone with an acoustic guitar, confronting traditional folk songs, his own tunes, and songs by the likes of Leonard Cohen, Glenn Danzig, and Tom Waits with biblical intensity. "Recorded in Rick's living room and at Johnny Cash's cabin," the credit reads (with two tracks recorded live last year at the Viper Room in Los Angeles). In those small spaces, Cash and Rubin got it all: *American Recordings* is at once monumental and viscerally intimate, fiercely true to the legend of Johnny Cash and entirely contemporary.

American Recordings is no joy ride, though. The album carves a brutal trail, marked by curses of fate (Glenn Danzig's "Thirteen"), unforgiving self-examination (Nick Lowe's "The Beast in Me," Leonard Cohen's "Bird on a Wire"), love wars ("Dehlia's Gone"), political wars ("Drive On"), and desperate bids for spiritual salvation (Kris Kristofferson's "Why Me, Lord" and Cash's own "Redemption" and "Like a Soldier"). In Rubin's ruthlessly unadorned, dry-as-dust settings, Cash moves with stoic fury. His voice is the best it has sounded in more than thirty years (think "I Walk the Line," think "Ring of Fire"), and he sings with a control reminiscent of Hemingway's writing: Not a feeling is flaunted, not a jot of sentimentality is permitted, but every quaver, every hesitation, every shift in volume, every catch in a line resonates like a private apocalypse.

The intermittent charm of *Duets* notwithstanding, Sinatra's magnificent career is over. *Sinatra and Sextet: Live in Paris* is a souvenir from his days of radiance, when the world knew no greater singer. Sixteen years younger than Sinatra, Cash has made what is unquestionably one of his best albums. *American Recordings* will earn him a time of well-deserved distinction in which his work will reach an eager new audience. But as different as their places are now—and as different as their lives have been—Sinatra and Cash are brothers, blood on blood. Proud, independent, unreconstructed, these two men did it their way.

Rolling Stone May 19, 1994

The Dream Fades

Bruce Springsteen's Born in the U.S.A.

An *original product* of counterculture aspiration and a boom economy that proffered better times for workers, Bruce Springsteen has watched two hopes wither and die in the last decade. Since *Greetings From Asbury Park* he has chronicled the translation of a dream into a memory; the "glory days" that once seemed to glisten before us are now a dimly recollected image of unfulfilled desire. *Born in the U.S.A.* finds the Springsteen pantheon of virtues—work, strive, endure, remember— still revered. What has disappeared is the promised land he once believed those virtues could earn.

Over pile-driving snare slams and a mournful, majestic synth theme that would do Aaron Copland proud, Springsteen wails about being "Born in a dead man's town" in the opening line of this LP's first (and title) track. "Born in the U.S.A." hits all the stops along the lost highway of the American death trip: Vietnam, unemployment, imprisonment, class oppression, alienation, the fading of the dream. "Nowhere to run, ain't got nowhere to go," this number's "cool rocking daddy in the U.S.A." concludes, despair becoming more bearable when you quote Martha and the Vandellas to evoke it.

Through the eleven years of his career, Springsteen's American landscape has darkened so much that it's hard not to see the flag he faces on *Born in the U.S.A.*'s cover as an immovable, unscalable wall. Earlier Springsteen anthems like "Born to Run" and "Badlands" depicted the culturally enforced dead-ends of working-class life as the everyday setting for epic heroism. People could shape their souls in the rise against social adversity, and redemption was an engine rev or a power chord away.

But the economically blasted family "talking about getting out / Packing up our bags, maybe heading south" in this album's last song, "My Hometown," has no vision of gas-powered paradise to fuel its hopes, no rock & roll manifest destiny to achieve. These folks are leaving a grim hometown past for a Sunbelt future that's both alien and uncertain.

Even the hell-raising rockers on *Born in the U.S.A.* are squeezed by the grip of their characters' circumstances. The "Cadillac Ranch"-styled guitar romp, "Darlington County," with its rollicking "sha la la" chorus, climaxes with the image of the narrator's buddy "handcuffed to the bumper of a state trooper's Ford." The love-hungry hero of the Buddy Holly-ish raver "Working on the Highway" ends up "swinging on the Charlotte County road gang." The raunchy, jaunty hand-clapped choruses of "I'm Goin' Down" endlessly reprise that song's title in an obsessive litany of decline.

More personally, "No Surrender" and "Bobbie Jean" on *Born in the U.S.A.*'s second side seem Springsteen's two-part tribute to departed E Street Band guitarist, Steve Van Zandt. Two young groovers swear a rock-based bond of blood-brotherhood in "No Surrender," but "young faces grow sad and old / And hearts of fire grow cold." The song ends with Springsteen echoing Dylan and offering a complementary vision to Van Zandt's new-found political fervor: "There's a war outside still raging / You say it ain't ours anymore to win / I want to sleep beneath peaceful skies in my lover's bed / With a wide open country in my eyes / And these romantic dreams in my head." In "Bobbie-Jean" the farewell is even more direct and plain-spoken: "Maybe you'll be out there on that road somewhere. . . . In some motel room there'll be a radio playing and you'll hear me sing this song / . . . You'll know I'm thinking of you."

Especially for a disc that credits four board men (Springsteen, Van Zandt, Jon Landau, and Chuck Plotkin), *Born in the U.S.A.* is a consistent, controlled, focused production that ably renders the full range of Springsteen's reach—from folky spareness to full-blown street orchestra romanticism. Musically, the more ambitious numbers on the album update Springsteen's sound without damaging its signature qualities. Pianist Roy Bittan's synthesizer parts are fully worked into the arrangements, avoiding both trendiness and excess. Drummer Max Weinberg is foregrounded in the virtual dance mixes of the LP's rock-outs, but a softer cut like "I'm On Fire" features him ticking out a stark and steady clockwork rhythm. Saxman Clarence Clemons tears off his patented screeching solos, but also takes a mellower turn in his sweet closing break to "Dancing in the Dark," reminiscent of Sonny Rollins's lovely fade-out on the Stones' "Waiting on a Friend."

But despite its musical heart and studio-craft, *Born in the U.S.A.*'s ultimate power resides in Springsteen's tough, cramped social vision. If

Woody Guthrie was the Dust Bowl laureate, Springsteen has emerged as the brave voice of workers in modern America's sunset industries. Many rock performers have spoken for one subculture or another, but none has ever defined the works and days of an entire class as their subject. Until now.

Record August, 1984

New Bruce: Lose Your Illusions

Human Touch and *Lucky Town*

With his two new albums —his first in nearly five years and first as a declared solo artist—Bruce Springsteen completes an emotional triptych begun in 1987 with *Tunnel of Love*. On that album, "Tougher Than the Rest" articulates the early Springsteen code on love: Commitment is a triumph of the will. You make a vow, you keep it. But at the center of that album stand three songs—"Tunnel of Love," "Two Faces," and "Brilliant Disguise"—that suggest the virtual impossibility of knowing yourself well enough (let alone another person) to make any vow meaningful forever. To enter the tunnel of love is to take a night journey on which the definitions of your identity dissolve and you encounter aspects of yourself that seem profoundly foreign and disturbing. In short, *Tunnel of Love* is a study of deception—and more chillingly, self-deception—in matters of the heart.

Human Touch (begun in 1989, completed in early 1991) and *Lucky Town* (recorded in a two-month burst shortly after *Human Touch*) describe the effort of building a realistic life after the code has been shattered, in Springsteen's case by an affair and a divorce. Intriguing companion pieces, they're *Lose Your Illusion I* and *II*.

Beginning with the pulsing title track, which stands among Springsteen's best work, the fourteen songs on *Human Touch* explore the movement from disenchanted isolation to a willingness to risk love and its attendant traumas again. At first the moves are tentative, motivated more by loneliness—a need for "a little of that human touch"—than by love's golden promise or, even more remote, the prospect of actual lasting happiness with another human being. Also, as the bluesy "Cross My Heart" makes clear, the certainties of the past ("Once you cross your heart / You ain't ever supposed to lie") are starting to be replaced by a more shaded outlook: "Well you may think the world's black and white / And you're dirty or you're clean / You better watch out you don't slip / Through them spaces in between."

Aptly, the introspective, self-questioning mood of *Human Touch* shifts near its midpoint with "Roll of the Dice," the most generic-sounding Springsteen rocker—glockenspiel and all—on either of these albums.

With renewed energy, even optimism, the singer accepts the emotional dangers of love and his own failings ("I'm a thief in the house of love / And I can't be trusted"), stops fretting, and determines to get on with living. The superb "Real World" then offers an inspiringly lucid vision of a love that can sidestep fantasy to take a dignified place in "the real world," and the slamming "All or Nothin' at All," graced by a soaring, catchy chorus, insists on commitment rather than flees it.

After that, however, both "Man's Job" and "Real Man" flirt perilously with soft, contemporary clichés about masculinity ("If I can find the guts to give you all my love / Then I'll be feelin' like a real man"). Fortunately, Springsteen stops short of songs about his inner child or flagging self-esteem. The slick, annoyingly seductive keyboard riff of "Real Man" also ventures closer to Phil Collins territory than anything Springsteen has done before. More positively, "Pony Boy," a traditional tune performed acoustically by Springsteen on guitar and harmonica, with his wife, Patti Scialfa, providing harmony, closes *Human Touch* on a tender, disarming note.

The childlike charm of "Pony Boy" provides an effective, understated transition to *Lucky Town,* on which Springsteen examines his life as a family man, negotiates a truce with his demons, and achieves a hard-won sense of fulfillment. Dedicated to Scialfa and the couple's two children, the album's ten songs paint a convincing—and only rarely cloying—portrait of domestic life and its contents. The rousing opener, "Better Days," ably sets the tone; it's a bracing antinostalgia blast that asserts: "These are better days baby / Better days with a girl like you." The song also takes on with impressive candor the Springsteen myth ("It's a sad funny ending to find yourself pretending / A rich man in a poor man's shirt") and the immeasurable degree of his material comfort ("A life of leisure and a pirate's treasure / Don't make much for tragedy").

With characteristic sure-footedness, however, Springsteen does not permit heartfelt satisfaction to slip into self-satisfaction. If "Leap of Faith," "If I Should Fall Behind," "Living Proof," and "Book of Dreams" all convey a nearly swooning appreciation of the pleasures that a settled home life affords, "The Big Muddy," "Souls of the Departed," and "My Beautiful Reward" intimate that, for Springsteen at least, the attainment of love is inextricable from the fear of its loss. A brooding blues evocatively colored by Springsteen's acoustic slide guitar, "The Big Muddy" takes a knowing look at infidelity, greed, and moral compromise, concluding, "There ain't no one leavin' this world buddy / Without their shirttail dirty / Or their hands bloody." The churning, guitar-driven "Souls of the Departed" depicts the singer, one of "the self-made men" in the Hollywood Hills, under siege as violence rages in the Middle East and, closer by, in East Compton. The death of a child in a barrio shooting causes him to wonder, in an aching drawl, "Tonight as I tuck my own son in bed / All I can think of is what if it would've been him instead."

"My Beautiful Reward," an elegant, folkish ballad, ends *Lucky Town* on an almost surreally unsettled note. The calm, gentle music belies dreamlike imagery of falling, wandering, and abandonment. The striking verse that closes the song and the album—"Tonight I can feel the cold wind at my back / I'm flyin' high over gray fields my feathers long and black / Down along the river's silent edge I soar / Searching for my beautiful reward"—harks back to the restlessness at the heart of *Human Touch* and hints of a darkness on the edge of *Lucky Town*.

Musically, neither of these two albums represents much of a departure for Springsteen, despite the breakup of the E Street Band. Produced by Springsteen, Jon Landau, Chuck Plotkin, and former E Street Band keyboardist Roy Bittan, *Human Touch* is more richly textured than *Lucky Town*, which Springsteen recorded in his home studio and pretty much produced himself, with help from the other three men. Along with the impeccable Bittan on keyboards, the studio pros on hand for *Human Touch*—bassist Randy Jackson and drummer Jeff Porcaro—do fine; Porcaro even manages on occasion to approach the muscle and finesse of the brilliant E Street Band drummer, Max Weinberg. Springsteen handles virtually all instruments except drums (played by Gary Mallabar) on *Lucky Town* with expressiveness and flair; on both albums his guitar playing is plentiful and gripping, a cry from the soul.

Without question, the aesthetic and thematic aims of *Human Touch* and *Lucky Town* would have been better realized by a single, more carefully shaped collection that eliminated their half-dozen or so least essential songs. But taken together, the two albums chart the fascinating progress of one of the most compelling artists of our time, a man who has found what he was looking for and who is searching still.

Rolling Stone April 30, 1992

10,000 Maniacs: This Side of Paradise

Our Time in Eden

Our *Time in Eden:* the title is an imagined memory as well as the statement of a Utopian ideal. In the vision of Natalie Merchant, the singer and primary songwriter of 10,000 Maniacs, the high-minded belief that somehow life—and our individual lives within it—is perfectible battles a deeper, Catholic assumption that we are fallen beings and no amount of effort on our part can re-create paradise, or possibly even a livable world, now. That struggle between fervent hope and a kind of wide-eyed despair propels the thirteen songs on this gripping new album, infusing it with a provocative, unnerving power.

First impressions of the album will not reveal those depths. As always, the Maniacs—guitarist Rob Buck, keyboardist Dennis Drew, bassist Steve Gustafson, and drummer Jerome Augustyniak—style instantly appealing musical surfaces. Buck's playful fascination with the shimmering sounds that can be coaxed from a variety of stringed instruments—lap and pedal steel guitar, electric sitar, banjo, mandocello—lend enticing strangeness to the band's otherwise straightforward smart-pop arrangements. Merchant herself plays a good deal of piano on the album, and her simple, searching melodies evoke mystery and yearning.

Strings add luster to three tracks; bassoons turn up on another. The J B Horns strut their funky stuff on two songs—as a concept (Natalie Merchant as the hardest-working woman in showbiz?), the collaboration may sound contrived, but they pull it off with ease. And with alternative all-star Paul Fox handling production—replacing Peter Asher, who did *In My Tribe* (1987) and *Blind Man's Zoo* (1989)—the Maniacs are far less restrained, though no less disciplined.

Merchant's voice, of course, provides continual sensual pleasure. She is one of the rare singer-lyricists—Van Morrison and Michael Stipe also come to mind—who, while obsessed by what they have to say and by words themselves, exult in the sheer physical delight of making vocal sounds. Given the choice—though she would prefer not to have to make the choice—Merchant will always opt for pleasure over verbal meaning in rendering a vocal line, and rightly so. This makes her songs difficult to understand in literal terms but easy to respond to emotionally.

The emotions called forth, however, are not always to be trusted. Coupled with the appealing textural feel of the band's music, Merchant's instinct for joy provides a jarring complement to the frequent darkness of her themes and her occasionally chilly moral earnestness. In other words, the sonic allure of the Maniacs' music and Merchant's voice is a seduction into songs that are charged, complex, and troubling.

As it typically does in Merchant's lyrics, biblical imagery runs throughout *Our Time in Eden*. That can give her songs the feel of parables, as do the questions that come up again and again, making the album both instructional and a kind of driven spiritual quest. "If You Intend," a challenge to live that might be addressed to a person suffering with AIDS, defends life's inherent worth and asks, "How can you be so near and not see?" In "Eden," Merchant confesses, "We're not honest, not the people that we dream," and then wonders, "Is there still time?" The JB Horns kick in fine R&B style on "Few and Far Between," but Merchant agonizes: "I'm a body frozen / I'm a will that's paralyzed / When will you ever set aside your pain and misery?"

Most dramatically, the gorgeous ballad "Circle Dream" takes an ancient symbol of perfection and transforms it into a horrifying emblem of entrapment. In a floating, childlike voice, over a delicate piano and keyboards accompaniment, Merchant sings: "I dreamed of a circle. . . . And in that circle was a maze, a terrible spiral to be lost in / Blind in my fear, I was escaping just by feel / But at every turn my way was sealed." In stunning contrast, the exuberant "These Are Days" summons up an almost mystical sense of ecstatic connection to a world that is wild and open: "When May is rushing over you with desire / Take part in the miracles you see in every hour / You'll know it's true that you are blessed and lucky / It's true that you are touched by something that will grow and bloom in you."

Such moments may be as close as we come to getting back to the garden, Merchant suggests on *Our Time in Eden;* paradise may indeed be forever lost. But in our minds and hearts, our time in Eden is as real as our days on Earth; it exists within us to inspire us to hope for better days ahead—and to be better ourselves.

Rolling Stone October 1, 1992

U2: "Zooropa," Mon Amour

Zooropa

Bosnia and Herzegovina. The resurgence of Nazism in Germany. Mafia terrorism in Italy. Escalating unemployment throughout the former Western Bloc. *Zooropa,* indeed.

None of those issues is explicitly addressed on U2's startling new album, of course. But the chilling emotional atmosphere of *Zooropa*—one of grim, determined fun, a fever-dream last waltz on the deck of the Titanic—is well suited to contemporary times in the Old World. "I fell like I'm slowly, slowly, slowly slipping under," Bono wails amid the dizzying disco rhythms of "Lemon." "I feel like I'm holding onto nothing." From that vantage of desperate spiritual dislocation, the vanished certainties of Cold War Europe look comforting.

Principally recorded earlier this year, *Zooropa* began as a toss-off EP to crank some juice into the European leg of U2's worldwide Zoo TV tour. Deeper inspiration struck, however, and with Brian Eno, the Edge, and Flood producing, this fifty-minute, ten-track album emerged.

Historically, U2 have always attempted to follow up breakthrough albums with less ostensibly ambitious efforts. Live EPs came hard on the heels of both *War* (1983) and *The Unforgettable Fire* (1984), and for the most part, they effectively eased the pressure on the band and left U2 free to explore whatever new aesthetic directions they pleased.

Unfortunately, the strategy backfired the last time U2 attempted a "spontaneous" one-off. In 1988, to get some distance on the prodigious success of *The Joshua Tree,* U2 perpetrated *Rattle and Hum,* an album-book-movie media blitz so self-conscious and contrived that it seemed about as unplanned as the invasion of Normandy.

With *Zooropa* the results are far more satisfying: The album is a daring, imaginative coda to *Achtung Baby* (1991), U2's first unqualified masterpiece. *Zooropa* defuses the daunting commercial expectations set by that album while closing off none of the band's artistic options. It is varied and vigorously experimental, but its charged mood of giddy anarchy suffused with barely suppressed dread provides a compelling, unifying thread.

The title track sets the tone from the very start. As the song opens, a stately piano figure, beautiful and foreboding, underlies indecipherable, static-stricken signals from the information-age inferno of Zoo TV. That alluring sonic chaos ultimately yields to the wah-wah blast of the Edge's guitar and the insistent groove of Adam Clayton's bass and Larry Mullen Jr.'s drums. Bono enters like a Mephistophelean seducer, offering jaded pleasures, nurturing dissatisfaction, and stoking desire, crooning the pander's eternal appeal, "What do you want?"

The exuberant paranoia of Bob Dylan's "Subterranean Homesick Blues" gets a postmodern twist on "Numb." Above a hypnotic rhythm track and a repetitive, industrial guitar screech, the Edge blankly intones a long string of disconnected injunctions, post-apocalyptic advice ("Don't move / Don't talk out of time / Don't think / Don't worry everything's just fine / Just fine") for stunned survivors. Meanwhile, Bono coos in a woozy falsetto, "I feel numb / Too much is not enough."

For "The Wanderer," *Zooropa*'s concluding statement, U2 usher in Johnny Cash to handle the lead vocal. It's a wildly audacious move that could so easily have proved a pathetic embarrassment—U2 overreaching for significance yet again—but it works brilliantly. Speak-singing with all the authority of an Old Testament prophet, Cash movingly serves as a link to a lost world of moral surety ("I went out walking with a bible and a gun / The word of God lay heavy on my heart / I was sure I was the one / Now Jesus, don't you wait up / Jesus, I'll be home soon"), literally replacing the various corrupted and confused personas Bono (and, on, "Numb," the Edge) had occupied in the course of the album.

Cash's "Wanderer" is no less lost than the album's other dead souls, but his yearning to be found and redeemed sets him apart. *Zooropa* never resolves whether that yearning is merely nostalgic—a wish for resurrection that has long ago been canceled—or a genuine intimation of hope. No matter: The album's true strength lies in capturing the sound of verities shattering, of things falling apart, that moment when exhilaration and fear are indistinguishable as the slide into the abyss begins.

Rolling Stone August 5, 1993

In the Crosshairs

N *ineteen eighty-nine* was a tough year for anyone who still clings to the belief that rock & roll is inherently liberating, a joyful noise rife with "the magic that can free your soul." For a confounding variety of reasons, rockers and rappers—far from being perceived as liberators of the soul—found themselves weathering a storm of controversy that raised profound questions about the very role of popular music in a free society. As the year and the decade draw to a close, those questions continue to sound with a disturbing resonance.

The first glimmering that the issue of bigotry would dominate the year in music occurred when the Gay Men's Health Crisis—an organization that formed in 1981 in response to the outbreak of AIDS—insisted that Guns n' Roses not be permitted to headline an AIDS benefit in New York because of derogatory lyrics about gays in the group's song "One in a Million." "Immigrants and faggots / They make no sense to me," the lyrics run. "They come to our country / And think they'll do as they please / Like start some mini-Iran or spread some fuckin' disease." In an interview in *Rolling Stone*, Axl Rose refused to disown the lyrics.

The GMHC's decision to boot Guns n' Roses was particularly brave and principled in that, despite the best efforts of entertainment-industry heavies like Arista Records president Clive Davis and actor Michael Douglas, the Gunners were the only rock & roll act that would come forward to headline the AIDS benefit. Asking them to step aside, in effect, postponed the benefit—and the receipt of the important funds it would raise—for more than a year. With all too rare exceptions, rock artists—typically so eager to stand up for trendier issues—have been reluctant to be publicly associated with raising money for AIDS. The rescheduled benefit, which will take place on March 17th, 1990, is now called a Celebration of 15 Years of Joy to Help End These Years of Sorrow and is, ostensibly at least, an anniversary fete for Arista.

A few months after the Guns n' Roses flap, Professor Griff, "minister of information" for the rap group Public Enemy, made a series of anti-Semitic remarks in an interview with the *Washington Times*. Jews are "wicked," Griff said, and "the majority of wickedness that goes on across the globe" can be laid at their door. In the furor that followed, Public Enemy by turn chastised and defended Griff, broke up, re-formed and awkwardly sought to calm the uproar Griff's statements had unleashed while simultaneously maintaining the group's credibility in the black community by not seeming to cave in to pressure from whites. At one point, Public Enemy frontman Chuck D. issued a statement affirming that his band was "pro-human-race" and suggesting, "Please direct all further questions to Axl Rose."

In the wake of the incidents with Guns n' Roses and Public Enemy, charges began to fly from all corners about bigotry in rock lyrics and rock attitudes. In the *New York Times,* Jon Pareles wrote an influential story that began, "Has hatred become hip? From isolated spots in pop culture, racial and sexual prejudice have slithered back into view." Gregory Sandow wrote in the *Los Angeles Herald Examiner,* "So twice in the past month or so I've found myself confronted with rappers—Ice-T and Slick Rick—who tried to arouse their crowds by saying, 'Everyone with AIDS keep quiet.' Can we agree, here on the civilized pages of this newspaper, that this is a dumb and ugly thing to say? . . . Meanwhile, back in Slick Rick's hometown of New York, AIDS spreads fastest in minority communities."

Of course, for better or worse, the songs, statements and actions of rock artists have incited controversy—including calls for government regulation and censorship—ever since the music was born. Rock & roll was perceived as synonymous with juvenile delinquency in the Fifties— much as rap is perceived as providing the soundtrack for gang warfare these days—and Elvis Presley's hip wiggling and Jerry Lee Lewis's marriage to his cousin caused scandals. John Lennon's declaration that the Beatles were more popular than Jesus caused the band's records to be burned throughout the South, and Jim Morrison's shenanigans with the Doors inspired "decency rallies" around the country.

The Rolling Stones earned the ire of feminists when ads for their album *Black and Blue* depicted a bound and beaten woman with the caption I'M BLACK AND BLUE FROM THE ROLLING STONES AND I LOVE IT. The Reverend Jesse Jackson called for a boycott of the Stones' music after their song "Some Girls" asserted that "black girls just want to get fucked all night." The Sex Pistols uncurled Britain's stiff upper lip when they swore and spat at a talk-show host on a live television show. And heavy-metal bands, with their cartoonishly adolescent celebrations of promiscuous sex and drugs—and, it should be noted, their politically unfashionable, white working-class audience—have been the repeated targets of parents' groups and law-enforcement agencies.

Nor were bigotry and offensiveness the exclusive province of rock & roll in this past year. Comedian Andrew Dice Clay trades on routines that single out women, gays, and Asians—in short, anyone who isn't white, male, and straight—for humiliating humor. Photographs by Robert Mapplethorpe and Andres Serrano triggered a fierce debate this year about federal funding of the arts.

Pressure groups on the right used economic leverage to bully advertisers into pulling out of network television shows. In the course of the New York mayoral race, comedian Jackie Mason insulted black Democratic candidate David Dinkins with racist jokes, and a Dinkins aide got fired for anti-Semitic statements. Even the flap about flagburning reflected a national preoccupation with establishing limits on freedom of expression.

What made the issue of bigotry come to the fore in 1989, however, is a sense that, after eight years of Reagan and the election of George Bush, relations among the classes and races in America are balanced on a knife point. While in the past, rock outrage typically served the interest of progressive ideas, it is now, at least in part, a vehicle for social hostility. Middle-class resentment of outsiders was stoked to a high, white flame during the Reagan years, and feelings that might never have found public expression earlier were spit out with pent-up force and a frightening sense of self-justification. Victories in the areas of civil rights and women's rights that had seemed invulnerably secure are being rolled back.

Minorities and working-class whites, eager to hold on to what little has trickled down to them, view each other as competitors and enemies; the borders between their neighborhoods are little more than battle lines. In giving voice to those otherwise disenfranchised communities, rappers and hard-rock bands are conveying important messages. Unfortunately, almost as a means of establishing their street authenticity, they too often and too freely give voice to the biased views of those communities, instead of challenging those views and channeling righteous anger into intelligent political action.

So which side are you on? It is not always easy to know. All civilized people would agree with Sandow about the stupidity of statements and song lyrics that insult victims of AIDS—or women or minorities or for-eigners. But words and songs can be offensive for many reasons, and rock & roll has drawn much of its power from its willingness to express the forbidden idea, to say the thing that should not be said, to shock. You may loathe the sexist lyrics of 2 Live Crew, but do you believe that store owners should be arrested and fined for selling the group's records, as happened in Alexander City, Alabama? Lining up with the organizations that want to cleanse rock of its offensive content can stand you shoulder to shoulder with some dubious comrades.

Like the Parents Music Resource Center (PMRC). For all the blather in its formative days about porn rock, the PMRC has a worthy record in speaking out against the demeaning portrayal of women in songs and videos. And the PMRC was among the first groups to notify the GMHC about the antigay lyrics in "One in a Million." Still, the chilling spectacle of the 1985 Senate hearings about rock & roll that influential PMRC organizers like Tipper Gore, the wife of Senator Albert Gore of Ten-nessee, and Susan Baker, the wife of Secretary of State James Baker, persuaded our nation's chief legislative body to hold provided a stark lesson in how genuine distress over the content of popular music can tip into a kind of McCarthyism.

And however earnest and understandable the PMRC's concern about the welfare of children may be, the group serves as a kind of wedge into the mainstream for conservative and fundamentalist groups whose agendas are by no means so wholesome. Susan Baker sits on the board of Focus on the Family, headed by the Reverend James C. Dobson, a prominent right-wing, anti-abortion activist; the *National Federation for Decency* magazine, a publication run by the Reverend Donald Wildmon, who has made anti-Semitic statements, reprinted a section from Tipper Gore's book *Raising PG Kids in an X-Rated Society* with the permission of the book's publisher.

But despite its call for record labeling, the PMRC is hardly the most dangerous force on the antirock front. Especially troubling this year was a letter sent by the Federal Bureau of Investigation (FBI) to Priority Records about a song called "Fuck tha Police" on the album *Straight Outta Compton* by the Los Angeles rap group N.W.A In the song, N.W.A—the initials stand for Niggers With Attitude, a moniker that raises issues of its own—dramatizes the harassment that the black community in Los Angeles and other cities has suffered at the hands of the police. The song ends with a vision of violent rebellion by black youths. In spirit and intent, the song is not far removed from Spike Lee's dedication of *Do the Right Thing* to black victims of police violence like Eleanor Bumpers and Michael Stewart or from Boogie Down Productions' indictment of police intimidation in "Who Protects Us From You?"

The letter, signed by an assistant director of the FBI, stated, in part, "A song recorded by the rap group N.W.A on their album entitled 'Straight Outta Compton' encourages violence against and disrespect for the law enforcement officer and has been brought to my attention. I understand your company recorded and distributed this album, and I am writing to share my thoughts and concerns with you. . . . Music plays a significant role in society, and I wanted you to be aware of the FBI's position relative to this song and its message."

The language of the letter is almost Orwellian. An agent of the federal government is "writing to share my thoughts and concerns" about a matter that, with no identification of a source, "has been brought to my attention." He is not threatening action of any kind, of course; he only wants to make you "aware of the FBI's position relative to this song."

Attorney Barry Lynn of the American Civil Liberties Union (ACLU)—a first-amendment-rights organization that was itself the target of McCarthyite tactics by the Bush campaign during the 1988 presidential race—has asked the FBI to withdraw the letter. The FBI thus far has not agreed to do so.

"Here you have an intimidating letter sent because officials know that as a constitutional matter there's nothing else they can do," Lynn says. "You cannot tell a record company that they can't sell rap music because it's insulting or offensive to some group. This song doesn't even come close to the advocacy of criminal activity, which would permit it to be regulated. I think the writer of the letter knows that, so he figures, 'I can go to the record company and tell them how upset we are'—and, if not create the fear of God in them, at least the fear of the FBI's continued scrutiny. You don't like to know that government agencies are conducting surveillance of what you do. It is a frightening experience."

Lynn sees the FBI's letter as part of "an atmosphere of hostility towards certain kinds of rock music, rock music on the edges of cultural norms." As for the voluntary industrywide rating or labeling systems advocated by the PMRC and other groups—systems to which many record companies have already conformed—Lynn perceives a danger to freedom of expression there, as well.

"We don't like industrywide labeling," Lynn says, citing the official ACLU position. "We don't like the MPAA movie code, because ultimately it inhibits the creativity of artists. It substitutes an industrywide regulatory scheme for one of the government, but you can't *sue* an industry for violation of first-amendment rights; you can only do that if the government's involved." As a practical matter, Lynn also believes that cynics in the entertainment media soon learn that sensation sells and that warning labels can be good advertising. Movies facing an X rating may occasionally be cut to achieve an R rating, but, Lynn says, "I'm personally convinced that some movies add material to achieve a PG-13 rating, for example, just so more teenagers, whom they're afraid are jaded and won't go see a PG movie, will go to the movie."

So what is the solution, or what is the most appropriate action when faced with statements in music or elsewhere that you find bigoted or insulting? The most important thing to remember is that freedom of speech is not simply something you grant to others, however reluctantly: It's something you must *exercise*. Racist or sexist statements from the stage should be met with hearty booing. Letters of protest and petitions can be written and sent to publications in which such statements appear. Children can be taught that certain attitudes or kinds of expression are not acceptable. It's also extremely important to keep in mind that music reflects social attitudes far more than it shapes them. If you want music to embody a vision of a more egalitarian, or even Utopian, world—work to create that world with your dollars, your votes, and your activism.

It's a tricky but necessary balance to achieve: Maximum vigilance must be combined with maximum tolerance. "The first amendment really works only if it works for everybody," Lynn says. "Unfortunately, there are a lot of people out there who believe that there should be *one* exception to the first amendment: whatever it is that bothers *them*. We've got to do away with that attitude if we're going to truly protect this bedrock of our constitutional system. Without free speech, we don't have freedom."

Rolling Stone December 14–28, 1991

Ice-T *fought the law,* and the law won. Unfortunately, that's the only assessment that can be made in the wake of Ice-T's decision to pull the track "Cop Killer" from his album *Body Count.*

By all accounts, Ice-T rescinded the song voluntarily, but you can be sure that Time Warner, the parent company of Ice-T's label, Warner Brothers, was relieved. The boycotts and stock divestments organized by law-enforcement groups were beginning to generate real heat—the kind of heat that melts corporate resolve. Along with those pressures came threats against Time Warner employees. Ice-T understands the distinction between putting your own life on the line and risking the lives of people who lack both your economic resources and your security guards, and that no doubt contributed to his decision. The larger issue facing Ice-T and every other artist at this point, however, is, what happens now?

In the short term, the heat is off. Time Warner will not impose the code of standards that was rumored to be in the offing if the company could find no other way to pacify its stockholders. The company and, ironically, those stockholders can now also enjoy the profits that are rolling in as *Body Count*—an album that was stone dead commercially before police groups decided it was a moral threat—storms up the charts and becomes a collector's item.

But yielding to censors is a strategy that never works in the long run. Agreeing to parental-advisory labels on records seven years ago, for example, was supposed to put an end to more extreme demands. It's obvious where that has led: The situation has only worsened. And code of standards or no, when one of the world's largest media conglomerates backs down on an indisputable First Amendment issue, what filmmaker, songwriter, author, or journalist can feel safe? Every pressure group in the country now knows that as long as it chooses its targets carefully, even the most powerful companies and the most outspoken artists can be forced to yield.

The key, of course, is choosing the right target. As Ice-T has repeatedly pointed out, this country was founded in a revolution, and at least one thread in the national weave is the urge to support outlaws and underdogs against the authorities. In song, this is one of our country's oldest and most consistent themes: Woody Guthrie's "Pretty Boy Floyd" and Johnny Cash's "Folsom Prison Blues" are only two relatively recent examples, and Eric Clapton had a Number One hit covering Bob Marley's "I Shot the Sheriff." No one sought to ban those songs. So what's the problem with "Cop Killer"?

The problem is that Ice-T is black and, although "Cop Killer" is a rock song, a rapper. That's also why he's an effective target. Gangsta rap—Ice-T's beat—is the voice of black insurgency and the primary art form through which the tense relations between the police and the black community have been dramatized. From "The Message," by Grandmaster Flash and the Furious Five, which ends in a police assault, to Boogie Down Productions' "Who Protects Us From You?" and N.W.A's "Fuck tha Police," rap has presented the street-side view of police corruption, harassment, and racism.

Though they do occasionally sensationalize them, rappers do not make these problems up. Can anyone deny the shameful record of the LAPD—the focus of Ice-T's rage—in serving the minority populations of Los Angeles? Significantly, black police organizations have supported Ice-T to the point of expressing disappointment with his withdrawal of "Cop Killer."

Rappers will continue to write songs about violent confrontations with the police because conditions have not changed. According to a sampler put out by their label, Tommy Boy, both Paris and Live Squad have such songs scheduled for their forthcoming albums. Tommy Boy is owned by Time Warner. Whether those tracks appear—and how police groups and Time Warner react if they do—will likely provide the first test of what one police spokesperson has defined as a "cease-fire" in the censorship wars.

One thing is certain: That cease-fire will never last. Police groups and other would-be censors, charged up by their victory in the "Cop Killer" case, are not going to be in any mood to back off. Rappers, rockers, and everybody else interested in freedom of speech will want to reclaim lost ground. That's not a cease-fire at all: It's the calm before the firestorm.

Rolling Stone September 17, 1992

By now even the most recalcitrant rock & rollers have stopped asking, "Who is Garth Brooks?" While record executives whine about the impact of the recession on sales, Brooks has moved well over twenty million albums in less than four years. Currently, he has four albums in *Billboard*'s Top Twenty, and a fifth sits just outside the Top Forty. His appeal is such that in early September his Christmas album, *Beyond the Season,* entered the charts at Number Five.

Whatever the merits of Brooks's records, that scale of commercial success suggests people are drawn to him for reasons that extend beyond music. What those reasons are has seemed mysterious because his primary audience—white people in their late twenties and older who live in the Midwest and the South—has never been fashionable and has been ignored by the rock-music industry.

The fact is that country music has become the refuge of older rock & roll fans who are put off by the anger, abrasiveness, and decibel level of the music favored by listeners in their teens and twenties: rap, alternative, and metal. At the same time, Brooks has won over a younger generation of country fans by spiking his music with a rock & roll kick. He is unafraid to challenge country verities by recording a muscular ballad like Billy Joel's "Shameless," performing Bob Seger's "Night Moves," and the Georgia Satellites' "Keep Your Hands to Yourself" in concert and peppering his live shows with such decidedly noncountry touches as smoke effects, guitar bashing, and rope swings out over the crowd.

Brooks also practices a virtue that he learned on the country-music circuit: respect for his audience. A recent Brooks concert in Chapel Hill, North Carolina, had a top ticket price of seventeen dollars. During the show Brooks repeatedly walked the edge of the stage shaking hands and accepting flowers and gifts. He also prefaced songs from his just-released album, *The Chase,* with requests that the crowd be patient as he played material they might not find familiar. When he finished the new songs, he thanked the audience and enthusiastically played his hits. Such gestures might sound hokey to rockers who have mistaken arrogance for hipness virtually since the music began. But if as sales of rock albums plummet, anyone is interested in determining why country audiences are so loyal, he or she might start with those small actions.

It's been said that Brooks's music—and by extension his audience—is reactionary, but it's not. Songs like "Unanswered Prayers," "What's She Doing Now," "The Dance," and "Somewhere Other Than the Night" address the domestic struggles and yearning for faith and meaning that have always been the stuff of country music—and that make up a significant part of most lives.

It's true that Brooks's audience—the *real* forgotten middle class, the *real* people worried about family values—is frightened, and their fears have been cynically fueled and exploited during the Reagan-Bush years. They are the people who worked hard and never complained, who went to church and trusted their leaders, who thought they knew the rules and believed that if they followed those rules, their lives would get better. They are neither oppressed minorities, whose needs have been etched into the nation's consciousness, nor members of the ruling elite, born with their hands on the reins of power.

Few artists have spoken for these people, but Brooks has with feeling and homespun eloquence. In song after homiletic song, he has encouraged them to be proud of themselves and tolerant of others, to honor their commitments to their families and communities, to nurture their dreams but to be strong and accepting when those dreams are broken. He's also encouraged them not to take themselves too seriously and to enjoy good times.

Onstage he will sometimes playfully refer to himself in the third person as Garth, as if to distance himself from the larger-than-life subject of all the acclaim, as if he were a member of his own audience. But he makes no secret that he enjoys the applause, breaking into a huge smile, throwing his head back, and pumping his fists as the crowd thunders its approval. He jokes about his weight and the size of his butt. He's no matinee idol.

But life is no matinee, and Garth Brooks understands that. That's why this ordinary guy trying to make ordinary lives a little bit better is held in his audience's heart long after the curtain has fallen.

Rolling Stone November 26, 1992

Opinion:
Mark David Chapman

❝ I *wished someone would write a book about me."*
The line comes in passing, in the middle of a much longer quote, seventy-five pages into *Let Me Take You Down: Inside the Mind of Mark David Chapman, the Man Who Killed John Lennon*. Chapman is speaking about *John Lennon: One Day at a Time*, by Anthony Fawcett, the book that despite its generally positive portrait of the artist, convinced Chapman that Lennon was a "phony" who deserved to die. The implications of Chapman's statement are obvious. Perhaps, to be generous, that's why Jack Jones, the author of *Let Me Take You Down*, fails to comment on it.

Now Chapman has his book—not to mention two television appearances, one each with the reigning masters of celebrity journalism, Larry King and Barbara Walters. The book and the television interviews were all done to commemorate the twelfth anniversary of Lennon's death. Six years ago, in his last burst of publicity, Chapman appeared on the cover of *People*.

It's no secret that Chapman killed Lennon to achieve precisely this kind of media notoriety. "I thought that by killing him I would acquire his fame," he told Walters. In a conversation with the imaginary Little People who Chapman believed lived inside his mind, he explained his decision to murder Lennon this way: "It's just because I've decided to be somebody. I've decided that I can't go on being a nobody."

Jones, a crime reporter who conducted more than two hundred hours of interviews with Chapman, presents *Let Me Take You Down* as an effort to understand the phenomenon of potentially violent celebrity stalkers. But he closes the book with a short story by Chapman, a story Jones describes as showing "the workings of an imaginative mind desperate for contrition, forgiveness, and recognition—a mind that is still driven to save the world." The implication is that Chapman is a kind of Lennon gone wrong, a writer himself, a kind of utopian artist "driven to save the world."

Despite Chapman's rantings in *Let Me Take You Down* about his frequent conversations with God, Satan, and the Little People—along with recurrent testimony about his ability to charm authority figures of various kinds—Walters commented that he seemed sane to her. She ended her *20/20* segment with Chapman's apologizing to Lennon's fans and, unbelievably, to Yoko Ono. "I wasn't killing a real person," he said. "I killed an image. I killed an album cover. I'm sorry." On the same show, Jones modestly suggested the likelihood that his chats with Chapman "brought him a little closer to reality."

Worse still are Jones's assertions in his book that Lennon himself "laid the groundwork for Chapman's deadly obsession." Drawing on the likes of Albert Goldman, author of the virulently mean-spirited biography *The Lives of John Lennon,* and Frederic Seaman, who stole Lennon's diaries from the Dakota after his death, Jones credits the idea that Lennon brought his murder upon himself.

This confusion of the victim with the aggressor—and this tarting up of commercial motivations like sales and ratings with high-minded clap-trap about "the razor-thin line between madness and art"—is reprehensible and plays directly into the hands of borderline personalities like Chapman. Certainly no aspect of human behavior should go unexplored, but neither Jones's book nor the *20/20* segment adds anything to our understanding of Lennon's tragic death.

These portrayals of Chapman demonstrate how our society has become a dangerous hall of mirrors. The relation of the "little people"—the language of Chapman's fantasy is telling—to celebrities is a combustible mix of worship and envy, admiration and secret rage. The line between reality and image has blurred; a person like Chapman, whose identity is not clearly defined, drifts across that line, sometimes with catastrophic results.

But such people must be made to understand at least one thing: Their outrages will not be rewarded by television interviews, magazine covers, or books that rest on myopic propositions like "Both Lennon and his assassin have shaken and forever altered twentieth-century history." Chapman may believe he was killing an image, but in fact he killed a man and an artist, a husband and a father. In his delusion, he aspires to be an image himself, but he should be treated exactly as what he is: a man who committed a murder.

Rolling Stone January 21, 1993

The Next Multiplatinum
Cash Cow

As *1992 draws to a close,* artists, fans, and the music industry as a whole are looking ahead to an extremely uncertain future. Sales are down and for reasons more complicated than the recession. Speculation that the rock era has run its course has escalated, though no one—not even that renowned bastion of pop-culture insight the *Wall Street Journal,* which declared in a page one story that ROCK IS SLOWLY FADING— will venture a guess about what, if anything, will rise to take its place. No one has a sure sense where music is heading or whether the fission of the "rock audience"—if it is any longer possible to use that term with any degree of precision—will ultimately prove to be a positive or a negative development.

For all the hand wringing and prognosticating going on, however, there is at least one genuine cause for optimism: Great music is still being made by artists new and old in every field—from Arrested Development to Wynonna Judd, from Morrissey to Lindsey Buckingham, from PJ Harvey to En Vogue. Listeners who didn't find any sounds to their taste last year simply weren't looking—to paraphrase the old blues song, it's your own fault. And though the current musical climate may occasionally seem confusing, times may never have been better for people whose palates are receptive to a wide range of flavors.

But for the most part, rappers, metal bands, country musicians, alternative and aging rockers, and more obscure artists in the dozens of subgenres splintering off in myriad ways seemed content to speak exclusively to their own specific audiences. With a few notable exceptions, like the U2-Public Enemy tour or the Lollapalooza extravaganza that ran the gamut from the Red Hot Chili Peppers to Ice Cube, no one was truly able—or much interested in making the effort—to reach across boundaries and address what many people have come to envision as the new multicultural America. Some people believe that a coming together of the tribes may not even be possible anymore.

But if popular music is eventually to play a cultural role in the next century of anything near the significance it has enjoyed in the second half of this one, a determination to bridge racial, generational, and gender gaps will be the principal reason why.

Before that can happen, however, the music industry will need to wake up and recover from the aftereffects of its Eighties hangover. The commercial expectations engendered during that decade—when the ascent of MTV, the dramatic development of CD technology and an economy racing on debt-driven energy combined to make multiplatinum sales a prerequisite for success—need to be scaled down to a more reasonable level. The past year has shown demonstratively that even the artists who established those inflated standards have not been able to meet them in the Nineties.

The clearest example of that is Michael Jackson, the self-designated and now deflated "King of Pop," whose 1982 blockbuster *Thriller* created the model for the modern album that was supposed to linger in the upper reaches of the charts interminably, spin off an endless series of hit singles, and achieve double-digit platinum sales. *Dangerous,* which was released late in 1991, never approached the numbers attained by *Thriller* or even the somewhat less prodigious showing of *Bad,* Jackson's 1987 follow-up. Nor is it likely that anything Jackson releases will perform that well ever again.

Does that mean *Dangerous* wasn't a good album or that Jackson is washed up as an artist? Not at all. Jackson has undermined himself not through his inability to match his earlier achievements—no rational person could expect the once-in-a-lifetime success of *Thriller* to be duplicated—but through his attitudes. Jackson made it clear that as far as he was concerned, nothing short of topping *Thriller* could make *Dangerous* a success. That isn't aspiration or ambition; it's simply substituting commercial goals for artistic ones. From the moment of its release, virtually all discussion of the album centered on its potential in the marketplace; whatever Jackson had to say with his music was largely lost.

As a result of all that, *Dangerous,* which has sold more than four million copies in the United States alone—roughly the same number as the initial sales of *Off the Wall,* the solo album that first propelled Jackson to superstardom in 1979—is widely perceived as a failure. Can Jackson possibly be pleased to be judged by so cold and unforgiving a standard— ironically, one that he himself has enshrined?

Bruce Springsteen is another Eighties icon who found himself confronting the harsh economic realities of the Nineties. *Human Touch* and

Lucky Town, the two albums he released last spring, delivered a deep, uncompromising assessment of emotional and family life on the far side of forty. At least partly because in these economically depressed times, putting out two albums at once confused and discouraged consumers (buy one and you're dissatisfied, knowing you're not getting the whole story; buy both and you have to brown-bag lunch for two weeks), the albums plummeted down the charts after a fast start.

So is Springsteen a failure? Not in the least—certainly not in artistic terms. But maybe *Born in the U.S.A.,* with its worldwide sales of ten million, was a peak that he will never again approach. Let's go even further and say it was an outright fluke. Does an artist who after twenty years still continues to challenge his audience and still manages to sell close to four million albums have anything to be ashamed of?

Springsteen never subscribed to Michael Jackson's code that sales are all that matters—in fact, his good humor about his slump in the marketplace provided some of the most charming moments on his tour. But he and his work were often wrongly judged by that same wildly inappropriate, Eighties-derived measure.

The industry's insistence on turning to established superstars for salvation may also stifle the growth of the most promising young artists, the very people on whom the future of the music depends. Can the staggering contracts offered in the past two years to aging acts like the Rolling Stones, ZZ Top, and Aerosmith possibly leave record companies in any position to take risks on a healthily diverse array of upcoming artists? Will they be able to commit their resources in any significant way to bringing the music of those artists to the public?

The answer is no. The vast commitment of the record companies to the music of the past does, however, whet their hunger for new superstars—after all, somebody has to pay the bills. Consequently, in the wake of the startling success of Nirvana and Pearl Jam, companies broke out their checkbooks last year and hunted far and wide for the next likely alternative—what can that term conceivably mean in this context?—breakout. The commercial pressures such deals bring to bear on young bands can be paralyzing, and they will likely lead to a quick turnover of rosters as labels search feverishly for the next multiplatinum cash cow. It can't possibly be good for a band like Helmet to begin its major-label career having to earn back a million-dollar guarantee.

Instead of investing in and nurturing a wide range of new talents, record companies are betting wildly like drunks at the roulette table, hoping that one big score—whether by an old favorite or a new lucky number—will cover all previous debts. That's all-or-nothing Eighties thinking, and that's the problem. It's an approach that makes for one winner and many losers, with each spin of the wheel just perpetuating the dizzying, desperate process.

Needing to up the ante continually is a phenomenon that unfortunately is not limited to the realm of sales. Madonna, for example, seeks to outdo herself not so much in terms of numbers—hers have remained consistently strong, though not up to the level of *Like a Virgin* (1984)—but in outrageousness. Before 1992 could slip unnoticed out the back door, Madonna launched the latest of her punishing biennial media assaults.

We've encountered many of the elements before, of course: a strong new album, *Erotica*, promoted by a sexually explicit video restricted to late-night airing by MTV (but played relentlessly on the Box, the refreshing video-jukebox cable channel that began to make a serious impact this year), and steamy advance word of a movie, *Body of Evidence*, due out in January, which in its original version fried the circuits of the rating board before it was cut to achieve an R.

So far, no news. The turn of the screw, so to speak, this time is *Sex*, a fifty-dollar "art" book in which Madonna and photographer Steven Meisel explore the nether world of psychosexual dominance and submission. That focus, which also runs through parts of *Erotica*, is potentially compelling, but the overwhelming effect of the book is numbing. The images are derivative, and Madonna herself seems far too eager to shock; that, not even prurient arousal, seems the ideal response the book tirelessly seeks. The potency of *Sex*'s subject matter is dissipated by Madonna and Meisel's self-congratulatory—and silly—sense of their own "bravery," as if their naughty games were somehow revolutionary.

All the hoopla about *Sex* suggests that Madonna's is the ultimate Catholic-schoolgirl rebellion—much as she rails about repressive American values, she needs that repression to lend definition to her identification of herself as a rebel. In that sense, she is as imprisoned by those values as the most strait-laced suburbanite. A world devoid of the notion of sexual sin—the polymorphous erotic world Madonna claims to

want—would render her provocations meaningless. And for Madonna,
those provocations are ends, not means.

As with Michael Jackson, Madonna's self-conscious desire to go further each time out must ultimately prove to be a losing strategy. It is an attitude that has nothing to do with the obligation artists have to urge themselves to new creative heights and everything to do with needing to bask in the vertiginous glare of media celebrity. It not only obscures the quality of her music in pointless discussions of "Has Madonna gone too far?" but it helps fuel the perception that she—and for some burned-out consumers, all contemporary music—is only about image and marketing.

Sinéad O'Connor, meanwhile, managed the seemingly insurmountable task of pushing the bondage-clad Madonna out of the headlines with her bizarre attacks on what she quaintly and archaically refers to as the Holy Roman Empire. The Catholic church is a perfectly legitimate target, particularly for an Irish single mother who grew up in an impoverished country in which Catholicism is virtually a state religion, contraception is discouraged, and abortion is banned.

But is O'Connor's aim to educate people about her point of view or to alienate them and insult their beliefs—as she did when she ripped up a picture of the pope on *Saturday Night Live,* ensuring that they will never take her seriously? However justified her critiques, O'Connor's conspiracy theories about the role of the church in world affairs are perilously reminiscent of the paranoid—and viciously anti-Semitic—fantasies of *Protocols of the Elders of Zion.* Very little about O'Connor—including her opinion that the woman raped by Mike Tyson is "a bitch"—suggests that she would be any more enlightened than the church fathers if real social power were in her hands.

Just as Madonna requires a backdrop of Puritanism to sharpen the thrill of her sexual antics, O'Connor needs to incite resistance—as she has done over and over again—in order for her to glow in the righteousness of her positions. It was painful to watch O'Connor onstage at the Bob Dylan tribute concert at Madison Square Garden in October not only because of the rudeness of the crowd, but for the way that she seemed in some perverse way to exult in the abuse. If Joan of Arc is her role model, martyrdom seems to be her goal.

We'll never know whether the fans at the Garden would have stopped booing if she had started to sing Dylan's "I Believe in You" as planned. The point is, she didn't even try, going so far as to stop the band twice. She also ended up dominating the news coverage of the tribute. Through her actions, O'Connor has overwhelmed her various causes with her personality, diminishing her effectiveness as a voice of protest.

Some artists, on the other hand, did not have to go out of their way to seek controversy in 1992—trouble fixed them in its crosshairs and fired. The furor over Ice-T's thrash-metal song "Cop Killer," which resulted in his pulling the song from his album *Body Count*, set a dangerous precedent, one that will be with us for some time to come. Is it now impossible for an artist to record a song in which a law-enforcement agent or a government official—however corrupt, however brutal, under whatever circumstances, in self-defense or not—is killed? Will that unspoken rule apply to Arnold Schwarzenegger as well as to Ice-T? Why should events in a song be held to a higher moral standard than those in a movie, a novel, a play, or any other work of art?

A crime committed in a work of art is different from a crime committed in the real world. Laws govern our public behavior, the acts we perform, but not what we are able to listen to, read, watch, or talk about. If the police groups were appalled by the actions dramatized in "Cop Killer," they should ask themselves why they are so mistrusted by so many people in minority communities. Rappers are certainly not above sensationalizing conditions in the inner city, but the police's collusion with drug dealers, harassment of urban youths, and indifference to the ravages of ghetto life are not issues made up by rappers for rhymes. They can be read about daily in the newspapers of any major city.

That law-enforcement groups were able, through the threat of a boycott against Time Warner, to pressure Ice-T into withdrawing "Cop Killer" means that it is open season on rap and any other music that attempts to address the gripping social and political realities of our time—and those are the concerns that make music matter. The word is already out that record companies are looking very closely at songs they deem to be controversial, no doubt making artists themselves more cautious and draining the blood from one of our society's most vital means of self-examination. This is not a favorable trend for anyone

interested in freedom of expression in the arts—and unfortunately, it
will not come to a halt with the arrival of the new year.

If rappers were coerced into the position of being First Amendment
fighters, a number of veteran artists who released albums in 1992 suggested approaches to the creation of rock & roll—broadly defined, as it
should be—that can help keep the music vital and important in people's
lives in other ways. Taken together, they show how this music can address the entire spectrum of human concerns with sophistication and
compassion.

Lou Reed's *Magic and Loss,* for example, demonstrated in arresting
terms rock & roll's ability to take on life's most urgent question—What is
the meaning of death?—and explore it with all the richness and complexity that great art has always brought to essential matters. For an artist who has often written about characters mesmerized by their self-
destructive urges, it was a bold, heartening statement.

Death also haunted *Automatic for the People,* R.E.M.'s autumnal meditation on the passage of time and the value of what lasts. It's a sadly
moving soundtrack for the age of AIDS, for a generation of people struck
senseless by the premature demise of many of their loved ones. The
album's eloquent string arrangements and eerily seductive melodies
dare to be simple and beautiful—a lesson in musical courage that should
not be lost on the up-and-coming noise-and-noise alone brigade.

Less ambitiously but no less admirably, Neil Young's *Harvest Moon*
took a searching look back at the two decades since he released what may
still be his most popular album, *Harvest.* The album's quiet, introspective tone showed, once again, Young's willingness to shift directions—
his last two outings, *Ragged Glory* (1990) and the *Arc/Weld* live set
(1991), threatened to violate decibel-safety standards—and follow the
imperatives of his art and his heart. Likewise the juicy funk and dreamy
ballads of Prince's ♀ bespeak the independence of spirit that continues
to make him inspirational. The album is not in a class with Prince's
greatest or most adventurous efforts, but it bristles with the energy of a
highly charged, individual vision.

That last quality is ultimately what distinguishes these albums. Whatever the specific merits of their work at any particular moment in their
careers, those four artists have neither pandered to gain large audiences

nor hidden from popularity when it came. They have made master-pieces, and in the course of following their own lights, they have stumbled into embarrassing mistakes. They have not been afraid to look foolish if that's the occasional price of achieving greatness. Their followings are loyal because their fans know that they are getting work that is honest and true, whether it is challenging, hard, and somber or ecstatic and fun. As younger artists with great potential—from Neneh Cherry to the Spin Doctors—step out into the fragmenting future, those are the kind of values they may want to keep in mind.

Rolling Stone December 10–24, 1992

I went to the blockbuster Broadway production of *The Who's Tommy* fearing the worst and, unfortunately, had nearly all those fears confirmed. First of all, it's not the Who's *Tommy* at all but something entirely different. The Who's groundbreaking rock opera, a generational tale of erotic, hallucinogenic, and spiritual questing, has been mainstreamed for the Nineties. Sixties rebels may have thought they were traveling the road of excess on the way to the Palace of Wisdom, but this new *Tommy* suggests that what they really wanted all along was comfortable, complacent, middle-class "normality."

Conveniently, that message is ideally suited to the well-heeled suburban boomers who are *The Who's Tommy*'s target audience and who are shelling out, in record-breaking numbers, as much as sixty-five dollars a ticket to see their glory days glorified on the musical stage. It's a perfect package, really. The loud (for Broadway) guitars, classic-rock songs, snappy staging and startling (for Broadway) special effects provide that always essential nostalgic whiff of rebelliousness. At the same time, the play's revised, reassuring ending—extolling family values and social conformity, neatly resolving the album's more troublesome conclusion—sends the audience home smiling and self-satisfied.

All this, of course, is a far cry from the Who's original *Tommy*, a sprawling, confused, ambitious, and altogether compelling album that brilliantly captures the hopes, fears, urgency, and inarticulate fury of 1969, the tumultuous year of its release. The story of a deaf, dumb, and blind kid who achieves transcendence through pinball wizardry, becomes an authoritarian rock star/guru for the yearning masses, and eventually plunges back into his frighteningly isolated, eerily enticing inner world proved a bold, bizarre metaphor for a period torn by the contradictory currents of revolution and reaction, of communal generosity and individual selfishness. Conservative and blandly heartwarming, *The Who's Tommy* is equally a sign of its far less inspiring times.

Visually, at least, *Tommy* makes a more than adequate transition to the stage. The use of scrims and video projections moves the plot along at a rapid, MTV-style pace. It also, appropriately, serves to blur the distinction between what's going on in the characters' imaginations and what's happening in the external world. At one exhilarating point the theater is transformed into a giant pinball machine. Particularly if, like most of the Broadway audience, you no longer go to rock shows, where such spectacular effects are far more common, the impact is impressive. But none of that inventiveness compensates for the ways in which Broadway smooths out *Tommy*'s rough edges and reduces it to the tale of an unhappy misfit who finally finds domestic happiness and acceptance.

For what seems like decades now people have been waiting for the musical that would bring rock & roll energy to Broadway—and that in the process would introduce a new, younger audience to the theater. And the enormous popularity of *Tommy*—not to mention its eleven Tony nominations—ensures that similar productions will be launched before very long. But the lesson *The Who's Tommy* teaches is that in coming to terms with the requirements of the theatrical stage, rock & roll must not allow its visceral power, its instinct for anarchy, to be blunted.

Take the case of Luther Rix, the orchestra drummer who performed the thankless task of having to reproduce Keith Moon's parts for *The Who's Tommy*. He's a first-rate musician, certainly well trained, probably, in strict terms, a "better" drummer than Moon. He did everything right, but what he couldn't manage—and was smart enough not even to attempt—was Moon's innate wildness, the vertiginous sense that he might take a song in any direction at any moment, just for the kicks. They can't teach that at the conservatory, just like they can't teach the splendid singers who sang *Tommy*'s songs so technically well the yearning, cord-ravaging strain of Roger Daltrey's and Pete Townshend's voices.

Broadway specializes in the literal, and the best rock & roll works on feel. In both spirit and execution, *The Who's Tommy* had plenty of the kind of talent that Broadway can provide but, fatally, not enough rock & roll, a form so raw and simple, so accessible on its surface and so elusive in its essence, that it confounds skill and yields only to genius.

Rolling Stone June 24, 1993

Culture Watch, Culture Wars

I'll Take My Stand

A Defense of Popular Culture

This essay served as the one contrarian argument in a collection titled *Dumbing Down: Essays on the Strip-Mining of American Culture*, edited by Katherine Washburn and John Thornton (Norton, 1996).

One recent evening a writer who occasionally freelanced for *Rolling Stone*, where I edited the record review section for five years, dropped by my apartment to listen to music. To say that techno—a hyperkinetic, electronic dance music that had become hugely popular in Europe and that was beginning to develop a following in the United States—was his specialty would be to vastly diminish the extent of his commitment to that genre and the ecstatic "rave" scene that surrounds it. He played some hard-to-find techno tracks for me, discussed them with insight and passion, explained the social ramifications of the music, and gave me some recommendations for future listening.

Because of his growing interest in ambient techno—a much slower and dreamier electronic music that ravers use to ease themselves down after their mad dancing—I put on some pieces by Erik Satie for him to hear. The idea was to connect Satie's notions about music that would mingle amiably with its environment and the intentionally atmospheric function of ambient techno. "Who is Erik Satie?" he asked.

I'll admit it: at first I was shocked. We'd touched on such a wide range of subjects that I assumed he'd be generally familiar with Satie, as I am; I just wasn't sure if he'd ever thought of him in this particular context. The evening had also included a viewing of *The Last Seduction* and a long talk about the history of film noir and the reasons for its current revival. We'd listened to Bob Dylan and Syd Barrett and rambled through a chat about the Beats and the intricacies of the most up-to-the-minute computer technology. How could this obviously intelligent, insatiably curious twenty-six-year-old product of a good university never have *heard* of Erik Satie?

For a moment, I found myself shedding my identity as an editor at a consumer magazine and reverting to my former role as a literature professor and, more or less by implication, ardent defender of academic "standards." What are they teaching these people nowadays?!?

That feeling, however, was quickly replaced by a more immediate delight. There was no question but that he would love Satie, and now I— while not an expert by the furthest stretch of the imagination—would have the pleasure of turning him on to that music. The antidote to my initial outrage seemed easy enough to achieve: I'll tell him, and then he'll know who Satie is. Somehow, that was a simple and fit end to a long evening of aesthetic exploration, sharing, and discovery.

Afterwards, at some remove from the actual event, I thought more seriously about whether or not my friend's ignorance of Satie constituted an indictment of our educational system—or even of him. I don't think it does at all—any more than I would like my ignorance of computer culture or the ramifications of techno to stand as an indictment of me. Somewhere my friend had learned how to be excited by knowledge and how to synthesize what he'd learned into fresh formulations. He'd learned how to listen, how to learn from someone else, and how to teach. His formal education must have played some role in all that, even if it wasn't an exclusive or even determinative one.

I also realized something else. Knowing about techno and not knowing much about classical music might be somebody else's very definition of dumbing down, but it certainly isn't mine. It's often struck me that many skeptics about popular culture succumb to one of its more obnoxious aspects—the reduction of complicated aesthetic issues to a hit parade— when setting forth what they think should or shouldn't be part of the curriculum or the canon, or even when just expressing their conviction about what is worth knowing. What is the point, though, of pitting one type of music, or one work of art, or one type of knowledge against another, as if in a popularity contest? That seems to me to betray even very traditional notions of the attitude an intellectual life should instill.

That type of thinking helps no one and really derives from issues that have little to do with aesthetic matters but everything to do with maintaining the cultural perquisites of class privilege. I remember feeling bifurcated in my intellectual passions when I was in college in the late 1960s and early 1970s. I'd loved rock & roll since I was a child, and in the mid-1960s I was delighted to find that, at least in the underground press, a serious, powerful brand of criticism was developing in response to the increased ambition evident in the music itself. That development paralleled my own burgeoning interest in literature; in fact, many early rock critics had been trained in the New Criticism that dominated university English departments in the 1950s and early 1960s. These writers approached the music *as* literature, concentrating on close readings and lyrical exegesis to the virtual exclusion of musical analysis.

In many ways, both the bohemian world of rock criticism and the erudite, upper-crust world of the literary Great Tradition and its students were equally foreign to me. I grew up in a working-class Italian family—neither of my parents graduated from high school—and, because of that, it's important to consider the different routes through which popular music and literature came into my life. Music, of course, was readily accessible to me through the media—I could hear it on the radio and, somewhat less frequently, watch performances of it on television. Singles were inexpensive and, once I reached the age of ten or so, I could buy them nearly as often as I would like.

Critical writing about the music was almost as easy to come by. Underground newspapers were inexpensive; some were given away free. Because my family lived in Greenwich Village—which in those days was as much an Italian neighborhood as a bohemian enclave—I had as much access to that type of publication as I could have wanted.

The social process of learning about literature, unfortunately, was far more complex and problematic, as it no doubt continues to be for people from backgrounds like mine. Within the family itself, things were fine. Education was regarded as an important route to a better life. My older brother and sister encouraged me to read; their schoolbooks and other reading material were readily available around the house. My father read three newspapers a day and argued loudly with what he read in the sports and political columns; that was its own encouragement and no small contributor to my eventual career in journalism.

But penetrating the mysteries of literature required teachers and a formal education primarily because access to the world of such "high art" was almost exclusively a function of class. To learn about Dion and the Belmonts all I had to do was flip my radio or television on. To learn about Shakespeare, I would have to reorient my entire life and challenge the full spectrum of social expectations for someone like me.

Fortunately, at the time, the City University of New York offered an excellent education for free—I never could have afforded to go away to school, nor did I have any of the social skills or emotional wherewithal to survive in such an environment, even if my family could somehow have come up with the money. As for my teachers' occasional condescension toward popular music—one of them as recently as a year ago wrote to the *New York Times* complaining about a critic's characterization of rap lyrics as "poetry"—who cared? I knew that Bob Dylan, Muddy Waters, and the Rolling Stones would always be as sustaining to me as any literature I would ever read—they still are—and I didn't need professors to tell me why, or why they shouldn't be.

Moreover, it simply didn't seem important whether my professors cared about popular music or not. Whenever our teachers attempted to reach across the then-much-brooded-upon generation gap by discussing popular music with us, my friends and I would laugh. As one exercise, the senior professor who taught my freshman honors seminary asked us to analyze the significance of *Abbey Road,* which had just come out, and I didn't even bother to write the paper. *He* was supposed to grade what I knew about the Beatles? Get real. (I did, however, write a term paper in that course on the Rolling Stones—this was 1970, after all. After giving me an A, the professor, unconsciously substituting his own criterion for mine, asked me if I thought it would be pleasant to sit down and have dinner with the band.)

I can now see that what I set out to get from my teachers was two things—one obvious, one subtle, a kind of cultural secret. The first was a literary and critical training that would enable me to do the work I wanted to go on to do—my ambition at the time was to become an English professor. For the second, I wanted to crack a social code, a way of speaking, dressing, acting, and even thinking that disguised my class origins and made me seem like the sort of person who *could* go on to become a professor.

It's not that I intended to adopt all the mannerisms I learned, but I needed to know where the points of differentiation were. It was "upward mobility time," as a friend later described it, and I needed people to point out to me, intentionally or not, where the ladder was, because I didn't have a clue. All I knew, after having watched any number of my incredibly savvy neighborhood friends slide down the societal chute to dead-end lives, was that it wasn't exclusively about intelligence or merit by a long shot.

A good deal has changed in the last quarter-century, but the lessons of those years about the profound degree to which knowledge—types of knowledge, access to knowledge, validation of knowledge, uses of knowledge—functions in a social context, sometimes to very brutal ends, still shape my vision of things. Class issues are rarely discussed in relation to the subject of "dumbing down"—in fact, they're rarely discussed at all without prompting absurd charges of "inciting class warfare"—but they are crucial to it. A "pure" understanding of what it is essential to know cannot be attained—it simply does not exist. As has always been true—and, at least in this country, nearly always disguised—that question must be answered from a position within the rapidly shifting dynamics of our society.

If it was ever possible to establish a clear, pragmatic hierarchy among types of knowledge—and I don't think it ever was—it's no longer possible now. There are too many things to know and too many ways of knowing. A genuine education today must consist of providing people with the skills to engage and enter the enormous number of worlds—aesthetic, intellectual, technological, scientific—that will increasingly be open to them. People must learn to converse across their differences, not learn the same rigidly defined things.

Despite reactionary arguments to the contrary, it is not content—opera as opposed to rock & roll, literature as opposed to film—but the nature of the critical approach that determines whether or not a specific discipline has been dumbed down. In the case of popular music, innumerable books, journal articles, newspapers, magazines, fanzines, documentaries, videos, and films address every issue of conceivable importance from every conceivable angle. Anyone who is interested enough to inquire will discover a level of cultural debate that is every bit as sophisticated and rich as that addressing any other subject.

Which is not to say that far too much popular music—not to mention much that is written or said about it—is not frighteningly stupid, and perhaps even dangerous. The escalating and overwhelming commercial imperatives of American culture dictate that only what is popular can survive. And what is popular will sometimes prove to be what is pandering.

That will be true as long as economics drives culture to the extent that we permit it to at this time, in this place. And that reality speaks to a paradox that the cultural Right in our country has yet to sort out. I debated Hilton Kramer at a college in Minnesota not too long ago, and he was attacking the Corporation for Public Broadcasting and National

Public Radio, on the one hand, while espousing traditional American free-market values, on the other. So who will pay for symphonies, museums, and opera? I asked. Rock & roll does not require government grants, I pointed out; it does quite well on the open market. As clearly as I could see, his politics completely undermined his aesthetics.

It is apparent to me that leveling charges of "dumbing down" is simply a way of asserting particular aesthetic preferences and a desire for social privilege. And the reactionary political agenda such charges routinely advance makes it virtually impossible to address matters of genuine cultural concern in our society in a civilized manner—questions like, How do we increase literacy and educate people for the society that awaits them in the future?

Ever since rock & roll first exploded onto the cultural scene in the 1950s, criticizing it has had more to do with anxiety about burgeoning social movements than anything remotely to do with artistic criteria. Responding to such critiques in his recent book, *Rock and Roll: An Unruly History,* critic Robert Palmer examines the musical sources of rock & roll and the aesthetic strictures of the Western classical tradition, and does not find a contrast between culture and decadence, but two different approaches to making music:

In traditional West African cultures, a piece of music is held to be satisfying and complete if there is sufficient rhythmic interest; to oversimplify, rhythm is as fundamental to African music as harmony in European tradition and melodic sophistication in the music of India. Indian music has no harmony as such, and nobody complains; much European classical music is rhythmically one-dimensional—one is tempted to say "primitive"—and you don't hear symphony subscribers complaining about that. But when pop music begins moving away from tin pan alley song forms and musical values and embracing the aesthetics of its African origins, suddenly our culture is seen as adrift, endangered, riven by decadence and decay. Some pundits write books bemoaning "The Loss of Beauty and Meaning in American Popular Music." Others assert that heavy metal, or punk, or gangster rap— whatever the latest pop-music bogeyman happens to be—imperils the very fabric of civilization! . . . It would help if these gloom-and-doom mongers could see the history of this music as a matter of cycles within cycles, or as a developing idiom that periodically refreshes itself by drinking from its own deepest wellsprings.

Does it still really need to be asserted after all this time that art—*all* art, classical as well as popular—does not float unsullied above reality in

some pure, eternal, universal realm, but is instead created and understood amid the gritty struggles and forced compromises of history? It is
no less satisfying, and certainly no less challenging, for that.

Anyone yearning for cultural certainty at the present moment must
face up to the curse of living in interesting times. Entire university
programs are devoted to popular culture, and gangster rap is written
about with great seriousness in the pages of the *New York Times*. At the
same time, opera and theater are performed for free in Central Park and
MTV underwrites speaking tours by young poets.

Culture is no less a battleground than it ever was, but now both sides
have aesthetics in their armory. As someone who has grown comfortable
moving from the art house to the club, from classic to contemporary
literature, from rock & roll to a wide variety of other types of music, I'm
saddened by the hardening of those lines, and I fight to break them
down.

But I live in history, too. And against the current climate of philistine
defense of high culture, cynical attacks on perfectly legitimate popular
art, and reactionary longing for cultural privilege, I'll happily, eagerly,
staunchly take my stand.

Anarchy in the U.S.S.R.?

I *magine the Sixties,* the depression, Watergate, and the Civil War going on all at the same time, and you'll get some sense of what's happening in the Soviet Union. All verities have been destroyed, and nothing has risen to replace them. No one can sense where things are heading. No one mood prevails; every social current generates an equally strong counterresponse. These are not the best of times; they are possibly the worst of times.

A journalist friend in Moscow whose English was serviceable, but no better, kept referring to my assignment in his country as a story about "real Soviet life." In the course of my three-week visit as a guest of the Soviet weekly newspaper *Arguments and Facts,* I could never tell if he was serious or just kidding me, mocking my ambitions as an American magazine writer looking—between museum visits and expense-account meals—for the inside story of the country he has lived in his whole life.

All I know is that he'd use the phrase whenever the grimly funny, daily surrealism of Soviet society would manifest itself. "This is real Soviet life," he'd say with an exasperated laugh when we were inexplicably refused tables at half-empty restaurants, when I discovered mice in the room of my supposedly top-of-the-line hotel in Moscow, when drunk American tourists, having failed to produce the requisite pass, sloppily grappled with armed guards—"What the fuck *is* this? I *live* here!"— outside their hotel in Leningrad. " 'What the fuck *is* this,' " he'd say, laughing, mimicking their American accents and their outrage. "This is not America," he'd say, as if in answer to the question. "This is real Soviet life."

In fact, among the people I met, the term *soviet* served essentially as a synonym for "fucked up." I'd been in the country about three days when a car that was sent to take me to an interview failed to start. After several attempts to get it going, the driver turned to me, smiled wearily, and explained: "Soviet car." By that time, that was all the explanation I needed.

The depth of the Soviet people's bitterness about conditions in their country is profound. They've been living for the past seventy-three years under socialism as it might have been conceived of by Groucho, not Karl, Marx, as it might be depicted in a novel by William Buckley. Quite simply, nothing in the country works. Broken chairs, for example, became something of a slapstick motif during my visit. A woman went to sit down at an editorial meeting: The chair crumbled. A young man picked up a chair in a restaurant to move it to his table: The seat fell off. Light in public places flickered on and off with distressing unpredictability. Phone service was spotty at best. Domestic mail was problematic, and sending something by overseas mail was considered tantamount to throwing it away.

What has brought matters to this extreme pass? "The October Revolution," Sergei Troitsky, the genially obnoxious twenty-three-year-old bass player for a Moscow band called Metal Corrosion, declared, alluding to Lenin's 1917 coup d'etat. One afternoon Troitsky was kind enough to show me a videotape of Moscow's first Thrash Metal and Sex Festival, which took place last year. The event achieved perfection of a sort when, during a song called "Let's Go Shake Shake" (the chorus, sung in English, ran: "Let's go shake shake / Let's go fuck and shake"), ten or so Soviet lovelies took the stage, stripped to bikini underpants, garter belts, and stockings and cavorted with Troitsky and his leering bandmates before a crowd of five thousand ecstatic young people. With unerring, if unintended, Soviet irony, the Moscow authorities had granted a permit for this show under the guise of its being an AIDS-awareness event—this, in a country in which condoms, not to mention disposable syringes, are virtually impossible to come by.

Understandably, Troitsky sees his country as gripped by decadence. His solution: the restoration of the monarchy. "At every concert, we play the old Russian hymn 'God Save the Czar,'" he said proudly through an interpreter. "We write out the lyrics of the hymn to give to our fans, and they sing with us." Troitsky's father, meanwhile, works at the Institute of Marxism-Leninism, an organ of the Central Committee of the Communist party. What does Dad think about his doings? "He has his own problems to keep him busy," Troitsky said wryly.

A far more serious critic of the current system than Troitsky is Alexander Podrabinek, the editor in chief of the *samizdat* journal *Express-Khronika*. "The biggest problem of our society is socialism," said Podrabinek. "And as we liberate ourselves from this, our problems will be solved." Podrabinek is a veteran of the days when papers like *Express-Khronika*—which routinely covers issues like the independence movements in the Baltic states, terrorist actions in the Soviet republic of Azerbaijan, and antigovernment actions in the Georgian capital, Tbilisi—could only be distributed in secret and at great risk.

As it is, the journal has moved its offices seventeen times in the past three years to keep a quick step ahead of the authorities; only a week before my visit, the paramilitary police entered the current offices, which are on the ground floor of a run-down apartment complex in Moscow, and questioned the staff for three hours while a police bus stayed parked ominously in the lot outside. Even so, the lean, intense Podrabinek was able to look around his office and smile. "Now to publish *samizdat*, we have computers, fax machines, telephones," he said.

Podrabinek does not mince words in describing the state of the Soviet Union. "All of our problems have one source: The reluctance and inability of the Soviet leadership to give the society political initiatives," he said. "It concerns everything—economics, the free definition of national policy.

"With the example of Lithuania," Podrabinek continued, "we see that the central powers are reluctant to give power to the republics to pursue their policies independently. So everywhere you see a dictatorship from the center. Now the authorities give many possibilities to the society, but within very clear-cut boundaries. Those who try to traverse those boundaries are going to be punished."

The limitations on the freedoms of the Soviet people after the heady initial promises of *glasnost* and *perestroika* have combined with the paralyzing shortages and inefficiencies of the Soviet economy to undermine President Mikhail Gorbachev's national standing completely. One European writer recently described Gorbachev as a centrist in a country that no longer has a center, and in capturing the degree of the president's isolation in a land that is flying apart in every conceivable direction, that description is apt. Virtually no one has a good word to say about him. Perhaps the only person less popular than Gorbachev is his wife, Raisa, who is seen as intrusive and uppity in a country in which it is assumed that, as one woman explained only half-jokingly, "Russian women are very obedient." The most sympathetic view of Gorbachev's plight is that *glasnost* and *perestroika* have opened a Soviet Pandora's box.

"It's a lot of mess going on," complained Sasha Gradsky, a trailblazer in the creation of Soviet rock & roll more than two decades ago and a prominent figure on the music scene today. "Those things that Gorbachev intended to do, that's not quite what we have in the results. I think he wanted to start with some slight reforms, but he didn't take into account that the people are awaiting permission to shout—and very much awaiting it. He half opened the door, and the people stuck their foot in. People say that he is unstable, unsteady, that he changes his views very often, because it is not he who has chosen the way. On the contrary, the way has chosen him."

Vladislav Starkov, the editor of the Moscow-based *Arguments and Facts,* was nearly removed from his position by Gorbachev late last year after the paper published a survey that suggested the leader's popularity was slipping. The paper's editorial board, heartily supported by more than thirty million subscribers, held firm, and Starkov was permitted to retain his position. Now the Communist party refuses to allot adequate paper and printing facilities to *Arguments and Facts*—a decision the paper's editors see as political, the paper shortage in the Soviet Union notwithstanding. Starkov remains a politic supporter of *perestroika*—and Gorbachev—nonetheless.

"Two alternatives are possible, and as often happens in life, they can overlap," Starkov said about the immediate future of his country. "I'll start with the worst one. The worst may come if the leadership and the conservative part of our society manage to curtail *perestroika*. That will mean a return to the previous way: to a dictatorship of the ministries, to censorship, to tightening things up, to wasting the national wealth.

"Such measures can work for a very short time, but, after all, they will end in failure, because it is like curing a malignant tumor with anaesthetic injections. The way out of such a situation is only in civil war, because the population has accepted *perestroika* and is looking forward to the results of *perestroika*. If the conservative forces try to interfere with and hinder *perestroika*, of course, civil war will become inevitable.

"The way that Gorbachev follows is to go along a very uneven road in a cart that goes very slowly," Starkov continued. "Sometimes it stumbles, sometimes it loses its wheels, but still it goes slowly forward. Of course, it's a very slow way, but it is the right way. It does not leave any room for civil war, and it allows for the expectation among the people that at some time in the future, they will go along the paved, even road."

Such moderate views are uncommon in the two major cities of the Soviet Union, where the failures of the old system and the shock of the new generate extremes. Tensions are running uncomfortably high, as worlds collide. People are feeling the strain. I understood this in an abstract sense even before I arrived, but it became dramatically clear on a personal level about halfway into my visit when, on a bright, cool April afternoon, my driver and my interpreter got into a fistfight as we drove down a broad, heavily trafficked avenue in Leningrad.

They hadn't been getting along since they'd met the previous day, and before the fight broke out, they'd been shouting at each other for some time. Since I don't understand Russian, couldn't fathom the problem, and was equally dependent on both of them, I maintained a diplomatic silence in the back seat. The din subsided for a moment, and then the interpreter, who was sitting next to me, uncorked two rights to the driver's shoulder, and our car careened into the next lane. I shouted at them to stop and, feeling a combination of shock and terror, bolted out of the car as it paused at the next traffic light.

I stood on the street, trying to collect myself amid the crowd of pedestrians strolling by. The interpreter leaped out of the car, ran over to me, and offered a terse apology. Evidently, he'd been called a motherfucker; "I don't like bad things said about my close relatives" is how he more delicately explained it. The two of us rode public transportation—buses, trolleys, and subway trains—in near silence for the rest of the afternoon.

For the remainder of the time I was in the Soviet Union, and for weeks after I returned to New York, I wondered about this incident. The sense of having been in physical danger far from home is one obvious reason the event stayed with me. But I also wondered about the pressures that could have driven these two men—each perfectly friendly in his own way—to violate so outrageously the strict Russian code of hospitality, not to mention risk their own lives and the life of their American guest.

I thought about how, one day before the fight, the interpreter—a proper, punctilious man in his early forties with blond, closely cropped hair—had returned from his first trip to the United States. The resident of a city in which you need to carry an identity card to purchase the few goods available in the shops, he had reeled at the world of consumer plenty he had encountered in Washington, D.C., New York, Boston, and Chicago.

Just a few hours after his return to Leningrad from the United States, he'd gotten a call asking if he could do some freelance work, beginning that afternoon, as an interpreter and guide for an American visitor.

Though suffering from jet lag and still on vacation from his full-time job, he accepted. Having had to watch his money "like a calculator" while in America, and given the current state of the Soviet economy, how could he pass up the chance to pick up a few extra rubles?

The driver, meanwhile, had his own complex story—really, no story in the Soviet Union is simple. In contrast to the rather prim interpreter—a fiend for efficiency, a true product of *perestroika*—the driver was a portly, white-haired, insanely garrulous man who had served in the Russian navy for thirty-five years. A great deal of fun and almost willfully useless as a driver—he refused to take directions and talked far too much to keep track of where he was going—he was obsessed with his car and its Italian-made engine, a virtually priceless commodity given the heaps of Soviet-made junk the vast majority of his countrymen felt lucky to own.

Fuel, it seems, was suddenly in short supply—perhaps because of the recent shutdown of oil pipelines to nearby Lithuania; typically, no one could say for sure. So when, on that fateful morning, we passed a queue of perhaps fifty cars at an apparently well-stocked gasoline station, the driver unilaterally decided that regardless of our schedule, he needed to tank up.

The interpreter, steaming at the delay, and I got out, hitched a ride to a hotel a few miles away in exchange for a pack of Marlboros, and had lunch. After we finished, we waited another hour or so before the driver turned up. He was late, he explained, because the attendants at the gas station—in perfect Soviet fashion—had decided to break for lunch themselves, despite the long line. On the drive back, the two men went at each other.

Mysterious shortages, short tempers, long lines, unnecessary problems, misunderstandings, visiting foreigners, old people in a changing world, glimmering visions of Western-style prosperity, opportunities for earning extra money in the *perestroika* economy, flirting with complete catastrophe: Welcome to the old, new Soviet Union, a huge, disunited giant of a nation balanced on a high, thin tightrope.

Contradictory impulses within Soviet society fuel the instability of contemporary times. The Communist party has been entirely discredited, while, particularly among older people, there remains an almost heartbreaking nostalgia for the certainties the party has provided. In the wake of Afghanistan and the upheavals in the outlying republics, the Red

Army may be seen as an oppressive force, but any resident of Moscow or Leningrad will tell you the history of every war memorial in those cities. Older men proudly wear their military decorations on their suit coats, and the army's heroism in World War II is palpably felt. The nation's horrifying history has been revealed; Stalin is now vilified, and even the officially sacrosanct Lenin is despised by many Soviet citizens. But people are beginning to tire of the sordid revelations and wonder why all the purgative truth telling isn't making their hard, everyday lives any easier. There is an ardent desire for more freedom but a hatred for leaders who vacillate. There is a dangerous yearning for order that some seem to believe only the iron hand of the past can provide.

The free market is seen as a panacea. It's really almost shocking to hear Russians, in their ravaged circumstances, spout all the huckster-isms of a Chamber of Commerce buffoon, to hear them go on and on about joint ventures, economic development, multinational deals, business infrastructures. "You have to understand the extremism of the Russian character," one woman explained to me. "If ten years ago everybody was an agent or a spy, today everybody is an entrepreneur."

The free market is also viewed with tremendous apprehension. After all, the price of bread, maintained at an artificially low level by the government, hasn't risen here in thirty years—though it will this summer. Housing conditions are by and large appalling, but everyone is guaranteed a place to live. The economy is absurdly inefficient, but everyone is guaranteed a job—and no one watches the clock too closely if you need to knock off work for a couple of hours to go stand on line for shoes or soap. Despite the current fascination with capitalism, people are deeply suspicious of individually acquired wealth and often associate the profit motive with the omnipresent black marketeers who run what amounts to an obscenely lucrative second economy. Everyone is eager for the consumer goods that capitalism seems able to provide so effortlessly in the envied West; no one is eager to face the hardships, social dislocation, and instability that the transition to an open market will bring.

There is a sense that people have suffered enough. How could they, *why should they,* be expected to suffer more? "It seems to me that in the United States, they do not take account of suffering as one of the most important themes of art," said Mikhail Levitin, chief producer of the aesthetically adventurous Hermitage Theater, in Moscow. "But we are suffering too much here. And this is probably the way we have shared the spheres in culture and art. You take the joy of life, and we take the suffering."

Suffering, of course, is an essential theme of traditional Russian art; it is the kiln in which the Russian soul was forged, and the Russian soul is a hot ticket these days. While Americans primarily hear of the more fashionable nationalist movements in the Baltic republics, the most fiercely—and dangerously—nationalistic group in the Soviet Union is the Russians. With the seven decades since the revolution largely perceived as an unmitigated failure, a longing for the purity of the noble Russian past is in the air. That past is viewed as Slavic and Christian—a point of view that does not signal good times ahead for Jews, Asians, or other non-Russian ethnic groups, who aren't exactly having a picnic even under the current conditions. Pamyat, the Russian nationalist group that is frankly anti-Semitic and fascist, has garnered a following, but even Russians who stop well short of such extremism openly speak of darker-skinned Georgians, for example, with a contempt just a hair shy of racism.

In line with those developments, Russian mysticism is experiencing a big revival, accompanied by an extraordinary fascination with the occult. Faith healers, astrologers, psychics, and fortunetellers are much in demand. Odd rumors abound, like those that float through America about Elvis or JFK. Cosmonaut Yuri Gagarin didn't really die when it was reported he did, one such story ran; he was held in a mental institution in the provinces and only died recently.

Because Russians tend not to come at things very directly, such interests often emerge in odd contexts. For example, a series of rock concerts along the Volga River was planned to raise awareness about environmental problems in the Soviet Union—a good idea, given that the air in Moscow is pretty much three-dimensional and many of the country's waterways are horribly polluted. (One Russian I met asked if he would be able to buy a Geiger counter on an upcoming visit to the United States, so concerned was he about exposure to radiation in the wake of Chernobyl.)

Rather than addressing any specific environmental problems, however, the money raised from this series of rock concerts would go toward the establishment of a Center for Nontraditional Healing—the broad connecting idea being "health."

What exactly is nontraditional healing, I asked. "It's becoming more and more popular," a spokesman explained. "There are these people who have the ability to heal with their hands, with herbs. They can heal with energy. It comes from an interaction with nature. They say that they get the energy from space, and then they can influence you with their energy in such a big amount that it makes your organs operate in the right way. That's major league!"

As an American, I was assumed by most Soviets to be an uncritical fan of *glasnost* and *perestroika,* an unquestioning supporter of Gorbachev. They took enormous, friendly delight in indulging my perceived illusions and then disabusing me of them.

"Do you want me to say what you want to hear from me, or do you want me to say what I think?" asked Mikhail Levitin with a broad smile when I asked his opinion about the effects of *glasnost* and *perestroika* and about his country's prospects.

First what I want to hear, I replied, then what he really thinks. "Very good," he said, laughing heartily. "So I will answer in the way you'd like it to be: 'There are great changes, of course, and they are irreversible! There is no way back.' The next is my answer: 'There have been no real changes, and life will be as it is now.' "

Alexander Podrabinek of *Express-Khronika* is similarly harsh in his assessment, echoing Vladislav Starkov's worries about the possibility of a civil war. "It is very difficult to make prognoses, to forecast under this regime," he said. "You'd need to be a fortuneteller or an astrologist in this situation. For the immediate future, I would say that the society demands possibilities for itself that the authorities do not provide. If they continue to resist those demands, it might end in civil war.

"To a certain extent, Gorbachev is a symbol of what is going on here, that is true," Podrabinek continued. "But in the West, they do not see everything that is happening here; they see only what propaganda presents. There are no structural changes in the state whatsoever. All the changes are within the framework of the policy of today. If the government changes, if policy changes, everything can easily go back to what we had. Of course, we ourselves *want* it to be irreversible, so our *wishes* are the same. But the world surrounding us, we look at it with different are no irreversible changes."

Foreigners often remark that the dreadful food shortages evident in Russian shops bear no relationship to the bounteous hospitality one receives in Russian homes. At the home of Olga Kalinina, a film archivist, and her husband, Alec, who directs a puppet theater, this contrast could not have been more dramatic. What was supposed to be, on my last night in Leningrad, a quick interview about the conditions of Soviet life was soon overwhelmed by endless offerings of splendid food and paralyzing amounts of vodka.

The conversation—Alec, Olga, and I were joined by the couple's daughter, a sister-in-law, my interpreter, and a Russian journalist— turned instead to the relative merits of American and Russian women, the beauty of Leningrad's Venice-style canals, the superiority of Leningrad (to this partisan crowd, at least) to Moscow. Eventually, however, the talk returned, as all talk eventually does in the Soviet Union, to politics. "Gorbachev is a product of the old system who wants to introduce new realities into society," Olga said.

"If we look back into history, we will see that the Soviet people have been frightened by that kind of experiment," Alec added. "As history shows, there has never been a single man who could turn things upside down and create something better. That's why people are so cautious about Gorbachev." So, once again, things could be changed back?

"We simply wait for that," Olga said, with matter-of-fact sadness. "We don't wait, we *expect* it," said Alec. "Unfortunately, a lot of things repeat themselves," said Olga. "This frightens us, because if it happens, things will go backwards." Then she gathered herself, brightened and raised her glass. "So let us drink that things will go forward," she said. "If the way things develop depends on this table, there will be no problems."

But there will be problems, and they will be ravaging. The redefinition of Soviet history sparked by *glasnost* has given the past a new, more immediate life—and, in something of a reverse prophecy, made it a threatening vision of the possible future. "It's rather dramatic," said Svetlana Makurenkova, a prominent Russian translator, "that this experience, accumulated through blood and tears, is coming back to us, also to bear new blood and new tears."

New blood and new tears. Leaving Moscow I was homesick and

274 heartsick—avid to come home to my loved ones, to my familiar life in America, troubled by the ruthless days lying in wait for my friends who must continue to live in real Soviet life. Some are born to endless night, wrote Blake. Good night, Moscow.

Rolling Stone July 12–26, 1990

Erotic Terrorism

The Enemy Is Us

When an op-ed editor at the *New York Times* contacted me in 1994 about writing a piece on the possible Beatles reunion, I passed and suggested this piece instead. It was rejected as "beautifully written, but unpersuasive." It appears here for the first time.

These are strange days in the ongoing sexual counter-revolution. In this time of settling down and nesting, of children and cocooning, of safe sex and monogamy, sex is stubbornly refusing to cooperate with our repentant, high-minded aims. As happens in all repressive eras, sex, unwilling to be contained, is now liable to rear its head anywhere, at any time, however unpredictably, however unwelcome.

Sex has certainly lost none of its power to command our attention and, whether we admit it or not, to titillate us. What it has lost is its ability to delight. Colored by contemporary fears (and guilt), the major sexual dramas in the media—our collective dream-state—are uniformly violent, perverse, grotesque, and disturbing. It is the force that motivates (and sometimes justifies) murder and betrayal, abuse and exploitation. It is the monster that has devoured us.

Over the past few years, this psychic environment has generated a seemingly endless series of sexual melodramas that have gripped the country and that share one distinctive element: a grim luridness, a sense of transgression that simultaneously transfixes us and enables us to feel superior both to the central figures in the action and to our voyeuristic pleasure in their plight. These sagas are soaked in sexual content but meet the needs of the zeitgeist by condemning sex as inevitably corrupting and perverse.

The Menendez trial provides only the most recent instance of this phenomenon—and the paralyzing moral confusion that comes in its wake. What initially appeared to be an open-and-shut case of two young men murdering their wealthy parents to gain their inheritance was plunged into chaos when Eric and Lyle Menendez claimed their father had sexually abused them as children and that they had killed him in self-defense. Two separate juries could not agree on a verdict; the case against each brother ended in a mistrial.

Similarly, in another riveting Court TV soap opera, Lorena Bobbitt justified castrating her husband—the wittily named John Wayne Bobbitt—on the grounds that she had been the victim of violent sexual abuse at his hands. One jury found John not guilty of marital rape; another jury found Lorena not guilty on the grounds of temporary insanity.

And, of course, let's not forget Michael Jackson. An out-of-court settlement, rumored in the millions of dollars, essentially ended the possibility that Jackson would be criminally prosecuted for sexually abusing a thirteen-year-old boy. Many thought the settlement cemented Jackson's guilt, but some wondered, "If you genuinely believed that someone abused your child would you be satisfied with a cash settlement?" Again, a surfeit of shockingly explicit details, and no clear verdict.

Fueling the national obsession with these and other cases—who would want, after all, to neglect those fun couples Amy and Joey, or Clarence and Anita?—are two profound, and relatively recent, cultural shifts. The first is the terrifying reality of AIDS. Regardless of whether people are acting in accord with their knowledge, everyone now knows that sex can be fatal. The result is deep suspicion and fear. The consequent desire to repress sex only serves to displace it, however; forced out of our lives, it permeates the very atmosphere in which we move.

The second cultural shift is the continuing redefinition of gender roles. As male prerogatives come under increasing scrutiny in every aspect of our society, the linkages between sex and power have become more evident. Sex has come to be seen not as the province of moony-eyed lovers, or even lustful coconspirators, but as another battlefield in which hierarchical relationships are brutally acted out. It is a realm of conquerors and victims, abusers and sufferers (children as well as adults, men as well as women), oppressors and the oppressed. The result: more suspicion, more fear, fewer models for behavior, less certainty from which to make clear judgments.

And it's certainly not clear where we're going from this disturbing moment. But one thing seems true. Until we come to trust each other more and allay our fears—a cure for AIDS? a more egalitarian society?— we will continue to be confronted in our public world with nightmarish scenes from the erotic theater of our imagination, scenes that fascinate and repel us. And leave us panting for more.

Pop Goes to College

It's a luscious, sunny April day in Bowling Green, Ohio, and along
Wooster Street, the southern border of the campus of Bowling Green
State University (BGSU), students are engaged in the time-honored
spring rituals of academic life: catching rays, tossing Frisbees, and
pumping rock & roll out the open windows of frat houses. Far from
being mere breaks from the rigors of study or ways to relieve tension as
final exams approach, however, these activities could well be subjects of
study at Bowling Green, "the only institution in the nation with a degree
program in popular culture," as a school brochure proudly states.

Naturally, rock & roll is a mainstay in the curriculum of Bowling
Green's Department of Popular Culture; the department offers a course
called Introduction to Popular Music, which examines "musical styles,
trends in popular music, popular performers and entertainers." It might
be a stretch, but sunbathing and Frisbee tossing could perhaps find a
home in another course, Popular Entertainments, which analyzes "cir-
cuses, carnivals, parades, vaudeville, professional and amateur sports,
camping, etc."

At both Bowling Green and other campuses, pop culture is a booming—and increasingly controversial—academic business. Last March in
New Orleans, more than three thousand professors, scholars, and students attended the annual joint convention of the Popular Culture Association and the American Culture Association, both of which are based
in Bowling Green. There the pop culturists, as they call themselves,
heard presentations like "The Reconciliation of Archie and Meathead:
All in the Family's Last Episode," " '*Carpe Diem*' in the Music of Jimmy
Buffet," and "The Tupperware Party and the American Dream."

It has been difficult for such pursuits to gain respectability in the ivory
tower. Academia is hardly noted for the speed with which it accepts new
fields of study, and as enrollment in pop-culture courses has risen,
scholars in the field have had to endure the snobbism of their more
conventional colleagues.

In fact, battle lines have been drawn. Perhaps the most significant
face-off took place at Stanford, where the faculty senate, after a ran-
corous debate, voted earlier this year to drop a required course called
Western Culture, which had essentially been a yearlong "great books"

survey. In its place is a new course called Cultures, Ideas and Values, which keeps roughly half of the Western Culture syllabus but also prescribes a work from "at least one non-European culture" and books by "women, minorities and persons of color." The canon busting at Stanford augurs well for pop-culture advocates.

Ray Browne, the founder and head of Bowling Green's popular-culture program, has been at the forefront of his discipline's battle for credibility for more than twenty years—a struggle he perceives as having ended in victory. A sixty-six-year-old man of unfailing optimism, Browne is like a civil-rights worker who remembers when segregation was the law of the land and who is proud and happy to be alive in a time when equality is legally guaranteed—even if, in practice, such equality is far from a reality.

Browne's cluttered office is in the basement of the popular-culture building—a small brick house located, appropriately enough, just off campus, across Wooster Street. Asked if popular culture is still an embattled field, Browne leans forward and says, "No, no longer. Fifteen years ago, if you'd asked that question, the answer would have been yes. Maybe even five or seven years ago. But not any longer." Browne's certainty is based on his sense of the mood at the convention in New Orleans. "I detected a sense of accomplishment and dignity and complete self-reliance which I had never felt before," he says. "The people there could stand up alongside any academic with the assurance that 'my field is just as important as your field.' "

Not everyone would grant popular-culture studies anywhere near that degree of intellectual status. Even members of Browne's own faculty say that their war is far from won. "I think that it's too early to declare victory," says Jack Santino, an assistant professor in the department. "What we have is a single master's program in a single department in a single university in one state in this country. I don't think that's the top of the mountain."

The climb, however, may begin to get easier. Debate has raged about what exactly the appropriate subjects for college study are. Over the past eight years, the consensus about what belongs in the curriculum has narrowed, for reasons that are political as well as educational. Although the campus upheavals of the Sixties and student demands for "relevance" reshaped college curricula in the Seventies, the Reagan administration swept into power with a far more conservative education policy.

As head of the National Endowment for the Humanities (NEH) during Reagan's first term, William J. Bennett, who would go on to become the secretary of education, established himself as a leading spokesperson for the "back to basics" movement, which advocates a return to a "core curriculum" based on traditional fields of study and a canon of great works. Considerable anxiety was raised by the 1983 Department of Education study *A Nation at Risk*, which depicted American students as ignorant of the most elementary facts of their nation's history and culture.

If that weren't enough, Allan Bloom's best-selling jeremiad *The Closing of the American Mind* and E. D. Hirsch Jr.'s *Cultural Literacy* heated the argument even more. Bloom's book asserts, among other things, that rock & roll "ruins the imagination of young people and makes it very difficult for them to have a passionate relationship to the art and thought that are the substance of liberal education." Meanwhile, Lynne Cheney, who succeeded Bennett at the NEH, is firmly in agreement with Bennett's vision, and she has used the enormous funding power of her agency to advance further the Reagan administration's agenda.

So it's no surprise that a prominent sign in the pop-culture building at BGSU reads, ALLAN BLOOM AND LYNNE CHENEY WILL BURN IN HELL. Browne sees the Reagan administration's attitude toward popular culture as out of step with what's happening at universities around the country. "The only thing they've done is deny us any kind of federal assistance," he says. "William Bennett and Lynne Cheney are just as intransigent and opposed as they've ever been, but their voices have not been heard. The number of courses is growing."

One reason schools are creating popular-culture courses is that, even in the era of the business major, students flock to them. "We may be or may not be halfway decent scholars," says Jack Nachbar, a professor of popular culture at Bowling Green. "But I think the department as a whole takes its teaching very seriously." At a time when many professors regard teaching as an annoying distraction from the research projects that can win them tenure and promotion, such dedication is no small attraction to students. In addition, pop-culture professors are often more willing to be imaginative in their instructional methods.

When Van Cagle—a young professor at Bowling Green who will be offering popular-culture courses this year at Tulane University, in New Orleans—was teaching Dick Hebdige's *Subculture: The Meaning of Style* in his popular-music class, he decided to take his subject to the streets. "The assignment for that night," Cagle says, "was to try to figure out the literal reactions in everyday life that punks got on the street in London in 1977. I asked the students to think about the clothing, think about what it meant, and dress that way for the class."

Cagle then led a group of students decked out in spiked hair, leather dresses, handcuffs, chains, safety pins, red Mohawks, and ripped fishnet stockings on a walk around campus. Cagle himself donned a dog collar, a leather jacket, and a shirt stained with fake blood. The group elicited quite a response. "Hebdige suggests that you'll either get the reaction that you're insane, people will want to draw you back into their own reality and make you seem normal, or they'll feel very threatened," Cagle says. "We had a group of fraternity guys follow us from the education building to the library, and they were talking about how much they wanted to kill us. They thought we were very real. . . . We got the reactions we needed, and we were able to go back to the class and talk about it."

At Bowling Green, a school of about fifteen thousand students, there are currently twenty undergraduates majoring in pop culture, eight undergraduates minoring in it, and fourteen graduate students working toward a pop-culture master's degree. Students can also pursue a Ph.D. in American culture with a concentration in popular culture. About two thousand students a year enroll in pop-culture classes, which are cross-listed with disciplines ranging from philosophy to home economics. Many students drift into the classes hoping to fill a humanities requirement with a course that demands little more than flipping on the tube or reading comic books. If they eventually find that these classes can teach them a good deal about the media-saturated world around them and decide to pursue their interest further, they often encounter the same condescending attitudes that afflict their professors.

"I think the main reasons the classes are looked upon as a blow-off is that the people who come to them enjoy them," says Brett Henne, a journalism student who has taken a few popular-culture courses. "If you enjoy a class, it doesn't necessarily make it a blow-off. It just means that you're interested in learning."

Popular-culture students tend to be people who are interested in college less as a means of career advancement than as a time of exploration. "College years are such a small percentage of your life—why not enjoy them?" asks Lora Marini, a double major in pop culture and psychology who has just given an energetic report on "death rock"—the Smiths, the Jesus and Mary Chain, and Siouxsie and the Banshees—in Cagle's popular-music class. "There are so many people who say they have to graduate in four years. They have to get diplomas so they can go out and get a job. I don't care if I'm here eight years."

Though pop-culture students tend to do no worse than other humanities majors on the job market, some students are hedging their bets. "I'm not a pop-culture major; I'm a communications major," says John McAlea, who is also in a local band called the Exchange. "I'm wading both streams, because I'm taking business classes but I'm also taking pop-culture classes. The reason why I take pop-culture classes is for *me*—I want to know this knowledge."

The traditional academic dogma would seem to say that the knowledge McAlea wants is not worth knowing. If disconcerting numbers of students don't know who T. S. Eliot was or when the Civil War was fought, should they really be permitted to fulfill requirements with a course on detective novels?

"The one thing that I think is important is that we don't necessarily say that T. S. Eliot shouldn't be taught," says Jack Santino. "It's not an either-or situation. I think people should know when the Civil War was and they should know about T. S. Eliot—but they should also be aware that the culture they live in is important and meaningful and operative.

"What we *don't* do is just flip on the television for an hour," Santino adds. "The point is to talk about it in terms of social context, in terms of creation and intentionality and audience—questions that, I would say, have never occurred to most of the students before. That's a legitimate perspective."

The growth of pop-culture studies is also related to another intellectual trend. Many young academics are less interested in establishing the "quality" of a particular book or song or movie than in discovering what it expresses about the society that created it. This approach is closer to sociology than to aesthetics, and it is one thread in the weave of "cultural relativism"—the belief that standards of value are embedded in specific societies and do not translate meaningfully from one culture to another.

"The whole argument of 'Is this great art?' is irrelevant to the framework in which we're studying," says Mickey Stephens, a Ph.D. student in the American-culture program and a guitarist in the Bowling Green band the Sygn, which formerly was known as the Sex Beatles. "The point would be that you can find the same amount of interest in any cultural product. We're not looking for aesthetic values. We're not looking for value judgments. What we're looking for is cultural indicators, how well you can feel the pulse of the culture by analyzing any artifact of the culture at a given time."

But according to Dieter Frank, another Ph.D. candidate in American culture and Stephens's partner in the Sygn, this cultural relativism, combined with the uncertain standing of popular culture in the academic hierarchy, makes for a credibility crisis in the field. "The last piece that finally defines what exactly it is that we're studying is, in my opinion, missing," he says. "A good example might be the questions for my M.A. exam, the comps I took last week. The questions were basically 'Tell me, what do you think about this program? Is it okay? Do you have suggestions?' There's still this uncertainty. 'Is this the right direction, or is there any direction at all? Do you feel that we're heading somewhere?'"

Whatever the final destination proves to be, popular culture is certain to be part of the academic landscape in the future. The great tradition of Western culture is increasingly seen as a white-male hegemony. As minorities and women achieve a greater say in the definition of that culture, it's inevitable that popular forms of expression—which, because they have been seen as less "serious," have allowed for broader participation—will be viewed as valid fields of study. Also, since the late Fifties, America itself has been a virtual laboratory of popular culture. Anyone who wants to figure out what's been going on in this society for the past thirty years simply must take television, the movies and pop music into account.

And sometimes popular-culture studies can lead to more personal insights. "Studying popular culture helped me find myself," says Rod Hatfield, a Bowling Green undergraduate and a member of a local performance-art band called Elvis Christ. "I was such a fan of pop culture, and I didn't even realize until I began studying it: 'Wow, this stuff applies to me—to my haircut, to my clothes.' I think it's a really valid study of society, what America's up to at a particular time."

Rolling Stone October 6, 1988

Popular Music

Political and Social Realities

Can Be Discovered in Serious

Criticism of the Medium

Last fall I attended a seminar on media coverage of Africa held at the Freedom Forum Media Studies Center at Columbia University. The two dozen or so participants represented an impressive range of backgrounds and ideological and professional viewpoints. The prevailing opinion seemed to be that coverage was highly inadequate, that it painted an incomplete and unfair portrait of Africa, quite possibly for reasons of an, at best, unconscious racism.

I essentially agree with both those conclusions. But, ultimately, what struck me as odd about the seminar was that coverage of Africa from a cultural perspective was—this time for reasons that might best be described as beneath consciousness—entirely excluded from the discussion. When I raised this point, I met with polite bemusement; it was considered, in near silence, for a moment then the conversation moved on, presumably to what were regarded as more serious issues.

Culture is not only as important as politics in its own right, but also one of the most profound ways in which political and social realities—and the fears and anxieties underlying those realities—find honest expression.

There is simply no question that for the past decade or so popular music has provided the most significant forum in which issues of importance to Africa could be explored and brought to the attention of millions of people. The "We Are the World" single and the Live Aid concert brought the story of famine in Africa into virtually every American home. A series of concerts organized by Amnesty International dramatized the plight of political prisoners in African countries and around the world. A daylong concert calling for the release of Nelson Mandela, attended by more than seventy thousand people in London in 1988, triggered a barrage of media debate about apartheid, corporate involvement with South Africa, and, after the broadcast in the United

States was stripped of its political content, the moral culpability of the international community.

And when Paul Simon released "Graceland" in 1986, no review of that album could ignore such charged questions as: Was it appropriate for a Western musician, whatever his stature and intentions, to travel to South Africa to record an album in violation of the United Nations boycott? Did Simon's use of black South African musicians and musical styles constitute cultural homage or cultural imperialism? How did his borrowings relate to the entire history of white artists, from Picasso to the Rolling Stones, who have drawn inspiration and perhaps more than that from African and African-derived sources?

In our own country, the current presidential campaign makes grimly palpable the extent to which popular music—and specifically rap—has become a cultural battleground. Is it possible to discuss the work of Ice-T or Sister Souljah in purely aesthetic terms, independent of the attacks on them by the likes of President Bush and Governor Clinton? And, as in the days of Elvis and before, every group interested in limiting freedom of expression—an issue of no small significance to the media— finds a ready target in the world of popular music, one of the few cultural arenas that has routinely admitted the voices of minorities and the working-class.

This is not at all to say that popular music criticism can somehow substitute for incisive, analytical coverage of news issues. High-minded actions by millionaire rock stars will not save the world, and rapping about a problem does not solve it. If artists wish to engage the world of public events either in their work or outside it, their motives and opinions need to be examined as stringently as those of any other public figures.

The most skillful writing about popular music is able to do this, to balance a full array of concerns—the intentions of the artists, the aesthetic worth of their efforts, and their meaning in the surrounding culture—with grace, intelligence, and insight.

The primary reason why so much writing about popular music is so bad is that, particularly at newspapers, pop music criticism simply isn't taken very seriously. A couple of years ago I ran into a childhood friend who had become a surgeon. When I told him I was an editor at *Rolling Stone,* he asked, with genuine curiosity, if I thought I might ever be interested in going into "real journalism."

Many newspaper editors, particularly outside major urban areas, share that sense of wonderment about why smart adults who appear normal in every other respect would pursue a career writing about popular music. Such editors don't know much about the music, don't like it, and couldn't care less. That attitude obviously cannot help but undermine the quality of coverage. Not only do editors tolerate the sort of bad or silly writing about pop music that they would never put up with in other sections of the paper, they subtly—or not so subtly—encourage it. In their staffing decisions and choice of assignments, they might even be said to create it.

Reporters who couldn't cut it in news or, even more certainly, sports—the area with the most demanding readership and in which the standards of first-rate writing and in-depth knowledge are upheld most rigorously—are routinely busted to the pop-music beat. Liking rock & roll and a tolerance for late nights in the hot clubs and crowded arenas in which the music is performed are thought to be the only relevant criteria for the critic's job. Consequently the music rarely receives the type of probing, authoritative evaluation that is accorded without a second thought to the more traditional arts—theater or classical music, for example—or even to the movies.

If I seem to be singling out daily newspapers for criticism, I definitely don't mean to. Publications that offer more specialized coverage of popular culture—monthly music magazines or so-called "alternative" weeklies—seldom do much better, though their problems are of a different sort. Such publications are typically more adventurous in their coverage, often to the point of being proudly and willfully obscure. The role of the critic is perceived to be something like "Ambassador to the Unhip"; the writing frequently is characterized by a chiding—even, despite all the voguish mannerisms—schoolteacherish tone. Attitude substitutes for perspective and opinions replace ideas.

The unstated question underlying such writing might be said to be: "But why don't you know all this already? It's so tedious to have to explain it to you." The stylistic excesses are sometimes justified as the writer's effort to mirror the energy of the music; in fact, they seem primarily designed to relieve the writer's boredom. Half-digested academic cultural theory combines with witless adolescent posturing and outrageously indulgent first-person rantings to create writing that can be of interest only to the most hardened or masochistic insiders.

Popular glossy magazines, on the other hand, often fetishize celebrity and hold matters of substance hostage to the trends of the moment. "Criticism" in any sense of the term can scarcely be applied to this "Lifestyles of the Rich and Famous" approach to coverage.

In the hands of witty, keen-eyed features writers, such profiles can be fascinating glimpses of lives trapped in the soft hell of notoriety—or they can just be fun, journalistic bonbons. Most often, however, they serve to inscribe more deeply the idea that the rich and famous are not only different from, but better than, you and me.

Some general observations can be made. The function and meaning of criticism are shifting dramatically in every aspect of our culture. The drama critic at the *New York Times* may be able to shut down a play with a negative review, but few individual or institutional voices wield that kind of power any longer, and that's almost certainly for the good. Providing guidance to potential consumers of the arts—"Is it thumbs up or thumbs down?"—is one legitimate function of journalistic criticism, but it absolutely is not the only one and it should not even be the primary one.

Besides, given the enormous cultural diversity of many of our country's communities, readers and viewers are becoming increasingly wary of placing their trust in one godlike critical figure. Consequently, the most honest and responsible critical writing these days does not hide behind the troubled, time-worn notion of "objective truth," but offers an informed, clearly stated view that the audience can understand and evaluate, accept or reject. Criticism, however penetrating, should not be regarded as the final word; it should mark the beginning of a dialogue with the audience, not the end of one.

Like all arts writing, popular music criticism should be driven by the power of the writer's ideas, not the real or imagined allure of the subject. That is to say, whether the subject is Madonna or the newest, least-known, least-scintillating band on the local scene, the writer's perspective should provide the story's most lasting impression. Like all writing in general-interest publications, critical writing about even the most rarefied, technically demanding, or avant-garde subjects should be accessible to nonspecialist readers.

Though *Rolling Stone* is primarily a music magazine, it does not cover music exclusively and its audience is extremely diverse. Some of our audience began reading the magazine at its inception in 1967 and are in their thirties or forties; others began reading it last year and are in their teens or twenties. Some people read it for the general-interest features or political coverage; others read it for a broader assessment of the pop-culture scene that includes movies and television, and still others do read it principally for its music coverage.

Moreover, particularly in recent years, significant fissures have developed in the music audience; these are changes in *Rolling Stone*'s readership that reflect changes in the society at large. Some of the magazine's readers are rap fans; others hate it. Some, both young and old, revere the titanic figures of the Sixties; others weary of tales about the good old days of peace, love, and granola.

Finding a way to address such a splintered audience is a challenge. To avoid being driven mad, I try, both in my editing of the album review section and in my own writing for the magazine, to summon up an imaginary figure I term "the smart, curious reader." By "smart" I mean possessing a reasonable degree of comfort with the process of engaging ideas; for critical writing especially, this seems the minimal requirement. By "curious" I mean possessing a reasonable degree of interest in the subject, even if that interest is entirely abstract and is accompanied by little or no specific prior knowledge. The aim of writing addressed to this reader is work that rewards anyone who comes to it with an open mind.

To reinforce the notion of criticism as an ongoing dialogue, I also try to keep the section open to a broad range of voices, styles, and viewpoints—assuming always that the critic is qualified and informed. A review by one writer will sometimes set forth an aesthetic vision entirely antithetical to the one put forward with equal conviction by another writer in an adjoining review. Some readers, like the sort of student who grows uneasy when, at the end of a vigorous class discussion, the teacher refuses to give the "right" answer, find this approach infuriating. Others, hopefully, find it liberating and enlivening, small but telling evidence of a democratic ideal in which differing ideas are all allowed valid expression.

Beyond this, there really is no magic prescription for ensuring first-rate critical writing about popular music or any other subject, cultural or political. The problems with coverage of the music result primarily from problems in how the music is perceived by the people who determine how it is going to be covered. Unless it is seen as a worthy subject that requires serious assessment in all its aspects by talented people willing to communicate with a general audience, the quality of the coverage will suffer. It isn't much more complicated than that. More than twenty-five years after Aretha Franklin sang the words of Otis Redding, defining in terms of an indelible pop song one of the crucial demands of the civil rights movement, the issue is still respect.

Nieman Reports Fall 1992

Just when it seemed about to keel over from the weight of its own irrelevance, the academic world has sprung to life again. Both left-wing and right-wing critics are raging about which subjects are fit to teach in colleges. Minorities and women are demanding that their stories be told in courses that have for decades been white-male domains. Students are protesting United States involvement in South Africa and Central America. Not since the Sixties and early Seventies have events on college campuses so commanded the attention of those outside the ivied walls.

This ferment is being reflected in—and further stirred up by—what students are reading. Not all students, of course. The typical university bookstore, after all, primarily moves books that are assigned for courses, best-sellers that one might find just as easily at the local mall, and cartoon time killers. Fortunately, however, the independently owned bookstores around schools or in college towns tell a far more intriguing story. Many students are venturing beyond the union building for reading matter that challenges accepted notions both within and outside the academy.

To find out what more adventurous college students are reading, *Rolling Stone* called twenty-six of these bookstores—from New York City's St. Mark's Bookshop to Salt Lake City's Cosmic Aeroplane Books, from San Francisco's City Lights Bookstore to Iowa City's Prairie Lights Books. We asked what books students are buying, outside of required reading for courses. Each store supplied a list of its best-selling out-of-the-mainstream books; from those reports, we've compiled the list that follows this essay.

Rather than diving into Stephen King or right-wing maven Tom Clancy, the student customers of independent bookstores are immersing themselves in cultural theory and postmodernist speculations, advanced scientific thought, hard-hitting political studies, and fiction from beyond America's borders.

Some of the books are or have been best-sellers, but you're not likely to find any of them resting on top of the keg at your next frat party. It takes a certain type of person to pass early adulthood pondering the mind-boggling complexities of *Postmodernism and Its Discontents: Theories,*

Practices—edited by E. Ann Kaplan, a professor at the State University of New York at Stony Brook (the book includes her remarkable essay "Feminism/Oedipus/Postmodernism: The Case of MTV")—while other students stick to their management textbooks.

One student who eschewed the Eighties emphasis on business-related studies for the joys of intellection is Rob Latham, a recent graduate of the University of Florida. "Well, you have to understand, I was a humanities major," says Latham, "so I'm already reconciled to the fact that the only kind of job I'm likely to get is within the academy." Jonathan Flatley, a senior at Amherst College, in Massachusetts, says, "If you're to the left and don't agree with a lot of stuff that's going on, one of the few marginalized spaces to move is in academia."

The margins can sometimes be a stimulating place—and they also have a surprising tendency to widen. The French existentialists who inspired the intellectual underground on campuses in the Fifties provided the philosophical underpinning for what became the beat movement. Students who were reading Herbert Marcuse and other Marxist theorists helped launch the political upheavals of the Sixties. The mystical concerns of Hermann Hesse, the Freudian utopianism of Norman O. Brown's *Life Against Death* and *Love's Body*, and even the wacky fantasies of J. R. R. Tolkien helped spur the spiritual questing of that decade.

After a lengthy period of enervation, the campus has once again become a magnet for ambitious, radical ideas—ideas that, however esoteric, may actually turn out to have an application or two. Fashionable theories of postmodernism—like poststructuralism and deconstruction—are giving students tools they can use to analyze the society they live in and study how power works at the universities they attend. If, to take a Marxist perspective, knowledge is the commodity produced and sold at the university, it makes sense to ask who determines which brand of knowledge is worth selling, who profits from the existing arrangement, and whether people's actual needs are being met by the product.

In an apt contradiction, deconstruction is both the purest flowering of an intellectual life untested by the world and a principal means by which academic concerns are having an effect outside the campus. Many academic theorists may write as if they want to repel comprehension, but their ideas have still managed to help undermine the foundations on which higher education in America has rested.

"I think we've been getting through," says Frank Lentricchia, a professor of English at Duke University and author of *After the New Criticism* and *Criticism and Social Change.* "The discourse itself is often esoteric, that's true. Unfortunately true, sometimes. But that's almost beside the point. If intellectuals have to talk to one another in specialized terms, so be it. The question becomes 'Does that get translated at some level into the classroom?' And if it *does,* then the barn door is open. Once you get into the undergraduate classroom successfully, then you're outside the ivory tower. You're into the culture."

The controversy over the goals of college study began in earnest a couple of years ago. Conservatives like Allan Bloom, author of *The Closing of the American Mind,* and former secretary of education William J. Bennett have been enraged by younger professors who have challenged previously sacrosanct notions about the classics and the curriculum. *Multi-Cultural Literacy: Opening the American Mind,* an anthology of essays by a rainbow coalition of authors, including novelists James Baldwin, Ishmael Reed, and Carlos Fuentes, is a direct response to the Western European bias of Bloom's book, the limited scope of E. D. Hirsch Jr.'s *Cultural Literacy,* and the narrowness of Bennett's vision of American education.

And then there is the theory mob. At their most vital, deconstructionists set out to reveal the array of assumptions that underlie the most seemingly objective statements. Some of these theorists look beyond language into society, and for them, social realities are not fixed and permanent but shifting and fluid; in a sense these realities are "texts" that can be analyzed, understood, and, possibly, changed.

Following Michel Foucault, the French poststructuralist who has shown how definitions of crime, madness, and sexuality vary from age to age and place to place to serve the interests of the powerful, many current thinkers have taught students to distrust the official line, to ask who benefits from "the way things are," to search for the many possible meanings beneath the received truth.

Such ideas have proven to be heady stuff in the Reagan decade, a time when questioning has been officially discouraged and accepting the system has been seen as the first step on the road to the universal goal of economic fulfillment. "With Foucault saying knowledge is power, for me it was a big and powerful realization," says Flatley. "The power that it gives you to think critically is exciting."

Such lessons can also help students discern the links between critical thought and public action. Feminist authors in particular have lessened the distance between words and the world. The conviction that the personal is political is still a subversive idea in a culture that typically enforces a strict split between private and public lives.

"I think there's a definite connection between the kinds of things I study and the demonstrations on campus—the CIA protest, the childcare protest," says Carl Martin, a senior at Duke. "For example, there's a lot of rape in Durham, and we had a 'take back the night' march as a consciousness raiser, an empowering event for women. Six hundred people marched. If you sit in class and talk about issues of sexism in the academy, that's not all you talk about. It starts to get very personal. The study of literature was a way into sharing ideas about sexism in our own lives. Taking that class was one of the reasons I showed up for that march."

Lentricchia sees a demographic explanation for the change of emphasis in the humanities. "The reason there's a lot of shift going on right now toward opening up the canon as it was taught by the old guys in the Thirties and Forties," he says, "is that after World War II a whole different type of person began to come into the profession of literary studies. We were not produced by that gentlemanly, Waspy New England tradition. I think we bring a whole new set of concerns. There's a lot more women in the profession now. Lots of minorities have gotten in. I think people necessarily bring their interests to bear."

Not every book is a call to arms, of course. *The Power of Myth*—a rendering of Joseph Campbell's conversations with journalist Bill Moyers for the PBS television series of the same name—is a discussion of mythological ideas that wanders across centuries and national boundaries. Although it is more spiritual in its concerns than many of the other books on the list, its popularity may derive from a similar source: the desire of students for something more satisfying and substantive than the consumer culture surrounding them.

Jean Baudrillard, the latest rage from France, where the method of deconstruction originated, presents another set of issues. His latest book, *America*, a compendium of jottings made while he was traveling through his favorite postmodern terrain, is occasionally provocative and almost always infuriating. Nat Herold of the Goliard Bookshop, in

Amherst, Massachusetts, describes it as "the first postmodern coffee-table book."

America is filled with perceptive, almost poetic observations, like this one about New York City: "That life begins again each morning is a kind of miracle, considering how much energy was expended the day before." Unfortunately, such insights alternate with annoying attempts to make every sentence a tour de force of insight and Gallic wit. Spotting some break dancers on a Manhattan street, Baudrillard writes, "You might say that in curling up and spiralling around on the ground like this, they seem to be digging a hole for themselves within their own bodies, from which to stare out in the ironic, indolent pose of the dead." *You* might say that, Jean—the rest of us might enjoy the skill of the show, drop a bill in the kids' hat, and be on our way.

Baudrillard's other writings, which have been highly influential, particularly in the art world, use terms like "simulation," "objective irony," and "strategy of indifference" to describe the effects of the media and consumerism on contemporary society. In another apt postmodern contradiction, it's often difficult to tell whether he's bemoaning or celebrating the passivity and confusion he's writing about.

That swirling quality of postmodernism—no position can be defined without immediately being destabilized and undermined—is deeply unsettling for those who believe that theory somehow ought to lead to meaningful action. "Everyone has a critique and no one has a solution, which is part of the postmodern condition," says Doug Jones of the Brazos Bookstore, in Houston. "Questions, but no answers."

Postmodernism, says Alexandra Leader, a senior at the University of Florida, "is the perfect subject for a college campus, where you can discuss things but not necessarily apply them. . . . I'm a little uncertain about what I can do with the theory I'm learning." Sarah Morris, a senior at Brown University and editor of a journal of criticism called *Defunct!*, hits this point harder still. "The more I study and try to understand poststructuralist thinkers," she says, "the more they seem to reflect a cynicism in our culture which doesn't lead to political action at all. It rather leads you to reconciling yourself with the reality you live under."

On other levels, postmodern theory seems also to be a magnificent expression of revenge: the Oedipal revenge of younger academics on their older, more conservative—and more powerful and entrenched—

colleagues; the defensive revenge of the academy as a whole on a bottom-line world that finds the life of the mind increasingly alien; the revenge of the post-Sixties generation on its self-righteous elders; the revenge of bookish humanities majors on more single-mindedly career-driven students; and, finally, the revenge of literary critics on the authors they write about.

"One of the things postmodern literary theory was supposed to do was undermine the hierarchy between literary theory and the notion of an original text," Herold says of the theorists who have declared "the death of the author." "What it has done in practice is to hold on to the hierarchy but invert it. So people now read theory, and they don't read what we used to call literature."

Perhaps the books students are reading indicate that the very notion of literature or the intellectual life is in the process of being deconstructed and re-created. "It's not that we don't read the classics anymore," Lentricchia says. "We still will. But this list constitutes a new image of the intellectual. There's literature on it, there's cultural theory, and there's scientific theory. At least where I teach, from out of the energy that I've been teaching and writing from, those three things are coordinated. They have kinship. . . . I think that's really exciting. The list indicates a kind of new person who's not going to be satisfied with the usual canonical things."

The prominence of such diverse, thorny, and irreverent books on college campuses is encouraging when the *New York Times*, in separate articles, reports that incoming freshmen "are increasingly interested in college as a way to land a high-paying job" and quotes one book editor as saying, "There is no meaningful audience in their teen-age years or people in their twenties" for serious books. To prevent universities from becoming nothing more than trade schools for corporations, we'll need the kind of serious fun these books provide.

The Hip Reading List

1. *The Power of Myth* by Joseph Campbell with Bill Moyers
2. *Love in the Time of Cholera* by Gabriel García Márquez
3. *Manufacturing Consent: The Political Economy of the Mass Media* by Edward S. Herman and Noam Chomsky

4. *Beloved* by Toni Morrison

5. *America* by Jean Baudrillard

6. *Chaos* by James Gleick

7. *The Care of the Self: The History of Sexuality, Volume Three* by Michel Foucault

8. *Corruptions of Empire* by Alexander Cockburn

9. *A Bright Shining Lie: John Paul Vann and America in Vietnam* by Neil Sheehan

10. *A Brief History of Time* by Stephen Hawking

11. *The Predicament of Culture: Twentieth-Century Ethnography, Literature, and Art* by James Clifford

12. *The Queen of the Damned* by Anne Rice

13. *Parting the Waters: America in the King Years, 1954–63* by Taylor Branch

14. *Multi-Cultural Literacy: Opening the American Mind* edited by Rick Simonson & Scott Walker

15. *The Bonfire of the Vanities* by Tom Wolfe

16. *The World as I Found It* by Bruce Duffy

17. *Life: A User's Manual* by Georges Perec

18. *Critique of Cynical Reason* by Peter Sloterdijk

19. *The Anti-Aesthetic: Essays on Postmodern Culture* edited by Hal Foster

20. *Invisible Cities* by Italo Calvino

21. *The Unbearable Lightness of Being* by Milan Kundera

22. *Guilty* by Georges Bataille

23. *Postmodernism and Its Discontents: Theories, Practices* edited by E. Ann Kaplan

24. *The Lyre of Orpheus* Robertson Davies

25. *Memory of Fire: Genesis* by Eduardo Galeano

Rolling Stone March 23, 1989

Village Idiots

I *had a dream the other night* —inspired by thoughts about this assignment [to write about the future of popular music], innumerable articles about interactive technology and the "information highway," my
girlfriend's current obsession with Bob Dylan, Michiko Kakutani's mus-
ings about the belief that truth is ultimately indiscernible, recent view-
ings of *Zelig* and a bootleg version of *Eat the Document,* and my fears that
in the future no one will read—in which someone took a print of *Don't
Look Back* and reconstructed it so that Madonna was the central character. In short, I had a dream about *Truth or Dare.*

Thinking about those two movies, I decided, in terms of writing this
piece, to get real: What conceivable point is there in attempting to speculate about the future of popular music? Is there anyone at any time in the
past who could have predicted Elvis, the Beatles, rap, MTV, or Seattle—
not to mention the seismic shifts that have displaced Bob Dylan as a
central cultural symbol and substituted Madonna? Besides, what seems
more dated—however poignantly—than a previous age's vision of the
future?

There is some point, however, in trying to imagine how music will be
presented to us in the future. The short answer is: visually to a greater
and greater extent. The issue, then, is what we will be given to interpret
and how we will respond both emotionally and analytically.

Let's go back to the two movies. Sure, the sophisticated cliché runs,
both Dylan and Madonna are constructed figures—Madonna's just
more honest about it. But, really, the primary difference between *Don't
Look Back* and *Truth or Dare*—that is, between 1966 and 1991—is that
while Dylan keeps his personal life entirely private but almost gleefully
shows his manager muscling promoters for money, Madonna reveals
every detail of her psychosexual life but slams the door shut when the
camera attempts to follow her into a business meeting.

The point is, though money is a far greater factor in the creation of
music now than it was twenty-five years ago, its influence, while much
more apparent on the glitzy surface, is also much more concealed. The
never-ending stream of free-floating images that critics so love to dissect
obscures the bottom-line world where the deals that determine who

makes music at all are made. Money walks, but never talks: postmodernism stops here.

Dreams of Madonna are one thing. But in my nightmare vision of the five-hundred-channel world to come, the images will continue to pour forth uncontrollably and the corporate rhetoric will declare that it's all happening in the name of diversity and individual preference. Viewers will be able to hone their tastes to a degree of purity that will never have to be violated by the tastes of anyone else.

The information highway will enable us to get the music we "want" faster than ever, but will raze communities of common musical vision. These media will introduce a world more radically isolated than the world before recorded music and television, when you would know the styles and songs of your particular community and nothing more. Limited as their knowledge may have been, those early communities were based on geography, shared ethnic history, and a common vision of the role music should play in people's lives.

No such ties will bind us in the brave new technological dystopia. Popular music will be the narcotic consolation for human beings irreparably defined as consumers and lost in the media maze, each person his or her own desolate global village.

Village Voice September 7, 1993

Talking Big

Can Eric Bogosian Tune In and Turn On

without Selling Out?

"**H**e's *going down in flames.*" That's how one character describes the predicament of Barry Champlain, the acerbic talk-show host whose psychic disintegration is the core of *Talk Radio*, the new movie directed by Oliver Stone and starring Eric Bogosian. Barry's chronically simmering crises reach a boil when a network offers to broadcast his Dallas-based show nationwide. Barry is intrigued by the notion of a bigger audience and greater stardom. But he's also worried about losing the freedom to say what he wants—and losing the slim hold he maintains on his sanity if the pressure of his job gets pumped up too high.

It turns out that the issue of "going national" is almost as unsettling for Eric Bogosian as it is for his character. Bogosian, who cowrote the play on which *Talk Radio* is based, is fond of saying, "Barry is me." Bogosian's first feature-film role dangles the prospect of mass exposure—and has forced him to ask himself what he wants.

"I'm not writing about anybody over there," Bogosian says. "I'm writing about myself. When I create Barry Champlain, I know him inside out. When he's tempted by something, I'm tempted. . . . My audience suddenly moves from two hundred people or three hundred people to *millions* of people. How can I make all these millions of people love me, and is that something I should try to do? That's when I start to get all torn up by it. It's an issue for me, and so it became an issue in the movie. I do believe that if you keep looking at the nasty stuff you don't want to look at, you can live with it better. It's better than just ignoring it."

Bogosian, who is thirty-five, and his collaborator Tad Savinar created the character of Barry Champlain in 1983, and *Talk Radio* was first done as one of Bogosian's one-man performances in 1985 at the Portland Center for the Visual Arts. It came to national attention in 1987 when producer Joseph Papp brought it to the Public Theater, in New York, rewritten as a full-length play, the first of Bogosian's career.

Reshaping *Talk Radio* as a play brought a fitting culmination to the series of edgy solo performances Bogosian had been giving since the late Seventies. First as the stand-up comedian Ricky Paul, whose racist and sexist comments stiffened backs in fashionably liberal New York clubs, and later in a series of roles he created for the one-man shows *FunHouse* and *Drinking in America,* Bogosian defined a style of performance art that was equal parts black humor, social confrontation, popculture exhibitionism, and psychological agitprop. Not an easy combination to bring to the big screen.

In a storefront office on Elizabeth Street, in Manhattan, that once served as his apartment—and in another era as a grocery store owned by Martin Scorsese's father—Bogosian describes the process of making *Talk Radio* into a film as "an enormous challenge, on many fronts.

"It wasn't just the writing, or the question of 'Can we make a movie?' but 'Can we make a movie and keep the thematic center of the play?' " he says, wearing a characteristic ensemble—a black sweat shirt and black jeans. "My central idea was not something which you could go into a Hollywood meeting and say, 'Here's my concept, *bang-o.*' "

Director Oliver Stone cowrote the screenplay for *Talk Radio* with Bogosian, and the credits also acknowledge Stephen Singular's book *Talked to Death: The Life and Murder of Alan Berg,* the story of a liberal talk-show host in Denver who was killed by right-wing fanatics. Bogosian had little screenwriting experience, and his only acting in major productions had been a role in *The Caine Mutiny Court Martial,* which was filmed for television by Robert Altman, and appearances on *The Twilight Zone* and *Miami Vice.* Consequently, he was daunted by the idea of working with Stone, the Oscar-winning director who had made *Platoon* and *Wall Street.*

"We had to have a collaboration or it wouldn't make any sense, as far as the writing went," Bogosian says. "So if I walked in the door and said, 'Okay, here's some pages,' and he just went, 'Feh, you call those pages?' and, like, threw them on the floor . . . I mean, that was probably my biggest fear going in.

"And in fact, things like that happened, because Oliver is very blunt, a very intense worker. But I also like to just get into it and work, let's not beat around the bush. Every time he would give me some kind of criticism, I would just try and pull myself together and come back as hard as I could." Despite—or perhaps because of—their mutual intensity, the two men ended up becoming friends, and *Talk Radio* was shot in twenty-six days for less than six million dollars.

The film fleshes out Bogosian and Savinar's rigorously concise play, adding flashbacks that show Barry's personal life and his progress through the world of radio. It also moves the story from Cleveland to Dallas—an apparent nod to the legacy of violence and media-related trauma of the Kennedy assassination.

More generally, *Talk Radio* uses the tale of WGAB disc jockey Barry Champlain and his show, *Night Talk,* to explore the mass media and their corrosive impact on people's lives—the lives of both the celebrities who need to keep a tight grip on their identity and the fans who invest their faith in figures who are often little more than projections of their own fantasies.

Amid chatter about nuclear war, the Holocaust, and racism, Barry's callers tell of problems that range from loneliness and substance abuse to paranoid fears about household appliances: "What if the garbage disposal came on while your hand was still down there?" one woman asks. Another listener sends Barry a dead rat wrapped in a Nazi flag.

Barry strings them along or cuts them off with the arbitrary imperiousness of a god—or is it just the cool judgment of a pro who instinctively knows which dilemmas will keep the folks out there in radio-land from turning the dial?

For his part, Barry is ever insecure and eager for approval. He begins to unravel under the strain of his job and insists to one caller, "The show *must* serve some kind of purpose for you." The caller's damning, off-hand answer, delivered in a quiet Southern accent, could have come out of a novel by Beckett or DeLillo: "Well, I wouldn't say that."

Bogosian listened to innumerable hours of talk radio in the course of inventing Barry, and to describe the dynamics of the medium, he launches into a monologue worthy of one of his characters. "It's important to remember that the guy who's hosting the show is a professional," he says. "He has a job. His job is not to the person calling; it's to all the people listening. Maybe twenty people are going to call in an evening; hundreds of thousands of people are going to listen. He's entertaining them, and he's *really, really* good at it. So we're watching an actor of sorts, a professional entertainer whose job is to find the drama in these live interactions. He's a character.

"This is where it really becomes interesting, because, as the public becomes more and more hungry for characters in the mass media— whether it be Barry Champlain or Mort Downey or Dan Rather or Bruce Springsteen—the audience wants to believe these guys are really who they say they are. The problem is that they are character actors. They are playing these roles—they get shitloads of money for doing it. And yet they're real people, and somewhere in their life they moved from the real person into the guy that everybody's watching. And it's kind of hard on them. People that have dropped their personas learn very quickly how pissed off the audience will get. If you're a guy whose job it is to blow his stack on the air, it can be one painful place to be day after day after day."

Bogosian, who grew up in an Armenian family in Woburn, Massachusetts, and graduated from Oberlin College, lives with his wife and sometime director, Jo Bonney, and their twenty-month-old son in a Manhattan apartment and a home in rural New Jersey. With *Talk Radio* behind him, Bogosian is working on his next solo performance, *Sex, Drugs & Rock 'n' Roll,* which will be staged off-Broadway in the spring and taped for HBO. Because he wants to concentrate on his film acting, that show will likely be Bogosian's last stage appearance for a while. He's also writing a screenplay in which he hopes to star. Tentatively titled *Blue Smoke,* it's set in the hipster jazz scene in New York in the Fifties.

For now, Bogosian will continue to look for ways to sharpen the subversive impulse in his work while reaching an audience larger than the New York underground. To illustrate the fate that must be avoided, he slips into an accent dripping with the knowing cynicism of the showbiz hack: "What slimy TV show do you want me to be on? I'll go do it. I don't care. Give me the money.

"If I do that, it isn't like I broke some law with God; I broke a law with myself," Bogosian says, speaking once again in his own voice, an uncanny blend of New York street toughness and broad Massachusetts inflections. "*I'm* going to have to suffer because of it. I'm just trying to keep myself happy for as long as possible. I think if I so-called sell out, then I lose."

Rolling Stone February 9, 1989

A Punk's Past Recaptured

T. Coraghessan Boyle

In many ways the scene is exactly what you would expect. The happening novelist of the moment—bearded, idiosyncratic, funny, and almost painfully articulate—is holding forth during lunch at the Algonquin Hotel, a longtime hotbed of literary hobnobbing in Manhattan. The room is sturdily elegant; the crowd tweedy and knowing; the maitre d' wrapped in a tuxedo. But the novelist's conversation—which does not revolve around royalty rates, agents, or the eternal editorial shuffle at New York's publishing houses—flashes an edge that cuts through the easy civility of the setting.

"You reach a point where you say, 'What am I gonna do? Am I gonna live, or am I gonna die?'" he says. "How many nights do you want to be sitting in somebody's apartment with the stereo blasting, saying nothing, at four o'clock in the morning?"

T. Coraghessan Boyle—plain old Tom to his friends—is talking about the period in the early Seventies, just after he graduated from college, during which he "did everything that was imaginable" in the way of drugs, including heroin. Though there was nothing privileged about his working-class upbringing or state-college education, Boyle regards that time as the height of his life as "a pampered punk," a self-indulgent rebel drunk on existentialist clichés and detached from any past that might lend his life meaning.

"It fits well with that teenage angst," he says now, laughing, about his philosophical pretensions, "where you want to die, and you're hoping to die any minute now, but, gee, maybe you should have just one more joint or go to bed instead. Existentialism is perfect for that."

It could be said that Boyle, despite being thirty-nine and a professor of creative writing for the past nine years, brought his punk phase to an end only recently, with the publication of *World's End,* his third novel and a genuine literary event. Set in the Hudson River Valley, the area of New York State where Boyle grew up and lived until he was in his midtwenties, the book sweeps up three hundred years of family and regional history into a swirling, panoramic narrative that encompasses the late

Sixties, the 1940s, and the Dutch community in the valley during the seventeenth century.

In its vision, ambition, and the sheer weight of its achievement, *World's End* is more reminiscent of the epic works of William Faulkner and Gabriel García Márquez than it is of most contemporary American fiction. While writers like Jay McInerney, Bret Easton Ellis, and Tama Janowitz focus on the tics of urban culture, Boyle seeks to capture something deeper than the present moment.

To help extend his reach, Boyle drew inspiration from another Hudson Valley writer, Washington Irving. "He wrote stories that are part of our mythos and our consciousness," Boyle says. "I wanted to be a purveyor of myths about the area myself. I wanted to invent myths and use his myths and play off them. And talk about history as myth, too, and weave it all together."

World's End—which takes its name from a passage on the Hudson River that became a nautical graveyard—also represents Boyle's effort to explore a past he was too self-involved to care about before he left the valley in 1972 to enroll in the prestigious Writers' Workshop at the University of Iowa. The seed for the novel was planted during one of Boyle's visits home. "Every day I'd take a walk down to the Hudson," he recalls. "The walk took me down this dirt path. There was a little historical marker by it. The marker said that the path was the one that Benedict Arnold had taken to flee to the British and get on the *Vulture*. I was just stunned that it's still there—for 200 years people have been walking on this dirt path in the woods. It's not paved, it's not a tourist site, it's nothing. It's just a path in the woods. It knocked me dead."

This anecdote about the silent power of history recalls a key scene in *World's End,* where Walter Van Brunt, a disaffected Sixties type given to measuring his actions against existential maxims, literally crashes into the past when his motorcycle slams into a historical marker. He loses his foot in the accident—he eventually loses the other foot as well—and the incident underscores one of the novel's central ideas. In Boyle's words: "If you don't know your history, you don't have your feet on the ground. You're not connected."

Boyle's growth into a sense of connection was, in many ways, no less troubled than Walter's. He grew up in Peekskill—called Peterskill in the novel—and his father, a school-bus driver, was an alcoholic who died as a result of his drinking in 1972. Walter's tormented search for his father, who had left him a legacy of betrayal and abandonment, propels one of the intertwining plots of *World's End*, and Boyle, in fact, dedicated the book to the "memory of my own lost father." Boyle's mother, who was a secretary, also became an alcoholic and died of liver failure several years after his father's death.

After indifferent experiences in grade school and high school, Boyle went off to the State University of New York at Potsdam. "I barely got through," he says. "I went to study music, but I couldn't hack it. I played saxophone and clarinet, but I really wasn't good enough and didn't have the discipline to do the practicing." At Potsdam, Boyle drifted into a creative-writing class, but a career as a writer still seemed a distant prospect.

Unfortunately, when Boyle graduated, the draft and possible service in Vietnam seemed perilously more imminent. Despite his nasty habits and almost preternatural thinness—he's six three and slim as a whip—Boyle passed his physical and was a prime candidate for induction. "I had no intention of going to the war," Boyle says flatly. "I was a wild, radical hippie. But also there were various avenues out, and I wanted to go the path of least resistance."

Consequently he decided to become a teacher. "I had never taken a teaching course, never even seen a child in my life, in fact," he says dryly. "I got my hair cut, bought a suit, and ran around to about sixty interviews in Westchester County. Finally got a job—now I realize it was through a connection of the father of my best friend. That saved my ass."

Boyle then taught English at a junior high school in Peekskill for a couple of years. "It was a shock to me," he recalls, "because this was a very tough slum school, mainly black and Puerto Rican. I had to rip their shirts, throw them against the wall, get physical. It was a violent, tough kind of thing. . . . At the same time this was when I started to get into heroin and hang out with all of those people. So I was up all night stoned, and I had to go in and do this job. It just about killed me."

Having taken a creative-writing course at Potsdam and developed a fondness for writers like Donald Barthelme, John Barth, and Thomas Pynchon, Boyle turned to fiction writing to sidestep the abyss and get his life on track. He published a story—aptly titled "The OD and Hepatitis Railroad or Bust"—in the *North American Review*. That success gave him the confidence to apply to graduate school. "The only one I'd every heard

of was Iowa," he says, "so I wrote to them, and they accepted me, **305**
because they accept you just on the basis of the work. I could never have
gotten in on my record."

Curiously, Boyle does not fully understand what drew him to writing
fiction. "I read comic books, like all kids, watched TV twenty-four hours a
day," he says. "I guess, looking back, I was just fascinated by stories. I
remember my mother used to read me stories from the newspaper. I
began to read books probably when I was eighteen or so, and it was just
like a new world opened up to me. It was what I could do and what I
should've been doing all along. I came to it late."

At Iowa, Boyle took classes with John Cheever, John Irving, and Vance
Bourjaily, continued to publish, and submitted the short-story collection
Descent of Man as his Ph.D. dissertation. *Descent of Man,* which was
published in 1979, established the ironic tone and black humor that
runs through much of Boyle's work. The title story, for example, is about
a woman who works at a primate center and leaves her boyfriend for a
particularly gifted chimp. In another the Ugandan president Idi Amin
Dada is invited to be the principal exhibit at a dada arts festival in New
York.

Descent of Man was strong enough to win Boyle a reputation in literary
circles and land him his job teaching creative writing at the University
of Southern California. But despite the positive reviews the collection
received, it only sold a few thousand copies—which is not bad for a
first book of fiction, but far below Boyle's somewhat unreasonable
expectations.

Boyle found the public response to *Descent of Man* "tremendously
disappointing," as he has with all his books—the short-story collection
Greasy Lake and the novels *Water Music* and *Budding Prospects*—until
World's End. "Each book I put out, I think, 'Goodbye, Updike and Mailer,
forget it,'" he says, laughing, but not entirely kidding. "I joke at Viking
that I'm going to make them forget the name of Stephen King forever,
I'm going to sell so many copies. I would like to be a guy like Vonnegut
for my generation, who could wake up people a little bit and show them
that literature is fun and entertaining and also serious at the same time.
So I expected *Descent of Man* to be in every pop household."

Boyle's populist instincts are perhaps best evident in his 1985 collection of stories *Greasy Lake,* which takes its name and the epigraph for the
title story—"It's about a mile down on the dark side of Route 88"—from

the Bruce Springsteen song "Spirit in the Night." Boyle says he was a Springsteen fan "from the beginning." "I really love the early albums a lot, really related to them," he says. "Particularly this 'greasy lake' kind of notion. I get the impression that Asbury Park and Peekskill were similar in a lot of ways. So that song was the departure point for the story."

A portrait of the hard, inevitable choices facing characters—like the youthful Boyle and his friends—who "read André Gide and struck elaborate poses to show that we didn't give a shit about anything," the story "Greasy Lake" is simultaneously merciless and sympathetic. "'Greasy Lake' is more realistic than Walter's nightmare," Boyle says, comparing the story with *World's End*. "Walter is caught in this turmoil of history and blood and inheritance. The narrator in 'Greasy Lake,' it's more the proposition of 'Just how tough are you really?' You strut around and think you're really tough, but, boy, there's always somebody a lot worse and a lot tougher, and do you really want to go that far? That's the proposition: Where is the bottom, and do you want to get there? No, you don't want to get there. It scares the shit out of you."

Having flirted with the bottom, Boyle has traveled a long way up. *World's End* has brought him a larger audience, and his short fiction is in greater demand than ever. His two earlier novels and one of his short stories have been optioned for films. He now lives in Woodland Hills, an upper-middle-class neighborhood in Los Angeles, with his wife, Karen, and their three young children. He's just begun working on a new novel, about "a Japanese man in Georgia." "It's extremely hilarious, but has a tragic ending," he says. "I see it as a musical, maybe. No. I wanted to create a character who's sweet and charming and whom you really love but who comes to a bad end."

In a time when much American fiction seems cramped and deadened, Boyle stands committed to pushing the boundaries back, as he did with *World's End*. "I don't want to do something small," he says. "I want to stretch as much as possible. . . . You think of these guys who burn out, and you wonder if it's going to happen to you, and you pray that it doesn't. I'd like to have a career like Updike's—you know?—where you keep getting better all the time, keep changing and doing different things."

The Product:
Bucky Wunderlick, Rock & Roll, and
Don DeLillo's *Great Jones Street*

Perhaps the best-known passage in Don DeLillo's *Great Jones Street*,
not one of his more highly regarded novels, occurs at the beginning
of the book. As the novel kicks off, rock star Bucky Wunderlick is holed
up in an apartment in a desolate industrial section of Manhattan—this is
the early Seventies; Manhattan had industrial sections then—having
abandoned his band midtour in Houston. Bucky's reflections on his
celebrity, which he is seeking to escape and examine, start the novel:

> *Fame requires every kind of excess. I mean true fame, a devouring neon, not the
> somber renown of waning statesmen or chinless kings. I mean long journeys across
> gray space. I mean danger, the edge of every void, the circumstance of one man
> imparting an erotic terror to the dreams of the republic. Understand the man who
> must inhabit these extreme regions, monstrous and vulval, damp with memories
> of violation. Even if half-mad he is absorbed into the public's total madness; even if
> fully rational, a bureaucrat in hell, a secret genius of survival, he is sure to be
> destroyed by the public's contempt for survivors. Fame, this special kind, feeds itself
> on outrage, on what the counselors of lesser men would consider bad publicity—
> hysteria in limousines, knife fights in the audience, bizarre litigation, treachery,
> pandemonium and drugs. Perhaps the only natural law attaching to true fame is
> that the famous man is compelled, eventually, to commit suicide.*
>
> *(Is it clear I was a hero of rock 'n' roll?)*

When I read that passage to a friend of mine—a friend who is, like me,
a rock fan and a reader—he said, "That's exactly what a writer would
think a rock star thinks like." He wasn't being complimentary. My friend
knows that rock stars' thoughts more often read like a Don DeLillo
parody of an interview—of which *Great Jones Street* contains several
funny examples—than like the sort of sociocultural analysis at the heart
of the passage I just quoted. Even Bob Dylan, who has made albums that
move me as much as any works of art I know and who is one of the
figures on whom DeLillo's portrayal of Wunderlick seems to be based,
typically doesn't seem to have very much to say about his own work. In

fact, in interviews, he often doesn't even seem to understand his own work, or at least he affects not being able to understand it, let alone the context that helped produce it. For example, here is an exchange between Dylan and former *Rolling Stone* writer Kurt Loder that appeared in *Rolling Stone* in 1986. They are discussing Dylan's Sixties albums, virtually every one of which is riveting and virtually every one of which seems to scream self-conscious intent:

> *Did you feel that you had tapped into the Zeitgeist in some special sort of way?*
> With the songs that I came up with?
> *Yeah.*
> As I look back on it now, I am surprised that I came up with so many of them. At the time it seemed like a natural thing to do. Now I can look back and see that I must have written those songs "in the spirit," you know? Like "Desolation Row"—I was just thinkin' about that the other night. There's no logical way that you can arrive at lyrics like that. I don't know how it was done.

Not even "I don't know how I did it," but "I don't know how it was done." Dylan goes on to describe how he feels his songs of that time came "through" him, which is about as characteristic a declaration from a rock songwriter as you will find. This mystical notion of creativity is one of the stances artists adopt to keep their own creative processes concealed from themselves, protected from a self-consciousness that they fear might prove paralyzing. It is also a way to maintain distance from audience expectations—one of the central, ongoing preoccupations of Dylan's career. Since artists have no control over what comes "through" them, the reasoning would seem to run, they can hardly be held accountable for deviating from the styles they previously worked in.

Wunderlick's relationship to his audience, and to the entire culture that is playing him, is central to *Great Jones Street*. In an interview, DeLillo said about Wunderlick: "The interesting thing about that particular character is that he seems to be at a crossroad between murder and suicide. For me, that defines the period between 1965 and 1975, say, and I thought it was best exemplified in a rock-music star." My friend's comment aside, Wunderlick, like so many of DeLillo's characters, is not meant to seem like a realistic, three-dimensional person; he is a notion around which DeLillo collects his ideas about how the culture was functioning at the time in which his novel is set. Wunderlick's actions, thoughts, and speech reflect those ideas, rather than anything that might conventionally be considered his own "motivations."

The interplay between murder and suicide that DeLillo mentions would seem to suggest the movement of American society from the political upheavals and turmoil of the late Sixties to the dreadful cynicism, deep alienation, and desperate privatism of the Seventies. Wunderlick's writing traces a similar pattern of drawing inward. His first album, a "special media kit" included in the novel informs us, is called *Amerikan War Sutra*—it's from 1968, natch, and his second, from 1970, is *Diamond Stylus*, an evident movement from political protest to a kind of aestheticism. By the time of his third album, *Pee-Pee-Maw-Maw*, in 1971—a "landmark work" in the estimation of one of the novel's characters—Wunderlick is trying to defeat language itself with a kind of minimalist gibberish.

Wunderlick's desire to strip away the rational meanings of language is related to his urge for self-attenuation—a response to the failure of the Sixties' promise of ever-expanding utopian possibilities, and the suicidal pole of the dichotomy DeLillo mentioned in discussing *Great Jones Street*. He speaks of himself as potentially becoming "the epoch's barren hero, a man who knew the surest way to minimize." Near the end of the book, his desire to elude the tyranny of language and achieve a pure, perfectly unimpeded relationship with his audience reaches the point of a desire to be disembodied: "I'm tired of my body. I want to be a dream, their dream. I want to flow right through them." He speaks of wanting to become "the least of what I was." In virtually the only comprehensible lyrics on *Pee-Pee-Maw-Maw*'s title track—DeLillo provides the full lyrics—Wunderlick states, in an eerie combination of Yeats and the depressed, pragmatic wisdom of the Seventies. "The beast is loose / Least is best."

What Wunderlick learns in his withdrawal is that it is finally impossible to withdraw. Great Jones Street is no different from Main Street or Wall Street; it offers no haven, no safe retreat. When he jumped off what he calls his "final tour"—though near the end of the novel he, like all good rockers with savvy managers, is contemplating going on the road again—Wunderlick had become convinced that suicide was the only meaningful performance still available to him. The basic rock-star paranoid fantasy—that the fans' wild love would somehow transform itself into murderous rage (a fantasy that proved all too real in the case of John Lennon and that is captured brilliantly on David Bowie's album, *The Rise and Fall of Ziggy Stardust*)—is turned around in Wunderlick's case.

On the "final tour," the mayhem Wunderlick's group could routinely inspire tapered off; the fans themselves withdrew, creating a vacuum that they expected Wunderlick to fill, or to internalize. "There was less sense of simple visceral abandon at our concerts during these last weeks," Wunderlick says, stricken with wonder. "Few cases of arson and vandalism. Fewer still of rape." He attributes this lessening of violence to his audience's realization that "my death, to be authentic, must be self-willed—a successful piece of instruction only if it occurred by my own hand, preferably in a foreign city"—that last detail, evidently, an allusion to the mysterious death of Jim Morrison in Paris. "It's possible the culture had reached its limit," Wunderlick speculates, "a point of severe tension."

This lessening of the fans' violence triggers a dual response in Wunderlick. The first is his suicidal, self-attenuating retreat to his room; he is one of the earliest of the "men in small rooms" that populate DeLillo's novels. The other response turns the violence toward the audience: "What I'd like to do really is I'd like to injure people with my sound," he says at a hilarious symposium at a prominent think tank, at which he is the featured guest. "Maybe actually kill some of them." Later on he says, "It's murder I've been burning to commit. I'm way beyond suicide."

But once Wunderlick retreats to the room on Great Jones Street, having reached his own limit within the context of the general cultural dissolution, it quickly becomes clear that the forces that really control events—quite independent of the whims of pop stars—have not relaxed their grip simply because he has decided to drop out. What happens is that the void he creates by his withdrawal makes the functioning of those forces more apparent—and more frightening—to him.

The first evidence of this is that Globke, Wunderlick's manager, turns up at the apartment even though Wunderlick has informed no one of his whereabouts. The very permeability of Wunderlick's room—the ultimate room of his own, an image of the sacrosanct internal world of the artist—is testimony to the failure of alternatives and escapes in this novel. On his visit, Globke informs Wunderlick that his management firm, Transparanoia, will stand by Wunderlick through this weird period—"What the hell, an artist's an artist," Globke reasons with the wisdom of a businessman who knows his product and which side his check is signed on. He also reveals that Transparanoia owns the building Wunderlick is living in. So much for escape; real estate never sleeps. Globke clearly does not share Wunderlick's desire to minimize: "It's a business thing. . . . Diversification, expansion, maximizing the growth potential. Someday you'll understand these things. You'll open your mind to these things." Transparanoia, it should be noted, is run exclusively on Wunderlick's earnings and investments. For Wunderlick's own purposes, of course, his money is "spent" or "tied up."

As in Pynchon's novels, the various undergrounds in *Great Jones Street* begin to intersect—and begin more and more to resemble flaky, sinister spin-offs on the dominant culture, rather than rebellious or subversive alternatives to it. Globke proves to be only the first of an endless series of visitors to what was supposed to be Wunderlick's secret hideaway. In the most important of those visits, Bucky, the messianic rock star turned urban hermit, is visited by a member of the Happy Valley Farm Commune—"a new earth-family on the Lower East Side that has the whole top floor of one tenement"—the book's major image of counterculture idealism gone beserk.

The Commune, whose members fled the rural life to try to find themselves in the city, holds Wunderlick in esteem for "[r]eturning the idea of privacy to American life," and asks him to stash a drug—alternately referred to as the "package" or the "product"—in his apartment. The product, as it happens, is "the ultimate drug," a drug that destroys the ability of people to speak. It was originally designed by the federal government to silence dissenters. "You'll be perfectly healthy," one character explains to Wunderlick, who eventually takes the drug. "You won't be able to make words, that's all. They just won't come into your mind the way they normally do and the way we all take for granted they will. Sounds yes. Sounds galore. But no words." In the desperate environment of a culture that has reached the breaking point, all extreme experience is desirable: "Everybody's anxious to get off on this stuff. If U.S. Guv is involved, the stuff is bound to be a real mind-crusher. . . . People are agog. It's the dawning of the age of God knows what."

More to the point: however many people want to get off on it, at least as many want to get their hands on it and sell it—or is that a false distinction? A culture under siege creates its own vital markets. The drug product becomes like the pornographic movie allegedly filmed in Hitler's bunker in *Running Dog:* an imagined commodity that, independent of its value or even its status as an object of desire, serves as a lightning rod for the greed and acquisitiveness pervading the cultural atmosphere. When the drug package becomes confused with another package containing Wunderlick's "mountain tapes"—a cache of songs Wunderlick had recorded in his remote mountain home a little over a year before his "final" tour (and based on the "basement tapes" Dylan made in Woodstock after his motorcycle accident in 1966)—the thematic center of the novel becomes clearly defined. The drug and Wunderlick's music, no matter how authentically conceived or individually created, are both products, and the buying and selling of products is what makes the world of *Great Jones Street* turn.

Eventually, every character in *Great Jones Street* is pursuing either the package containing the so-called "ultimate drug" or the one containing Wunderlick's mountain tapes. And every relationship that Wunderlick thought he had is finally seen to revolve around the possibility of business deals (legitimate or illegal, underground or mainstream, related to drugs or music: distinctions among these pairings are purely conceptual, finally) and profits. Each person is simultaneously on the make for himself and representing shadowy others. Azarian, a member of Wunderlick's band, appears one day and, after quizzing Bucky about his intentions for the group, gets around to his real point: "Happy Valley Farm Commune is holding something I'm willing to lay out money for. I represent certain interests. These interests happen to know you're in touch with Happy Valley. So they're making the offer to you through me."

When Opel Hampson, Bucky's girlfriend and the person who normally lives in the apartment on Great Jones Street, returns from her travels in "timeless lands," it is, she says, because "I've got business." That business is, of course, the product. Like Azarian, she is representing "people." "I'm bargaining agent for Happy Valley," she explains. "I have bargaining powers. I wheel and deal." Azarian and Opel eventually die for their troubles.

Fenig, the funny, failed writer who lives above Wunderlick, is likewise on the make, continually seeking to figure out the literary market—this, despite the wonderful fact that his one-act plays "get produced without exception at a very hip agricultural college in Arkansas." In the course of the novel, Fenig's wanderings through the world of genres take him through science fiction to pornographic children's literature ("Serious stuff. Filthy, obscene and brutal sex among little kids"). The object of his obsession is fame. His meditations on the subject are somewhat less penetrating than Wunderlick's: "Fame. . . . It won't happen. But if it does happen. But it won't happen. But if it does. But it won't." But if it does: "I'll handle it gracefully. I'll be judicious. I'll adjust to it with caution. I won't let it destroy me. Fame. The perfect word for the phenomenon it describes." The final genre that captivates Fenig is, needless to say, "[f]inancial writing. Books and articles for millionaires and potential millionaires." This money literature is his "fantastic terminal fiction."

The urge to entrepreneurship also infect Hanes, a messenger for Transparanoia and an emissary for the Happy Valley Farm Commune. He takes the drug package from Wunderlick and, drugged with the power of possessing such a precious object, attempts to double-cross the Commune and make a deal for the drug on his own. As does Dr. Pepper, the scientific genius of the underground whose name is a clever conflation of the counterculture utopianism of the Beatles' *Sgt. Pepper's Lonely Hearts Club Band* and the soft-drink commodity. Pepper first signs on to analyze the drug for the Commune and then attempts to obtain and market it himself. "Everybody in the free world wants to bid," is how Pepper describes the drug's desirability. Bohack, a representative of the Commune whose name derives from a supermarket chain, threatens Wunderlick when he cannot produce the drug. Meanwhile Globke steals the mountain tapes from his own client and plots to release them. Finally, the double-dealer Hanes, in order to save his own life, informs the Commune of the whereabouts of the mountain tapes, which the Commune then destroys. The members of the Commune are angry that Wunderlick, who, after all, had restored the notion of privacy to American life, was planning to violate his own privacy and tour again.

The character who has the most to say to Wunderlick about what his life has been—and what it has become, and what determines it—is Watney. Watney is a former pop star—he pulls up to Wunderlick's building in a limousine that includes "[t]hree rooms and a dining alcove. But at the same time fairly inconspicuous"—and stands as a kind of Alice Cooper figure, an image of the decline of rock into shock spectacle, as opposed to Wunderlick's Dylan/Jagger fusion. Watney's wild, androgynous band, Schicklgruber, epitomized the notion of rock & roll as a mad, pointless threat to the social order: "wherever they went the village elders consulted ordinances trying to find a technicality they might use to keep the band from performing or at the very least to get the band out of town the moment the last note sounded." When he visits Wunderlick, however, it turns out Watney is done with rock & roll and is—in a perfect transition—"into sales, procurement and operations now. I represent a fairly large Anglo-European group." Like everyone else, he visits the former band leader to bid on the drug product.

In the course of his discussion about the product with Wunderlick, Watney explains the reasons for his move into sales:

> "I had no real power in the music structure. It was all just show. This thing about my power over kids. Watney the transatlantic villain. Schicklgruber the assassin of free will. It was just something to write, to fill up the newspapers with. I had no power, Bucky. I just dollied about on stage with my patent leather pumps and my evil leer. It was a good act all right. But it was all just an act, just a runaround, just a show."

Later on in the novel, Watney explains to Wunderlick how real power works.

> "Bucky, you have no power. You have the illusion of power. I know this first-hand. I learned this in lesson after lesson and city after city. Nothing truly moves to your sound. Nothing is shaken or bent. You're a bloody artist you are. Less than four ounces on the meat scale. You're soft, not hard. You're above ground, not under. The true underground is the place where power flows. That's the best-kept secret of our time. You're not the underground. Your people aren't underground people. The presidents and prime ministers are the ones who make the underground deals and speak the true underground idiom. The corporations. The military. The banks. This is the underground network. This is where it happens."

By the end of the novel, Wunderlick takes the ultimate drug, which provides him with "weeks of deep peace," but proves "less than lasting in its effect." Like all consumer goods, it is ultimately disappointing. The failure of the drug to transport him to a place beyond language—its failure to achieve a kind of suicide for him—is part of what Wunderlick calls his "double defeat." The other part of that defeat is the frustration, with the destruction of the mountain tapes, of his murderous desire to get back on the road. As Wunderlick himself frames the dichotomy of his failure: "first a chance not taken to reappear in the midst of people and forces made to my design and then a second enterprise denied, alternate to the first, permanent withdrawal to that unimprinted level where all sound is silken and nothing erodes in the mad weather of language." As the rumors surrounding his disappearance continue to swirl, he is back in numb isolation on Great Jones Street, sounding almost like a character out of T. S. Eliot: "When the season is right I'll return to whatever is out there. It's just a question of what sound to make or fake."

"Your life consumes itself," Watney tells Wunderlick, and the revelation of Wunderlick himself, and all artists, as objects of consumption, commodities like the ultimate drug or the mountain tapes, is part of the point of *Great Jones Street*. Like the Happy Valley Farm Commune, which moves from utopian ruralism to vicious drug dealing, each of the book's characters, with the exception of Wunderlick, who is essentially paralyzed, abandons whatever alternative seemed to be available and willfully enters the market economy. In 1990 it may not seem like much of an exercise to explore how much the Sixties counterculture and its utopian hopes did or did not threaten the dominant culture. In 1973, however, such an exercise was well worth undertaking, and may still have value today. What DeLillo depicts in *Great Jones Street* is a society in which there are no meaningful alternatives, in which everyone and everything is bound in the cash nexus and the exchange of commodities, outside of which there stands nothing. Everything is consumed, or it consumes itself: murder or suicide, exploitation or self-destruction. After a decade of rampant market economics and amid regular announcements of the worldwide triumph of capitalism—smug, dumb declarations of how the West was won—can the world DeLillo portrays in *Great Jones Street* not seem painfully familiar?

In a recent interview in *Rolling Stone*, Axl Rose, lead singer of Guns n' Roses, the fuck-you, rebellious band of the moment—and one of the most popular bands in the world—made questionable remarks about gays, blacks, women, and immigrants, and then offered these observations about his artistic life: "I was figuring it out, and I'm like the president of a company that's worth between $125 million and a quarter billion dollars. If you add up record sales based on the low figure and a certain price for T-shirts and royalties and publishing, you come up with at least $125 million, which I get less than two percent of." A little while later Rose advises youngsters aspiring to his lifestyle of rock & roll revolt: "What I'd tell any kid in high school is 'Take business classes.' I don't care what else you're gonna do, if you're gonna do art or anything, take business classes."

Is it clear he is a hero of rock & roll?

South Atlantic Quarterly Spring, 1990

Dharma Bums
and Other Friends
Ginsberg's Photos

T*he poignancy of a photograph* comes from looking back to a fleeting moment in a floating world," writes Allen Ginsberg in the commentary accompanying *Photographs,* a collection of pictures that documents Ginsberg's own life and the progress of the Beat Generation from the late Forties to the present. None of the photographs were shot by "professional" photographers, but almost all were shot by artists—Ginsberg himself took most of the pictures, in fact—and the freshness of the visionary eye is apparent in every image. "There is a mythology," Ginsberg goes on to say of the lives of his mostly famous friends, "but finally people are just themselves." That's true, and that's exactly how *Photographs* portrays them.

But what does "just themselves" mean in a context like this? Moving through the fleeting moments in a floating world, a person becomes and undoes many selves. Perhaps part of the poignancy of these photographs lies in their ability to chart without sentimentality the changes wrought by time. So Jack Kerouac—the author of *On the Road,* the defining work of the Beat Generation—stands on a fire escape in New York in the early Fifties, smoking a cigarette and looking intent, sensitive, and forceful, the openness of the city sky above him, an urban vista ahead. A decade later he is slumped in a chair—a "corpulent W. C. Fields shuddering with mortal horror," in Ginsberg's chilling phrase—imprisoned in a room, the once-open sky framed in a narrow window. Which image, then, is just himself?

In another photograph, LSD guru Timothy Leary sits laughing with Neal Cassady—the inspiration for Dean Moriarity in *On the Road*—on Ken Kesey's Merry Prankster bus, which drove the Fifties along the road of excess into the Sixties. Twenty-five years later, still wearing the top hat of an impresario, Kesey poses for Ginsberg in a shabby hotel room and tells of a crisis of faith brought on by the death of his son.

In between the narrative end points defined by those pairs of photographs are lives lived in the streets of American cities, in Marrakesh,

318   Dakar, and Tangier, and, transported by a pharmacopeia of mind-altering chemicals, in the wilderland of the imagination. These are the faces of the desolation angels, the sacramental companions, the wild boys, howling and in response, being just themselves. As Ginsberg says, "We loved and saw each other as in 'a one and only' time in eternity. . . . Appreciation is the sacrament." Appreciate.

Rolling Stone March 21, 1990

An Ambitious History Lesson:
Greil Marcus's *Lipstick Traces*

*I**n his 1975 book** Mystery Train: Images of America in Rock 'n' Roll Music,* critic Greil Marcus set out "to deal with rock 'n' roll not as youth culture, or counter culture, but simply as American culture." Smart, probing, and splendidly written, the book proved to be—and continues to be—powerfully influential, a milestone achievement in the effort to establish rock & roll as a fit subject for serious cultural criticism.

Marcus's new book, *Lipstick Traces: A Secret History of the Twentieth Century,* is more ambitious still. Joining the burgeoning ranks of thinkers who are exploring subjects excluded from mainstream history, Marcus takes his obsession with the Sex Pistols as a jumping-off point to ask provocative questions about how—and by whom—history is defined and made.

Assessing his own profound and lasting response to the band in relation to its brief existence and commercial insignificance, Marcus asks, "Is it a mistake to confuse the Sex Pistols' moment with a major event in history—and what is history anyway? Is history simply a matter of events that leave behind those things that can be weighed and measured—new institutions, new maps, new rulers, new winners and losers—or is it also the result of moments that seem to leave nothing behind, nothing but the spectral connections between people long separated by place and time, but somehow speaking the same language?"

When writers ask such questions, it's a good bet they already think they know the answers, and Marcus clearly stands on the latter side of the either-or dichotomy he constructs. Still, his hand rarely weighs heavy as he traces "spectral connections" that extend far beyond rock & roll into avant-garde art movements, radical political groups, and millenarian religious sects in this century and in earlier times, in Europe and in the United States.

The book's overall tone is speculative, generous, and open, with Marcus offering interpretations that are meant to excite the reader to further imagining and thought rather than mere agreement or disagreement. Given the abstruseness of his subjects, it's also a pleasure that Marcus manages to find a language that is neither condescending to his audience—virtually all of whom will be unfamiliar with the people and events he discusses—nor defensive.

The movements Marcus writes about rival each other both in their obscurity and in the extremity of the demands they made on the societies that spawned them. "Oblivion is our ruling passion," declared one radical Parisian group Marcus examines, while the Sex Pistols' "God Save the Queen," he says, "suggested demands no art of government could ever satisfy."

In Marcus's view, such limitless desires "blur the lines between idealism and nihilism," mock the alienating control mechanisms of official culture, and seek to restore emotional autonomy to individual citizens. In addition to punk bands like the Pistols, the Germs, and the Slits, Marcus examines the crazed utopianism of the dadaists, the grandly titled Lettrist International and Situationist International, and the revolutionaries who nearly toppled the French government in the insurrections of May 1968.

The Situationists—especially their founder, Guy Debord—are in many ways the center of Marcus's story. Descended from the dadaists and the Lettrists (whose founder, an Elvis look-alike, sought to create a poetry that would, Marcus explains, "rescue the letter from the word"), the Situationists were initially "dimly perceived as a Pan-European association of megalomaniacal aesthetes and fanatical cranks, despised on the left and ignored by everyone else."

But from their start in 1957, the Situationists' revolutionary critiques, brilliantly represented in Debord's 1967 work *The Society of the Spectacle*, contributed greatly to the intellectual climate that produced the Days of May in Paris in 1968. French president Charles de Gaulle himself denounced the group's baleful influence, demonstrating for Marcus the degree to which "the disgust of a few, even the refusal of one, could bring a government to the verge of dissolution." The shadowy Situationist legacy was passed along to the Pistols, Marcus shows, through the band's manager, Malcolm McLaren, who helped publish a collection of Situationist writings in England in 1974.

But the linkages among such groups, which Marcus limns with humor and grace, constitute only one of the virtues of *Lipstick Traces*. The insightful analysis Marcus provides in passing of the Jacksons' *Victory* tour in 1984, of punk iconography, of art and its sources, of his own experiences in the Free Speech Movement at the University of

California at Berkeley, and of the purpose of criticism serves almost as a
leitmotif in the book.

The description of Sonny Til's vocal on the Orioles' 1948 single "It's
Too Soon to Know" epitomizes the impressive blend of precision and
lyricism Marcus is regularly able to muster: "Framed by high, drifting
moans that faded almost before they could be registered," Marcus
writes, "Til's fragile tenor was so emotionally distant, so aurally cre-
puscular, that it did not sound like singing at all. It was a voice that
seemed to treat the forming of a word as a concession, a voice less of
someone singing than of someone thinking about the possibility of
singing, as if to say, 'What would it mean to care?' "

Marcus, of course, is aware that *Lipstick Traces*—the title is taken from
a line in a Benny Spellman song—will enter the very subterranean
realms the book chronicles. Its intellectual heft—and its hefty price—
ensures that this text won't turn up on airport racks or best-seller lists.
But such relative obscurity does not circumscribe the importance of the
book, dull its impact, or distance it from Marcus's more widely known
rock criticism. In a half-heard conversation of "voices cut off or falling
silent," Marcus has cranked up the volume. That's a rock & roll gesture,
and as Marcus says, *Lipstick Traces* "is, finally, a rock 'n' roll story."

Rolling Stone May 4, 1991

Hot Writers

Neil Sheehan and Taylor Branch

*I**n contemporary popular culture,** the Sixties have become the subject of a kind of free-floating nostalgia—the decade is portrayed as an emotionally resonant *Happy Days* for the once hip. Television shows and movies brim with attractive, stressed people in their thirties and forties who have important—no, better, *creative*—jobs and who see their lives as bitterly circumscribed by the adult cares their parents had the good sense to take for granted. In this milieu of disappointed dreams, a Temptations song or a well-worn photograph from college can take on the transporting power of Proust's madeleine and become the medium for inchoate, half-forgotten feelings of generational significance.

But what, finally, do such moist reminiscences amount to? The earnest recollection that it was once possible to care about a world beyond the self conceals the assumption that such caring is no longer possible. The disjuncture between a youth of commitment and a grown-up life of disaffection hints that commitment is a function of youth, a heady adventure that inevitably must be set aside, however sadly, for the more "sophisticated" ambivalence of adulthood. Protest comes to seem a campus prank—flagpole sitting and panty raids overlaid with absurd, self-rationalizing rhetoric. All too often these days, evocations of the Sixties avoid the tough questions and issues that period raised, substituting soft-focus fantasies of youthful rebellion for clear-eyed analysis, personal events devoid of their social context or history.

Last year, however, two books were published that restored a fullbodied historical sense to the two great political events that shaped the Sixties: the civil rights movement and the Vietnam War. Taylor Branch's *Parting the Waters: America in the King Years, 1954–63* and Neil Sheehan's *A Bright Shining Lie: John Paul Vann and America in Vietnam* each gains its force from the rich examination of a specific individual in a major historical setting.

Both books won Pulitzer Prizes: Sheehan won in the category of General Nonfiction, while Branch shared the prize in History with James M. McPherson, who wrote *Battle Cry of Freedom: The Civil War Era.* Quite beyond their extraordinary strengths as narratives and their important contributions to knowledge, the Branch and Sheehan books articulate a crucial message for an alienated time: The individual life and the larger public world are inextricably linked.

Interestingly, the books had similar beginnings. Branch, who is forty-two, and Sheehan, who is fifty-two, were both wrenched out of the confident bliss of post-World War II America by their initial encounters with their subjects. "I grew up very much uninterested in politics," says Branch over lunch one afternoon in a restaurant close by his home in the Mount Washington section of Baltimore, where he lives with his wife and two children. "I was politically underdeveloped until the spring of '63, when I was a junior in high school and Birmingham happened. It shook me out of my Norman Rockwell, baby boomer's view of the world: that America had licked polio and soon would lick cancer and all was right with the world—a Pax Americana view. It made me ask, 'How could this happen?'—which was the first political question I ever asked."

If seeing the goons of the Birmingham police commissioner, Bull Connor, hosing down children during civil rights marches stunned Branch, who grew up in Atlanta, into a new awareness of the world around him, Sheehan's awakening was more gradual. Born in Mount Holyoke, Massachusetts, Sheehan attended Harvard, where he joined the Republican Club and majored in Middle Eastern history. After graduation, he signed up for a three-year stint in the army, serving in Korea and Japan, where he edited his division's weekly newspaper, which was based in Tokyo.

While still an enlisted man, Sheehan took a part-time job at the Tokyo office of UPI, offering to work for free to learn the business of journalism, which was starting to replace the prospect of an Arabist post in the State Department as his career interest. His introduction to big-time journalism could have come from a Forties film: "You want to work for nothing, kid?" the bureau chief asked him. "When do you want to start?"

Sheehan soon got on the payroll, though, and two weeks after he got out of the army, he pulled his first major assignment: head of UPI's Vietnam bureau in Saigon. He arrived in Saigon in April of 1962 at the age of twenty-six. The United States was limited to an advisory role in the country at that time, but the war was heating up. Sheehan was thrilled to be there.

"The filter through which I saw Vietnam was that filter of American ideology, that age of the Fifties and Sixties, when this country was at the height of its powers," says Sheehan in the living room of the Washington, D.C., home where he lives with his wife, Susan Sheehan, who is herself a Pulitzer Prize-winning staff writer for the *New Yorker.* "We were going to set things right in this country. I saw it as another in a long list of American challenges. You had a very keen sense that you were a citizen of this great world power which was establishing a benevolent world order—and maintaining it. I believed we were *certainly* going to win that war. First of all, I believed that we *ought* to win that war."

After having his political conscience quickened by the events in Birmingham, Branch went to college at the University of North Carolina at Chapel Hill and became involved in the antiwar movement. "By '66 or '67, I dropped all my premed courses and got caught up in campus activism, which by then was about Vietnam and not really about civil rights," he recalls. "But I always remembered that it had been Birmingham and the civil rights movement that framed all those questions and opened up that whole vocabulary of applying morality to politics."

At that point, Branch also began to develop a sense of the complexity of the Reverend Martin Luther King Jr., whose stature had been diminished somewhat by the rise of the black-power movement. "I didn't openly challenge or openly espouse the notion among white and black radicals, really, by the middle Sixties, before King was killed, that he was passé and that he was kind of an Uncle Tom figure," Branch says. "Yes, the reasoning ran, he deserved credit for getting things started, but he got things started based on ordinary homilies of being nice to one another; now we were dealing with economics and international politics and superpower relations and, on the far left, revolution itself, whereas King was much more of a reformist figure. Part of me always said, 'I know it's not that simple.'"

Through the person of John Paul Vann, Sheehan learned that what was happening in Vietnam was not so simple, either. Despite the fact that he had never done field reporting before his arrival in Saigon, Sheehan quickly began to understand that the grim realities in Vietnam did not correspond to the rosy reports and optimistic predictions of the military command and the State Department. "What you saw and what the advisers in the field told you was in complete contradiction to what you were being told by the command in Saigon and by the higher levels of the embassy," Sheehan says. "So there was immediate antagonism and distrust."

An ambitious, visionary lieutenant colonel in the army, Vann was frustrated by the obtuseness of his superiors, the bureaucracy in Washington and the cowardice and corruption of the South Vietnamese forces with which the United States was allied. He began leaking information and providing military analysis to Sheehan and his colleagues, like David Halberstam of the *New York Times,* in the hope that their stories would prove so embarrassing to the American government that a more rational—and successful—policy would become inevitable. Vann never opposed the war; he was simply convinced that he knew exactly how to win it.

Armed with Vann's information, Sheehan could challenge the official American line with absolute confidence. "He'd tell you what to look for," Sheehan recalls, mimicking one of Vann's lectures: "'Ask 'em. When you go down to a district and they tell you that X Road is secure, ask them: Do they drive it at night? Can we go out and drive it now? Let's go—and *see* if they go!'" Sheehan laughs, in memory of the sorts of responses he would get from frightened advisers—"'Oh, *no.* Oh, no, no!'

"Vann had an extremely important effect in shaping reporting, and he had an impact on policy through shaping reporting," Sheehan continues. "He was very valuable to us. That's one of the reasons why those of us who knew him then retained such high esteem for him. The moral heroism was very important, but it was also the memory of this man who had helped you to tell the truth, which as a young reporter was very difficult to do."

Branch got his start in journalism while attending graduate school at the Woodrow Wilson School of Public and International Affairs, at Princeton. After working with civil rights activists at the 1968 Democratic convention, in Chicago, Branch spent the summer of 1969 working on a voter-education project in rural Georgia. He was also supposed to be doing research for his graduate program at Princeton, but instead of producing the policy paper his professors had asked for, he turned in a diary of his experiences doing voting-rights work, "in kind of a fit of rebellion—it caused quite a controversy."

One professor, however, was sufficiently taken with Branch's writing that he sent the diary to the *Washington Monthly,* which accepted it for publication. Branch eventually joined the staff of the magazine and later worked for both *Harper's* and *Esquire.* He also cowrote *Second Wind,* the memoirs of basketball star Bill Russell, and ghostwrote *Blind Ambition,* the story of former Nixon aide John Dean, a central figure in the Watergate scandal.

While writing on other subjects, Branch found himself keeping an eye on what was being published about the civil rights movement. What he saw did not impress him much. "I was very disappointed with what I read," he says. "Everything seemed to be at more than arm's length from the real ground level. Everything was analytical or sentimental or argumentative. None of it seemed right. That frustration planted the seed of ambition to try to do something that would re-create the characters as they were so I could build up to the drama as it was."

Sheehan's determination to write about Vietnam formed in a different way. He covered the war for UPI between 1962 and 1964 and returned to the country as a correspondent in 1965, this time for the *New York Times*, for about a year. As American policy came to seem increasingly deranged, Sheehan's position on the war shifted 180 degrees. When military analyst Daniel Ellsberg, who had met Sheehan in Vietnam, decided to release the top-secret studies of the war known as the Pentagon Papers, Sheehan was the reporter he gave them to.

Still, by 1972 Sheehan had not yet come upon a way to frame the definitive book he hoped to write about the Vietnam War. When he attended the funeral of John Paul Vann in June of that year, he found it. "I never expected John to die," Sheehan says. "After a while, I think his friends began to believe in this myth of his invulnerability. I realized that he and I had gone in totally different directions on the war. And I realized also that the war had devoured John. The old John I had known had disappeared into the war." Vann had died in a helicopter crash in South Vietnam, and the mourners at his funeral ran the spectrum from CIA covert operatives like Edward Lansdale and William Colby to doves like Daniel Ellsberg and Ted Kennedy, from General William Westmoreland to Vann's son Jesse, who placed half of his torn draft card in his father's grave.

"I was very moved by the funeral," Sheehan recalls. "It was just an extraordinary event. . . . I realized that if you wrote a book about John, you could tell the story of the war in Vietnam. And it would be a human story, so people would be willing to come to grips with Vietnam, which was so painful and divisive."

Determining a subject and finding a focus turned out for both Branch and Sheehan to be only the most preliminary step toward actually writ-

ing their books. *Parting the Waters,* which runs over one thousand
pages—Branch's original manuscript totaled more than nineteen hundred pages—is merely the first of a two-volume study; the second will cover King's life from the end of 1963 to his death in 1968. Asked if he realized when he started how long it was going to take him to write the first volume, Branch says, "Well, the original contract was for three years to go through '68. Now it's been seven years through '63. So, no, I didn't have any idea."

Parting the Waters offers startlingly three-dimensional portrayals of life in the black church—what Branch calls "preacher culture"—and behind the scenes in the civil rights movement. In addition to focusing on King's activities, Branch gives full play to the efforts of other groups, like the Student Nonviolent Coordinating Committee and the National Association for the Advancement of Colored People, who alternately cooperated and competed with King's organization, the Southern Christian Leadership Conference. The political maneuverings of the Kennedy administration and the FBI are also detailed in striking terms.

The ground-level view Branch achieved resulted from a massive amount of research, including hundreds of interviews with people who knew King at every phase of his life. "What worried me the most was going in there and not knowing enough to get past the standard civil rights interview, which you would get from all kinds of people," says Branch, who then summarizes what such interviews consist of: " 'Oh, it was terrible, but we persevered. You can't believe how fearful it was, but we went prayerfully forward, and we triumphed. And by the way, I was Martin's best friend.' "

The tortuous sixteen-year path to completing *A Bright Shining Lie* led to considerable speculation that, like John Paul Vann, Sheehan himself had been devoured by the war. "I was as arrogant as Robert McNamara— I thought it would get done in three or four years," Sheehan says with a rueful laugh when asked about how long he initially felt it would take him to finish his book, which is more than eight hundred pages long. "It turned out to be a total miscalculation, obviously." As secretary of defense, Robert McNamara continually supported escalation as the speedy means to an American victory. His eventual doubts and guilt about that policy led, in part, to his commissioning the Pentagon Papers, which Sheehan says is still "the most complete and informative official archive on the Vietnam War."

As with Branch, part of the difficulty of completing the book stemmed from Sheehan's characteristic desire for thoroughness. He returned to Vietnam twice in the early Seventies, and in total he interviewed nearly four hundred people, many of them at least twice. He ended up having to trim 110,000 words from his completed manuscript. External factors also made for lost time. In 1972 the subject of Sheehan's first book, *The Arnheiter Affair,* sued him for libel. Sheehan's defense was successful, but the case dragged on until 1979, when the Supreme Court refused to take it up and the lower-court decision in Sheehan's favor was allowed to stand. And in 1974, Sheehan was sidelined for a year by the serious injuries he sustained when his car crashed head-on with an automobile that was being driven on the wrong side of the road.

Sheehan acknowledges these difficulties but says that "basically the problem was that the task was far greater than I'd ever imagined it to be." Early interviews with Vann's wife revealed that in 1959, Vann had been brought up on charges of statutory rape by the army—charges he successfully refuted, despite their being true, when he beat a polygraph test and pressured his wife to lie in his defense.

Vann's reporter friends thought he was taking a moral stand when he left the army in 1963 and spoke out against the ineptness of American policy in Vietnam, but in fact Vann knew that the rape charge on his record would prevent him from ever achieving his ambitions in the army. He had planned to leave all along. Consequently, when Vann returned to Vietnam in 1965, it was under the aegis of the Agency for International Development. Despite his image of military probity, Sheehan learned, Vann was illegitimate, the son of a prostitute; despite having a wife and five children at home in the States, Vann was a compulsive womanizer who had two full-time mistresses in Vietnam and often had sex with two or three different women a day during his time in that country.

"I thought I knew John Vann," Sheehan says, nearly whispering. "And all of his friends thought they knew John Vann. None of us knew John Vann. He was so complicated he probably didn't even know himself." After speaking to Vann's wife, says Sheehan, "I realized that I'd be writing the book about more than John Vann and the war in Vietnam. I realized that I'd be writing an American saga. I'd be writing the story of how a man's youth, origins, views, early years, had led him to this war in which he would do his best and he would be destroyed. And I was writing the story of a country whose historical development had led it to inflict this tragedy on itself and on the peoples of Indochina."

Of course, Martin Luther King had his secret life as well, one that became public primarily as the result of the wiretaps and surveillance that FBI director J. Edgar Hoover ordered maintained on King beginning in 1963. As a minister and a political leader who relied almost exclusively on moral force to achieve his nonviolent ends, King was certainly aware that his adulterous activities could have had a disastrous effect if they had ever become widely known. Yet he was unable to control that impulse in himself.

Describing King as a man who "reviled himself to some degree for his personal failings," Branch sees King's philandering as "a cat-o'-nine-tails for him to use against himself. . . . I know from his sermons, from the timing and from what people have told me, that the moods of his unhappiness with himself over this correspond with the peaks and valleys of his commitment to the movement. It's his great fascination with Saint Augustine, who reviled himself and tried to redeem himself by public acts. His favorite quote from Saint Augustine—it's from the *Confessions*—is 'Lord, make me pure—but not *yet*.' "

Even after all the work they have already done, neither Branch nor Sheehan has set his subject to rest. Branch, of course, is working on the second volume, *Pillar of Fire*, and consequently is still deeply immersed in King's life. As he relaxes in a wicker chair on the porch of his Victorian-style home—built in 1854, it's one of the oldest houses in his neighborhood—Branch discusses the challenges facing him. "I wrote this book not knowing really if anybody was going to want to read it," he says about *Parting the Waters*. "A lot of despair, worry, and angst can build up around that, but on the other hand, there's a clarity of purpose: The only reason you're writing it is to satisfy yourself. That's changed, because there is an audience for the book now. Obviously, that makes me more self-conscious. There's a lack of purity, maybe."

Branch also feels that while *Parting the Waters* traces the inspirational rise of the civil rights movement, *Pillar of Fire* will deal with a time of great internal struggle and confusion. The book's emotional momentum will be more complex, creating problems of craft and emphasis. "Obviously, the hardest thing is that this is when King's personal life becomes a political issue, and so writing about that in a way that is honest and truthful and yet doesn't completely obscure what has built through the first book is a great challenge," he says. "People are going to start falling off the stage. You're going to have movement casualties right and left, and things start to fly apart. There's more of a downer in this— even though there are great heights, too. There's *nothing* more inspirational than Selma, including the fact that it was created out of such despair. So it's a rocky road."

Writing *Pillar of Fire,* Branch says, will take "at least a couple of years," though he adds, with a knowing laugh, "I don't foresee as long a book. After all, it's only four and a half years—but a *hell* of a four and a half years!"

For his part, Sheehan sits in his living room—whose suburban ambiance of pastels, glass, and chrome is disturbed only by the fierce animal figures in the Asian art on the walls—and speaks of going back to Vietnam. A golden Buddha sits serenely in a corner. "What Susan and I plan on doing is, we're going to go back to Vietnam in June for research, a reporting trip, to write a series of two or three pieces for the *New Yorker,*" Sheehan explains. "They'll be retrospectives on that country and on the war. We'll probably go for a couple of months this summer, and then go back again in December."

Sheehan is also considering a return to newspaper work and eventually undertaking another book. The Vietnam articles, which would be the first time Neil and Susan Sheehan have written under a dual byline, may eventually be put together into what Sheehan pointedly calls "a short book." "There will be no more long books on Vietnam from Neil Sheehan," he says, laughing. "There's no encore to *A Bright Shining Lie.*"

Sheehan is also concerned that there be no encores to Vietnam, either—in Central America or anywhere else. "When President Bush says, 'Let's put Vietnam behind us,' or as he said in the inaugural address, 'The statute of limitations has run out on Vietnam'—first of all, I don't think we *ought* to put it behind us," Sheehan says, growing increasingly intense. "Vietnam will have been a bad war, a war in vain, only if we *don't* learn the lessons from it.

"Second—you *can't* put Vietnam behind us. There's no way to put Vietnam behind us. Because it's changed us. There's no way he can call a statute of limitations on Vietnam. It's not going to happen. He just doesn't have the capacity of his predecessors. The people are going to question his Nicaraguan policy. They're not going to give him a blank check."

Despite strained race relations in contemporary America, Branch also believes the civil rights movement has left an important legacy. He sees significant parallels between these times and the enclosed post-World War II self-satisfaction that sparked a counterresponse in civil rights protests from people excluded from the country's new-found prosperity.

"Most people know that there's an atmosphere of cornered materialism and there tends to be a hunger for something deeper, not just in our public life, but in our personal lives," Branch says. "There's a lot of denial. People know that the upper echelons of American society are living way beyond their means—that basically our credit card has run out, but it hasn't been confiscated yet. They also know that there's a connection between that and the fact that homeless people are showing up on the streets. There's some obvious comeuppances due, but they're frightening, in the same sense that getting rid of segregation was frightening."

The impressive popular and critical success of Taylor Branch's *Parting the Waters* and Neil Sheehan's *Bright Shining Lie* suggests that facing up to our problems and our history, at home and abroad, might be hot in the Nineties. If that proves wrong, the heat will be forged by forces far less under our control. And we will be compelled to relive the crises of a history that was far more convulsive to experience than to imagine in nostalgic fantasy.

Rolling Stone May 18, 1989

Epilogue

The Naked Transcript

In the course of twenty-five years, a mythology has grown about the glamorous life of the wild *Rolling Stone* reporter. Famous, semifamous, infamous, and forgotten writers who have worked for the magazine promulgate it. Movies and works of fiction nurture it. Critics of the magazine, in the very zeal of their attacks, unwittingly encourage it. And the magazine itself revels in it.

The myth has some foundation in reality. Virtually all the staff writers for *Rolling Stone* have had the opportunity to do extraordinary stories in spectacular settings, to meet many of the artists who have affected them most deeply. It happens so often that after a while you lose sight of how rare those opportunities are in most lives.

Sometimes it takes the reaction of other people to remind you. In 1989 I was involved with a woman who lived in Boston, which made getting together difficult. I called one day to say that I might be coming to Boston that weekend to interview the Rolling Stones—"It depends on what Mick decides." Expecting excitement, I got silence. "Is anything wrong?" I asked. "No, that's great," she said. "It's just that I never thought I might be personally affected by a decision Mick Jagger made."

At other times the experience itself is overwhelming enough to make a genuine impact. When I interviewed George Harrison at his home in England in 1987—his first major interview with *Rolling Stone* in thirteen years—it took the greatest strength of will to maintain a semblance of professional detachment and not just blurt out, "Don't you realize how profoundly the Beatles affected my life?" Okay, I was a bit overwrought—after all, I had just interviewed Paul McCartney the day before.

And after I finished interviewing Keith Richards for a 1988 cover story—an interview in which he went into provocative detail about his feuds with Mick Jagger—I was so charged up that I started running along Fifty-seventh Street in the crushing August heat. I went out for a champagne dinner with my then girlfriend to celebrate and afterward sat up into the early morning listening to the tapes, making sure I had not somehow deceived myself, making sure he had really said those things.

Obviously, then, the myth is based in reality. But the myth is not all there is to working at *Rolling Stone,* as I've done since 1986. The myth, for example, does not take into account the critical voice of the record-review section, which I edit and which inspires an edgier dialogue with artists. Nor does it acknowledge the everyday joy, poignancy, surreality, office-life lunacy, and, yes, even occasionally, tedium of making your living writing about rock & roll.

How does tracking down Robbie Robertson for an interview after Richard Manuel of the Band committed suicide fit into the myth? The exhaustion, confusion, and grief in Robertson's voice as he spoke of his old friend is something I will remember for the rest of my life. This was not a celebrity interview in an exotic clime; this was twenty minutes in my office on the telephone one afternoon in 1986. The rest of my life.

And what about the embarrassing moments, when the veil is lifted and you, not your subject, are revealed, as in this shockingly inarticulate exchange with Peter Gabriel about his album *So:*

ME: Well, it's sort of interesting. . . . In connection with . . . one of the things about the record . . . in sort of closing with "Big Time" and "We Do What We're Told," it almost sort of seemed to me as almost like this kind of . . . I mean, "Big Time," for all of its humor and stuff like that, sort of seems to me, you know, kind of a song about, you know, kind of *ego run rampant,* you know?

GABRIEL: Yes.

ME: The analogy is kind of letting yourself go completely, just, kind of, almost—it's *one* sort of danger. Whereas "We Do What We're Told" sort of represents almost the sort of opposite.

GABRIEL: Yes.

ME: Where you just kind of allow yourself to be totally the, uh . . .

GABRIEL: Yeah. One is ego dominant, and the other ego submissive. Yeah. I think that's right.

ME: It just kind of leaves the record off in this, in this, in this real sort of intriguing place of, um, uh, you know, of trying to find some, I think, some sort of middle ground between those things.

GABRIEL: Yeah. I think that's right.

334   Whatever. The naked transcript—the reality beneath the myth—is rarely
a beautiful sight.

The myth also proclaims that everything gets into the magazine for
the reader to see. But there are experiences that fall through the cracks,
events that don't make it into stories, because no one would care about
them except you, stories that for one reason or another don't happen at
all. Who except my friends knows about my sitting up all night with
Peter Buck in a Charlotte, North Carolina, motel room in early 1984, an
ice storm freezing the landscape outside and *Foxes* running silent on the
television as we spoke, incessant and inspired, about the promise of
R.E.M.? Who was there when Bono walked over to me one late night in a
London hotel bar and asked what it was like to go to graduate school to
study literature, prompting a long, funny, touching conversation about
poets and poetry? No one ever read about my crazily emotional interview
with Ray Davies, one of my early idols (in my teens he'd turn up in my
dreams), for a story that never made it into the magazine.

The blockbuster stories are like the public events of a relationship—
the weddings, the births, the housewarmings. They are meaningful, and
your friends and family remember them because they are realizations of
the mythology of what we all hope relationships will be. You remember
those events, too, of course, but you mostly remember making love for
the first time in the hot upstairs room of her brother's house that summer; sitting on a bench one April afternoon under lush trees and a calm,
blue sky, confessing emotions that made you feel frightened and exalted;
the way the light would fall through the blinds in her bedroom in the late
morning; hailing a taxi home after dinner one cold winter night, smiling
to yourself as you climb into the car together because running through
your head is "The Night I Fell in Love" by Luther Vandross.

You enjoy the myth, but for better, for worse, you do the work and live
the life each day. The mythology is fun, important, and rich. The life,
though harder to convey to others, is richer still.

Rolling Stone October 15, 1992

Index

Anthony DeCurtis is a Contributing Editor to *Rolling Stone*. He is the editor of *Present Tense: Rock & Roll and Culture* (Duke, 1992) as well as coeditor (with James Henke and Holly George-Warren) of *The* Rolling Stone *Illustrated History of Rock & Roll* and *The* Rolling Stone *Album Guide*.

Library of Congress Cataloging-in-Publication Data

DeCurtis, Anthony.

Rocking my life away : writing about music and other matters /

Anthony DeCurtis.

p.   cm.

Includes index.

ISBN 0-8223-2184-x (cloth : alk. paper)

1. Popular music—History and criticism.   I. Title.

ML3470.D43   1998

781.64'0973—dc21   97-9717